WITHDRAWN

Processing Instruction
Theory, Research, and Commentary

Second Language Acquisition Research
Theoretical and Methodological Issues
Susan Gass and Jacquelyn Schachter, Editors

Tarone/Gass/Cohen • Research Methodology in Second Language Acquisition

Schachter/Gass • Second Language Classroom Research: Issues and Opportunities

Birdsong • Second Language Acquisition and the Critical Period Hypotheses

Ohta • Second Language Acquisition Processes in the Classroom: Learning Japanese

Major • Foreign Accent: Ontogeny and Phylogeny of Second Language Phonology

Monographs on Research Methodology

Gass/Mackey • Stimulation Recall Methodology in Second Language Research

Yule • Referential Communication Tasks

Markee • Conversation Analysis

Dörnyei • Questionnaires in Second Language Research: Construction, Administration, and Processing

Of Related Interest

Gass/Sorace/Selinker • Second Language Learning Data Analysis, Second Edition

Gass/Selinker • Second Language Acquisition: An Introductory Course, Second Edition

Processing Instruction
Theory, Research, and Commentary

Edited by

Bill VanPatten
University of Illinois at Chicago

LAWRENCE ERLBAUM ASSOCIATES, PUBLISHERS

2004   Mahwah, New Jersey   London

Copyright © 2004 by Lawrence Erlbaum Associates, Inc.

Lawrence Erlbaum Associates, Inc., Publishers
10 Industrial Avenue
Mahwah, New Jersey 07430

Library of Congress Cataloging-in-Publication Data

Processing instruction : theory, research, and commentary / edited by
Bill VanPatten.
    p. cm. — (Second language acquisition research)
    Includes bibliographical references and index.
ISBN 0-8058-4635-2 (cloth : alk. paper)
1. Language and languages—Study and teaching. 2. Second language acquisition. I. VanPatten, Bill. II. Series.
P53.P736 2003
418'.0071—dc22   2003049449
                                                             CIP

Printed in the United States of America
10 9 8 7 6 5 4 3 2 1

And I am all alone
There is one here beside me
And my problems have all gone
There is not one to deride me
But ya got to have friends ...

—*Mark Klingman and Buzzy Linhart*
as sung by the Divine Miss M, Bette Midler

This volume is dedicated to all my friends and to the late
Murphy Wolf Lee VanPatten, who kept me company up until
he just couldn't anymore. He was a great cat and I miss him.

Contents

Acknowledgments   x

About the contributors   xi

Part I Foundations   1

Chapter 1. Input Processing in SLA
Bill VanPatten   5

Chapter 2. The Nature of Processing Instruction
Wynne Wong   33

Chapter 3. Commentary: What to Teach? How to Teach?
Patsy Lightbown   65

**Chapter 4. Commentary: Input Processing as a Theory of
Processing Input**   79
Michael Harrington

Part II Processing Instruction Versus Other Types of Instruction   93

**Chapter 5. Processing Instruction and the French Causative:
Another Replication**
Bill VanPatten and Wynne Wong   97

**Chapter 6. Processing Instruction and Spanish Ser and Estar:
Forms With Semantic-Aspectual Values**
An Chung Cheng   119

**Chapter 7. The Relative Effects of Processing Instruction and
Meaning-Based Output Instruction**
Andrew P. Farley   143

**Chapter 8. Commentary: Where PI Research has Been and
Where It Should be Going**
Joseph Collentine   169

Part III The Roles of Structured Input and Explicit Information 183

**Chapter 9. Processing Instruction in French:
The Roles of Explicit Information and Structured Input**
Wynne Wong 187

**Chapter 10. The Effects of Structured Input Activities and
Explicit Information on the Acquisition of the Italian
Future Tense**
Alessandro Benati 207

**Chapter 11. Processing Instruction and the Spanish
Subjunctive: Is Explicit Information Needed?**
Andrew P. Farley 227

**Chapter 12. Computer Delivered Implicit Versus Explicit
Feedback in Processing Instruction**
Cristina Sanz 241

**Chapter 13. Commentary: When PI is Focus on Form it is Very,
Very good, but When it is Focus on Forms ...**
Catherine J. Doughty 257

Part IV Long-Term Effects of PI 271

**Chapter 14. The Long-Term Effects of Processing
Instruction**
Bill VanPatten and Claudia Fernández 273

Part V Final Commentaries 291

**Chapter 15. Some Comments on Input Processing and
Processing Instruction**
Susanne Carroll 293

**Chapter 16. On the Generalizability, Limits, and Potential
Future Directions of Processing Instruction Research**
James F. Lee 311

**Chapter 17. Several Reflections on Why There is Good
Reason to Continue Researching the Effects of Processing
Instruction**
Bill VanPatten 325

Author Index 337

Subject Index 343

Acknowledgments

This volume came about for one major reason; I realized early in 2002 that my 1996 book was already out of date. Since the original publication of VanPatten and Cadierno (1993), there has been considerable empirical work within the processing instruction framework. At the same time, critical voices have arisen to challenge the tenets and findings of processing instruction research. Given the considerable empirical work conducted since 1993 coupled with the need to rethink and restate some ideas, I decided it was time to do another book. However, I did not want to do one alone and I also wanted a book that included a number of studies that could be grouped around particular topics related to processing instruction. In this way, the volume would have a built-in replication feel to it. At the same time, I also recognized that particular people could offer important critical insight and commentary. For the most part, those asked to write commentaries have no particular allegiance to processing instruction or its research. The result would be a more balanced perspective and allow readers to determine for themselves the merits of the theory, research, and commentary. I contacted the various people in this volume and, much to my delight, they all readily agreed to participate. The rest, as they say, is history.

So, my first acknowledgments go to the contributors. Although I thank them in Chapter 17, they deserve thanks again. They truly have made this book what it is. I owe extra thanks to Wynne Wong. Wynne discussed a number of points with me regarding the content of this book and contributed to three different chapters. She is always there to lend an ear. I hope she likes the dedication to this book. Thanks also go to Greg Keating, one of my doctoral students. Greg had the lucky task of formatting the volume to turn it into camera-ready copy and also of checking and rechecking references and citations. (I'm sure he doesn't want the blame if there are any errors.) My thanks also to Susan Gass and Jacquelyn Schachter for supporting this volume in its embryonic stage and for getting it into the hands of the publisher. Thanks also to Cathleen Petree, Bonita D'Amil, Nadine Simms, and all the other folks at Lawrence Erlbaum Associates for making this volume happen.

Finally, I owe thanks to my own Ya Ya Sisters: Bryan, Joey, and Mike. The martinis helped a lot.

—Bill VanPatten

About the Contributors

Alessandro Benati is Senior Lecturer in Applied Linguistics and Italian at the University of Greenwich, UK. He has researched and published in the area of second language acquisition and processing instruction.

Susanne Carroll is Professor of English Studies and Applied Linguistics in the Institute of English and American Studies of the Universität Potsdam (Germany). She has published widely on input in second language acquisition, various topics in English and French syntax and is currently working on word segmentation in SLA (and cleaning up her office).

An Chung (Anita) Cheng is Assistant Professor of Spanish in the department of Foreign Languages at the University of Toledo, Ohio, where she also serves as coordinator of Elementary and Intermediate Spanish Program. Her research goal is to link the disciplines of second language acquisition theory and language teaching; her research interests lie in input processing, grammar instruction, discourse analysis, and the application of technology in language teaching and its impacts on second language acquisition.

Joe Collentine is Associate Professor of Spanish at Northern Arizona University and current chair of the Department of Modern Languages. He has researched the acquisition of the Spanish subjunctive and complex morphosyntax, the efficacy of input-oriented instructional techniques and computer assisted language learning, as well the comparative effects of different learning contexts on SLA, such as study abroad and immersion. Joe is also the associate editor of the Applied Linguistics sections of *Hispania*.

Catherine Doughty is Associate Research Director for Second Language Acquisition at the Center for the Advanced Study of Language (CASL), The University of Maryland at College Park. She is widely known for her work in instructed SLA, including issues related to cognition, language processing, and research design. She is co-editor (with Michael H. Long) of *The Handbook of Second Language Acquisition* published in 2003 by Basil Blackwell.

Andrew P. Farley is Assistant Professor of Spanish and Director of Spanish Language at University of Notre Dame. Andrew has authored articles and book chapters on processing instruction and a forthcoming book on structured input for McGraw-Hill's Second Language Professional Series. He and his wife Katharine live in South Bend, Indiana.

Michael Harrington is a Senior Lecturer in Linguistics and Second Language Acquisition at the University of Queensland, Australia. He has published in the areas of second language processing, cognitive models of second language development, computer-mediated second language acquisition, and the acquisition of Japanese as a second language.

James F. Lee is Professor of Spanish at Indiana University. He is well known for his research on second language reading and for his work on input processing, second language instruction, and language program direction. He is currently balancing his career with being a single parent of pre-school triplet daughters.

Patsy M. Lightbown is Distinguished Professor Emeritus of Concordia University. Her research in classroom second language acquisition has focused on learners of elementary school age, especially in Quebec. Now a resident of the United States, she has turned her attention to second language learning and first language maintenance by young Spanish speakers.

Cristina Sanz is Associate Professor at Georgetown University. She has published articles and book chapters on input, technology, and research methodology, and has edited *Cognition and Spanish Bilinguals* and *Spanish Applied Linguistics at the Turn of the Millennium* (co-edited).

Bill VanPatten is Professor of Spanish and Second Language Acquisition at the University of Illinois at Chicago. He has written extensively on input processing, processing instruction, and on the acquisition of Spanish. In his spare time he writes novels and performs standup comedy.

Wynne Wong is Assistant Professor of French and Director of French Basic Language Instruction at The Ohio State University. She has published articles and book chapters on the topics of textual enhancement, processing instruction and the role of attention in SLA. She has a forthcoming book on input enhancement with McGraw-Hill's Second Language Professional Series.

Part I

Foundations

A series of publications (Lee & VanPatten, 1995, 2003; VanPatten, 1993, 1996, 2000, 2002a) has described and discussed both the nature of *input processing* and the nature of *processing instruction* (PI). Sometimes confused in the literature (one sometimes finds reference to input processing when the instructional treatment is meant, and it is not uncommon for some to call processing instruction input processing instruction), input processing refers to the strategies and mechanisms learners use to link linguistic form with its meaning and/or function. The description of these strategies and mechanisms are considered to be context neutral (i.e., the principles described in the model do not change depending on classroom or nonclassroom context). The roots of input processing research stem from early L2 work that was informed by some of the processing principles first described in Slobin (1973) and Bever (1970) for child L1 acquisition. Earlier L2 work (Lee, 1987; LoCoco, 1987; Nam, 1975; VanPatten, 1984) was principally interested in the assignment of function to nouns (e.g., subject/agent vs. object/patient), but work on input processing has subsequently led to questions about how learners link particular forms (e.g., inflections) to their meanings and functions. More recently, issues of sentence parsing in L2 research have surfaced and it is perhaps here that the greatest challenge faces a model of input processing. As I discuss in this section, it is not quite clear how L1 models of parsing can be applied to L2 context to consider the notion of acquisition of form and meaning or function. Because the L1 models are concerned with ambiguity resolution, their potential for explicating acquisition is not clear. Nonetheless, what is clear is that at some point a model of how the L2 parser develops will take on increased importance as we look at the nature of sentence comprehension by L2 learners.

Processing instruction, of course, is the pedagogical intervention that draws insights from a model of input processing. In the same way that some within a Universal Grammar (UG) perspective have asked "If we know what the problem is based on, can we provide instruction that will facilitate parameter resetting?," those working with PI ask "If we know something about input processing, can we use this information to structure activities to improve processing?" VanPatten (2002a) has provided an update on PI research, but it is actually in this volume that recent unpublished research on PI has been gathered for publication. Because of the controversy and debate that has surrounded the PI research (e.g., DeKeyser, Salaberry, Robinson, & Harrington, 2002; DeKeyser & Sokalski, 1996; Salaberry, 1997; Sanz & VanPatten, 1998; VanPatten, 2002b), readers will want to read carefully the descriptions and comments in all chapters given that part of the controversy is at least partially based on interpretations of certain constructs and assumptions about PI.

Chapters 1 and 2 in this volume update and expand on previous descriptions of input processing and PI. Chapter 1 (VanPatten) reconsiders some of the basic principles from VanPatten (1996) and also addresses some of the criticisms of the input processing model that have appeared since then. Chapter 2 (Wong) describes in detail the nature of PI, in particular, structured input activities, offering a good deal of examples from several languages and structural features. The section concludes with insightful comments by Patsy Lightbown and Michael Harrington, each of whom brings a different perspective to the task of commenting on the model and the pedagogical intervention.

REFERENCES

Bever, T. G. (1970). The cognitive basis for linguistic structures. In J. R. Hayes (Ed.), *Cognition and the development of language* (pp. 279–362). NewYork: Wiley.

DeKeyser, R., & Sokalski, K. (1996). The differential role of comprehension and production practice. *Language Learning, 46,* 613–642.

DeKeyser, R. M., Salaberry, R., Robinson, P., & Harrington, M. (2002). What gets processed in processing instruction: A response to Bill VanPatten's "Update." *Language Learning, 52,* 805–823.

Lee, J. F. (1987). Morphological factors influencing pronominal reference assignment by learners of Spanish. In T. A. Morgan, J. F. Lee & B. VanPatten (Eds.), *Language and language use: Studies in Spanish* (pp. 221–232). Lanham, MD: University Press of America.

Lee, J. F., & VanPatten, B. (1995). *Making communicative language teaching happen*. New York: McGraw-Hill.

Lee, J. F., & VanPatten, B. (2003). *Making communicative language teaching happen* (2nd ed.). New York: McGraw-Hill.

LoCoco, V. (1987). Learner comprehension of oral and written sentences in German and Spanish: The importance of word order. In B. VanPatten, T. R. Dvorak & J. F. Lee (Eds.), *Foreign language learning: A research perspective* (pp. 119–129). Cambridge, MA: Newbury House.

Nam, E. (1975). Child and adult perceptual strategies in second language acquisition. Paper presented at the 1975 TESOL Convention, Los Angeles.

Salaberry, M. R. (1997). The role of input and output practice in second language acquisition. *The Canadian Modern Language Review, 53,* 422–451.

Sanz, C., & VanPatten, B. (1998). On input processing, processing instruction, and the nature of replication tasks: a response to M. Rafael Salaberry. *The Canadian Modern Language Review, 54,* 263–273.

Slobin, D. I. (1973). Cognitive prerequisites for the development of grammar. In C. Perguson & D. Slobin (Eds.), *Studies of child language development* (pp. 175-208). New York: Holt, Rinehart, & Winston.

VanPatten, B. (1984). Learners' comprehension of clitic pronouns: More evidence for a word order strategy. *Hispanic Linguistics, 1,* 57–67.

VanPatten, B. (1993). Grammar teaching for the acquisition-rich classroom. *Foreign Language Annals, 26,* 435–450.

VanPatten, B. (1996). *Input processing and grammar instruction: Theory and research.* Norwood, NJ: Ablex.

VanPatten, B. (2000). Processing instruction as form-meaning connections: Issues in theory and research. In J. F. Lee & A. Valdman (Eds.) *Form and meaning in language teaching* (pp. 43-68). Boston: Heinle & Heinle.

VanPatten, B. (2002a). Processing instruction: An update. *Language Learning, 52,* 755–803.

VanPatten, B. (2002b). Processing the content of input processing and processing instruction research: A response to DeKeyser, Salaberry, Robinson, and Harrington. *Language Learning, 52,* 825–831.

Chapter 1

Input Processing in Second Language Acquisition

Bill VanPatten
University of Illinois at Chicago

Without a doubt, second language acquisition (SLA) is complex. It is complex for at least two reasons. It involves the acquisition of a complex implicit linguistic system consisting of lexical entries and their features and forms, an abstract syntactic system, a phonological system, and rules on pragmatic use of language, among other components related to language. In addition, acquisition cannot be reduced to a single process. SLA is best conceived of as involving multiple processes that in turn may contain subprocesses that work at every stage of acquisition.

This chapter is concerned with only one of the processes involved in SLA, the initial process by which learners connect grammatical forms with their meanings as well as how they interpret the roles of nouns in relationship to verbs. This process is termed *input processing* (cf., Chaudron, 1985). In earlier work, I have discussed input processing vis à vis four principles that guide learner attention to linguistic form in the input. Here I will review those principles and expand on them. Before doing so, several points need clarification. The first is that any model of input processing is not per se a model or theory of acquisition. As mentioned previously, acquisition consists of multiple processes. Thus, the mechanisms responsible for how learners restructure grammars (e.g., reset parameters, regularize forms and structures) fall outside the domain of input processing. Likewise, how learners come to be able to produce language for communicative purposes also falls outside the domain of input processing, as do whatever factors or mechanisms are involved in the acquisition of fluency and accuracy in output.

A second very important point is that a model of input processing such as the one presented here is not intended as a final state model; that is, I am not attempting to describe an L2 parser and how it operates. L2 parsers develop over time. The present model attempts to capture under what conditions learners may or may not make connections between a form in the input and a meaning and the processes they initially bring to the task of acquisition. (I take this point up in more detail later.)

A third important point is that a focus on input does not suggest that there is no role for output in acquisition in its more general sense as some have come to wrongly conclude after reading work on input processing. Both input and output have roles in acquisition and I touch upon this later in this chapter. As a preview, I argue that input and output play complementary roles but that we cannot get around the basic fact that the fundamental source of linguistic data for acquisition is the input the learner receives.

A fourth and final point before beginning is that input processing is not about instruction or about classroom-based learning only. As a model of one process involved in acquisition, what we observe about input processing should be true regardless of context. It is true that research on input processing with so-called "naturalistic" learners is scant, at best. But as Gass (1990) argued, there is no reason to believe that the internal mechanisms learners bring to acquisition should somehow be different based on context or language to be learned. To be sure, insights from input processing research can be and have been used to develop intervention techniques for instructed SLA (VanPatten, 1996; Wong, chap. 2, this volume). But instructional developments are not equivalent to a theory or model on which the developments draw.

FIRST, SOME DEFINITIONS

Given the plethora of terms used in SLA these days to talk about similar and related phenomena, it would be appropriate here to discuss the term *processing*. As I use it, processing refers to making a connection between form and meaning. That is, a learner notes a form and at the same time determines its meaning (or function). The connection to meaning may be partial or it may be complete (for example, given the complexity of verb endings in Spanish, a learner may "realize" that a form denotes pastness but has not grasped the aspectual meaning also encoded in the inflection).

Processing is not the same as *perception* of a form or *noticing*. Perception of a form refers to the acoustic signal registration that happens to all auditory stimuli. This occurs prior to assignment of meaning and in a number of cases something perceived may get deleted before assignment of meaning to a sentence (see, for example, the discussion in Wolvin & Coakley, 1985). Noticing, as I understand it, refers to any conscious registration of a form, but not necessarily with any meaning attached to it (Schmidt, 1990). Terrell (1991), for example, very clearly illustrates his ability to notice a form in the input but an inability to assign any meaning (or function to it). In my terms, he noticed the form but did not process it. Thus, processing implies that perception and noticing have occurred, but the latter two do not necessarily imply that a form has been processed (linked with meaning and/or function).

I should also define what I mean by intake. I use the term *intake* to refer to that subset of the input that has been processed in working memory and made available for further processing (i.e., possible incorporation into the developing system). As we will see, intake is not just filtered data (i.e., a mere subset of the input) but it may include data processed incorrectly (i.e., the wrong form-meaning connection may be made). I do not use intake to refer to internalized data. How data makes it into the developing system and the impact this has on the grammar is the subject of what I term *accommodation and restructuring* and lie outside the present discussion.

In short, processing is about making form-meaning/function connections during real time comprehension. It is an on-line phenomenon that takes place in working memory. I turn attention now to the "what" of input processing.

GETTING MEANING WITH THE RESOURCES YOU HAVE

I take as a point of departure the following claims: that during interaction in the L2 (1) learners are focused primarily on the extraction of meaning from the input (e.g., Faerch & Kasper, 1986; Krashen, 1982), (2) that learners must somehow "notice" things in the input for acquisition to happen (Schmidt, 1990 and elsewhere), and that (3) noticing is constrained by working memory limitations regarding the amount of information they can hold and process during on line (or real time) computation of sentences during comprehension (e.g., Just & Carpenter, 1992). We begin with the most basic and overarching principle in input processing:

Principle 1. Learners process input for meaning before they process it for form.

What this principle says is that learners are driven to look for the message or communicative intent in the input. Although this is true of all human communication, for the second language learner undergoing acquisition this "push to get meaning" combined with limited resources for processing input, means that certain elements of form will not get processed for acquisitional purposes. This observation is consistent with a number of perspectives on both first and second language acquisition (e.g., Faerch & Kasper, 1986; Klein, 1986; Sharwood Smith, 1986; Peters, 1985; Wong Fillmore, 1976; among others).

That learners would process input for meaning before form would lead one to ask, "Well, just what is it that learners are processing, especially in the early stages of acquisition?" Again, consistent with observations in both first and second language acquisition, the most logical place for learners to extract meaning is in content words. Although children may come to the task of acquisition with a universal grammar (UG) that distinguishes between lexical and functional categories, they do not come to the task like second language learners who already have the cognitive construct of "word" based on their first language experience (see, for example, the discussion in Peters, 1985, on "units of acquisition"). In short, second language learners in particular know there are "big words" that can help them get the meaning of what is being said to them and their internal processors attempt to isolate these aspects of the speech stream during comprehension. "Little words", inflections on verbs and nouns, may be skipped over or only partially processed and then dumped from working memory as the processing resources in working memory are exhausted by the efforts required to process lexical items. (Some little words and inflections may be processed but not in isolation; that is, they may be fused with the content word they occur with. This is called *chunking* and results in formulas and routines.) The focus on processing content lexical items, then, leads us to posit a sub-principle of Principle 1, one that we might call "The Primacy of Content Words."

> *Principle 1a. Learners process content words in the input before anything else.*

To be sure, the primacy of lexical items in learners' search for meaning in the input is aided by prosodic factors. In most natural languages, content lexical items tend to receive stronger stress than noncontent items and very often, the roots of content items receive stronger stress than any surrounding particles, functors or inflections. Thus, learners may use prosodic cues as a means of helping them locate and process the major "units of meaning" in a given input string.

The primacy of processing lexical items, although helping learners get meaning, creates a secondary problem when it comes to acquisition. Natural languages often involve a great deal of redundancy of meaning. By this I mean that semantic notions are often encoded more than once in either a sentence or in discourse (across sentences). One of the clearest examples is standard English present tense third person singular marking. A basic rule of English is that if a sentence contains a third person singular subject, the verb "must agree" (i.e., *repeat the same semantic and/or functional information*). If we examine the following sentences, we see how.

(1) John (third-person sing) talks (third person sing) too much.
(2) What does (third person sing) John (third person sing) do?
(3a) He (third person sing) talks (third person sing) too much.
(3b) Talk (non finite) too much.
(3c) *Talks (third person sing).

In (1)-(3a), the third person singular referent is marked twice; once by the (pro)noun and once by the verb form. This is called redundancy. Note how only (3a) and (3b) can be answers to (2). (3b) is fine without a noun or pronoun because the verb is nonfinite. (3c) is ruled out because the *–s* on the verb cannot stand alone in a declarative; it requires the obligatory presence of a noun or pronoun that marks the same meaning. This is redundancy.

A fallout, then, of relying on content lexical items is that if a content lexical item and a grammatical form both encode the same meaning, the learner's processing mechanisms need only rely on the lexical item for that semantic information and not the form. In the case of third person *–s*, the noun or pronoun subject is the content lexical item that carries the information that someone else is being talked about. To be sure, not all forms are redundant nor do all forms carry semantic meaning (see the discussion in VanPatten, 1996) but a good many do. The point is that learners may not have to rely on grammatical markers to get the semantic information. Thus, a second subprinciple of Principle 1 would be:

Principle 1b. Learners will tend to rely on lexical items as opposed to grammatical form to get meaning when both encode the same semantic information.

This is a slightly restated version of the original Principle P1b which used the term "prefer" (instead of "tend to rely on") and simply "semantic information" (instead of "same semantic information"). In short, the original wording did not capture the nature of redundancy by omitting the use of "same." This particular subprinciple can be called "The Lexical Preference Principle."

To be clear, it is not the case that learners "choose" to ignore form (one reason to change the word "prefer") any more than it is the case that learners "choose" to process one form over another. Like most aspects of acquisition, learners may voluntarily pay attention to language in order to comprehend, but processing basically happens to the learner. It is also not the case that the processing mechanisms sweep through an input string and eliminate all grammatical form and attend only to lexical items as some have (mis)interpreted (e.g., DeKeyser, Salaberry, Robinson, & Harrington, 2002). To interpret this subprinciple and the next one correctly, one must keep in mind what we mean by *process* and *processing*. To process a form means to connect that form with its meaning and/or its function. The position taken here is that because of the constraints on working memory, these connections may not happen (or may happen only under certain conditions). The learner may very well perceive the form and notice it, but because no connection to meaning or function is made, the form is dropped from further processing. One must keep in mind how effortful comprehension and processing are for beginning and even intermediate learners. Processing lexical items simply drains the resources in working memory that would allow for making a connection to meaning for any possibly perceived form. (Again, this may vary under conditions, a point I discuss later.)

In previous work, I have discussed a third subprinciple for Principle 1. This particular principle is based on the idea that not all forms are equal in terms of the meaning they express. Specifically, some forms carry meaning and some do not. Adjective agreement in languages such as the Romance languages does not carry semantic information when the object of agreement is a noun expressing an inanimate object, as in the following example:

(4) *La* **casa** blanc*a* fue pintad*a*.
The white house was painted.

In this sentence, the head noun *casa* is of feminine grammatical gender. Gender may have originated as a semantic notion (e.g., biologically or socially determined maleness/femaleness), but as a grammatical feature is devoid of semantic information: inanimate nouns such as "house" and "rock" are not biologically or socially constructed with gender. The grammatical form as an inflection, then, is meaningless in terms of semantic information it carries.

Previously we saw that third person *–s* carries a semantic notion (another person that is neither the speaker nor the person the speaker is addressing). However, it is redundant and learners may not make the particular form-meaning connection in the input right away. Alternately, the progressive marker *–ing* is not redundant; it tends to be the sole marker of progressive aspect (a semantic notion) in English as in sentences such as "What are you doing?" "I'm baking a cake. Why are you asking?" There are no lexical items that carry the same information. In the third subprinciple to Principle 1 I suggested that learners would attend to more meaningful items before less meaningful items with the scale being this:

- items with semantic information are meaningful that are not redundant with lexical items bearing the same semantic information;
- items with semantic information that are redundant are less meaningful;
- items with no semantic information are not meaningful.

The particular subprinciple was stated as follows:

P1c. Learners prefer processing "more meaningful" morphology before "less meaningful" morphology.

At the time, I defined "meaningfulness" as the relative communicative value a form had, which meant the overall meaning that form contributed to sentence comprehension. *Communicative value* was operationalized by an intersection of the features [+/- semantic information] and [+/- redundancy] as described above (see Lee, 1987a, for an excellent study that demonstrates how learners skip items of low communicative value during processing). However, this subprinciple is misleading as stated. First, not all grammatical form is morphological in the sense that it is inflected on nouns and verbs. As described soon, form can also exist at the sentence level in terms of word order. In addition, the subprinciple failed to separate redundant form with meaning and form (whether redundant or not) that does not carry meaning. (Meaning, again, refers to a semantic notion.) Here I refine the subprinciple to be two different ones:

> *New P1c. The Preference for Nonredundancy Principle. Learners are more likely to process nonredundant meaningful grammatical form before they process redundant meaningful forms.*
> *New P1d. The Meaning-Before-Nonmeaning Principle. Learners are more likely to process meaningful grammatical forms before nonmeaninful forms irrespective of redundancy.*

The question arises, once one discusses that forms have differential levels of "meaningfulness" (or what I used to term *communicative value*), "If learners are driven to get meaning, how is it that they process the form that does not contribute much to overall sentence meaning?" Recalling that processing form (i.e., linking it with meaning or function) is constrained by the limits of working memory and the taxing nature of comprehension for early and intermediate stage learners, I developed a second principle that said:

> *P2. For learners to process form that is not meaningful, they must be able to process informational or communicative content at no or little cost to attention.*

This principle fell out of the theorem in SLA that increased comprehensibility of input may result in increased acquisition (e.g., Blau, 1990; Hatch, 1983; Long, 1985); in this case, however, we would restate the matter as increased comprehensibility results in increased likelihood of a form being processed in the input. However, as stated, the principle fails to capture that there is also the matter of redundant but meaningful forms that may be difficult to process (a fallout of P1c). What is more, the principle is actually not a principle in its own right, but a derivative of the preceding subprinciples. For these two reasons, the principle is restated here as a new subprinciple:

> *New Principle P1e. The Availabity of Resources Principle. For learners to process either redundant meaningful grammatical forms or nonmeaningful forms, the processing of overall sentential meaning must not drain available processing resources.*

Just what provides for the availability of processing resources? One obvious answer is proficiency level and the nature of learners' ability to access lexical items they have already incorporated into their developing linguistic systems. If lexical retrieval is not laborious during comprehension, in principle resources are not as strained as they would be at an earlier stage. At the same time, familiarity of words in the input would make a difference. Simply put, fewer unknown words in the input string requires less processing of novel lexical items that in turn means releasing resources to process grammatical form.

One Role for Output

Less obvious to some is that task demands also affect processing resources. It is here that one of the roles of output in acquisition becomes evident. Some have argued that negotiated interaction facilitates acquisition. Gass (1997), for example, has said "negotiation is a facilitator of learning; it is one means but not the only means of drawing attention to areas of needed change. It is one means by which input can become comprehensible and manageable" (pp. 131–132). What Gass is arguing, it seems, is that interaction alters the task demands placed on a learner during input processing. The change in task demands frees up attentional resources allowing learners to process something they might miss otherwise. It must be made clear that this position does not suggest that by producing the form in question during the interaction the learner is acquiring or has acquired the form; the position is that by interacting the learner gets crucial data from another interlocutor (more on this later). The following example is illustrative and was overheard in a locker room after a tennis match. "Bob" is a native speaker of English and "Tom" is a non-native speaker with Chinese as a first language.

> Bob: So where's Dave?
> Tom: He vacation.
> Bob: He's on vacation?
> Tom: Yeah. On vacation.
> Bob: Lucky guy.

In this particular interaction, Bob's clarification/confirmation request allowed Tom to notice the use of *on* with *vacation*. Why? Bob's second question did not contain a new message. That is, Tom did not have to process it for its informational content. This freed up the resources in working memory for him to process the preposition. That Tom incorporated it subsequently into a confirmation does not mean that he has acquired it; what it shows us is that he has noticed it, something that Gass claims may be part of the process of acquisition or, in this case, input processing (see also Schmidt, 1990, 1995).

Consistent with Gass's position is one articulated by Swain (1998). She states the following:

> "I have hypothesized that, under certain circumstances, output promotes noticing. This is important if there is a basis to the claim that noticing a form in input must occur in order for it to be acquired." (p. 66)

In addition to altering the attentional demands of the task and thereby getting important data from the input, the learner may also notice that something he or she says is not the same as what was just heard in the input. Thus, the immediacy of juxtaposing one's output with another's input may trigger noticing that is useful for making form-meaning connections. This is one way to explain, for example, the possible benefits of recasts (Ortega & Long, 1997) and the interactions that surround them (see the Bob/Tom just described).

Back to Principles

In later writings (e.g., VanPatten, 1997), I reviewed research on processing that is related to but not the same as a change in task demands. That research focuses on the location of formal elements within a sentence. The research (e.g., Barcroft & VanPatten, 1997; Klein, 1986; as well as some of the literature in cognitive psychology) strongly suggests that elements that appear in certain positions of an utterance are more salient to learners than others, namely, sentence initial position is more salient than sentence final position that in turn is more salient than sentence internal or medial position. Translated into processing grammatical form in SLA, what this observation means is that grammatical form or linguistic elements in sentence initial position are more likely to be processed than elements in other positions (all other processing issues being equal). Why would this be so? Again, the explanation may reside in processing resources. Elements at the beginning are, by definition, the first on which available resources are applied to process an input string. If the resources are constrained then that means the resources may be gobbled up to process that initial item(s) and may not be available for medial items. As the learner approaches the end of the input string (i.e., once again redirects attention to processing the string), the resources may now be available and thus an element in final position gets processed or has chances of being processed. Of course, sentence length may interact with this principle. Processing something like "Is it cold outside?" is a lot different for the early stage or "resource depletion prone" learner than "Is it cold outside or do you think I can go out with just a shirt on?"

The principle of location, then, can be captured in a principle such as P1f:

New Principle P1f. The Sentence Location Principle. Learners tend to process items in sentence initial position before those in final position and these latter in turn before those in medial position.

To summarize so far, we have discussed one major principle and five subprinciples that fall under the general matter of the primacy of meaning in input processing. I list all of the principles here in their most current incarnation for the benefit of the reader.

Principle 1. The Primacy of Meaning Principle. *Learners process input for meaning before they process it for form.*

>   **Principle 1a. The Primacy of Content Words Principle**. *Learners process content words in the input before anything else.*

>   **Principle 1b. The Lexical Preference Principle**. *Learners will tend to rely on lexical items as opposed to grammatical form to get meaning when both encode the same semantic information.*

>   **Principle 1c. The Preference for Nonredundancy Principle**. *Learners are more likely to process nonredundant meaningful grammatical form before they process redundant meaningful forms.*

>   **Principle 1d. The Meaning-Before-Nonmeaning Principle**. *Learners are more likely to process meaningful grammatical forms before nonmeaninful forms irrespective of redundancy.*

>   **Principle 1e. The Availability of Resources Principle**. *For learners to process either redundant meaningful grammatical forms or nonmeaningful forms, the processing of overall sentential meaning must not drain available processing resources.*

>   **Principle 1f. The Sentence Location Principle**. *Learners tend to process items in sentence initial position before those in final position and those in medial position.*

WHO DID WHAT TO WHOM?

Until now we have discussed grammatical form as inflections and noncontent words ("little words"). However, if we expand the notion of form, we see that sentences can also have form. Languages can have different word orders when it comes to relationships of nouns to a verb. English, for example, is almost exclusively SVO in both declaratives and questions. Languages like Spanish and

Hungarian are not so rigid, allowing for SVO, SOV, OVS and others. Thus, as a sentence is processed, learners must assign both grammatical (e.g., subject vs. nonsubject) and semantic (e.g., agent vs. nonagent) roles to nouns in order to get the intended meaning of the speaker.

A good deal of research on L2 sentence processing suggests that learners begin acquisition by tagging the first noun in an NP-V-NP sequence as the subject or agent. We see learners of various first languages tending to interpret (5) as (6).

(5) The cow was kicked by the horse.
(6) The cow kicked the horse.

We suspect that this misinterpretation is not due simply to L1 transfer. First, the L2 learners tested come from various L1 backgrounds, some of which include passives and some that don't. Some allow for flexible surface word order (e.g., in addition to being SVO they may also allow OVS, for example). In one study (Ervin-Tripp, 1974), learners of L1 English going into L2 French tended to interpret the first noun of a passive structure as the agent even though English and French have the exact same sentence structure for passives. Finally, we also know from typological research that SVO and SOV are overwhelmingly the preferred canonical patterns of languages from around the world suggesting that the human mind may be predisposed to placing agents and subjects in a first noun position.

This particular tendency to tag the first noun or noun phrase as the subject or agent is called the first noun principle.

P2. The First Noun Principle. Learners tend to process the first noun or pronoun they encounter in a sentence as the subject or agent.

In terms of consequences for language learning, this principle may cause a delay in the acquisition of passives, any OVS structures, case marking, among others. L2 learners of French, for example, are known to misinterpret causative structures (e.g., Allen, 2000; VanPatten & Wong, this volume). In French, the causative is formed with the verb *faire*.

(7) Jean fait nettoyer la chambre à Marc.
    John makes Mark clean the room.
    (lit: John makes to clean the room to Marc.)

When asked, "Who cleans the room?" learners tend to respond that John does, thereby interpreting the sentence as something like "John cleans the room for Mark." L2 learners of Spanish are known to misinterpret object pronouns when the subject is omitted or placed after the verb (e.g., Lee, 1987b; VanPatten, 1984). Thus, they misinterpret sentences such as the following:

(8) Lo conoce María.
    him—OBJ knows Mary—SUBJ
    incorrect interpretation: He knows Mary.
    correct interpretation: Mary knows him.

(9) Se levanta temprano.
    self-REFL raises early.
    incorrect interpretation: He (= se) gets up early.
    correct interpretation: He (= self) gets up early [as opposed to someone getting him up early].

LoCoco (1987) found that learners of German ignore case markings and misinterpret sentences in German. Sentences such as *Den Lastwagen schiebt das Auto* ('the-OBJ truck pushes the-SUBJ car' 'The car pushes the truck') are incorrectly interpreted by learners as "The truck pushes the car." This occurs even after learners have formally studied case marking in German and have been formally tested on it. (See Gass, 1989, for a study on L2 learners of English and L2 learners of Italian.)

In short, this particular principle may have a variety of consequences in a variety of languages. It is not just that learners may get word order wrong, it is also that they may not process case markings for some time, will have difficulties with the pronoun system in some languages, and so on.

However, there is also research showing that the First Noun Principle can be attenuated in certain circumstances. For example, lexical semantics may come into play. Our earlier example of the passive, repeated as (10) involves two entities equally capable of performing the act of kicking. However, in (11) the lexical semantics of the verb require that an animate being with legs be the subject/agent of the verb ruling out a misinterpretation of who did what to whom.

(10) The cow was kicked by the horse.
(11) The fence was kicked by the horse.

The effects of lexical semantics can be captured as a subprinciple to P2.

P2a. The Lexical Semantics Principle. Learners may rely on lexical semantics, where possible, instead of on word order to interpret sentences.

Another way in which the First Noun Principle may be attenuated is with event probabilities. Event probabilities refer to the likelihood of one noun being the subject/agent as opposed to another. Given two nouns such as *man* and *dog* and the verb *bite*, it is more likely in the real world that a dog would bite a man than the other way around. Thus, learners would likely interpret a sentence such as (12) correctly given what they know about the real world.

(12) The farmer was kicked by the horse.

The principle that captures this aspect of sentence interpretation is the following:

P2b. The Event Probabilities Principle. Learners may rely on event probabilities, where possible, instead of word order to interpret sentences.

In previous work I combined P2a and b into one principle but because lexical semantics and event probabilities are really two different semantic concepts, I have come to realize it is best to discuss them separately. At the same, time we have conducted research based on contextual cues in L1 sentence processing that show that contextual cues in L2 sentence processing may also attenuate the First Noun Principle. In this research (VanPatten & Houston, 1998), we gave learners sets of identical sentences with the only difference being that one set had contextual information that would push them away from interpreting the targeted clause the wrong way. For example, we gave them sentences like (13) and (14). The targeted clause is underlined.

(13) Gloria contó a su amiga que la atacó Ramón en casa.
     Gloria told her friends that her-OBJ attacked Ramon-SUBJ at home.
(14) Roberto está en el hospital porque lo atacó María con un cuchillo.
     Robert is in the hospital because him-OBJ attacked Mary-SUBJ with a knife.

In (14) "Robert is in the hospital" suggests he is there because something has happened to him. This would lead to more interpretations of Mary attacking him with a knife rather than the other way around; that is, "Robert is in the hospital because he attacked Mary with a knife" makes little sense. In (13) the preceding phrase "Gloria told her friends" does not constrain interpretation; the following phrase could equally be that she attacked Ramon or that Ramon attacked her. Our results were overwhelmingly clear. Participants' reliance on the First Noun Principle was significantly less for the sentences with constraining context and some participants showed no reliance at all on the First Noun Principle when a constraining context was present. I have thus added another subprinciple to P2.

P2c. The Contextual Constraint Principle. Learners may rely less on the First Noun Principle if preceding context constrains the possible interpretation of a clause or sentence.

The reader will note the use of the term *preceding*. We have yet to research any effects that a post target context may have on sentence interpretation. For example, if we took (14) and reversed the order of presentation, we would get something like (15). Again, the targeted clause is underlined.

> (15) <u>A María la atacó Ramón</u> y por eso ella está en el hospital.
> Mary-OBJ her-OBJ attacked Ramon-SUBJ and that is why she is in the hospital.

We cannot predict based on our results that learners would necessarily also interpret the first part of the sentence correctly because there is context present. In this case, given aspects of working memory limitations, it is open to empirical investigation whether learners would have the capacity to backtrack and re-process what they heard in the first part of the sentence, and under what conditions they can.

To summarize this section, I have outlined the principles that account for basic sentence interpretation (who did what to whom). These consist of a First Noun Principle and three subprinciples that account for its possible attenuation. The principles are all listed below:

P2. The First Noun Principle. *Learners tend to process the first noun or pronoun they encounter in a sentence as the subject/agent.*

> **P2a. The Lexical Semantics Principle**. *Learners may rely on lexical semantics, where possible, instead of word order to interpret sentences.*

> **P2b. The Event Probabilities Principle**. *Learners may rely on event probabilities, where possible, instead of word order to interpret sentences.*

> **P2c. The Contextual Constraint Principle**. *Learners may rely less on the First Noun Principle if preceding context constrains the possible interpretation of a clause or sentence.*

OTHER MATTERS

In this section, I examine and discuss a number of issues related to input processing that have either arisen in discussions with colleagues or have arisen in scholarship by others.

Looking at More Than one Principle

I should clarify here two aspects of input processing that merit attention. First, the principles do not operate in isolation; sometimes (if not often) several may act together or one may take precedence over the other. It should be clear, for example, that The Availability of Resources Principle allows for learners to process something they might normally miss if the task demands alter the demands placed on processing resources. As the Bob and Tom episode clearly suggests, interactional aspects of language may free up resources when no new information is conveyed. Thus, learners may process something in the input they had missed before. (Remember that process here is not equal to acquisition; we cannot say that just because something is processed that it becomes part of the implicit L2 linguistic system.)

In languages such as Spanish, we have evidence that L2 learners may skip over a non-redundant case marker that is in initial position because the First Noun Principle is such a powerful guide for sentence interpretation. Learners hearing a sentence like *A María no la ha visto Juan por muchos años* 'John has not seen Mary for many years' often miss the object marker *a* (which is not redundant in this particular case; the clitic pronoun *la* is). Even the Sentence Location Principle does not help them to process the case marker (the marker *a* is in initial position). Instead, they are guided completely by the First Noun Principle (VanPatten, 1984).

In some cases, principles "collude" to delay acquisition. The subjunctive in French, for example, is hindered by at least two processing problems; The Lexical Preference Principle (mood is indicated in the matrix clause by a phrase rendering the subjunctive redundant in noun clauses) and The Sentence Location Principle (it tends to occur in medial position in a sentence).

The point here is that one must look at a variety of factors that influence processing rather than at one single principle or problem to determine why a form may be difficult to process in the input. Obviously, such things as frequency in the input ultimately come to bear on acquisition, but we also know that frequency cannot be the only factor (e.g., various papers in N. Ellis, 2002; Larsen-Freeman & Long, 1991).

The Developmental Nature of Processing

Some have taken the model of input processing to be similar to an L1 parsing model and thus should follow the same constraints in terms of construction and theory (e.g., DeKeyser, Salaberry, Robinson, & Harrington, 2002). They have argued that the input processing model makes use of an outdated model of attention as well as a parser that does not consider the standard accounts in L1 parsing, namely, that parsing is structure based. The present model of input processing clearly has a strong meaning-based foundation as Principle 1 and all the subprinciples within it suggest. At first glance, the criticism that this model looks far different from any L1 model of sentence processing seems to be true. However, my argument is that we cannot import wholesale models from L1 studies without concern whether such wholesale importation is appropriate for SLA (we learned this from behaviorism). Let's take parsing first.

That L1 parsing relies on structure precedence is predicated upon ambiguity resolution in L1 sentence processing (e.g., Clifton, Frazier, & Rayner, 1994; Cuetos, Mitchell, & Corley, 1996). These models attempt to account for how native speakers get tripped up and resolve processing problems such as that presented by the verb *raced* in *the horse raced past the barn fell*. The problem here is that the verb can either be a main verb or part of a reduced passive in a relative clause. Other parsing ambiguities in L1 studies include whether people use early or late closure in processing sentences such as *Mary bought a present for the nephew of the man who speaks French*. When asked "Who speaks French?" the answer could be either the nephew or the man and the response depends on whether one has a preference for early closure or late closure. One final example of a parsing issue occurs in languages like Spanish and Italian that allow null-subjects. The Spanish sentence *Vi a Juan cuando [pro] iba a la playa* is ambiguous in that it could mean "I saw John when I was walking to the beach" or "I saw John while he was walking on the beach." (The verb *iba* can be used with either first person or third person singular.)

Although important matters for L1 parsing models, such issues hardly speak to the basic L2 question of "What forms get processed under what conditions?" In addition, developing L2 learners do not have intact L2 parsers like L1 speakers. L2 learners may *eventually* wind up with a parsing mechanism that can be described and tested using L1 models but this does not mean they *begin* with those parsers. Child L1 acquirers certainly don't (e.g., Crain, Ni, & Conway, 1994). Likewise, L2 learners must build L2 parsers. If we briefly examine the research of Fernández (1999), for example, we see one of the limitations of the application of parsing research to SLA. Fernández investigated native, early non-native and advanced non-native interpretations of sentences with ambiguous prepositional phrases such as *Roxanne read the review of the play that was written by Diane's friend*. When asked the question *What was written by Diane's friend? The review or the play?* native speakers of English tend (about 60%) to answer *the play*, revealing what is called a "late closure strategy." Native Spanish speakers, with the exact same sentence in Spanish (literally, word for word) respond (again, about 60%) *the review* revealing a preference for "early closure." What she found was that the learners tended to use the L1 preference in interpreting the L2 sentences. She answers her main research question—Do adult learners process L2 linguistic input in the way monolingual speakers of the target language do?—"No, they don't." The question for us in this chapter is "What does this have to do with making form-meaning connections?" Certainly nothing regarding the *initial* processing of inflections, functors, and other surface features of language and certainly not the *initial* processing of basic syntax. It does tell us that learners have L1

preferences for interpretation of ambiguous sentences, something that may or
may not be important in the long run. But note that the preferences of native
speakers hovers around 60%. Do we want to say that the remaining 40% of
native speakers' responses are wrong because they don't fit the pattern? Clearly
both interpretations are possible in both languages and both sets of native
speakers use them. My point is that although I find this study highly interesting
for its basic premise (that we must study processing in order to understand
acquisition), and it is certainly a solid piece of research uncovering processing
preferences for ambiguous sentences, I am not sure where this line of parsing
research will lead in relation to the basic questions: "What do learners process in
the input and why to they process that and miss something else?" Perhaps as we
get more sophisticated in relating parsing to form-meaning connections, my
skepticism will change.

It should be noted that my skepticism does not contradict the cautious
optimism of Harrington (2001) who believes that the application of L1
processing frameworks to L2 processing contexts may prove insightful. After
reviewing three different approaches to sentence processing research (a
principle-based approach, a constraint-based approach, and a referential
approach) he concludes, "Research on ambiguity resolution has generated a
large body of [L1] empirical findings and has been a primary source of evidence
for current [L1] models of sentence comprehension. However, with more
interest directly on learning processes, the focus is starting to shift to modeling
acquisition processes in which the focus is on modeling normal learning
processes" (pp. 123–134). The current model of input processing is attempting
to do precisely this by starting with the premise that comprehension and
processing for natives cannot and is not the same process as that for beginning
non-natives who must not only comprehend but also come to discover linguistic
data in what they comprehend.

Harrington (2001) is useful here to help us understand the domain of input
processing. He discusses three components or mechanisms of sentence
comprehension: algorithms, heuristics, and representations. Algorithms are
stated as IF–THEN procedures for processing outcomes and as Harrington states
"are responsible for transforming linguistic input into meaning" (p. 98).
Heuristics are pre-existing principles that constrain how the algorithms work.
Harrington offers the examples of the late closure principle (related to the
Fernández study described above) and Slobin's operating principles such as
"Pay attention to the ends of words" (Slobin, 1973). Representations refer to the
linguistic and non-linguistic knowledge structures of the learner. As Harrington
puts it "[representations] are the 'stuff' on which algorithms and heuristics
operate" (p. 99).

If we take something like our Lexical Preference Principle in L2 input
processing by which learners tend to rely on lexical items as cues to meaning
rather than their corresponding grammatical markers, this is clearly not an
algorithm or a representation. It functions much like the heuristics Harrington

refers to. But what is important to note here is that the Lexical Preference Principle is *not meant to be a final state principle* for sentence comprehension but a *constraint on processing* (making form-meaning connections) during acquisition. It attempts to describe a particular strategy that learners take to the task of comprehension that affects processing.

To be sure, the current model of input processing does not address the issue of how learners come to process syntactic information such as co-reference and reduced clauses vs. main verbs. (I discuss this in the section on L1 influence.) Thus, the concept of *input processing* cannot be equated with the term *sentence processing* as it is normally used in the psycholinguistic literature.

As for capacity, although it may be true that some models of attention no longer describe fixed resources, the issue of capacity is simply inescapable in current discussions of attention. In his 1998 book, Pashler reviews attention in great detail as well as the various models that have evolved over several decades of research. At almost every level of discussion in his book, the issue of capacity (that is, limited resources) surfaces in the terms "gate keeping" (to describe what gets excluded during processing), "selective attention," "interference of one detected stimuli with another," "competition," and others. What is clear from his conclusions is that limited resources and limited capacity, as constructs within attention, are alive and well: "Assuming these conclusions are roughly correct, many basic questions still remain to be resolved. One question is the nature and source of the capacity limitations that arise with perceptual overload" (Pashler, 1998, p. 403).

The issue of attentional limits and capacity constraints in language processing has been addressed by Just and Carpenter (1992). They have proposed a model of capacity limitations that is comprehension-oriented. One of their most fundamental claims is that language comprehension is one of the most capacity robbing behaviors that humans engage in and that capacity affects skill in terms of reading and listening (see also the discussion in Gathercole & Baddeley, 1993). Their claim is that capacity is not the same for everyone and that there are individual differences in capacity that affect the on-line computations a reader or listener makes during comprehension. In short, some people have greater capacity than others. If a language-based L1 model suggests that comprehension is capacity robbing, we can only begin to imagine the drain on resources for the L2 learner attempting to comprehend in a new language and the impact this has on input processing. In short, any model of L2 input processing would have to consider in some way the impact of capacity issues in working memory on what learners can do at a given point in time.

As one more point, no matter what weaknesses reside in the explanations behind learner processing behaviors, the fact remains that the processing principles do describe what L2 learners actually do. There is published and unpublished research using on- and off-line measures that show that learners do indeed prefer lexical items to grammatical markers for getting semantic information (e.g., Lee, Cadierno, Glass, & VanPatten, 1997; Mangubhai, 1991;

Pondea & Wong, 2003; Musumeci, 1989), that a First Noun Principle is active (e.g., see Allen, 2000; VanPatten, 1996), that there are position preferences for processing (e.g., Barcroft & VanPatten, 1997; Klein, 1986; Rosa & O'Neill, 1998), and so on.

To conclude, a model of L2 input processing must capture the developmental and non-static nature of how learners get form from input and how they process basic syntax. The model must address the basic questions of what gets processed, why it gets processed, and the conditions that affect the processing. The current model attempts to do this.

First Language Influence

The problem of L1 influence in SLA has long been acknowledged, but its manner of operation is debated. Within input processing one might ask the question "Doesn't the nature of the L1 influence how learners process input?" This is a legitimate question. For example, shouldn't French speakers process the subjunctive sooner and better in Spanish than learners with English as the L1? Given they already have grammars with the subjunctive they can use this knowledge to process the subjunctive in the input. Although this may be true, it does not mean that the learners will process the subjunctive before non-redundant forms, for example. It does not mean that the learners do not have preference for location in sentences, for example. It simply means that when they finally do *notice* the form in the input, they are more likely to process it (connect form and meaning/function) than their English L1 counterparts.

Several other questions about L1 influence surface in the present discussion: what about the First Noun Principle? Isn't this principle dependent on the first language? What about learners whose L1 is object first (e.g., OVS)? Wouldn't they process sentences thinking the first noun is the object? These, too, are legitimate questions. Those working within the Competition Model would certainly claim that learners begin with L1 processors. The Competition Model says that sentence processing involves the use of weighted cues and that in a given L1, certain cues are preferred over others because in that language they are more reliable and valid. For example, in English word order is preferred over cues such as animacy as a cue to agency and patience because in natural language data English word order is highly reliable as a cue. MacWhinney (1997) has made the following claim about SLA and processing: "We find, uniformly, that the learning of sentence processing cues in a second language is a gradual process. The process begins with L2 cue weight settings that are close to the L1" (p. 129). To cut to the chase, L2 learners transfer L1 cue weights.

Although this claim is backed by considerable research (see MacWhinney, 1997, for the summary), I have wondered about the foundation of the Competition Model. Cue weight preferences are determined by giving speakers sentences in which cues are put into *deliberate conflict*. For example, NVN sentences are fairly unrevealing to understand how people assign agency or subject-status to nouns because the world's languages are overwhelmingly subject-first, or rather subject-before-object, in terms of canonical order. So what those working with the Competition Model do is *create* conflicts with NVN in which animacy is thrown in as the conflict. For example, participants are asked to respond to sentences such as *rock-throw-monkey*. What the Competition Model research finds is that English speakers tend to select the rock as the subject more often than speakers of other languages, thus showing a strong preference for word order. Italian speakers would select the monkey more often because it is animate (see the Lexical Semantics Principle earlier in this chapter).

What puzzles me about this research is what it actually says about non-conflict situations. When given sentences such as monkey-bite-baboon, all speakers regardless of language, pick the monkey as the subject. This suggests to me that there is something much more primitive and default about word order (the first noun as the subject) and that differences only surface when we deliberately put conflict into sentences. Thus, some languages develop cues in addition to word order but everyone has word order at the core. If this interpretation is correct, then English speakers do not transfer word order to L2 processing; they simply use the default cue. Speakers of other languages have cues in addition to the basic cue and thus may transfer those while retaining the core cue of word order.

The only way to test this hypothesis, of course, is to work with learners of OVS languages. I do not see this happening in the near future. We do have research on learners from SVO and SOV languages. But as mentioned above, even when word orders are the same as in the case of English and French passives, we do not see *positive* transfer.

In more general terms, it is certainly possible that learners transfer language specific aspects of their parsers. That is, they may transfer strategies such as the late/early closure strategy or other co-reference preferences (Fernández, 1999). If their L1 parsers cannot handle such things as gaps (e.g., Juffs & Harrington, 1995), they may have difficulty processing sentences with extractions; the difficulty being that they have to backtrack to reanalyze a sentence and may not have the capacity to do so. These functional areas of syntax in processing are certainly worthy of exploration but, again, we must remember the fundamental question that has driven current input processing research: What form–meaning connections do learners make and why do they make those and not others at a given point in time? Input processing may evolve into two subareas, one that deals with form-meaning connections and another that deals with issues of syntax or sentence processing.

The Relationship of Input Processing to Restructuring

Some might consider or conclude that a model of input processing is a model of acquisition. This is not so. In previous publications I describe acquisition as something consisting of different processes, each bringing something to bear on acquisition. In Figure 1.1, I offer a shorthand sketch of these processes. (Although this figure captures the basic processes in acquisition, it is not meant to convey that acquisition is linear with no interaction between some of processes and/or products.) As this shorthand depiction suggests, input processing is the "first hurdle" a form or structure must jump through on its path toward acquisition. If a form is processed (there is a connection of form and meaning, whether right or wrong from a target standpoint), it becomes available for further processing and may be accommodated into the developing linguistic system. Accommodation may be complete, partial, or it may not happen at all (for reasons not well understood). An accommodated form may cause repercussions in the grammar and trigger some kind of restructuring, such as a parameter resetting within a UG framework or something like U-shaped development, documented in cognitive and behavioral research. Thus, input processing only offers data for the internal mechanisms that store and organize language in the brain; it does not do the organization and storage itself. As one example, English-speaking learners of Spanish get unequivocal data early on that Spanish has verb movement. The data come in the form of VSX questions such as *¿Almorzó María con Juan?* (Did Mary eat lunch with John?). The verb appears before the subject and can only have done so if the language allows verb movement. Input processing tags the content lexical item in initial position, *almorzó,* with the meaning *ate lunch* and assigns it the status of VERB. Input processing tags the content lexical item *María* with its meaning and assigns it the status of NOUN and SUBJECT. Thus, the input processing mechanisms make available the VS word order to the processors responsible for parameter resetting (if one believes in a UG account of things) and it is there where the restructuring begins. Spanish speaking learners of English get consistent SVX word order and so there are no data disconfirming verb movement delivered to the internal processors given that SVX is possible in verb movement languages.

Output is the result of the acquisition and development of separate processes such as access and production procedures (e.g., Pienemann, 1998). Again, input processing is the starting point for acquisition; it is not the end point nor can it be equated with acquisition itself. Figure 1.2 captures in shorthand what I have discussed regarding input processing in this chapter. Note that Figure 1.2 zeroes in on that part of acquisition that involves the derivation of intake from input.

I   II   III
input → intake → developing system → output

I = input processing
II = accommodation, restructuring
III = access, production procedures

FIG. 1.1. A Sketch of Basic Processes in Acquisition.

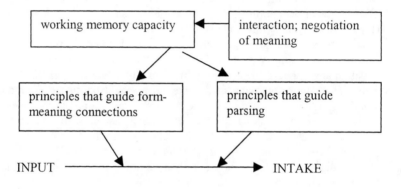

FIG. 1.2.   A Detail of Process I from Figure 1.1.

The Role of Output in Acquisition, Again

Because of the fundamental role I place on input in making form-meaning connections for the development of an underlying system, I have often been juxtaposed to interactionist positions or the position taken by Swain on the role of output in SLA. The suggestion is that I dismiss output or do not think it is important simply because it does not figure into my research. As my discussion regarding P1e above clearly shows, one role for output in acquisition may be the effect it has on the task demands. Interaction may make input more manageable by creating shorter sentences for learners to process, by repeating information so that the demands to get meaning are lessened, by moving elements into more salient positions, and so on. Greater manageability can lead to increased resources for processing.

What I disagree with in terms of a possible role for output is that using a form in one's output is a direct path to acquisition. In some approaches to SLA, such as skill acquisition theory (e.g., DeKeyser, 1997, 1998), the claim is that SLA follows the same rules that skill learning in general follow, namely, learners begin with some kind of declarative knowledge that is proceduralized and automatized via output (e.g., Anderson, 2000). Learners acquire forms and structures by using them repeatedly in communicative situations. My belief is that skill development is a separable phenomenon from the creation of an implicit linguistic system (see VanPatten, 2003). I believe that learners do create linguistic systems based on input processing, accommodation, restructuring, interaction, and the mechanisms involved in these processes. I also believe that learners have to acquire appropriate procedures for accessing forms and phrases and also for stringing them together to make utterances (Pienemann, 1998; Terrell, 1986). In short, the creation of a linguistic system does not in and of itself guarantee fluency and accuracy in production. At the same time practicing forms and structures in output does not result in acquisition as I (and probably most others) define it. Thus, I distinguish between output as interaction with others and output as production of forms and structures. Although learners may need to produce output to develop the types of procedures Pienemann describes and only through output can they automate these procedures, making output does not create an implicit system. (For more detailed discussion, see VanPatten, forthcoming).

CONCLUSION

In this chapter I have updated and clarified various aspects of input processing from previous publications (e.g., VanPatten, 1996, 2002a and b). We are far from understanding everything we need to know about L2 input processing. My hope is that psycholinguists in SLA continue to work in this fertile area of investigation. Understanding how learners deal with initial and subsequent encounters with formal features in the input can offer great insights into the creation of an L2 linguistic system. As the rest of this book suggests, there are insights to be gained for L2 pedagogical intervention as well.

To be absolutely clear, my hope for continued work in input processing is not a call for researchers to abandon other areas of SLA. As the opening sentence to this chapter says, SLA is a complex process. It cannot be reduced to one simple theory or one simple mechanism. In a sense, understanding SLA is like understanding how a building works. There is the electrical system, the plumbing, the foundation, the frame, the heat and air system, and so on. All are necessary; one alone is insufficient. But like those who work in house construction and are electrical contractors or plumbing contractors, in SLA some of us are interested in matters dealing with input. Others are interested in output.

Others are interested in universal aspects of language. Others have focused on interaction. This is a good thing.

REFERENCES

Allen, L. Q. (2000). Form-meaning connections and the French causative: An experiment in processing instruction. *Studies in Second Language Acquisition, 22,* 69–84.

Anderson, J. R. (2000). *Learning and memory* (2nd ed.). New York: John Wiley & Sons.

Barcroft, J., & VanPatten, B. (1997). Acoustic salience of grammatical forms: The effect of location, stress, and boundedness on Spanish L2 input processing. In A. T. Pérez-Leroux & W. R. Glass (Eds.), *Contemporary perspectives on the acquisition of Spanish: Vol. 2. Production, processing, and comprehension* (pp. 109–121). Somerville, MA: Cascadilla Press.

Blau, E. K. (1990). The effect of syntax, speed and pauses on listening comprehension. *TESOL Quarterly, 24,* 746–753.

Chaudron, C. (1985). Intake: On methods and models for discovering learners' processing of input. *Studies in Second Language Acquisition, 7,* 1–14.

Clifton, C. Jr., Frazier, L., & Rayner, K. (Eds.). (1994). *Perspectives on sentence processing.* Hillsdale, NJ: Lawrence Elrbaum Associates.

Crain, S., Ni, W., & Conway, L. (1994). Learning, parsing and modularity. In C. Clifton, Jr., L. Frazier & K. Rayner (Eds.), *Perspectives on sentence processing* (pp. 443–467). Hillsdale, NJ: Lawrence Elrbaum Associates.

Cuetos, F., Mitchell, D. C., & Corley, M. M. B. (1996). Parsing in different languages. In M. Carreiras, J. E. García-Albea & N. Sebastián-Gallés (Eds.), *Language processing in Spanish* (pp. 145–187). Mahwah, NJ: Lawrence Elrbaum Associates.

DeKeyser, R. M. (1997). Beyond explicit rule learning: Automatizing second language morphosyntax. *Studies in Second Language Acquisition, 19,* 195–221.

DeKeyser, R. M. (1998). Beyond focus on form: Cognitive perspectives on learning and practicing second language grammar. In C. Doughty & J. Williams (Eds.), *Focus on form in classroom second language acquisition* (pp. 42–63). Cambridge: Cambridge University Press.

DeKeyser, R. M., Salaberry, R., Robinson, P., & Harrington, M. (2002). What gets processed in processing instruction: A response to Bill VanPatten's "Update." *Language Learning, 52,* 805–823.

Ellis, N. (Ed.). (2002). Frequency effects in language processing: A review with commentaries. Special issue of *Studies in Second Language Acquisition, 24.*

Ervin-Tripp, S. M. (1974). Is second language learning really like the first? *TESOL Quarterly, 8,* 111–127.

Faerch, C., & Kasper, G. (1986). The role of comprehension in second language learning. *Applied Linguistics, 7,* 257–274.

Fernández, E. (1999). Processing strategies in second language acquisition: some preliminary results. In E. Klein and G. Martohardjono (Eds.), *The development of second langauge grammars: A generative approach* (pp. 217–239). Philadelphia: John Benjamins.

Gass, S. M. (1989). How do learners resolve linguistic conflicts? In. S. Gass & J. Schacter (Eds.), *Linguistic perspectives on second language acquisition* (pp. 183–199). Cambridge: Cambridge University Press.

Gass, S. M. (1990). Second and foreign language learning: Same, different, or none of the above? In B. VanPatten & J. F. Lee (Eds.), *Second language acquisition and foreign language learning* (pp. 34–44) Clevedon: Multilingual Matters.

Gass, S. M. (1997). *Input, interaction, and the second language learner.* Mahwah, NJ: Lawrence Elrbaum Associates.

Gathercole, S. E., & Baddeley, A. D. (1993). *Working memory and language.* Hillsdale, NJ: Lawrence Elrbaum Associates.

Harrington, M. (2001). Sentence processing. In P. Robinson (Ed.), *Cognition and second language instruction* (pp. 91–124). Cambridge: Cambridge University Press.

Hatch, E. (1983). Simplified input and second language acquisition. In R. W. Andersen (Ed.), *Pidginization and creolization as language acquisition* (pp. 64–88). Rowley, MA: Newbury House.

Juffs, A., & Harrington, M. (1995). Parsing effects in second language sentence processing: Subject and object asymmetries in Wh-extraction. *Studies in Second Language Acquisition, 17,* 483–516.

Just, M. A., & Carpenter, P. A. (1992). A capacity theory of comprehension: Individual differences in working memory. *Psychological Review, 99,* 122–149.

Klein, W. (1986). *Second language acquisition.* Cambridge: Cambridge University Press.

Krashen, S. D. (1982). *Principles and practice in second language acquisition.* Oxford: Pergamon Press.

Larsen-Freeman, D., & Long, M. H. (1991). *Introduction to second language acquisition research.* London: Longman.

Lee, J. F. (1987a). The Spanish subjunctive: An information processing perspective. *The Modern Language Journal, 71,* 50–57.

Lee, J. F. (1987b). Morphological factors influencing pronominal reference assignment by learners of Spanish. In T. A. Morgan, J. F. Lee & B. VanPatten (Eds.), *Language and language use: Studies in Spanish* (pp. 221–232). Lanham, MD: University Press of America.

Lee, J. F., Cadierno, T., Glass, W. R., & VanPatten, B. (1997). The effects of lexical and grammatical cues on processing tense in second language input. *Applied Language Learning, 8*, 1–23.

LoCoco, V. (1987). Learner comprehension of oral and written sentences in German and Spanish: The importance of word order. In B. VanPatten, T. R. Dvorak & J. F. Lee (Eds.), *Foreign language learning: A research perspective* (pp. 119–129). Cambridge, MA: Newbury House.

Long, M. H. (1985). Input and second language acquisition theory. In S. M. Gass & C. Madden (Eds.), *Input in second language acquisition* (pp. 377–393). Rowley, MA: Newbury House.

MacWhinney, B. (1997). SLA and the Competition Model. In A. M. B. de Groot & J. F. Kroll (Eds.), *Tutorials in bilingualism* (pp. 113–142). Mahway, NJ: Lawrence Elrbaum Associates.

Mangubhai, F. (1991). The processing behaviors of adult second language learners and their relationship to second language proficiency. *Applied Linguistics, 12*, 268–297.

Musumeci, D. (1989). *The ability of second language learners to assign tense at the sentence level.* Unpublished doctoral dissertation, University of Illinois, Urbana-Champaign.

Ortega, L., & Long, M. H. (1997). The effects of models and recasts on the acquisition of object topicalization and adverb placement in L2 Spanish. *Spanish Applied Linguistics, 1,* 65–86.

Pashler, H. E. (1998). *The psychology of attention.* Cambridge, MA: MIT Press.

Peters, A. M. (1985). Language segmentation: Operating principles for the perception and analysis of language. In D. I. Slobin (Ed.), *The cross-linguistic study of language acquisition, vol 2.* (pp. 1029–1067). Hillsdale, NJ: Lawrence Elrbaum Associates.

Pienemann, M. (1998). *Language processing and second language development: Processability theory.* Philadelphia: John Benjamins.

Pondea, L., & Wong, W. (2003). Assigning tense at the sentence level in second language acquisition. Unpublished manuscript. The Ohio State University.

Rosa, E., & O'Neill, M. (1998). Effects of stress and location on acoustic salience at the initial stages of Spanish L2 input processing. *Spanish Applied Linguistics, 2,* 24–52.

Schmidt, R. W. (1990). The role of consciousness in second language learning. *Applied Linguistics, 11,* 129–158.

Schmidt, R. W. (1995). Consciousness and foreign language learning: A tutorial on the role of attention and awareness in learning. In R. W. Schmidt (Ed.), *Attention and awareness in foreign language learning* (pp. 1–63). Honolulu: University of Hawaii Press.

Sharwood Smith, M. (1986). Comprehension versus acquisition: Two ways of processing input. *Applied Linguistics, 7,* 239–274.

Slobin, D. I. (1973). Cognitive prerequisites for the development of grammar. In C. Ferguson & D. I. Slobin (Eds.), *Studies in child language development* (pp. 175-208). New York: Holt, Rinehart, & Winston.

Swain, M. (1998). Focus on form through conscious reflection. In C. Doughty & J. Williams (Eds.), *Focus on form in classroom second language acquisition* (pp. 64–81). Cambridge: Cambridge University Press.

Terrell, T. (1986). Acquisition in the natural approach: The binding/access framework. *The Modern Language Journal, 70*, 213–227.

Terrell, T. (1991). The role of grammar instruction in the communicative approach. *The Modern Language Journal, 75*, 52–63.

VanPatten, B. (1984). Learners' comprehension of clitic pronouns: More evidence for a word order strategy. *Hispanic Linguistics, 1*, 57–67.

VanPatten, B. (1996). *Input processing and grammar instruction: Theory and research.* Norwood, NJ: Ablex.

VanPatten, B. (1997). On the relevance of input processing to second language acquisition theory and second language instruction. In A. T. Pérez-Leroux & W. R. Glass (Eds.), *Contemporary perspectives on the acquisition of Spanish: Vol. 2. Production, processing, and comprehension* (pp. 93–108). Somerville, MA: Cascadilla Press.

VanPatten, B. (2002a). Processing instruction: An update. *Language Learning, 52*, 755–803.

VanPatten, B. (2002b). Processing instruction, prior awareness, and the nature of second language acquisition: A (partial) response to Batstone. *Language Awareness, 11*, 240–258.

VanPatten, B. (2003). *From input to output: A teacher's guide to second language acquisition.* New York: McGraw-Hill.

VanPatten, B. (forthcoming). Input and output in establishing form-meaning connections. In B. VanPatten, J. Williams, S. Rott & M. Overstreet (Eds.), *Form-meaning connections in second language acquisition.*

VanPatten, B., & Houston, T. (1998). Contextual effects in processing L2 input sentences. *Spanish Applied Linguistics, 2*, 53–70.

Wolvin, A. D., & Coakley, C. G. (1985). *Listening*, 2nd edition. Dubuque, IA: William C. Brown Publishers.

Wong Fillmore, L. (1976). *The second time around.* Unpublished doctoral dissertation, University of California, Berkeley.

Chapter 2

The Nature of Processing Instruction

Wynne Wong
The Ohio State University

Processing Instruction (PI) is a type of focus on form instruction that is predicated on a model of input processing (see VanPatten, chap. 1, this volume, and elsewhere). The goal of PI is to help L2 learners derive richer intake from input by having them engage in structured input activities that push them away from the strategies they normally use to make form-meaning connections. This chapter describes in detail the nature of PI. I describe the three major characteristics of PI: (1) explicit information about the target structure, (2) explicit information about processing strategies, and (3) structured input activities. I pay particular attention to the nature of structured input activities because, as is clear from attempted replication research by others (e.g., Allen, 2000; DeKeyser & Sokalski, 1996; Salaberry, 1997), the purpose and nature of structured input activities is not always clear to readers. As part of my discussion, I also examine the guidelines suggested for developing structured input activities as first outlined in VanPatten (1993) and then expanded on in Lee and VanPatten (1995), VanPatten (1996) and Wong (2002a). Of particular interest and critical to PI is the sixth guideline, "Keep learners' psycholinguistic processing strategies in mind."

INPUT PROCESSING AND PROCESSING INSTRUCTION

PI is a type of explicit grammar instruction that is informed by a model of how L2 learners initially process L2 input to make form-meaning connections, that is to say, VanPatten's model of input processing (1993, 1996, 2002, this volume).

I   II   III
Input   →   Intake   →   Developing System → Output
                  [Working Memory]

I = input processing: the conversion of input to intake
II = accommodation, restructuring: incorporation of intake into developing system
III = access

FIG. 2.1. Three Sets of Processes in Second Language Acquisition
(based on VanPatten, 1996).

VanPatten conceptualizes second language acquisition (SLA) as the result of internal mechanisms acting on meaning-bearing input. These mechanisms are conceptualized as consisting of sets of processes (Fig. 2.1.). The first process, called input processing, involves the conversion of input into intake. Intake is defined as input that learners pay attention to and from which form-meaning connections have been made (VanPatten, 1996). This subsequent processing involves the actual incorporation of the data into the system (called "accommodation"), which may be partial or complete. Depending on the nature of the data, accommodation may have an effect on the developing system such that some kind of restructuring may occur. Finally, linguistic data that have been incorporated into the developing system may be eventually accessed by the learner as output or production. This process is called "access."

VanPatten's model of input processing focuses on the first process, that is, input processing. The model provides various principles with corollaries to explain (1) what learners attend to in the input and why, (2) what strategies direct how they make form-meaning connections, and (3) why they make some form-meaning connections before others.

The model postulates that L2 learners will initially pay attention to items in the input that are crucial for understanding referential meaning before items that are less important for doing so (Principle 1).[1] This means that more meaningful items in the input will initially get processed before less meaningful ones and implies that content words are probably the first things that learners process (e.g., see research by Musumeci, 1989; Lee, Cadierno, Glass, & VanPatten, 1997). Principle 1e explains that learners will also be able to attend to forms that are less meaningful if they do not have to struggle with understanding the meaning of the message.

Principle 2, also known as the first noun principle, deals with how word order affects processing strategies, particularly when the L2 does not follow a strict SVO order. Research (e.g., Lee, 1987; VanPatten, 1984) has documented

---

[1]See VanPatten (this volume, chap. 1) for a complete list and description of the principles.

that learners tend to assign the role of agent to the first noun that they encounter even when the first noun is not the subject. Thus, the model predicts that when learners initially attempt to parse sentences, they have a tendency to assume that the first noun is always the subject.

Principle 1f concerns how the position of the form in question may have an effect on whether or not it is likely to get processed. Supported by research by Barcroft and VanPatten (1997) and Rosa and O'Neill (1998), this principle postulates that forms that are in initial position in a sentence get processed first followed by those in sentence final position. Forms in medial position tend to be the most difficult to process.

As can be seen from this model, the strategies that L2 learners use to process input are not always efficient and may sometimes be wrong. The goal of PI is to push learners away from these processing strategies toward more optimal ones. What makes PI unique compared to other focus on form techniques is that it first identifies the processing strategy that hinders learners from processing a particular form or structure correctly. Once the strategy has been identified, activities are created to help learners process input more efficiently. For example, according to Principle 1, learners tend to process input for meaning before they do so for form and will consequently pay less or no attention to forms that are not critical to the propositional content of utterances or sentences. How can we manipulate the input so that they will pay attention to these items? According to Principle 2, learners tend to rely on a first noun strategy and assign the role of agent/subject to the first noun in a sentence. What forms and structures does this strategy affect and in what ways can we structure the input to ensure that learners do not rely on the strategy?

To summarize, PI is a pedagogical tool that is informed by a model of input processing. Input processing is a model of how L2 learners initially parse L2 input to make form-meaning connections. Based on this information about how L2 learners process input on their own, PI pushes learners to abandon their inefficient processing strategies for more optimal ones so that better form-meaning connections are made.

THREE CHARACTERISTICS OF PI

PI has three basic characteristics. First, learners are given information about how the linguistic form or structure works, focusing on one form or use at a time. This explicit information (EI) also informs learners about a particular IP strategy that may lead them to process the input incorrectly. This is the second characteristic of PI. An example of what the EI may look like in PI is found in Figure 2.2. The target of instruction here is the French causative and the processing problem is a word order problem. Note that in order to alert learners of their processing problem, this explanation includes information about learners' processing strategies (i.e., "don't use a first noun strategy").

We often ask or get people to do things for us by telling them to do something.

Paul says, "John, would you mind doing the dishes?"

If you and I were to describe what is happening we might say:

We say, "Paul gets John to do the dishes."
or
"Paul makes John do the dishes."

This is called a causative construction (because someone is causing a behavior in someone else). French has a similar structure using the verb *faire*. Let's repeat our examples from above.

Paul says, "Jean, pourrais-tu faire la vaisselle?"
We say, "Paul fait faire la vaisselle à Jean."

How would we describe the following scenario?

Wynne says, "Sara, pourrais-tu promener le chien?"

We would describe Wynne getting Sara to do it like this.

We say, "Wynne fait promener le chien à Sara."

Often we don't mention who we get to do something; we might simply say we have something done.

"Paul fait nettoyer la chambre."

In this case, Paul has the room cleaned, but we don't know who or how.

One of the problems the *faire causatif* presents is in listening comprehension. Second language learners of French often misinterpret what they hear because the word order is different from English. For example, it is not uncommon for learners of French to make the following mistake:

They hear: "Jean fait faire la vaisselle à Paul."
They incorrectly think: John is doing the dishes for Paul.
or
They hear: "Marc fait couper les cheveux.
The incorrectly think: Marc cuts hair.

In the activities that follow, we will practice hearing and interpreting the *faire causatif.*

FIG. 2.2. Example of Explicit Information in PI.

The third characteristic of PI involves giving learners "structured input" (SI) activities. They are termed *structured input* activities because the input has been manipulated so that learners are pushed away from the less-than-optimal strategies described earlier. (An incidental byproduct is that learners' attention is drawn to the relevant form–meaning connection.) Furthermore, because the goal of these activities is to help learners create intake from input, they do not produce the target structure. Instead, learners are pushed to make form-meaning connections by requiring them to rely on form or sentence structure to interpret meaning. The fact that learners do not produce the target structure in SI activities, however, should not be taken to mean that output has no role to play in SLA (e.g., see Swain, 1997, VanPatten, 2003, and Wong & VanPatten, in press) for discussion on the roles of output). Output practice is not a component of PI simply because PI is concerned with input processing, the process responsible for converting input to intake. Output practice is related to the process of accessing internalized language for production (see VanPatten 2002, 2003, and this volume for discussions and Lee & VanPatten, 1995 and in press, for what they refer to as "structured output" activities and their complementary role to structured input).

DEVELOPING SI ACTIVITIES

To develop appropriate and effective SI activities, certain procedures should be kept in mind. It is important to point out that SI activities cannot be equated with just any kind of input-based activity. In other words, the fact that an activity does not require the learner to produce the target form does not automatically make that activity an SI activity. For an activity to be an SI activity, that activity must somehow push learners to circumvent an inefficient processing strategy. In the next sections, I give a detailed description of procedures to follow in developing SI activities.

Step 1: Identify the Processing Problem or Strategy

The first and perhaps most important step in developing SI activities is to identify and understand what the processing problem is for the form in question. Why are learners having problems processing a particular form? What strategies are they using that is causing them to process this form inefficiently or incorrectly? Is it due to a tendency to rely on lexical items (i.e., Principle 1)? Is it due to a word order problem (i.e., Principle 2)? Is location a problem (P1f)? Or is some combination of factors involved? Remember that the goal of PI is to push learners away from their less than optimal strategies for processing input. If the processing problem or strategy is not identified, we will not be able to create SI activities to help reach this goal.

Once the processing problem has been identified, then the development of SI activities can begin. The input in these activities should be structured so that learners cannot rely on inefficient strategies to successfully complete the activities. The activities should force them to use more optimal strategies to process the form in question. Guidelines for developing SI activities are described in the next section.

Step 2: Follow Guidelines for Developing SI Activities

Guidelines for developing SI activities were first outlined in VanPatten (1993) and then expanded on in Lee and VanPatten (1995), VanPatten (1996) and Wong (in press). We will discuss these in detail in the following sections.

1. Present one thing at a time. In order to maximize intake efficiency, only one function and/or one form should be the focus of instruction at any given time. As explained in Lee and VanPatten (1995), this means that only one rule of usage and/or one form of a paradigm should be presented at a time. The reason for this guideline is simply this: when there is less to pay attention to, it is easier to pay attention. Because learners have a limited capacity to process information, we want to make sure that we do not overtax their processing resources. Presenting one rule at a time and breaking up paradigms help maximize the chances that learners will pay more focused attention to the forms that they need to for intake. Furthermore, presenting one thing at a time helps ensure that learners will not be bogged down with too much description and explanation about rules (Lee & VanPatten, 1995).

2. Keep meaning in focus. Acquisition cannot happen without exposure to meaning-bearing input, that is to say, input that contains some kind of referential meaning or communicative intent. Therefore, meaning must be kept in focus at all times. This means that meaning-bearing input must be used in SI activities and learners must successfully process the propositional content of the input in order to successfully complete the activities. If the activity can be completed without attention to the referential meaning of the input (as in the case of mechanical drills), then it is not an SI activity.

3. Move from sentences to connected discourse. When grammar is taught via SI activities, it is preferable to begin with sentences first. The rational for this goes back to the fact that learners have a limited capacity to process input, especially at the beginning stages. As outlined in Principle 2 of VanPatten's model of input processing, learners process input for form only if their processing resources have not been depleted after they have processed the input for meaning. Because short sentences are easier to process than connected discourse, learners will be more likely to pay attention to the relevant grammatical information that is the target of instruction (see, for example, Wong, 2002b). This guideline is exemplified in the following activities (from Lee & VanPatten, 1995, pp. 106–107). The target structure in these activities is third person present tense verbs and is a translation of the original Spanish version. Note how the activities move from sentences to connected discourse (short narration).

Activity A. Alice and Ray. Look at the drawings of events from a typical day in the lives of Alice and Ray. Listen as your instructor reads a sentence. Say whether that activity is part of Alice's routine or Ray's.

MODEL: (you hear) This person eats lunch with friends.
        (you say) That is Ray.

Activity B. In What Order? Without referring to the drawings about Ray's day, put the following activities in the correct order in which he does them.

____ a. He goes to bed late.
____ b. He sleeps in his math class.
____ c. He works at the pizzeria.
____ d. He goes to music class.
____ e. He gets up late.
____ f. He watches some TV.
____ g. He eats lunch with friends.
____ h. He tries to study.

Now compare with the drawings. Did you get them all in the right order?

Activity C. The Typical Student. Read the following sentences. Are they true for a typical student at your school?

The typical student ...	True	False
1. gets up at 6:30 a.m.		
2. skips breakfast.	____	____
3. drives to school.	____	____
4. sleeps in at least one class.	____	____
5. studies in the library, not at home.	____	____
6. works part time.	____	____
7. eats a microwaved dinner.	____	____
8. watches David Letterman at night.	____	____
9. goes to bed after midnight.	____	____

Your instructor will now read each statement and then ask you to raise your hand if you marked it as true. Someone should keep track of the responses on the board. In the end, how did the class respond to each statement?

Activity D. John's Day.
Step 1. Break into groups of three and listen as your instructor reads a short narration.

Step 2. With your group members, give as many details as you can remember by completing the following sentences. The group with the most details wins. You have three minutes.
1. John gets up at _____ .
2. He requires at least _____ to wake up fully.
3. He prefers not to _____ in the morning.
    [the list continues]

Step 3. Look over the details that you have recalled. Read a sentence to the class and then say whether or not you do the same thing.

MODEL: John gets up at 8:00, and so do I.
          John gets up at 8:00, but I don't.

[*Part of narration read by instructor*. "John is a student at X university. On most days, he gets up at 8:00 but the mornings are very difficult for him because he just isn't a morning person. He needs to drink at least three cups of strong coffee to wake up. And more often than not he reads the newspaper in silence since he prefers not talking to anyone until he is fully awake ..."]

4. Use Both Oral and Written Input. Both oral and written input should be used in SI activities because learners should have opportunities to receive input in both modalities. Although all learners need oral input, more visual learners would benefit from "seeing" the input as well. Not giving these learners exposure to written input could put them at a disadvantage in learning situations (Lee & VanPatten, 1995). Note how both oral and written input was used in Activities A through D.

5. Have Learners Do Something With the Input. In line with major tenets of communicative language teaching, the activities should not only be meaningful, they should also be purposeful. This means that learners must have a reason for attending to the input. Therefore, the activities should have learners responding to the input in some way to ensure that they are actively processing. This guideline is illustrated in Activity E.

Activity E was constructed to help learners of French process *de* with the verb *avoir* (to have) correctly in order to derive the meaning of negation in the sentences. In French, indefinite articles (*un/une/des*) must change to *de* or *d'* (if in front of a vowel) if they are used in negative sentences with the verb *avoir*. Thus we have *Marie a une voiture* (Marie has a car) in the affirmative but *Marie n'a pas __de__ voiture* (Marie does not have a car) in the negative. The processing problem here is that learners will skip over the *de* vs. *une* distinction and will rely instead on the *ne ... pas* to get negation.

Activity E was structured so that learners had to rely on the *de* vs *une* distinction to get meaning.

Activity E. Chez les LeBlanc

Étape 1. Pierre and Lise LeBlanc are talking about things they have and don't have in their house. Pay attention to the articles to determine whether they have or do not have the things mentioned. Complete each sentence with either "**Nous avons** ..." or "**Nous n'avons pas** ..."

_____ **une** salle de séjour.
_____ **de** télévision.
_____ **de** lit.
_____ **un** fauteuil.
_____ **une** cuisinière.
_____ **de** réfrigérateur.
_____ **une** table.
_____ **une** toilette.
_____ **une** douche.
_____ **de** baignoire.
_____ **de** lampes.
_____ **de** chaises.
_____ **des** souris (mice).

Étape 2. Based on these descriptions, decide with a partner how rich or poor this couple is and explain why.

Pierre et Lise sont....*très riches/ riches/ assez riches/ assez pauvres/ pauvres/ très pauvres* (circle one) parce que....

INSTRUCTOR'S SCRIPT
Give students a few minutes to work on step one on their own. Then go over each answer with them. Go on to step two. Have them discuss their answers with a partner and then share with whole class to see if everyone wrote the same thing.

In this activity, the learners' task is to determine whether the couple, the LeBlancs, has the household items listed by filling in the blanks with either "*Nous avons*" (we have) or "*Nous n'avons pas*" (we do not have). The guideline of having learners do something with the input is observed by requiring learners to draw a conclusion about the couple's economic status at the end of the activity. In other words, learners have to share with their classmates their thoughts about how rich or poor they think the LeBlancs are based on the input they just processed. The answers shared may vary. The LeBlancs don't have a bathtub (*baignoire*) or a bed (*lit*) but they do have a shower and mice. Would that make them poor? Somewhat poor? Very poor? Learners may have different opinions. The point here is that learners were given a reason for attending to the input, that is, they had to report to their classmates about the economic status of the LeBlanc's. And to be able to provide this information, they had to have correctly processed the target forms in the first part of the activity.

6. *Keep the learner's processing strategies in mind.* The goal of PI is to help learners move away from inefficient processing strategies so that they adopt more optimal ones. Therefore, the processing strategies that learners use to process a particular form must be kept in mind at all times in developing SI activities. If the activity is not constructed to preempt an inefficient processing strategy, then it is *not* an SI activity. This is why it is critical that the processing problem or the processing strategies that learners use for a given form be clearly identified *before* SI activities are constructed. For example, if learners are relying on lexical items to interpret tense (Principle 1), then we may want to structure the activities so that learners are pushed to rely on grammatical morphemes instead of lexical adverbs to get tense.

Recall that the processing problem in Activity E is that learners tend to rely on *ne ... pas* to get negation and will skip over the *de/d'* vs. *un/une/des* distinction. Keeping this processing strategy in mind, we would want to push learners to make the connection that *de/d'* with *avoir* denotes negation. Notice that in Activity E, the *ne ... pas* was removed from the phrases so that learners had to rely on the articles to determine whether the sentence should be affirmative or negative. By removing *ne...pas*, learners were forced to pay attention to *de/d'* vs. *un/une/des* to get meaning.

Another difficulty with the target structure in Activity E is that it occurs in medial position, the least salient position so learners are even more likely to miss it (as explained by Principle 4). Notice that in Activity E, the input is structured so that the articles are in initial position (the most salient position) and are bolded to increase their perceptual salience. The first item learners see in each phrase is either *un/une/des* or *de/d'*. It is through successfully processing these forms that they are able to fill in the beginning part of each phrase (*Nous avons* or *Nous n'avons pas*) and determine whether the couple has or does not have each of the household items mentioned.

TWO TYPES OF STRUCTURED INPUT ACTIVITIES

Two types of SI activities are used in PI: referential and affective. Referential activities require learners to pay attention to form in order to get meaning and have a right or wrong answer so the instructor can check whether or not the learner has actually made the proper form-meaning connection. Affective activities, on the other hand, do not have right or wrong answers. Instead, they require learners to express an opinion, belief or some other affective response as they are engaged in processing information about the real world.

Activity E discussed above is an example of a written referential activity. Learners had to process form correctly in order to get meaning and there was only one correct answer in the first part of the activity. Activity F is an example of an oral referential activity for the same target form.

> **Activity F. In the Classroom.** The following sentences describe objects that may or may not be in a classroom. You will hear the last part of each sentence. Listen carefully to the article in order to determine if each object mentioned is in the classroom or not. Circle the correct response. Then based on the answers, comment on whether you think this is a well-equipped classroom.
> 1. La salle a...   /   La salle n'a pas...
> 2. La salle a...   /   La salle n'a pas...
> 3. La salle a...   /   La salle n'a pas...
> 4. La salle a...   /   La salle n'a pas...
> 5. La salle a...   /   La salle n'a pas...
> 6. La salle a...   /   La salle n'a pas...
> 7. La salle a...   /   La salle n'a pas...
> 8. La salle a...   /   La salle n'a pas...
>
> Would you say that this is a well-equipped classroom? Share your response with a classmate.
>
> INSTRUCTOR'S SCRIPT
> Read each sentence once. After each sentence, ask for an answer. Do not wait until the end to review answers. Students do not repeat or otherwise produce the structure.
> 1. ...un tableau.
> 2. ...un ordinateur.
> 3. ...de fenêtre.
> 4. ...des affiches.
> 5. ...de téléphone.
> 6. ...une télévision
> 7. ...des chaises.
> 8. ...de magnétoscope

As in Activity F, learners are required to process form correctly in order to get the correct meaning and must form a conclusion about how well-equipped this classroom is (i.e., do something with the input).

Activity G is an example of a written affective activity for the same target form. In this activity, there is no right or wrong answer. Learners are instead asked to process sentences about housing in Columbus, Ohio and Beverly Hills, California to give a personal reaction and opinion. Notice, however, that the input is once again structured so that attention to form is privileged: The target form is in a salient initial position and is visually enhanced through bolding. The activity makes learners do something with the input by requiring them to form their opinions and share them with classmates.

> **Activity G**. The following sentences describe what a typical student apartment in Columbus may have or not have. Read each sentence and indicate whether you think each statement about student apartments in Columbus is true or false.
>
> Un appartement d' étudiant typique à Columbus a ...
> | | |
> |---|---|
> | **une** cuisine (kitchen). | vrai / faux |
> | **une** salle de séjour (living room). | vrai / faux |
> | **un** grand jardin (garden). | vrai / faux |
> | **des** chambres (bedrooms). | vrai / faux |
>
> Un appartement d' étudiant typique à Columbus n'a pas ...
> | | |
> |---|---|
> | **de** garage. | vrai / faux |
> | **de** salle à manger (dining room). | vrai / faux |
> | **de** balcon. | vrai / faux |
> | **de** piscine (swimming pool). | vrai / faux |
>
> Now, repeat the above activity but this time imagine it is a house in Beverly Hills. Do any of your answers change?
>
> Une maison à Beverly Hills a ....
> | | |
> |---|---|
> | **une** cuisine (kitchen). | vrai / faux |
> | **une** salle de séjour (living room). | vrai / faux |
> | **un** grand jardin (garden). | vrai / faux |
> | **des** chambres (bedrooms). | vrai / faux |
>
> Une maison à Beverly Hills n'a pas ...
> | | |
> |---|---|
> | **de** garage. | vrai / faux |
> | **de** salle à manger (dining room). | vrai / faux |
> | **de** balcon. | vrai / faux |
> | **de** piscine (swimming pool). | vrai / faux |
>
> Did you and your classmates write similar or different things?

Because referential activities allow instructors to make sure that learners are focusing on the relevant grammatical information to derive meaning, instruction should begin with these activities. The purpose of affective activities is to reinforce those connections by providing them with more opportunities to see or hear the form used in a meaningful context. Furthermore, by requiring learners to express an opinion or some other kind of personal response, we can keep instruction in line with an important tenet of communicative language teaching: *a focus on the learner.*

PI VS. TRADITIONAL INSTRUCTION

There is a substantial amount of empirical evidence to suggest that PI is an effective pedagogical tool. In a series of studies that have compared PI to traditional instruction (TI), overall results show that PI is superior to TI.

TI typically involves giving learners explicit explanation of a form followed by controlled output practice. The practice activities usually begin with mechanical drills followed by meaningful and communicative drills (Paulston, 1972).[2] TI has been criticized in VanPatten (1996) and elsewhere for being an approach that does not take into consideration the crucial role that meaning-bearing input plays in SLA. Because TI involves immediate production practice of forms, learners do not get the input that they need to construct mental representations of the structure (p. 6).

The first study on PI was done on Spanish object pronouns and word order by VanPatten and Cadierno (1993). This study set out to compare PI to the traditional approach to instruction described above. Subjects were randomly assigned to three groups (1) a PI group, (2) a TI group and (3) a control group that received no instruction. In the PI group, learners first received EI about how object pronouns work in Spanish. They were also told that learners of Spanish have a tendency to think that the first noun they encounter is the subject. They were told that this is not an effective strategy because Spanish has a more flexible word order and the first noun is not always the subject. After receiving this EI, learners engaged in a series of SI activities that pushed them to interpret word order and object pronouns correctly. The following are SI activities from VanPatten and Cadierno's study.

> **Actividad A.** Select the picture that best corresponds to the sentence. (Keep in mind that Spanish does not follow a rigid subject-verb-object word order and that object pronouns may go before a conjugated verb or at the end of an infinitive.)
>
> [Learners see a set of two pictures for each item]
>
> [picture 1: parents calling son]
> [picture 2: son calling parents]
> 1.   Sus padres lo llaman por teléfono.

---

[2]See Lee and VanPatten (in press) and Wong and VanPatten (in press) for discussions on how TI is manifested in current L2 textbooks and classrooms.

[picture 1: Manuel inviting two girls to the movies]
[picture 2: two girls inviting Manuel to the movies]
2. Las invita Manuel al cine.

[picture 1: nephew listening to grandmother]
[picture 2: grandmother listening to nephew]
3. La abuela lo escucha.

[picture 1: little boy waves at little girl]
[picture 2: little girl waves at little boy]
4. Lo saluda la niña.

[picture 1: little boy looks for little girl]
[picture 2: little girl looks for little boy]
5. El chico la busca.

Actividad B. Indicate whether each statement about your parents applies to you. Share your responses with a classmate.

Sí, me aplica   No, no me aplica

_____   _____ 1. Los llamo con frecuencia por
                                      teléfono.
_____   _____ 2. Los visito los fines de semana.
_____   _____ 3. Los visito una vez al mes.
_____   _____ 4. Los abrazo cuando los veo.
                                      (abrazar = *to hug*)
_____   _____ 5. Los comprendo muy bien.
_____   _____ 6. Los ignoro completamente.
_____   _____ 7. Los aprecio mucho.

Did you notice that there are no explicit subject nouns or subject pronouns in each sentence? Because the *yo* form of the verb can only refer to *yo*, no subject pronoun is needed. All of the sentences are of the simple word order object pronoun-verb.

Actividad C. Select a female relative of yours (*madre, hermana, tía, abuela, prima,* etc.) and write her name below. Which of the statements describes how you feel about her?

Pariente: _____   Nombre: _____
_____ 1. La admiro.
_____ 2. La respeto.
_____ 3. La quiero mucho.
_____ 4. Trato de imitarla.

_____ 5. La detesto.
_____ 6. La _____ ? _____ .

Now select a male relative and do the same.
       _____ 1. Lo admiro.
       _____ 2. Lo respeto.
       _____ 3. Lo quiero mucho.
       _____ 4. Trato de imitarlo.
       _____ 5. Lo detesto.
       _____ 6. Lo _____ ? _____ .

Compare with two other people. Did you select the same relative(s)? Did you mark the same items?

Actividad D. Listen to each statement and select the appropriate picture.

1.
[picture a: Juan is calling some other guy]
[picture b: Some guy is calling Juan]
2.
[picture a: man listens to woman]
[picture b: woman listens to man]
3.
[picture a: mother hugs daughter]
[picture b: daughter hugs mother]
4.
[picture a: two men greet woman]
[picture b: woman greets two men]
5.
[picture a: girl looks at boy]
[picture b: boy looks at girl]

For activity D, the instructor reads the following statements.
1.   Lo llama Juan por teléfono.
2.   La escucha el señor.
3.   La abraza la mamá.
4.   Los saluda la mujer.
5.   El niño la mira.

Actividad E. For each paso of this activity, work in pairs.

Paso 1. Look over the following reading then answer the questions afterward. The following vocabulary may help you.

seguir (to follow)
asustarse (to become frightened)
aconsejarse (to advise)
jurar (to swear)
el colmo (the last straw)
paz (peace)

DEBATE

Un drama familiar muy común: ella se siente dominada, perseguida por su hermano (que puede ser menor, pero con aires de grandote) y no sabe cómo zafarse de él. Alicia y Manuel son el caso típico.

ALICIA CUENTA SU PARTE

"Manuel es muy posesivo. No me deja respirar. Cada vez que voy a salir, me pregunta con quién, a dónde voy, qué vamos a hacer.... A veces me sigue. Lo juro. Cuando un chico viene a visitarme Manny lo interroga y él se asusta. El colmo: mis padres me dejaron ir con unas amigas a un concierto de Bon Jovi... Y Manuel les aconsejó que uno de ellos fuera con nosotras, para supervisarnos. Por eso peleamos mucho, le he dicho más de mil veces que él no es mi papá y que me deje en paz. Pero Manuel no me suelta."

1. The main problem here is Manny. Alicia thinks he is…
    a. uncaring. b. domineering.
2. Which of the following words summarizes a major theme in Alicia's comments?
    a. love   b. friendship   c. trust

Paso 2. Find the following in the reading:
me dejaron ir
me pregunta
me sigue
no me suelta
viene a vistarme

In each instance, Alicia is saying that someone is doing something to her or for her. Can you identify the subject of the verb?

Paso 3. Find the following in the reading:

lo juro
lo mato
lo interroga

Who is the subject of each verb? Who or what does *lo* refer to?

Actividad F. Manny responde

Paso 1. In the following selection, Manuel responds to his sister's claims. Read it now for general meaning. Then do the activities that follow. Here is some vocabulary to help you.

no queda más remedio	(no choice is left)
confiar	(to trust)
mentir	(to lie)

MANNY HACE UNA ACLARACIÓN

"No quería decirlo, pero no me queda más remedio. Si vigilo a mi hermana, es porque me ha dado motivos para sospechar de ella. En varias ocasiones la sorprendí con un tal Sergio, que es uno de reputación por el suelo. Una vez le dijo a mis padres que iba al cine con las amigas y después un buen amigo me contó que la había visto en el cine ... pero con Sergio. Cómo puedo confiar en mi hermana si miente a todos en la casa? Ella no conoce a los chicos. Ese tipo sólo busca una cosa. Y yo no quiero que a mi hermana le suceda nada 'feo.'"

For the next **pasos** in this activity, you should first work alone and then share your responses with someone else.

Paso 2. Find all the uses of a third-person object pronoun. To whom or what do they correspond? What is the subject of each verb next to which you found each pronoun?

Paso 3. Which of the following best describes Manny's feelings for his sister?

_____ *La quiere mucho.*
_____ *La admira.*
_____ *La detesta.*

Paso 4. Which of the following does Manny probably do on a Friday night if his sister goes out?

_____ *La sigue para ver lo que hacer y con quién.*
_____ *La deja en paz porque es una adulta.*
_____ *La espera en casa.*

Object Marker *a*

Recall that Spanish has the object marker *a*.
*Los padres miran **a** los hijos.*
*Llamba **a** mis padres.*

This object marker has no equivalent in English but is important in Spanish since it provides an extra clue as to who did what to whom. Since Spanish has flexble word order, the *a* reminds you that even though a noun appears before the verb it doesn't have to be the subject!

A María la llama Juan.
A María Juan la llama.
(John calls Mary)

Note that when an object appears before the verb, the corresponding object pronouns must also be used. If you think that this is redundant, it is! But redundancy is a natural feature of languages, right? (Hint: Think about how we put tense endings on verbs when most of the time we also say "yesterday," "last night," and so on.) What does the following sentence mean? Who is doing what to whom?
A la chica la busca el chico.

Right. The boy is looking for the girl.

Actividad G. Select the English rendition of each sentence.

1. A mi mamá la besa mucho mi papá.
   a. My mother kisses my father a lot.

b.   My father kisses my mom a lot.
2.   A mi papá no lo comprendo yo.
    a.   I don't understand my father.
    b.   My father doesn't understand me.
3.   A la señora la saluda el señor.
    a.   The woman greets the man.
    b.   The man greets the woman.
4.   A los chicos los sorprende la profesora.
    a.   The professor surprises the boys.
    b.   The boys surprise the professor.

Activities A, D, E, F, and G are referential activities and Activities B and C are affective activities. These activities were constructed to help learners abandon their reliance on the first-noun strategy to process the input. Notice that learners do not produce the target forms but they must process object pronouns correctly to get meaning and to successfully do these activities. The input is also structured so that the target forms are in initial position, the most salient position, when possible. Both oral and written input are used and learners must complete some kind of task with the input, that is, form an opinion, discuss responses with classmates, among other activities. Furthermore, the activities begin with sentence level input before moving on to discourse level input (Activities E and F) and the activities frequently remind learners of the processing strategy that they should use when doing the activities (e.g., "Keep in mind that Spanish does not follow a rigid subject-verb-object word order and that object pronouns may go before a conjugated verb or at the end of an infinitive").

Subjects in the TI group received an explanation of object pronouns followed by mechanical, then meaningful, then communicative output drills (based on Paulston, 1972).[3] This group did not engage in any interpretation activities.

The researchers found that on a sentence level test of interpretation that required subjects to select pictures that best corresponded to what they heard, the PI group made significant gains whereas the TI and control group did not. These gains were maintained on a delayed posttest one month later. On a production test that required learners to complete sentences based on pictures that they saw, both the TI and PI groups made significant gains on the immediate and delayed posttest and these gains were not significantly different from each other. The control group did not make significant gains.

---

[3]TI was operationalized using Paulston's (1972) classification of drills. The activities began with mechanical drills, then moved to meaningful drills and finally to communicative drills. This is important to point out because some researchers have misinterpreted the TI treatment in VanPatten and Cadierno's study as comprising strictly of mechanical activities (see DeKeyser, Salaberry, Robinson, & Harrington, 2002, p. 816).

The results from VanPatten and Cadierno (1993) suggest that PI is more beneficial than TI because not only did subjects in the PI group gain in ability to interpret object pronouns, their input processing of this structure resulted in some kind of change in their system that could be accessed for production. This is an important finding because at no time during treatment did subjects in the PI group ever practice producing object pronouns. Yet on the production task, they were able to perform as well as subjects in the TI group who received lots of practice in producing this structure. The subjects in the TI group on the other hand, could not do the interpretation task. Their performance on this task was no better than those in the control group who received no instruction. Subjects in the TI group were only good at doing what they practiced doing during treatment. Other studies that follow the same research design and have reported similar superior results for PI include Benati (2001) for the Italian future tense, Cadierno (1995) for Spanish preterite tense, Cheng (1995) for Spanish ser vs. estar, and VanPatten and Wong (this volume) for the French causative.

VanPatten and Sanz (1995) demonstrated that the effects of PI can also be generalized to assessment measurements that involve more complex cognitive processing such as a video narration task. In another study, VanPatten and Oikkenon (1996) separated out the effects of SI activities and EI from PI and found that the positive effects of PI were due to the SI activities. A recent longitudinal study by VanPatten and Fernández (this volume) shows that the effects of PI are durable for at least eight months.

Recently, some SLA researchers have remarked that of the focus on form techniques that are in the literature, PI appears to yield some of the most promising results (e.g., Carroll, 2001; Doughty, 2002; N. Ellis, 2002; Norris & Ortega, 2000). These researchers attribute the positive results of this focus on form technique to the fact that PI was designed with the goal of altering learners' processing strategies. According to these researchers, in L2 learning situations where input alone may not be enough, the best kind of intervention appears to be one in which input is structured so that learners can perceive and process/parse L2 stimuli more effectively and accurately (Doughty, 2002; N. Ellis, 2002).

PI AND REPLICATION STUDIES

We cannot overemphasize the nature and purpose of SI activities. It is tempting to see the activities in PI as simply being "more input" or "embedding a structure in input" because the underlying psycholinguistic strategies of learners may not be thought about by many researchers (and certainly not by a lot of instructors). Thus, to illustrate what constitutes appropriate SI activities, the next section will present activities from certain replication studies that purport to contradict VanPatten and Cadierno's findings. My point in reviewing these is not to criticize the authors for their research, but rather to contrast their activities with those used by VanPatten and his colleagues to demonstrate how easy it is to misinterpret what SI activities are and what they are supposed to do. Those who wish to implement or even test the effects of SI activities with their own learners or under different contexts will benefit by such a presentation.

DeKeyser and Sokalski (1996)

DeKeyser and Sokalski (1996) state that they set out to replicate VanPatten and Cadierno's study. They compared two treatment groups, an input group and an output group, to a control group. The target items were Spanish object pronouns and the conditional tense in Spanish. The EI for the two experimental groups was the same. This information was adapted from sections of *Dos Mundos* (Terrell, Andgrade, Egasse, & Munoz, 1994), the text used by the participants' classes. The practice exercises in both groups began with a few mechanical activities and then progressed to meaningful and communicative ones (p. 626). Sentence length and vocabulary were held constant for both groups. Essentially, the only difference between the practice exercises for the two groups was that it was input-based in one version and production-based in the other version. The following is an example of one of the exercises that the input group and output group received (from DeKeyser & Sokalski, 1996, pp. 640–642).

> **Input Group.**
> Read the following exercises. Circle all possible things that the direct object can refer to.
>
> Example: Yo lo tengo
>   me   you (sg.)   him her it   you (pl.)/them
>
> 1.   La escuchas conmigo
>   me   you (sg.)   him her it   you (pl.)/them
>
> 2.   Nosotros te vemos
>   me   you (sg.)   him her it   you (pl.)/them
>
> 3.   Ellos los lavan en la cocina
>   me   you (sg.)   him her it   you (pl.)/them
>
> 4.   Yo lo prefiero de color azul
>   me   you (sg.)   him her it   you (pl.)/them
>
> 5.   Lo tocan ellas muy bien
>   me   you (sg.)   him her it   you (pl.)/them

For the next 5, listen to the sentences your teacher reads and circle all possible things the direct object can refer to.

6. me   you (sg.)   him her it   you (pl.)/them
7. me   you (sg.)   him her it   you (pl.)/them
8. me   you (sg.)   him her it   you (pl.)/them
9. me   you (sg.)   him her it   you (pl.)/them
10. me   you (sg.)   him her it   you (pl.)/them

Output Group
Fill in the missing blanks with the corresponding Spanish direct object pronoun for the pronoun given in parentheses.

Example: Yo <u>lo</u> tengo.   (him)

1. _____ visitas conmigo   (her)
2. Nosotros _____ llevamos.   (you, sg.)
3. Ellos _____ reciben.   (them, masc.)
4. Yo _____ lavo.   (it, masc)
5. _____ necesitan ellas.   (you, pl. masc)
6. Nunca _____ llamas tu.   (me)
7. Ellas _____ buscan en la cocina.   (them, masc)
8. Nostros no _____ invitamos.   (them, masc)
9. El nunca _____ visita.   (you, sg.)
10. _____ escuchas tu.   (us)

Note how the sample input activity differs from the activities presented earlier from VanPatten and Cadierno's study. Learners are not pushed to process form correctly to get meaning here. In fact, this activity does not even require any attention to meaning.

The assessment tasks for this study were a comprehension task and a translation/fill in the blank production task. DeKeyser and Sokalski found that for object pronouns, the input group was better than the output group on the comprehension task but that the output group was better than the input group on the production task. These results were not maintained on a delayed posttest. For the conditional, there was an overall advantage for the output group in both tasks but results were not maintained on delayed posttests. Based on these results, DeKeyser and Sokalski concluded that PI is not superior to TI.

This conclusion, however, is not sustainable. As discussed in VanPatten (2002), it must be underscored that the input-based treatment group in DeKeyser and Sokalski was not PI. This becomes evident when we examine the instructional treatment used in their input-based group. Recall that the goal of PI is to alter learners' processing strategies so that they process input better. Therefore, for instruction to be PI, the processing problem or inefficient strategy that learners use to process the target form must first be identified. In DeKeyser and Sokalski's study, there was no mention of any strategy that the researchers were trying to circumvent through their instructional treatment. Given that there was no strategy to circumvent, the practice activities were consequently not designed to push learners away from their natural processing strategy. Therefore, the practice activities in the input-based group cannot be classified as SI activities and would not necessarily have the same effect that SI activities would if they did what they were supposed to do. Furthermore, the sample activity taken from DeKeyser and Sokalski shows that another of the essential guidelines for creating SI activities was not adhered to: "Keep meaning in focus." For an activity to be an SI activity, that activity must require that learners process the input for both meaning and form because learners should be pushed to rely on sentence structure or form to derive meaning. However, as DeKeyser and Sokalski pointed out themselves, not all the activities in their input-based instructional treatment required learners to attend to meaning. Therefore their study did not replicate VanPatten and Cadierno's study. They were essentially comparing their version of an input-based instruction to their version of output-based instruction.

Salaberry (1997)

Salaberry (1997) also claimed to have evidence to refute the findings of VanPatten and Cadierno (1993). His target form was also Spanish object pronouns. Salaberry compared two experimental groups, that is, input processing and output processing, to a control group and found no differences between the two treatment groups. Therefore, he concluded that PI is not better than TI. However, an examination of the treatment groups reveals that the instruction the input processing group received was input-based but did not contain SI activities that attempted to push learners away from faulty processing strategies. It is clear that the researcher misinterpreted the guidelines in Lee and VanPatten (1995) because he incorrectly cited the guidelines as saying that the SI activities should move from mechanical to communicative language:

> For example, Lee and VanPatten (1995) argue that in IP instruction teachers should (a) present one thing at a time (sequencing) and (b) move from sentences to connected discourse (from mechanical to communicative language). (Salaberry, 1997, p. 426)

What the guidelines actually say is that because meaning must be kept in focus at all times, "learners should not engage in the mechanical input activities of traditional grammar instruction" (Lee & VanPatten, 1995, p. 104). In short, the instructional treatment in Salaberry (1997) was not PI and his activities were clearly not trying to circumvent a processing strategy because the only difference between his two treatment groups was that one set of activities required participants to produce the target form while the other set did not. It is no surprise that Salaberry obtained results different from those of VanPatten and Cadierno. If the reader compares the VanPatten and Cadierno activities with those of Salaberry (and those of DeKeyser and Sokalski), it is clear that we are dealing with quite different treatments in terms of their underlying purpose.

Allen (2000)

Allen (2000) claimed to have evidence that conflicts with the findings of VanPatten and Cadierno (1993). Her target structure was the French causative with *faire*. The processing problem associated with this structure is a word order problem. The verb faire means "to do" or "to make" in French but is also used in causative constructions to say that someone is causing a behavior in someone else:

> (1) *Jean fait laver la voiture à Marie.*
>   Jean makes to wash the car to Mary.
>   John makes Mary wash the car.
> (2) *Mes professeurs me font travailler beaucoup.*
>   My professors me make work a lot.
>   My professors make me work a lot.

In (1), the subject of the first verb *fait* is *Jean*. The subject of the second verb *laver* is *Marie,* obligatorily placed postverbally and marked by the preposition *à*. It is the subject of the second verb that poses problems for learners of French. When learners are asked to process sentences such as (1) and are asked "Who washes the car?" they tend to say "Jean." They would translate the sentence into something like "John washes the car for Mary" (based on pilot data from Allen, 2000).

In (2) the subject of the second verb appears preverbally. However, in this case, it is not a subject pronoun but an object pronoun. When learners are asked to provide a rough translation of (2), they tend to say something "My professors work hard for me."

These examples illustrate learners' reliance on the first noun principle. In (1), learners tend to think that *Jean* washes the car because he is the first noun that appears before the verb. In example (2), they incorrectly assume the professors work a lot because *professeurs* is the first noun before the verb.

Allen (2000) compared a control group to two experimental groups: a PI group and a TI group. A sentence-level interpretation task revealed that both the PI and the TI groups made gains and they were not different from each other. On a sentence-level production task, results showed that both groups made gains but the gains made by the TI group were higher. Therefore, Allen concluded that the results of VanPatten and Cadierno are not generalizable to the causative structure.

Both the results and conclusions in Allen's study are questionable vis à vis what PI is and what it means to assess the effects of PI. Unlike DeKeyser and Sokalski (1996) and Salaberry (1997), Allen does identify a processing strategy that must be overcome, that is, the first-noun strategy, and she does attempt to help learners move away from this strategy through her activities (i.e., she reminds learners in her activities not to rely on the first-noun strategy). However, her SI activities are problematic because they do not force learners to rely on sentence structure to get meaning. First, as exemplified in Activity A below, only causative sentences were used in her activities. Thus, her activities did not push learners to make a distinction between causative and non-causative sentences with *faire* (see the discussion in VanPatten and Wong, this volume). Therefore, we cannot be sure what learners were actually learning. It is possible that they were being led to memorize a pattern with these activities rather than rely on sentence structure for meaning.

> **Activité A**. Select the correct interpretation of the sentences. Circle a or b. Keep in mind that the word order in French is not exactly the same as English.
>
> 1.   Tom fait faire les valises à Marc.
>   a. Tom packs the bags.   b. Tom gets Marc to pack the bags.
>
> 2.   Les enfants font faire du bateau à leurs parents.
>   a. The children go boating.   b. The children get their parents to
>   go boating.
>
> 3.   Je fais faire du vélo à ma soeur.
>   a. I get my sister to go bike riding. b. I go bike riding.
>
> 4.   Tu fais faire de l'alpinisme à ton ami.
>   a.   You get your friend to go   b. You go mountain
>   climbing.   climbing.
>
> 5.   Jason fait faire de la gymnastique à son frère.
>   a. Jason does gymnastics.   b. Jason gets his brother to do
>   gymnastics.
>
> 6.   Le professeur fait faire des devoirs aux élèves.
>   a. The teacher does homework.   b. The teacher makes the
>   students do homework.

7. Sara fait faire un voyage à ses parents.
    a. Sara gets her parents to take a trip.   b. Sara takes a trip.

A second problem has to do with the response choices for each practice item. In Activity A, learners must select the correct interpretation for each sentence. Note that there are two possible choices: a or b. One choice mentions only one person and that person is the one performing the action. The other choice mentions two people; one of the people mentioned is having the other person do the action. These choices are problematic because they allow learners to successfully complete the activity simply by matching names in the response choices to the sentence. For example, in item 1, *Tom fait faire les valises à Marc*, we see two names: Tom and Mark. The correct answer is b: Tom gets Marc to pack the bags. Note that the learner does not even have to know any French to successfully do this item; response b *has to be* the correct answer here because only b contains both names, Tom and Mark. The same goes for the rest of the items. In item 2, we see *Les enfants font faire du bateau à leurs parents.* The correct response is b: The children get their parents to go boating. Again, b has to be the correct choice because only b mentions both the children and the parents. Thus, we cannot tell if the learners selected this response because they successfully processed this sentence or simply because only b mentions the two people in the sentence. A third problem of this activity has to do with event probabilities. For example, in item 6, learners see *Le professeur fait faire des devoirs aux élèves.* The correct response is b: The teacher makes the students do homework. In the real world, it is almost always professors who make students do homework and not the other way around. Therefore, learners may select b as the response because it is more likely that professors get students to do homework and not because they have made any kind of form-meaning connection from the structure (not to mention the fact that only response b mentions both professors and students). Therefore, it should be clear that this activity cannot be considered an SI activity because learners are not pushed to rely on sentence structure to get meaning. Because the goal of SI activities is to get learners to process sentence structure for meaning, we must remove things from the activities that may allow learners to give correct responses without relying on sentence structure. Similar problems can be observed in subsequent referential activities in Allen's study. Other problems include requiring learners to process the full verb paradigm rather than on focusing on one form at a time (Guideline 1). Learners were required to pay attention to all conjugations of the present tense of the verb *faire* rather than focusing on one form (e.g., *Je fais, tu fais, Paul fait, nous faisons*, etc).

In VanPatten and Wong (this volume) we replicated Allen's study with SI activities that did push learners to process sentence structure in order to get meaning and obtained different results. In fact, our results were similar to those of the original VanPatten and Cadierno (1993) study. Results revealed that on the interpretation task, the PI group improved significantly more that the TI group from the pre- to posttest. The no-instruction control group did not improve. On the production task, both the PI and TI groups made gains from pre- to posttest and there was no difference between the two groups. The control group showed no improvement. All results were maintained on the delayed posttests (see VanPatten & Wong, this volume). The following is a referential SI activity taken from VanPatten and Wong's study:

> Listen to each sentence, then indicate who is performing the action by answering each question.
>
> 1. Who cleans the room? _____
> 2. Who packs the bags? _____
> 3. Who watches the movie? _____
> 4. Who plays the flute? _____
> 5. Who does the dishes? _____
> 6. Who buys wine? _____
> 7. Who watches the show? _____
> 8. Who reads the instructions? _____

INSTRUCTOR'S SCRIPT

Read each sentence once. After each sentence, ask for an answer. Do not wait until the end to review answers. Students do not repeat or otherwise produce the structure.

1. Claude fait nettoyer la chambre à Richard.
2. Marc fait les valises pour Jean.
3. Sandra fait voir le film à Pierre.
4. Louis fait jouer de la flute à Suzanne.
5. Georges fait la vaisselle pour Louis.
6. Louise fait acheter du vin à Diane.
7. Ma mère fait regarder le spectacle à mon père.
8. Sally fait lire les instructions à Jean Luc.

Notice that in this SI activity, both causative and non-causative sentences with *faire* are used so learners have to pay attention to respond correctly (item 2 and item 5 are not causative). Furthermore, unlike the translation task used in Allen's activity presented above, this activity requires learners to indicate who is performing the action so learners cannot simply match names to get the correct response. Rather than present the whole verb paradigm, only one form, the third person singular, was presented. Finally, event probabilities were controlled for. In each item, either person mentioned could logically be performing the action. In this way, students are required to rely on sentence structure in order to determine who is doing each action.

The following example is an example of a written affective activity taken from VanPatten and Wong.

In this activity you will compare and contrast what someone gets a child to do with what someone gets a dog to do. For each item, indicate whether it refers to the small child (**à l'enfant**), the dog (**au chien**), or possibly both (**à tous les deux**).

Un adulte …

1. fait chercher l'os (*bone*) à/au _____ .
2. fait faire la vaisselle à/au _____ _____ .
3. fait manger les restes à/au _____ .
4. fait jouer du piano à/au _____ .
5. fait prendre un bain à/au _____ .
6. fait dormir au plancher (*floor*) à/au _____ .
7. fait se comporter bien (*behave*) à/au _____ quand il y a des invités.
8. fait boire du lait à/au _____ .

Does everyone in class agree?

INSTRUCTOR'S SCRIPT
"Ok. On va voir. Numero 1. Un adulte fait chercher l'osse à qui? Sharon?" "Au chien." "OK. Tout le monde est d'accord?" (students respond) "Et qu'est-ce qu'un adulte fait chercher à son enfant?" Students may volunteer things like their books, a toy, etc.; students do not say or repeat the verbs. They just provide nouns and so on.

VanPatten and Wong concluded from their study that there is evidence to show that PI is generalizable to the causative structure. When activities are structured to push learners to make the necessary form-meaning connections, they do successfully alter learners' inefficient processing strategies.

SUMMARY AND CONCLUSION

The purpose of this chapter was to describe in detail the nature of PI, the only type of focus on form instruction to date that is informed by the strategies that learners use to initially parse input to make form-meaning connections. Research has shown that this type of grammar instruction is effective in helping L2 learners adopt better processing strategies so that they can derive richer intake from input. I described the three characteristics of PI as well as the procedures and guidelines to follow in the development of SI activities. Particular attention was paid to Guideline 6: "Keep learners'psycholinguistic processing strategies in mind." This point is underscored because it is evident from some attempted replication studies that PI has sometimes been mistakenly reduced to be any kind of input practice. To reiterate, not all input-based activities are SI activities and not all input-based instruction is PI. For instruction to be PI, the processing strategy that learners use to process a particular form must be identified. In order for an activity to be an SI activity, that activity must be designed with that ineffective strategy in mind so that the activity can help learners use more efficient strategies to process the input. Furthermore, an SI activity must make learners process form correctly to get meaning. If learners do not need to pay attention to meaning or if they do not need to rely on form to get meaning, the activity is not an SI activity (e.g., see the previous discussion regarding Allen, 2000).

To be clear, I am not saying that other activities that are not designed to preempt an ineffective processing strategy cannot be useful. However, it should be evident that the more we know about what learners do with input, the better we will be at helping them process input better. Because SI activities are designed with learners' processing strategies in mind, they probably stand the most chance at altering learners' inefficient strategies so that optimal input processing can take place. Creating activities without first identifying a processing strategy is like a doctor passing out medication without knowing what is wrong with the patient. Sometimes it may work and sometimes it won't but we won't know why. With PI, the doctor (researcher) always knows why.

REFERENCES

Allen, L. Q. (2000). Form-meaning connections and the French causative: An experiment in processing instruction. *Studies in Second Language Acquisition, 22,* 69–84.

Barcroft, J., & VanPatten, B. (1997). Acoustic salience: Testing location, stress and the boundedness of grammatical form in second language acquisition input processing. In A. T. Pérez-Leroux & W. R. Glass, (Eds.), *Contemporary perspectives on the acquisition of Spanish: Vol. 2. Production, processing, and comprehension* (pp. 109–121). Somerville, MA: Cascadilla Press.

Benati, A. (2001). A comparative study of the effects of processing instruction and output-based instruction on the acquisition of the Italian future tense. *Language Teaching Research, 5,* 95–127.

Cadierno, T. (1995). Formal instruction in processing perspective: An investigation into the Spanish past tense. *The Modern Language Journal, 79,* 179–194.

Carroll, S. (2001). *Input and evidence: The raw material of second language acquisition.* Philadelphia: John Benjamins.

Cheng, A. (1995). *Grammar instruction and input processing: The acquisition of Spanish ser and estar.* Unpublished doctoral dissertation, University of Illinois, Urbana-Champaign.

DeKeyser, R., & Sokalski, K. (1996). The differential role of comprehension and production practice. *Language Learning, 46,* 613–642.

DeKeyser, R., Salaberry, R., Robinson, P., & Harrington, M. (2002). What gets processed in processing instruction? A commentary on Bill VanPatten's "Update." *Language Learning, 52,* 805–823.

Doughty, C. (2002, March). *Effects of instruction on second language acquisition.* Paper presented at the Conference on Form-Meaning Connections in SLA, Chicago, IL.

Ellis, N. (2002, March). *The processes of second language acquisition.* Paper presented at the Conference on Form-Meaning Connections in SLA, Chicago, IL.

Lee, J. (1987). Comprehending the Spanish subjunctive: An information processing perspective. *The Modern Language Journal, 71,* 50–57.

Lee, J., Cadierno, T., Glass, W., & VanPatten, B. (1997). The effects of lexical and grammatical cues on processing tense in second language input. *Applied Language Learning, 8,* 1–23.

Lee, J., & VanPatten, B. (1995). *Making communicative language teaching happen.* New York: McGraw-Hill.

Lee., J., & VanPatten, B. (in press). *Making communicative language teaching happen* (2nd ed.). New York: McGraw-Hill.

Musumeci, D. (1989). *The ability of second language learners to assign tense at the sentence level: A cross-linguistic study.* Unpublished doctoral dissertation, University of Illinois, Urbana-Champaign.

Norris, J., & Ortega, L. (2000). Effectiveness of L2 instruction: A research synthesis and quantitative meta-analysis. *Language Learning, 50,* 417–528.

Paulston, C. B. (1972). Structural pattern drills: A classification. In H. Allen & R. Campell (Eds.), *Teaching English as a second language* (pp. 239–138). New York: McGraw-Hill.

Rosa, E., & O'Neill, M. O. (1998). Effects of stress and location on acoustic salience at the initial stages of Spanish L2 input processing. *Spanish Applied Linguistics, 2,* 24–52.

Salaberry, M. R. (1997). The role of input and output practice in second language acquisition. *The Canadian Modern Language Review, 53,* 422–451.

Swain, M. (1997). The output hypothesis, focus on form, and second language learning. In V. Berry, B. Adamson & W. Littlewood (Eds.), *Applying linguistics: Insights into language in education* (pp. 1–21). Hong Kong: University of Hong Kong, English Centre.

Terrell, T., Andrade, M., Egasse, J., & Munoz, E. M. (1994). *Dos mundos* (3rd ed.). New York: McGraw Hill.

VanPatten, B. (1984). Learners' comprehension of clitic pronouns: More evidence for a word order strategy. *Hispanic Linguistics, 1,* 57–67.

VanPatten, B. (1993). Grammar teaching for the acquisition-rich classroom. *Foreign Language Annals, 26,* 435–450.

VanPatten, B. (1996). *Input processing and grammar instruction: Theory and research.* Norwood, NJ: Ablex.

VanPatten, B. (2002). Processing instruction: An update. *Language Learning, 52,* 755–803.

VanPatten, B. (2003). *From input to output: A teacher's guide to second language acquisition.* New York: McGraw-Hill.

VanPatten, B., & Cadierno, T. (1993). Explicit instruction and input processing. *Studies in Second Language Acquisition, 15,* 225–243.

VanPatten, B., & Oikkenon, S. (1996). Explanation vs. structured input in processing instruction. *Studies in Second Language Acquisition, 18,* 495–510.

VanPatten, B., & Sanz, C. (1995). From input to output: Processing instruction and communicative tasks. In F. Eckman, D. Highland, P. Lee, J. Mileham & R. Rutkowski Weber (Eds.), *Second language acquisition theory and pedagogy* (pp. 169–185). Mahwah, NJ: Lawrence Erlbaum Associates.

Wong, W. (2002a). Linking form and meaning: Processing instruction. *The French Review, 76,* 236–264.

Wong, W. (2002b, October). *Decreasing attentional demands in input processing: A textual enhancement study.* Paper presented at the meeting of the Second Language Research Forum, Toronto, Canada.

Wong, W., & VanPatten, B. (in press). The evidence is IN: Drills are OUT. *Foreign Language Annals.*

Chapter 3

Commentary: What to Teach? How to Teach?

Patsy M. Lightbown
Concordia University, Montreal

Some years ago, I argued that SLA research could not tell teachers *what* to teach or *how* (Lightbown, 1985a). In the 1970s and early 1980s, SLA research had touched on only a few isolated language features, and there was no general framework for deciding which of the nearly innumerable details of a language could or should be the focus of instruction. Furthermore, I suggested that, although there was much in SLA research to support the movement away from rigid audio lingual instruction to more communicative language teaching, it seemed that such trends regarding *how* to teach were confirmed—not caused—by SLA research. Over the years, many SLA researchers have emphasized their separateness from language pedagogy, insisting, with considerable justification, that SLA was a field in its own right, and that it was appropriate for SLA researchers to seek to understand how language is acquired, without always having to answer the question, "but what does that say about teaching?" They left the pedagogy to others. Bill VanPatten was an exception to this. His research and that of a circle of colleagues and graduate students always had one foot firmly planted in the classroom. That commitment to improving second language teaching has not changed and the chapters that are the subject of my commentary provide a rich resource for teachers, researchers, and teacher/researchers whose goal is to find ways to help classroom language learners get beyond roadblocks that limit their progress in second language development.

The questions of what input is available to L1 and L2 learners, as well as how they perceive and process that input, have been a focus of my research for a long time (Lightbown, 1980, 1983, 1984, 1985b, 1987, 1991, 1992a, b; 2001; Lightbown & d'Anglejan; 1985, Lightbown et al, 2002). In 1991, my colleagues Nina Spada and Lydia White and I organized a colloquium in Montreal on the role of instruction in SLA. We brought together researchers who agreed that instruction could play a role in second language learning, but who had quite different interpretations of that role. The study that Bill VanPatten presented appeared as VanPatten and Cadierno (1993) in the issue of *Studies in Second Language Acquisition* (Volume 15, No. 2) devoted to papers from that colloquium. The pedagogical implications of his ideas about focussed input became an important component of every SLA course I taught thereafter—to undergraduates in teacher training courses and to post-graduate students with a research focus. So, for years, I have reviewed and discussed these ideas (VanPatten shows up in the reference lists of nearly everything I've published since that time). I have found his ideas to be both useful and provocative, and students have always found the work fascinating and intuitively appealing. We often say that the best way to learn something is to teach it. But preparing this commentary on chapters 1 and 2 has led me to new appreciation of what seemed so familiar.

I found that, in reading and rereading both previously published work and the chapters I will comment on here, my understanding of IP and PI has deepened. With that deeper understanding of both the theoretical background and the details of the research methods and findings have come a greater awareness of the specificity of the pedagogical proposals as well as new insights into the possible limitations of PI—limitations that have always been acknowledged by VanPatten. In this commentary, I will reflect on some aspects of the potential value of PI for second language pedagogy, especially in "the acquisition-rich classroom" (VanPatten, 1993).

All theories of second language acquisition recognize a crucial role for input (Gass, 1997). There are disagreements, however, about a number of issues, including *frequency, salience*, and *comprehensibility* of the input. The acquisition of some language features is undoubtedly affected by their frequency and salience in the input that learners are exposed to. While there is much evidence that low-frequency features are difficult to acquire (Ellis, 2002), there is evidence that some high-frequency features with low salience and/or high redundancy (VanPatten, this volume, chap. 1) are also late and/or difficult acquisitions. The salience of features is affected by a number of things—whether they are full syllables or bound morphemes (Wode, 1981), whether they are in initial, medial, or final position in sentences (Meisel, Clahsen, & Pienemann, 1981; Pienemann, 1999; VanPatten, this volume). First language patterns also affect learners' ability to perceive patterns in the L2 lexicon and morphosyntax (e.g., Kellerman, 1983; Schachter, 1974; Zobl, 1980).

With regard to comprehensibility, Krashen (1985, 1994) argues that input that is comprehensible and that contains language features just beyond the learner's current interlanguage will, if affective conditions are right, provide the necessary and sufficient conditions for acquisition to proceed. Sharwood Smith (1986) distinguished between input for comprehension and input for acquisition, suggesting that not everything that is available in the input becomes intake for acquisition or leads to changes in a learner's interlanguage. White (1987) suggested that comprehensible input might lead learners to conclude that they already know what they need to know. She argued that it is when input is *incomprehensible* that learners realize they need to pay attention to formal aspects of the language (see also Carroll, 1999). VanPatten (1990) showed that learners had difficulty focussing on certain types of language form while their attention was oriented primarily toward meaning.

In second language classrooms where language is seen primarily as a carrier of information rather than as the object of instruction in itself (content-based instruction, immersion instruction, certain types of "communicative language teaching"), there is ample evidence that learners can successfully understand much of what they hear and read, without acquiring all the language features that are present in the input. Some of the features that learners fail to acquire through activities that are primarily meaning-based prove to have low frequency in the classroom input (Lyster, 1994; Swain, 1988). Others, however, may have high frequency, but high redundancy and low salience, allowing learners to ignore them as long as contextual cues or event probabilities provide enough information to permit accurate guessing. This suggests that, in much language interaction outside the classroom and in meaning-based instruction, comprehension may interfere with acquisition in the sense that learners are misled into thinking that they have processed and understood language form, when in fact, they have relied on contextual or cotextual cues (see Batstone, 2002). As VanPatten points out (2002; this volume, chap. 1), it is only when learners are confronted with the necessity of using those non-salient features to grasp meaning that they come to realize that they have either misunderstood what they heard or read or that they have understood the general idea without knowing how language encoded the meaning. VanPatten has proposed processing instruction as one way to increase learners' chances of making correct form/meaning connections.

For nearly twenty years, most of my SLA research has been done in language teaching/learning contexts where teachers were committed to a type of communicative language teaching in which any focus on language itself other than a gentle "recast" was considered counterproductive (e.g., Lightbown & Spada, 1990). The instructional environment was one in which francophone children, 11–12 years old, were enrolled in "intensive ESL classes" where, for a period of five months of one academic year, they spent most of each school day participating in activities in English. The emphasis was always on "meaning" and it was expected that, with time and motivation, learners would eventually acquire both fluency and accuracy in their use of the target language. Anything that might be construed as "teaching grammar" was seen as potentially de-motivating and, in any case, something that would take time away from the more important activity—using the language in communicative interaction. It would be hard to overstate the extent to which students in these classes (with the encouragement of their teachers) confirmed VanPatten's Principle 1 and its subprinciples: *Learners process input for meaning before they process it for form; they process content words before anything else, and they tend to rely on lexical items rather than redundant, non-salient grammatical morphemes and function words* (my paraphrasing). Activities were designed in such a way that students were not only enabled, but actively *encouraged* to "go for meaning", not worrying about the details, that is, not worrying about function words or grammatical morphology.[1]

Our research in these classes showed that, after several months of intensive exposure to English (3–5 hours a day), most learners had either not noticed or, in any case, had not incorporated into their developing interlanguage a number of high frequency language forms. Two examples are inversion in question forms (Spada & Lightbown, 1993) and the use of possessive determiners *his* and *her* (Lightbown & Spada, 1990; White, 1998). We recently reported on a study in which we introduced form-focussed instruction on these two language features (Spada, Lightbown, & White, in press), and it is useful to review both the experimental methodology and the findings of that study in light of VanPatten's principles of input processing and Wong's (this volume, chap. 2) elaboration of the "structured input" activities that are at the heart of processing instruction. Before describing the research procedures and the findings of our study, I will briefly describe these language features, suggesting the processing problems that might explain students' difficulty in acquiring them.

For French-speaking learners, the choice of the correct third person possessive determiner is complicated by the fact that in French, as in Spanish and many other languages, the determiner agrees with the grammatical gender of the possessed entity, not with the natural gender of the possessor.[2] Thus, the sentence *J'ai posé sa règle sur son bureau* could have four possible translation equivalents in English:

> *I put his ruler on his desk.*
> *I put her ruler on his desk.*
> *I put his ruler on her desk.*
> *I put her ruler on her desk.*

Only contextual information tells us whether the possessor of the ruler and the desk is the same person and whether his/her/their gender is masculine or feminine. Even after French-speaking learners of English have started to use both *his* and *her* (after an initial period of using the definite article or an undifferentiated possessive determiner—often "your"), they run into trouble

---

[1]Similar findings have been reported in other instructional environments, including French immersion (Lyster, 1994, 1998).

[2]In fact, there is a further complication in the fact that, in referring to body parts, French often uses the definite article rather than a possessive form. (See Spada, Lightbown, & White, in press, and White, 1998, for further treatment of this aspect of the learners' development.)

when the possessed entity has natural gender. That is, they may produce sentences such as *The little girl talk to his father*, choosing *his* to agree with the natural gender of the father (Lightbown & Spada, 1990; White, 1998; Zobl, 1985). White and Ranta (in press) show that students' explanations for their choices confirm that they are operating on the basis of the French rule for choosing the gender marking of the possessive determiner.

With regard to inversion in questions, we had found in previous studies (Spada & Lightbown, 1999) that learners had relatively little difficulty in learning to recognize the ungrammaticality of questions without subject-[auxiliary] verb inversion when the subject was a pronoun. However, they continued to accept questions without inversion, if the subject was a full lexical noun. For example, most accepted *Can we watch television?* and *Why do you want to go outside?*, but at the same time, they accepted *Why fish can live in water?* and **Why children like McDonald's?* as grammatical. We hypothesized that the problem lay in learners' assumption that English, like French, does not allow inversion with noun subjects. That is, *Peut-il jouer dehors?* (literally, *Wants-he to-play outside?)* is grammatical, but **Peut-Jean jouer dehors?* (literally, *Can John to-play outside?)* is not.[3]

There are several reasons why learners might "hear" English as allowing pronouns but not nouns in inversion. They may have filtered the input on the basis of a pattern that they know from their first language (Lightbown, 2001). VanPatten points out, quite correctly, that the existence of a pattern in L1 is not a sufficient basis for predicting L2 developmental patterns. For one thing, learners need to reach a certain level of development before they can even recognize similarities and differences between the target language and previously learned languages. Nevertheless, it has been shown that L1 interacts with developmental sequences in a variety of ways—speeding or slowing progress, constraining generalization, adding sub-stages (Zobl, 1980). In the case of these students, they had reached a stage where they recognized the pattern of inversion in English questions that matched the French pattern, but could not see that it extended to nouns as well as pronouns.

Another possible reason for learners' failure to recognize the grammaticality of inversion with noun subjects is that, in informal speech, the auxiliary verb often has very little salience. Having had little or no form-focussed instruction, the students did not realize that in both yes/no and wh-questions in English, a verbal element must precede the subject, although the lexical verb remains in its post-subject position (Indeed, I assume this is what

---

[3]It has long been noted that inversion is rare in informal spoken French (Lightbown, 1980; Picard, 2002). However, students of this age will have had considerable exposure to written French and to more formal varieties of spoken French. They will also have been taught to use inversion in their own writing. Therefore, when they are asked to judge the grammaticality of sentences, we may assume that their judgements are based on their knowledge of more formal varieties as well as their own informal spoken French.

VanPatten is referring to when he says that English has predominantly SVO order, even for questions.) We can see evidence that students simply do not hear the auxiliary preceding the subject in the changes that some students made to sentences such as *Why children like McDonald's?* They "corrected" the question by inserting *the*, yielding *Why the children like McDonald's?* This seemed to suggest that if they heard the *do* at all in the many correct questions present in the classroom input, they heard it as a plausible pronunciation of the definite article, a required element in the corresponding question in informal spoken French *Pourquoi les enfants aiment McDonald's?* In normal language, delivered at a normal rate, the difference between "Why do children..." and "Why the children..." is minimal, and no doubt extremely difficult for low proficiency learners to hear. Furthermore, failure to recognize or produce the grammatical auxiliary in pre-subject position is very unlikely to interfere with communicative effectiveness. Not surprisingly, this type of error persists in the English of students even after long periods of exposure to the language.

Thus, in this study, we had identified two problems that we knew to be long-term challenges for francophones learning English, and we designed an instructional intervention that was intended to help them improve their ability to recognize these features and to use the correct forms in their own production. Looking back on this study in terms of processing instruction, several things are worthy of note. We did follow Step 1 in Wong's list of the steps in designing structured input activities by identifying a plausible strategy to explain how learners were misinterpreting the input and using their incorrect interpretation to shape their output. We also followed the first guideline in Step 2, providing the teachers with activities that focussed on "one thing at a time." Students in both groups (those being taught question inversion and those being taught possessive determiners) were told what the problem was. That is, they were shown how French and English differ with regard to the feature they were learning, and they engaged in activities that kept the focus on these features.[4]

To a certain extent, some of the remaining guidelines in Step 2 were also met by the instructional activities. Both oral and written input were provided, and students performed a variety of tasks that required them to "do something with" the features in focus. The learners' processing strategies, as we understood them, were the basis of all the materials, and teachers were asked to provide feedback when students showed that they were relying on the incorrect strategies. Nevertheless, the study was not planned in terms of the guidelines for the structured input required for processing instruction, and the fit is not perfect.

---

[4]The study had been planned as an opportunity to compare the learning success of students who were told about the French/English contrasts and those who were simply taught the English pattern. After the study was under way, we realized that the teachers in the intact classes participating in the study had, either before or during the experimental treatment, provided their students with information about the contrast. Thus, all students had at least some direct instruction that drew their attention to the processing problem they needed to overcome.

There was not strict adherence to the guideline to move from single-sentence focus to discourse focus, and activities included opportunities for students to produce as well as hear and read the target features. The most significant point where our instructional intervention differed from processing instruction was with regard to the guideline "Keep meaning in focus." The overall emphasis of the classroom activities (including those that were part of the experimental intervention) was almost always on meaning, and using language in context. However, there was a difference in meaning focus for the two language features. For the activities in which possessive determiners were the target feature, success in carrying out the various tasks, answering questions, and playing games usually required the correct use and interpretation of *his* and *her*. However, while a learner's misinterpretation of a possessive determiner or use of the wrong one in production can lead to misunderstanding, there is little likelihood that failure to invert in questions led to communication difficulty or to an inability to continue with the tasks. Thus, in the activities focused on inversion, the instructional intervention targeted correct *form* rather than crucial form/meaning relations.

In pretest/posttest comparisons, we found that the experimental intervention was very effective in changing learners' ability to interpret and use possessive determiners. Changes in their recognition of grammaticality in questions and their use of inversion in questions were also affected by the instruction, but the effect was less substantial. We offered several possible interpretations for this finding (see Spada, Lightbown, & White, in press). The one that is relevant here is that the instruction in question inversion was not based on a fundamental form/meaning connection, while instruction on possessive determiners was. Although it is important to emphasize again that this study was not designed to replicate or mimic PI instruction, the differences in outcomes seem to be quite consistent with the predictions that VanPatten and Wong would make regarding the effectiveness of the instructional intervention. The inference that I draw from this is that one of the limitations of PI will be in its relative effectiveness in helping learners overcome problems with language features that lead to errors that interfere with meaning, compared to those that do not. In previous research, we have seen learners improve their accuracy in recognizing and using questions, but these studies have involved relatively long periods of intervention, explicit focus on accuracy, and sustained teacher feedback (Spada & Lightbown, 1993; White, Spada, Lightbown, & Ranta, 1991).

VanPatten has been clear that PI is aimed at bringing learners to process a form/meaning relationship that they have either not previously processed or that they have processed incorrectly. Not only is there no claim that PI leads to flawless production in spontaneous communication, there is not even a claim that the intake that results from PI leads to a change in the structure of a learner's interlanguage. PI is proposed as a first step, a way to start something that needs many more components before the feature in focus becomes a natural part of the learner's use of the second language.

Most experimental PI instruction (like the instruction in most other experimental SLA studies) has taken place over a very short period of time—minutes, hours, days. And, by definition, instruction and exposure to the target features have been carefully controlled. It may be that longer periods of PI—or frequent refresher lessons that remind learners of their processing problem—would eventually lead to correct, fluent use. However, it seems more likely that a great deal more time and a great many more opportunities to retrieve and use the feature in communicative settings are likely to be necessary.

Processing instruction is a valuable first step in helping learners to make connections between language forms and their meanings or their uses. Once this step has taken place, learners need to encounter the language features again and again in discourse-rich contexts where their use is appropriate. Psychological research on transfer-appropriate processing suggests that we recall something most easily when we are in the same situation in which we learned it (see Segalowitz & Lightbown, 1999). VanPatten repeatedly emphasizes that the *processing* that takes place in the narrow scope of PI is not, in itself, learning (nor, to acknowledge Krashen's contrast, is it *acquisition*). Rather, this initial processing permits recognition, practice, and learning to take place subsequently in "transfer-appropriate" contexts (see also Schmidt, 1992).

Throughout the learning process, classroom learners may also benefit from sustained feedback on the errors in their use of many language features, even after they have a good foundation—whether that includes formal grammatical explanation or only structured input without explanation (see Sanz, this volume; Wong, chap. 2, this volume). Sustained feedback is especially likely to be important if the linguistic feature is one of those that does not affect meaning—either in general, or an environment where students (and teachers) share the same L1 and many interlanguage patterns. This brings me to a brief comment about the example that VanPatten gives for the effectiveness of a certain type of feedback. In the "Bob and Tom" example, a clarification request (in the form of a recast with rising intonation) seems to lead the second language speaker to notice something about the way the target language works. There's plenty of evidence to show although such "conversational" recasts sometimes alert learners to differences between their original version of a sentence and the one offered in the recast, they may also pass unnoticed outside the classroom or in classrooms where the learners (and the teacher) have the habit of focusing primarily on meaning (Lyster, 1998). To date, the research suggests that recasts are most effective when they include some signal to make it clear that the recast focuses on form rather than (or in addition to) meaning (Doughty, 1999). Recasts have been shown to work in laboratory dyads where interaction is very focused or in classrooms with small numbers of adult learners where the instruction includes a substantial metalinguistic component (see Nicholas, Lightbown, & Spada, 2001 for review). Even in these contexts, learners may misread recasts, especially if they are offered by classmates (Morris, 2002).

A question that inevitably comes to mind regarding not only PI research but also any research on assisting language learning is the extent to which it can be adopted or adapted for use by classroom teachers. The research findings are sufficiently clear to persuade me that PI is an effective tool for helping learners zero in on form/meaning relationships that they have previously overlooked or misinterpreted. In translating the research findings to classroom application, I am aware of how wishful thinking leads some educators to hope that there is a magic formula that will work across the board for solving pedagogical problems. I am reminded of the strong reservations I have expressed elsewhere about the possibility of planning teaching sequences to match developmental sequences that have been observed in second language acquisition (Lightbown, 1985c; 1998). VanPatten and Wong have been very clear that they do not see PI as the best or only approach to teaching all language features. They have also left no doubt that PI is not proposed as the basis for taking learners all the way to spontaneous, accurate, automatized production of any language features. In reflecting on the role of PI in "ordinary classrooms", I'd like to focus on two concerns. First, how can we identify language features that are (or are not) good candidates for the PI approach? Second, are teachers prepared to use this tool in their classrooms?

There are probably many language features that are not good candidates for PI instruction. This would include those that learners acquire without apparent difficulty while they engage in interactive communicative language. At the other end of the continuum are those that learners continue to have difficulty with, because of their inability to distinguish between correct and incorrect language forms. These are features that do not ordinarily lead learners to misinterpret what they hear and read, and accuracy in producing these features leads to a more polished performance rather than to changes in the meaning. Although some of the components of PI may be effective in helping students notice the difference between correct and incorrect versions of a language feature, a full-scale application of the guidelines that Wong proposes is either impossible or requires an unreasonable amount of effort at creating structured input. One example of this may be the inserted auxiliary *do* in questions.[5] Another would be the kinds of complex syntactic features that are often the focus of SLA research with a Universal Grammar orientation. The finding that structured input works as well as structured input plus explanation (VanPatten & Oikkenon, 1996; the various papers in Part 3 of this volume) may be the key to whether PI can be used to guide learners' acquisition of more complex linguistic features as well as features in which errors do not lead to problems with interpreting meaning. It also shows how PI can be effective with learners whose lack of metalinguistic

---

[5]VanPatten (1996) has suggested, however, that PI might be used to help learners process *do* as a carrier of tense and number information, thereby making the form more salient and possibly available for further processing and learning. (See VanPatten, this volume, chap. 17 as well.)

awareness or training (including young learners and those with low levels of literacy) limits the usefulness of "explanations" that are given using unfamiliar terminology.

Are teachers prepared to use the insights and procedures of PI in their classrooms? Wong's carefully detailed guidelines certainly improve the chances that in future "replications" of PI, researchers can scrutinize the design of their intervention studies in terms of their conformity to that approach. But, even with these guidelines, is it reasonable to expect teachers to be up to the challenge? Although university foreign language instructors may continue to receive extensive training in both the grammar of the language(s) they are to teach and SLA research findings, teachers working with younger learners as well as many teachers of English as a second language to both children and adults have far less knowledge of the language itself and of the language acquisition research. Their backgrounds often include more training for teaching in general or for foreign/second language teaching methods in particular (both of which are often sadly lacking in the training of university foreign language instructors). My experience with teachers working in second and foreign language instruction in primary and secondary schools is that they are often unaware of the reasons students make certain errors or have difficulty with particular language features. Indeed, in some cases, they do not even notice the errors—either because they make them themselves (in the case of teachers who have less than excellent command of the second language) or because they look "through" the error to the *meaning* that is their focus. This is not, of course, a problem with PI. Rather, it is a potential limitation on its application in situations where it could be an effective pedagogical tool if only teachers were equipped to use it.

For years, I told students that my SLA course was not a "teaching methods" course and that I would not be telling them "what to teach or how to teach." I told them, however, that I hoped they would find the course "useful" in helping them to set appropriate expectations for what their students could learn and what they could teach within the context of classroom instruction. Over time, the course content changed as more and more SLA researchers *were* doing research with a pedagogical focus (see Lightbown, 2000, for a review of some of this work). Some research that was not classroom-based also contributed significantly to our understanding of why teaching didn't always have the effect teachers hoped it would have. Gradually, some of the work students read did begin to point to answers to questions about what to teach and how. The work of VanPatten and his colleagues has evolved to include some of the most explicit responses to both these questions. The clear and detailed principles and guidelines that are available in the VanPatten and Wong chapters will make a further contribution to answering them.

In recent years, I've become bolder in claiming that the SLA course makes a "practical" contribution to teacher education. Now I almost always end the term by giving students a set of guidelines for classroom practice that I think are supported by the research they have read about during the course. Knowing that

Lightbown, P. M. (1992a). Getting quality input in the second/foreign language classroom. In C. Kramsch & S. McConnell-Ginet (Eds.), *Text and context: Cross-disciplinary and cross-cultural perspectives on language study* (pp. 187–197). Lexington, MA: D. C. Heath.

Lightbown, P. M. (1992b). Can they do it themselves? A comprehension-based ESL course for young children. In R. Courchêne, J. St. John, C. Therrien & J. Glidden (Eds.), *Comprehension-based second language teaching: Current trends* (pp. 353–370). Ottawa: University of Ottawa Press.

Lightbown, P. M. (1998). The importance of timing in focus on form. In C. Doughty & J. Williams (Eds.), *Focus on form in classroom second language acquisition* (pp. 177–196). Cambridge: Cambridge University Press.

Lightbown, P. M. (2001). Input filters in second language acquisition. In S. Foster Cohen & A. Nizegorodcew (Eds.), *EUROSLA Yearbook. Volume 1: 2001* (pp. 79–97). Amsterdam: John Benjamins.

Lightbown, P. M., & d'Anglejan, A. (1985). Some input considerations for word order in French L1 and L2 acquisition. In S. Gass & C. Madden (Eds.), *Input in second language acquisition* (pp. 415–430). Rowley MA: Newbury House.

Lightbown, P. M., & Spada, N. (1990). Focus-on-form and corrective feedback in communicative language teaching: Effects on second language learning. *Studies in Second Language Acquisition, 12,* 429–448.

Lightbown, P. M., Halter, R., White, J., & Horst, M. (2002). Comprehension-based learning: The limits of "do it yourself."*Canadian Modern Language Review, 58,* 427–464.

Lyster, R. (1994). Négotiation de la forme: Stratégie analytique en classe d'immersion. *Canadian Modern Language Review, 50,* 446–465.

Lyster, R. (1998). Recasts, repetition and ambiguity in L2 classroom discourse. *Studies in Second Language Acquisition, 20,* 51–80.

Meisel, J. M., Clahsen, H., & Pienemann, M. (1981). On determining developmental stages in natural second language acquisition. *Studies in Second Language Acquisition, 3,* 109–135.

Morris, F. (2002, October). *How foreign language learners of Spanish perceive implicit negative feedback.* Paper presented at the Second Language Research Forum, Toronto.

Nicholas, H., Lightbown, P. M., & Spada, N. (2001). Recasts as feedback to language learners. *Language Learning, 51,* 719–758.

Picard, M. (2002). L1 interference in second language acquisition: The case of question formation in Canadian French. *IRAL, 40,* 61–68.

Pienemann, M. (1999). *Language processing and second language development: Processability theory.* Amsterdam: John Benjamins.

Schachter, J. (1974). An error in error analysis. *Language Learning, 24,* 205–214.

Schmidt, R. (1992). Psychological mechanisms underlying second language fluency. *Studies in Second Language Acquisition, 14,* 357–385.

Segalowitz, N., & Lightbown, P. M. (1999). Psycholinguistic approaches to SLA. In W. Grabe (Ed.), *Annual Review of Applied Linguistics, 19,* 43–63.

Sharwood Smith, M. (1986). Comprehension versus acquisition: Two ways of processing input. *Applied Linguistics, 7*, 239–256.

Spada, N., & Lightbown, P. M. (1993). Instruction and the development of questions in L2 classrooms. *Studies in Second Language Acquisition, 15*, 205–224.

Spada, N., & Lightbown, P. M. (1999). Instruction, L1 influence and developmental readiness in second language acquisition. *Modern Language Journal, 83*, 1–22.

Spada, N., Lightbown, P. M., & White, J. (in press). The importance of form/meaning mappings in explicit form-focussed instruction. In A. Housen & M. Pierrard (Eds.), *Instructed second language learning* (Mouton de Gruyter, SoLA series).

Swain, M. (1988). Manipulating and complementing content teaching to maximize second language learning. *TESL Canada Journal, 6*, 68–83.

VanPatten, B. (1990). Attending to form and content in the input: An experiment in consciousness. *Studies in Second Language Acquisition, 12*, 287–301.

VanPatten, B. (1993). Grammar instruction for the acquisition rich classroom. *Foreign Language Annals, 26*, 433–450.

VanPatten, B. (2002). Processing instruction: An Update. *Language Learning, 52*, 755–803.

VanPatten, B., & Cadierno, T. (1993). Explicit instruction and input processing. *Studies in Second Language Acquisition, 15*, 225–243.

VanPatten, B., & Oikkenon, S. (1996). Explanation versus structured input in processing instruction. *Studies in Second Language Acquisition, 18*, 495–510.

White, J. (1998). Getting learners' attention: A typographical input enhancement study. In C. Doughty & J. Williams (Eds.), *Focus on form in classroom second language acquisition* (pp. 85–113). Cambridge: Cambridge University Press.

White, J., & Ranta, L. (in press). What you know and what you do: The relationship between metalinguistic performance and oral production in a second language. *Language Awareness.*

White, L. (1987). Against comprehensible input: The input hypothesis and the development of second language competence. *Applied Linguistics, 8*, 95–110.

White, L., Spada, N., Lightbown, P. M., & Ranta, L. (1991). Input enhancement and L2 question formation. *Applied Linguistics, 12*, 416–432.

Wode, H. (1981). *Learning a second language: An integrated view of language acquisition*. Tübingen: Gunter Narr.

Zobl, H. (1980). The formal and developmental selectivity of L1 influence on L2 acquisition. *Language Learning, 30*, 43–57.

Zobl, H. (1985). Grammars in search of input and intake. In S. Gass & C. Madden (Eds.), *Input in second language acquisition* (pp. 205–221). Rowley, MA: Newbury House.

Chapter 4

Commentary: Input Processing as a Theory of Processing Input

Michael Harrington
The University of Queensland, Australia

In this article I examine the input processing (IP) model as part of a cognitive theory of second language acquisition (SLA). The model has attracted considerable interest as a psycholinguistic account of second language grammar development and also provides the theoretical foundation for *Processing Instruction*, an influential approach to second language pedagogy (VanPatten, 1996; Wong, this volume, chap. 2). Although instructional issues have attracted the most attention (Cadierno, 1995; DeKeyser & Sokalski, 1996; VanPatten, 2002), they are not examined here. Rather, the focus in this chapter will be on IP as a testable psycholinguistic construct. However, issues raised in this regard will ultimately have implications for instructional applications of the model.

I will begin by specifying what the IP model does not attempt to do. This is useful because the acquisition of second language (L2) grammar is an extremely complex process. A complete account of L2 grammar development will have multiple dimensions, and the IP model must be considered as part of that larger enterprise. Specifying what the IP account does not attempt to do also helps define key terms used in the model. *Form, meaning* and *processing* are all used in ways that permit multiple, sometimes conflicting, interpretations. Close attention will be given to these terminological issues and the implications they have for the testability of the IP claims. I will then consider what the model aims to do, namely to provide an explanation for why beginning learners often have more difficulty with surface forms that signal structural relations (e.g., bound inflections) than with those that carry more transparent semantic content (e.g., nouns). This difficulty is evident in both first language (Clark, 1993) and second language acquisition (Ellis, 1994). As the ability to comprehend and produce these forms is integral to (if not synonymous with) grammar development, an account of why they pose difficulties for the learner is at the heart of any SLA theory.

In this chapter I will examine key IP claims in terms of their testability and explanatory power. The model is complex and I will only be addressing what I see as key issues. The model's explanatory power depends in the first instance on its *internal validity*, that is, the degree to which it accounts for the observed difficulties that beginning learners have with learning certain grammatical morphemes. In this regard I identify three significant challenges to the internal validity of the IP model as it is currently formulated. The first concerns the form-meaning connections the learner is assumed to make in the course of comprehension. This connection making, which occurs under the pressure of real-time comprehension demands, *is* input processing. According to the IP model, the order in which forms are connected to meanings (that is, are processed) is a function of the processing resources available to the individual at the time of comprehension and the relative *meaningfulness* of the form. Meaning has multiple dimensions in the IP model, which makes it a difficult notion to operationalize and test. The second challenge to the IP account concerns the proposed locus of input processing within the larger comprehension event. The difficulty a learner encounters with certain grammatical forms in the input is assumed to arise at the initial encoding of the form-meaning connection, rather than at the earlier stage of perceptual processing or the latter stages of storage and retrieval. As an empirical claim this claim is untestable in its current form, and the observational and experimental evidence used to date to support it is largely irrelevant. The final challenge the IP model faces concerns the use of processing capacity constraints to explain processing/learning outcomes. The explanatory value of capacity differences depends crucially on identifying the specific processing demands being made during comprehension, how these demands interact with existing knowledge, and finally the nature of the capacity constraints on this process. These constraints must be, at least partially, independent of domain knowledge; otherwise the explanation becomes circular (Miyake & Friedman, 1998). The current model addresses these issues in very general terms, if at all (DeKeyser, Salaberry, Robinson, & Harrington 2002). I close with more general comments on the IP model as a cognitive account of SLA.

WHAT THE IP MODEL IS NOT

In this section I briefly spell out what the model does not intend to do. This is not intended as a list of shortcomings, nor is it meant to imply that the IP model –or any single account of SLA—could or should account for all the points raised. Rather the list is meant to locate IP in the larger SLA enterprise, and to also anticipate possible confusions that might arise from the model-specific ways in which key terms are used. In brief, the IP model is not a comprehensive theory of second language development or second language grammar development, nor is it an account of sentence processing as it is usually understood.

Not a Comprehensive Theory of Second Language Development

The IP model focuses on the initial stages of the process that leads to the creation of an "implicit linguistic system" in the mind of the learner (p. 25). This process is not concerned with the development of L2 fluency or accuracy as represented in skill learning (DeKeyser, 1998), and output-based approaches (Gass, 1997; Swain, 1998). The model thus maintains a fundamental distinction between acquisition and learning. IP is part of implicit acquisition and does not contribute to the development of fluency, while practice and explicit rule learning does not result in acquisition (Krashen, 1982, p. 23, this volume, p. 26).

Not a Comprehensive Theory of Second Language Grammar Development

The IP model is not intended as a comprehensive theory of L2 grammar development. Rather, it limits itself to explaining how raw linguistic input becomes potentially internalisable intake, or more specifically "... under what conditions learners may or may not make connections between a form in the input and a meaning, and the processes they initially bring to the task of acquisition" (p. 6). In particular, the model does not attempt to explain how these form-meaning connections might ultimately become part of the learner's developing grammar. Thus input processing is an act of comprehension or realization of a form-meaning mapping, the output of which may or may not ultimately be learned. To underscore this point, throughout the chapter I will refer to the individual doing the putative input processing as the *comprehender* and not the learner, as the latter presumes an outcome that is technically beyond the scope of the model.

Not an Account of Sentence Processing

Despite the model's label, VanPatten explicitly cautions against interpreting the IP model as an account of L2 sentence processing, and specifically one of parsing (p. 5–6). The form-meaning connections made during the input processing stage are assumed to feed into the parser, whose job it is to identify the structural constituents in the input string (p. 25). The interaction between input processing and more general processing mechanisms is a tricky issue for the model. Although in theory separable from the overall speech processing mechanisms, the specific mechanisms that subserve input processing need to be consistent with what we know about sentence processing, a point made in (DeKeyser et al., 2002).

WHAT THE IP MODEL IS

The IP model seeks to provide a psycholinguistic explanation for the widely-observed fact that early in development, L2 (and L1) learners often encounter difficulty with certain grammatical forms, particularly bound morphemes (e.g., case markers in Japanese) and "little" words carrying grammatical information (e.g., auxiliary *do* in English). There are a number of possible reasons why these forms might cause difficulty for the beginning learner. Perceptually they are difficult to handle, being short, fast, unstressed and phonologically reduced. Research shows that even competent adults have difficulty processing these forms, which can be recognized out of context less than 30% of the time (Goodman & Nusbaum, 1994). These forms also signal the relationship between words within the input utterance and the organization of the larger linguistic system. The acquisition of these relational forms depends on the prior, or at the very least simultaneous, learning of the content words they link (Bates, Dale, & Thale, 1995).

The IP model attributes the observed learning difficulties to a single underlying cause, namely, processing capacity limitations. Real-time processing demands are assumed to force the learner to be selective in processing the input string, resulting in a focus on words that carry identifiable referential meaning at the expense of those signaling more abstract structural relations. The effects of capacity limitations are also minimized by the use of processing heuristics that focus the learner's attention on items early in the utterance, and may also bias the learner toward interpreting the first noun as the subject or agent of the utterance. I will not be discussing the latter here, although these heuristics play a major role in other processing models (see especially MacWhinney, 1999).

MAKING THE FORM-MEANING CONNECTION

At the heart of the IP model is the connection the learner makes between form and meaning, and the attendant constraints on that process. Although the meaning of the terms *form* and *meaning* may appear straightforward, in fact they are used in multiple, sometimes conflicting, ways in the IP model.

Form

Form is used in two distinct ways in the IP account. In the first instance it is used to refer to the *surface forms* the learner encounters in the input. These written or spoken forms are what the learner perceives, notices, processes, and potentially internalizes. Form in this sense is interchangeable with the term *items* (p. 8). But the term is also used to refer to non-content words in the input, or what is called *grammatical form* (this volume, p. 9). Grammatical form is a linguistic category and is defined by its role in the abstract linguistic system. In earlier work these grammatical forms included bound morphemes, prepositions, articles, and pronouns (VanPatten, 1996, p. 10), but are limited in the current model to bound grammatical morphemes and word order (this volume, p. 7).

Form is a key term in the IP principles and it is important to understand what is meant by its use. Consider Principle 1, the overarching principle on which all the other principles rest (this volume, p. 7).

Principle 1. Learners process input for meaning before they process it for form.

Which sense of *form* is intended here? If input processing is defined as making connections between a form and a meaning, then it must involve the simultaneous pairing of form and meaning – one cannot precede the other. Thus, making a connection *between* form and meaning invokes the surface form sense, while processing input *for* form (as in Principle 1) involves grammatical form. This distinction is clearer if we paraphrase Principle 1 by substituting the phrase "comprehend the form-meaning connection" for the verb "process":

Principle 1, (paraphrased). Learners comprehend the surface form-meaning connection for meaning before they comprehend the surface form-meaning connections for grammatical forms.

Or, in less cumbersome terms:

Principle 1a. Learners process content words in the input before anything else.

Taken literally, Principle 1a seems to say that the comprehender will comprehend *all* the form-meaning connections for content words before she comprehends *any* of the form-meaning connections for grammatical morphemes. Such a literal reading is apparently not intended, but the actual claim being made is unclear. Principles 1 & 1a say that content forms are input-processed/comprehended before grammatical forms, but neither principle indicates how we might interpret the notion of *before anything else*. The principles are only testable if we assume they mean something like the following. When learning a new linguistic rule (which expresses some communicative notion or function) in the target language, the comprehender will process (and possibly learn) the content words involved in the surface form realization of that rule before the relevant grammatical morphemes.

Note the prediction only makes sense in the context of a specific linguistic rule or domain. Current support for the model, however, comes from general observations about the apparent ease with which certain forms are comprehended, independent of the role the forms play in the development of L2 grammatical competence (VanPatten & Cadierno, 1993; VanPatten, 1996, 2002). As an example, consider 1a and 1b.

(1a) *He is eating the apple*
(1b) *He eats the apple.*

The model predicts that the *-ing* form in 1a is easier to (input) process than the third person singular *-s* in 1b (p. 10). This is presumably because the *-ing* form is more meaningful (despite the fact that, in propositional terms, it is more complex). However, the claim is largely irrelevant to understanding how learners develop knowledge of the second language linguistic system, implicit or explicit. Of interest is not whether the *-ing* form is learned before the third person *-s* in absolute terms. Rather, what is crucial is how these surface forms map onto the systematic L2 grammar knowledge developing in the mind of the learner. See Pienemann (1998) for one such attempt to relate processing effects to grammatical development.

To test the central IP claim concerning the form-meaning connection, a means must be found to (1) independently classify surface forms as either grammatical forms or content forms and (2) just as important, to identify how these forms relate to the learning of specific rules. The current model addresses the first issue in part by the construct of meaningfulness, which will be considered next. To date it has not addressed the second.

Meaning

Problems with terminological ambiguity in the IP model are even more apparent in the multiple uses of the term *meaning*. At the most general level, *overall meaning* refers to the intended meaning of the utterance. It is what the comprehender attempts to get in the course of processing the utterance. Although not specified, overall meaning apparently encompasses the range of propositional and illocutionary meanings an utterance can express. This overall meaning is extracted by the comprehender principally by the *semantic meaning* conveyed by surface forms in the text. Semantic meaning results either from the retrieval of stored knowledge representations, or by making a novel connection between a surface form and an underlying meaning (i.e., input-processing). The likelihood of this form-meaning connection being made is a function of the "meaningfulness" of the mapping. Meaningfulness is defined by the *communicative value* of the form, which reflects the amount of overall meaning that form contributes to the output of comprehension (this volume, p. 10). Different surface forms have different amounts of meaning. All content words by definition have meaning, while the meaningfulness of grammatical forms varies, and in some cases is entirely absent. In VanPatten's words "… some forms carry meaning and some forms do not" (p. 10). For example, the third person singular *-s* in English conveys the semantic meaning of "another person that is neither the speaker nor the person spoken to" (p. 10), but it also signals number agreement between the noun and the verb. The latter grammatical information, like gender markings in Spanish, are deemed "devoid of semantic information" (p. 10) and thus meaning. This is despite the fact that, in this instance, agreement cues help the comprehender figure out who is the actor and what is being done. A categorical distinction is thus made for grammatical forms between the possible (semantic) meanings a form can convey and the role it plays in signaling grammatical information. The first is meaningful, the latter is not. Some grammatical forms can convey both semantic meaning and grammatical information (e.g., English third person –s) and some only grammatical information (Spanish gender).

Another key dimension of meaning in IP is *redundancy*. This notion reflects the degree to which meaning conveyed by a given form is signaled elsewhere in the utterance (p. 10). The IP model assumes that the more redundant a form, the less likely it will be input processed, particularly in instances where processing resources are being stretched. Unlike the qualitative distinction made between content and grammatical form, redundancy is a quantitative concept, with the degree of redundancy conveyed by a form dependent on the particular context in which it appears and the other forms it appear with. Although not specified, redundancy appears to affect only the processing of grammatical form (e.g., the third person –s is often dropped in sentences like 1b *He talks too much* because the semantic meaning [person] is already expressed in the pronoun *He*).

Meaning in its manifold senses is central to IP processing claims. Consider Principle 1d (this volume, p. 11).

Principle 1d. Learners are more likely to process meaningful forms before nonmeaningful forms irrespective of redundancy.

What is the prediction here? Again we encounter a problem if we attempt too literal a reading: To define input processing as the mapping of a surface form onto some meaning requires that there be some meaning to map onto the form for processing to take place. In the strictest sense nonmeaningful forms (= forms without meaning, that is, forms signaling only grammatical information) *cannot be* processed. Grammatical forms like Spanish gender and English number agreement fall outside the scope of the IP model. Also, if redundancy always—or even usually—involves grammatical forms, then in Principle 1d is, well, redundant. A grammatical form that is nonmeaningful is processed after meaningful forms. Whether it is also redundant is irrelevant. A grammatical form like third person –s that also conveys some kind of referential real-world meaning (here, agency) is also processed second, given that content words are always processed first (see Principle 1a). These surface forms, which can at once be both meaningful *and* meaningless, are processed second, regardless of redundancy.

A literal reading of Principle 1d does not work and, again, the interpretation given here was probably not intended. What is the intended reading? One immediate problem is with the term "nonmeaningful." Rather than denoting "without meaning," or "meaningless," the term is apparently meant in a less categorical sense, that is, as something like "more or less meaningful." In this case the prediction is that, in relative terms, meaningful elements will tend to be learned first, (which of course implies they were input-processed at some point). If this were a legitimate gloss of Principle 1d (and indeed overriding Principle 1), there would be little argument—although testing the account remains problematic.

However, this probabilistic reading is inconsistent with the categorical distinction made between content and "anything else" in Principles 1 and 1a. That is, the distinction between semantic meaning (which has communicative value conveyed both by content and grammatical forms) and grammatical information (which is signaled by grammatical forms alone). The latter, for example an inflection, "… is meaningless in terms of the semantic information it carries (p. 10)." The wording here hints that inflections may have other, non-semantic, meanings. These presumably contribute to the overall meaning of the utterance. However, reference to meaning in the IP principles *does not* encompass these other (structural) senses of the term. As VanPatten cautions the reader "Meaning, again, refers to a semantic notion (this volume, p. 11)." Meaningful versus nonmeaningful thus become semantics versus grammar. The IP model asserts that, when attempting to understand an utterance, the comprehender is more interested in semantic information than grammatical information, especially at the beginning stages of learning. This is probably true, if nothing else than for the fact that the comprehension of forms conveying semantic information (e.g., "content" words) has a logical priority over grammatical form. Number, tense, aspect, and so on are attributes of a given noun, verb, and so on. They cannot exist independently. But for a model to provide insight into the psycholinguistic factors responsible for this outcome we need at the very least, an operational definition of what is meant by semantics and grammar and their relationship to such notions as "overall meaning" and "communicative value." This has yet to be done.

The issue as to whether meaning should be characterized in discrete or relative terms reflects a more basic issue with IP as a model of cognition. It currently has a split personality in terms of whether it is a discrete or probabilistic model of language processing and knowledge. The distinction reflects a fundamental division in approaches to language processing and cognition in general, and has profound implications for how models are developed and what evidence is adduced in support of these models (Harrington, 2001). The major IP principles are stated in categorical terms (Principles 1 and 1a), while remaining sub principles are couched in probabilistic terms, *preference* (*P1b* and *P1c*), *likelihood* (*P1c* and *P1d*) and *tendency* (*P1f*). As a probabilistic model the IP account has obvious parallels with Bates & MacWhinney's Competition Model (VanPatten, 1996). In this approach surface forms are characterized as cues to meaning that vary in strength according to the likelihood with which they signal a specific meaning (MacWhinney, 1999). An attractive feature of the Competition Model for IP is that cue strength is independent of such notions as content and grammatical forms, and provides a consistent means by which to assign meaning across semantic and grammatical forms. However, identifying those cues remains a significant challenge

The issues raised in this section have been mostly terminological, but it should be evident that the lack of definitional precision makes evaluation and testing of the key IP claims difficult. The use of terms like content, meaning, redundancy does make the account accessible to a wide audience, but the very familiarity of these terms in more general usage makes it doubly important that they be explicitly defined.

WHAT IS PROCESSED?

The third challenge to the internal validity of the IP account concerns the notion of *processing*. As was the case with "form" and "meaning", "processing" is also used in several ways. In most instances it is used as a synonym for input processing itself. VanPatten states that "...processing refers to making a connection between form and meaning" (this volume, p. 6). This restricted sense contrasts with the use of processing in other contexts to refer to the overall comprehension and learning process, as in reference to the "... availability of processing resources" (this volume, p. 11). The two senses must be distinguished, obviously, if the IP model is to be distinguished from general sentence processing mechanisms

It is unclear what exactly is being processed in the input. The IP model does not specify whether the "making of form-meaning connections" refers solely to the initial mapping of novel form-meaning links, or whether this connection-making occurs, as a matter of course, for all items in the input utterance, known and new. The novel-mapping sense is apparently intended, as evident in the statement that "a [Spanish] learner may "realize" (quotes original) that a form denotes pastness but has not grasped the aspectual meaning also encoded in the inflection" (p. 6), and that, in addition to input processing, learners also ".... have to acquire appropriate procedures for accessing forms and phrases" (p. 27). Note that "realize" means "input-process," if we assume under the novel reading. The scope of processing is not an idle question because, as noted, if IP is not restricted to novel mappings, then the model becomes indistinguishable from other approaches to sentence processing.

But the novel mapping reading begs the considerable question as to how the input processor interacts with the parser and the other language processing/learning mechanisms. Suppose, for example, that a beginning ESL learner encounters the utterance in (2).

(2) *He is baking a cake.*

If the learner has already learned the "rule" (something like the *is* + VERB+ *-ing* form maps onto the meaning "doing something in the present progressive"), then by definition no "input processing" would take place. She would simply retrieve the correct form-meaning links and come up with the appropriate overall meaning. This is the work of the (second language) parser, and outside the scope of the IP account. More likely the learner would have encountered a similar utterance along the way and possibly retained a partial mapping of the form and meaning from that encounter. The parser would presumably retrieve the partial mapping and provide it as input to the input processor which might, depending on processing capacity demands, make the more complete form-meaning mapping (which, incidentally, is opposite of the information flow indicated in Figure 1.2, this volume, p. 26). Such a parallel, highly interactive mechanism is not impossible, but it would need far more specification than it currently receives.

The IP model seeks to capture what happens on-line as the learner attempts to make sense of an utterance. Input processing is confined to the encoding stage where the form-meaning link is perceived and converted to some code that can potentially be learned, that is, to intake. It does not concern the storage or subsequent retrieval of the link (this volume, p. 5). This is an empirical claim, but there is no experimental evidence either for or against it. The studies reported by VanPatten and his colleagues that purport to show greater processing demands for grammatical forms when performing ancillary tasks provide no insight into when and how these mappings might take place on-line (VanPatten, 1990; VanPatten & Cadierno, 1993; VanPatten & Oikkenon, 1996; Wong, 2001). The decrement in performance on grammatical items evident in these studies can be due to a range of perceptual or structural factors at play at various stages of the comprehension process, perception, storage or retrieval. See DeKeyser et al. (2002) for a more thorough discussion of this body of research.

The role of redundancy in input processing is also questionable. Redundant elements are those parts of the message that can be removed without the loss of essential information. Redundancy is an attribute of the message and is pervasive in human language. It facilitates communication by lowering the processing load through minimizing the amount of new information the system has to deal with. Some redundancy in the message allows the meaning to get through despite noise in the signal.

It is not clear how the notion of redundancy relates to the processing of novel input. The third person *-s* in for example, *He eats the apple* is only redundant if the comprehender knows that both *He* and *-s* share the feature "a person talked about but not face-to-face." To say that redundant grammatical forms will be input-processed only when they do not drain available processing resources directly implies that the processor can somehow identify forms as redundant or nonredundant. How can redundancy play a role at the initial stages of learning, when the learner does not know the form?

The IP model as a psycholinguistic account of second language processing appears to be between a rock and a hard place. Under the novel-mapping reading it is too narrow, being restricted to initial processing of novel items and providing no account of how the input processor might interact with other language processing mechanisms and existing knowledge. If input processing is seen as applicable more generally then it becomes indistinguishable from other becomes a model of sentence processing and evaluated in those terms (DeKeyser et al., 2002). Although I have not discussed the possible effects of the assumed first noun and location heuristics, their presence or absence does not affect this conclusion.

CAPACITY EXPLANATIONS OF PROCESSING AND LEARNING

The IP model is based on the fundamental assumption that the learner has limited resources or capacity available during real-time comprehension. These limitations drive the tradeoffs identified in the principles, especially the preference for processing semantic information before grammatical information. The use of limited resources as an explanatory factor has a long tradition in cognitive psychology in general and language processing in particular (Just & Carpenter, 1992). There is also a growing understanding of the role these constraints play in L2 learning outcomes (Harrington, 1991; Miyake & Friedman, 1998).

Although widely used, resource explanations have also been criticized by some for having the explanatory power of the proverbial soupstone, in reality adding nothing to what is already known about the domain in question (Navon, 1984). A convincing capacity account must show that these limitations are, at in least in principle, independent of knowledge in the domain. This can be an extremely difficult task in research on learning and development, where domain knowledge is often not available, and if it exists can be highly unstable. The claim that a beginning learner is not be able to process an inflectional form as readily as a content form *because* of capacity limitations can only be tested against the learner's existing knowledge. In the case where the learner has no prior knowledge of the form (which is the only time that input processing happens under the novel-mapping reading), a capacity account of input processing has to show that the outcome was due to capacity limitations and not just to lack of L2 knowledge, implicit or otherwise. In other words, the researcher would have to exclude the possibility that the learner doesn't know the specific form/rule in question *or* have the needed knowledge in the L2 to infer the novel form-meaning mapping from other cues linguistic and extralinguistic in the immediate utterance. Although VanPatten rightly observes that the availability of processing resources and proficiency interact, there is no way to separate the two in the current account.

A pressing need in the IP model is a more explicit account of the relationship between processing (in its broader and more restricted input sense) and L2 knowledge. A fundamental distinction is made throughout between input processing on one hand, and various aspects of L2 knowledge on the other. These include storage "internalized data" (p. 7), learning "accommodation," "restructuring," and processing "access" or "production procedures" (this volume, p. 25). The intake that results from input processing is characterized as potential input for these other aspects, which it may well be, but the input processing that produces it is also directly dependent on them. Until the role of existing L2 knowledge in input processing is more clearly articulated, the notions "processing resources" and "capacity limitations" will be interchangeable with for "the relative amount of L2 knowledge available."

This is not to say that capacity does not play a role in L2 grammar learning. Individual differences in working memory capacity have been correlated with performance in a number of L2 areas, including global reading (Harrington & Sawyer, 1992); syntactic processing (Miyake & Friedman, 1998); lexical processing (Atkins & Baddeley, 1998); and on-line inferencing behaviour (Estevez & Calvo, 2000). It would be surprising if the same kind of relationship were not evident in input processing. As the IP account focuses on the initial stages of acquisition, the role of individual differences in capacity may be particularly manifest, as the mediating effects of domain knowledge are relatively small (Harrington, 1992). What is important is that the domain knowledge and capacity measures are distinguished.

IP AS A COGNITIVE ACCOUNT OF SLA

In this chapter I have raised a number of issues that affect the internal validity, and hence explanatory power, of the IP model. Given the complexity of second language grammar development and the aims of the model, it would be surprising if no such difficulties existed. The IP model is part of a cognitive theory of SLA. Such a theory is concerned with articulating the knowledge that develops in the mind of the learner, the mechanisms responsible for the development of that knowledge, and the nature of environment in which that development occurs (Gregg, 1996).

The IP model is a serious and ambitious attempt to address all three criteria, especially the mechanisms the learner uses to deal with novel input and the conditions that will favor this process. The claim made for the model, that "the processing principles do describe what L2 learners actually do" (this volume, p.

22), like a number of terms discussed here, can be read in different ways. Learners do tend to make form-meaning connections earlier for words that are more salient and carry more meaning than for words that are not and do not. The IP model has made an important contribution to SLA theory by trying to explain why this is the case. But it remains open as whether these outcomes reflect meaning-driven processing demands or whether they have a range of sources: cognitive, linguistic and pragmatic.

REFERENCES

Atkins, W. B., & Baddeley, A. D. (1998). Working memory and distribute vocabulary learning. *Applied Psycholinguistics, 19,* 537–552.

Bates, E., Dale, P. S., & Thale, D. (1995). Individual differences and their implications for theories of development. In P. Fletcher & B. MacWhinney (Eds.), *The Handbook of Child Language* (pp. 96–151). Oxford: Blackwell Publishers.

Cadierno, T. (1995). Formal instruction from a processing perspective: An investigation into the Spanish past tense. *The Modern Language Journal, 79,* 179–193.

Clark, E. V. (1993). *The lexicon in acquisition.* Cambridge: Cambridge University Press.

Caplan, D., & Waters, G. (1999). Verbal working memory and sentence comprehension. *Behavioral and Brain Sciences, 22,* 77–126.

DeKeyser, R. M. (1998). Beyond focus on form: Cognitive perspectives on learning and practicing second language grammar. In C. Doughty & J. Williams (Eds.), *Focus on form in classroom second language acquisition* (pp. 42–63). New York: Cambridge University Press.

DeKeyser, R., & Sokalski, K. (1996). The differential role of comprehension and production practice. *Language Learning, 46,* 613–642.

DeKeyser, R., Salaberry, R., Robinson, P. J., & Harrington, M. (2002). What gets processed in processing instruction? A commentary on Bill VanPatten's "Update." *Language Learning, 52,* 805–823.

Ellis, R. (1994). *The study of second language acquisition.* Oxford: Oxford University Press.

Estevez, A., & Calvo, M. G. (2000). Working memory capacity and time course of predictive inferences. *Memory, 8,* 51–61.

Gass, S. M. (1997). *Input, interaction and the second language learner.* Mahwah, NJ: Lawrence Erlbaum Associates.

Gregg, K. R. (1996). The logical and developmental problems of second language acquisition. In W. C. Ritchie & T. Bhatia (Eds.), *Handbook of second language acquisition* (pp. 49–81). San Diego: Academic Press.

Goodman, J. C., & Nusbaum, H. C. (Eds.). (1994). *The development of speech perception: The transition from speech sounds to spoken words.* Cambridge, MA: MIT Press.

Harrington, M. (2001). Second language sentence processing. In P. Robinson (Ed.), *Cognition and second language instruction* (pp. 91–124). Cambridge, UK: Cambridge University Press.

Harrington, M. (1992). Working memory capacity as a constraint on L2 development. In R. J. Harris (Ed.), *Cognitive processing in bilinguals* (pp. 123–135). Amsterdam: North Holland.

Harrington, M., & Sawyer, M. (1992). L2 working memory capacity and L2 reading skill. *Studies in Second Language Acquisition, 14,* 25–38.

Just, M. A., & Carpenter, P. A. (1992). A capacity theory of comprehension: Individual differences in working memory. *Psychological Review, 99,* 122–149.

Krashen, S. (1982). *Principles and practice in second language acquisition.* Oxford: Pergamon.

MacWhinney, B. (1999). The Competition Model: The input, the context, and the brain. In P. J. Robinson (Ed.), *Cognition and second language instruction.* Cambridge: Cambridge University Press.

Miyake, A., & Friedman, N. P. (1998). Individual differences in second language proficiency: Working memory as "language aptitude". In A. F. Healy & L. E. Bourned (Eds.), *Foreign language learning: Psycholinguistic studies on training and retention.* Mahwah, NJ: Lawrence Erlbaum Associates.

Navon, D. (1984). Resources—a theoretical soup stone? *Psychological Review, 91,* 216–234.

Pienemann, M. (1998). *Language processing and second language development.* Philadelphia: John Benjamins.

Swain, M. S. (1998). Focus on form through conscious reflection. In C. Doughty & J. Williams (Eds.), *Focus on form in classroom second language acquisition* (pp. 64–81). New York: Cambridge University Press.

VanPatten, B. (1990). Attending to form and content in the input. *Studies in Second Language Acquisition, 12,* 287–301.

VanPatten, B. (1996). *Input processing and grammar instruction: Theory and research.* Norwood, NJ: Ablex.

VanPatten, B., & Cadierno, T. (1993). Explicit instruction and input processing. *Studies in Second Language Acquisition, 15,* 225–243.

VanPatten, B., & Oikkenon, S. (1996). Explanation versus structured input in processing instruction. *Studies in Second Language Acquisition, 18,* 495–510.

Wong, W. (2001). Modality and attention to meaning and form in the input. *Studies in Second Language Acquisition, 23,* 345–368.

Part II

Processing Instruction Versus
Other Types of Instruction

This section presents the findings of a number of studies in Spanish, French, and English that are conceptual replications. The first three examine whether the findings of VanPatten and Cadierno (1993) can be obtained if the linguistic item is changed (although Cadierno, 1995, has already reported that the findings held for complex morphological structures such as the Spanish preterite tense as does Benati, 2001, for the Italian future tense). The fourth study, by Farley, examines whether the findings hold if the nature of the output-based instruction is changed from traditional instruction to what he terms *meaningful output based instruction*.

To understand the background for these studies, it is essential to review VanPatten and Cadierno's research in detail here. In this study, we set out to answer the following research questions:

1. Does altering the way in which learners process input have an effect on their developmental systems?
2. If there is an effect, is it limited solely to processing more input or does instruction in input processing also have an effect on output?
3. If there is an effect, is it the same effect that traditional instruction has (assuming an effect for the latter)?

We compared three groups of learners: a PI group (n = 27), a traditional instruction (TI) group (n = 26), and a control (n = 27). The processing group received instruction along the lines presented in Chapter 2 (Wong) of this volume. The focus was word order and object pronouns in Spanish. Previous research (summarized in VanPatten, 1996) had demonstrated that learners of Spanish misinterpret OVS and OV structures as SVO and SV structures, respectively. In Spanish, object pronouns precede finite verbs and subjects may be optionally deleted or may appear postverbally. Thus, learners misinterpret structures such as *Lo ve María* as He sees Mary rather than the correct Mary personal answers. At no point did the learners in this group produce the structure and forms in question.

In the TI group, learners received a treatment based on the most popular Spanish college-level text at the time. The treatment involved a typical explanation of object pronouns, the complete paradigm of the forms, and then was followed by mechanical, then meaningful, then communicative practices (see Paulston, 1972). At no time did this group engage in any interpretation activities. This particular approach to grammar instruction was selected because it is the dominant approach to grammar in foreign language classrooms in the U.S. and is the model followed by almost every major language textbook published for the secondary and post-secondary market. This is important to underscore since criticism of research on PI has questioned the use of TI as a comparative treatment on both its operational level as well as its actual use in classrooms (see, e.g., DeKeyser, Salaberry, Robinson & Harrington, 2002). However, as I have argued elsewhere (VanPatten, 2002a, 2002b; Wong & VanPatten, in press), TI as an approach to classroom instruction can hardly be questioned. In terms of operationalization, Paulston (cited above) provided the model upon which TI rests and is the one which we have followed in our research. There is nothing "wishy washy" about what TI means in our study. As for its presence in actual classrooms, one need only read the major books on teacher education in language instruction to see that the use of drills and mechanical activities prior to meaningful and communicative activities is a widespread belief and one that is propagated by professionals (see the review in Wong & VanPatten, forthcoming).

Both experimental treatments were balanced for tokens, vocabulary, and other factors that could affect the outcome. In addition, all instruction was performed by one instructor and lasted two days. This instructor believed that there would be differential outcomes; that the processing group would learn to interpret better and that the traditional group would be better at production (an important point to bring up given the results). This is also important to underscore since the results do not reflect the instructor's beliefs. The control group did not receive instruction on the target structure and instead read an essay and discussed it in class.

To prevent an assessment bias for any particular treatment, all groups received assessment consisting of two tests: a sentence-level interpretation test and a sentence-level production test. These were administered as a pretest, an immediate posttest, a two-week delayed posttest and a four-week delayed posttest with various versions used in a split block design (e.g., if a subject received version A as the pretest, he would receive B as the first posttest, C as the second posttest, and D as the final posttest while another subject might receive D as the pretest, C as the first posttest, and so on). The interpretation test consisted of 10 target items and 10 distracters; the production test consisted of five items with five distracters. The interpretation test was based on a referential activity performed by the processing group (e.g., "select the picture that best goes with what you hear") whereas the production test was based on an activity the traditional group performed during their treatment phase (e.g., "complete the sentence based on the pictures you see"). The interpretation test was scored as right or wrong answers for one point each (total = 10 points) and the production test was scored as two points each (2 points if correct use of object pronoun with correct word order, 0 points for no object pronoun, 1 point for incorrect use of object pronoun or problem with word order).

The results were clear. An ANOVA on the pretests yielded no differences among the groups on the two tests prior to treatment. In the post-testing phase, the processing group made significant gains on the interpretation test but the traditional and control groups did not. The gain was maintained for the month that post-testing was conducted. On the production test, both the traditional and processing groups made significant gains but were not significantly different from each other. These gains were maintained over the month post-testing phase. The control group did not make significant gains.

In terms of our research questions, we took our results to mean three things. First, that altering the way learners process input could alter their developing systems. The processing group showed evidence of this on both interpretation and production tests. Second, the effects of PI are not limited to processing but also show up on production measures. Third, the effects of PI are different from TI. With PI, learners get two for one: by being pushed to process form and meaning simultaneously in the input, they not only could process better but could also access their new-found knowledge to produce a structure they never produced during the treatment phase. The traditional group made gains only on production and did not make gains in the ability to correctly process form and meaning in the input. We took these latter results to mean that the TI group learned to do a task while the PI group experienced a change in their underlying knowledge that allowed them to perform on different kinds of tasks.

It is worth pointing out that at no time did our conclusions refer to comprehension vs. production. Our final conclusion was that instruction that was directed at *intervening in learners' processing strategies* should have a significant impact on the learner's developing system.

The papers gathered in this section depart from this initial research. We will see that although PI is overall superior to TI, the results of VanPatten and Cadierno are not duplicated exactly in each experiment. This is to be expected as different researchers in PI introduce slight variations in the treatments without knowing or because it is impossible to control for such variations across studies (e.g., number of items, time on task, rate of delivery of aural assessment, nature of the sentence-level production tests, and so on). These variations may have a cumulative effect and thus impact the results in different ways. In the case of Farley, the results are quite different. His results do support the generalizability of PI to various languages and structures but perhaps not its superiority to all other kinds of instruction or intervention. Farley's study, then, suggests that although PI is clearly a viable and effective pedagogical intervention, there may be others that can offer similar results. But as he argues, it may not be that the results are different from those of VanPatten and Cadierno simply because both his treatment groups were completely meaning based, a point VanPatten (2002a) notes when he discusses the disappointing results of text enhancement. VanPatten notes that research on text enhancement, a meaning-based approach to input enhancement, does not yield consistent positive effects and in most cases yields no effects at all. There is something additional in Farley's meaning-based output treatment and his suggestion is that it contains incidental structured input.

Regardless of the above differences in outcomes, what is clear is this: the original claim by VanPatten and Cadierno that intervention in learners' processing strategies should have a significant impact on the learner's developing system is still supported. Although it is not clear that all output-based approaches always make a difference, PI always does. Our claim is that the consistently positive effects of PI are due to the effect(s) it has on learner processing of input.

REFERENCES

Benati, A. (2001). A comparative study of the effects of processing instruction and output-based instruction on the acquisition of the Italian future tense. *Language Teaching Research, 5,* 95–127.

Cadierno, T. (1995). Formal instruction from a processing perspective: An investigation into the Spanish past tense. *The Modern Language Journal, 79,* 179–93.

DeKeyser, R. M., Salaberry, R., Robinson, P., & Harrington, M. (2002). What gets processed in processing instruction: A response to Bill VanPatten's "Update". *Language Learning, 52,* 805–823.

Paulston, C. B. (1972). Structural pattern drills: A classification. In H. Allen & R. Campell (Eds.), *Teaching English as a second language* (pp. 239–138). New York: McGraw Hill.

VanPatten, B. (1996). *Input processing and grammar instruction: Theory and research.* Norwood, NJ: Ablex.

VanPatten, B. (2002a). Processing instruction: An update. *Language Learning, 52,* 755–803.

VanPatten, B. (2002b). Processing the content of input processing and processing instruction research: A response to DeKeyser, Salaberry, Robinson, and Harrington. *Language Learning, 52,* 825–831.

VanPatten, B., & Cadierno, T. (1993). Explicit instruction and input processing. *Studies in Second Language Acquisition, 15,* 225–243.

Wong, W., & VanPatten, B. (in press). The evidence is IN; drills are OUT. *Foreign Language Annals.*

Chapter 5

Processing Instruction and the French Causative: Another Replication

Bill VanPatten
University of Illinois at Chicago

Wynne Wong
The Ohio State University

Allen (2000) attempts to replicate the results of previous PI studies using the French causative construction as the target structure. Her results differ from those of previous PI studies in that PI did not prove to be superior to traditional instruction (TI) on the two measures she used. Because we question certain aspects of Allen's treatments and assessment tasks, we have conducted a replication study that also targets the French causative as the object of acquisition. We ask the same general question that Allen asked: whether or not the results of previous PI research generalize to other structures. In addition, we address the same three research questions posed in her study.

1. Will there be any statistical differences in how learners who receive processing instruction, learners who receive traditional instruction, and learners who receive no instruction on the French causative interpret sentences containing the French causative?
2. Will there be any statistical differences in how learners who receive processing instruction, learners who receive traditional instruction, and learners who receive no instruction on the French causative produce sentences containing the French causative?
3. If an effect for instruction is found, will it hold on a delayed posttest?

BACKGROUND

The Processing Problem

Of relevance to the present study is the First-Noun Principle of VanPatten's input processing model. bECAUSE it deals with word order, the strategy reflected by this principle may have important effects on the acquisition of a language that does not follow strict SVO word order or may have an impact on non-canonical structures for languages that do have an SVO word order. In each of the following sentences in Spanish, the first noun-phrase the learner encounters is not a subject but the learner may very well attempt to encode it as such:

> (1) A Juan no le gusta esta clase mucho. (OVS)
>   John-IOBJ does not please this class-SUBJ very much.
>   John does not like this class much.
> (2) La vi yo en la fiesta anoche. (OVS)
>   her-OBJ saw I-SUBJ at the party last night.
>   I saw her at the party last night.
> (3) Se levanta temprano. (OV)
>   REFLEXIVE-gets up early.
>   He/She gets up early.
> (4) Nos faltan varios libros. (OVS)
>   us-IOBJ are missing several books-SUBJ.
>   We are missing several books.

Research has shown that learners do indeed encode such pronouns and noun phrases as subjects (e.g., Juan is the subject of (1), la is the subject of (2) and means 'she') thus delivering erroneous intake to their developing linguistic systems (see VanPatten, 1996, Chapter 2 as well as Chapter 1 of the present volume for a summary of this and other research related to IP).[1]

Research has also shown that the First-Noun Principle describes how learners initially process the French causative. The causative generally takes the form seen in examples (5)-(6).

> (5) Jean fait promener le chien à Marie.

---

[1]It is not clear from the research whether the first-noun strategy is a universal or is based on L1 processing procedures. For the purposes of a model of input processing, this is an important point. The vast majority of languages for which we have data, two word orders dominate: SVO and SOV, underscoring the primacy of the first-noun as subject. For the purposes of the present study, whether this processing strategy is universal or not is irrelevant. Nonetheless, we shall proceed with caution and say that English learners of L2 French tend to use the first-noun strategy when processing causative structures with *faire*.

> John makes to walk the dog to Mary.
> John makes Mary walk the dog.
> (6) Mes professeurs me font travailler beaucoup.
> My profs me make work hard.
> My profs make me work hard.

In (5), there are two verbs and two subjects/agents. The first verb is *fait* with its obligatorily preposed subject/agent *Jean*. The second verb is *promener* with its subject/agent, *Marie*, obligatorily placed postverbally and marked by the preposition *à*. (At the surface level this noun appears as the object of the preposition; its subject function is a feature of an underlying sentence structure that reflects the semantics of the sentence.) It is the subject/agent of the second verb that is the problem for learners of French. When asked "Who walks the dog?" learners overwhelmingly say "Jean" since he is the first noun that appears before the verb, thus demonstrating their reliance on the First-Noun Principle. When asked to give a rough translation, learners will say the sentence means something like "John walks the dog for Mary." In (6) the causative structure is different because the underlying subject of the second verb appears preverbally; not as a subject pronoun but as an object pronoun. When asked "Who works hard?" learners will tend to say "My professors," once again demonstrating reliance on the principle. Their overall interpretation of the sentence is something like "My profs work hard for me." In short, learners tend to gloss over the verb *faire* and process the second verb. At the same time they assign the first noun as subject of the second verb. (See MacDonald and Heilenman, 1992, as well as the pretest data in Allen, 2000 for research on second language learners sentence processing in French.)

Note that learners may make correct interpretations even though they may not be able to parse the sentence correctly. VanPatten's model allows learners to use lexical semantics and event probability to interpret sentences as well. Lexical semantics refers to what verbs require as agents for the action to occur (e.g., +/- animacy) while event probability refers to the likelihood of events in the real world. Thus, if learners hear a French causative such as *Le professeur fait faire les devoirs à ses élèves* (The professor makes his/her students do homework) learners are more likely to think that the students are doing homework for the professor since in the real world students do homework and not professors.

Motivation for the Present Study

The present study is motivated by the research presented in Allen (2000). In her study, Allen offers what is called a conceptual replication of VanPatten and Cadierno's 1993 study. Citing Polio and Gass (1997), Allen points out that a conceptual replication alters various features of an original study to test for generalizability or external validity. As Polio and Gass state it, "Researchers will attempt replication to see if the results hold for a different population, in a different setting, or for a different modality" (p. 502). In her study Allen claims to have maintained treatment fidelity to VanPatten and Cadierno and that both the PI and TI in her study are consistent with the two treatment types as defined in the original study. In previous research of ours, we defined and operationalized TI as the presentation of explicit information concerning the form or structure followed by a move from mechanical, through meaningful, and finally to communicative exercises. Our reason for the selection of TI for the experiments was (and still is) that TI is the *dominant form of grammar instruction in foreign languages in the U.S.* We were thus exploring PI vs. TI in order to couch our research within some kind of ecological validity. In this way, we could speak to researchers as well as practicing instructors regarding our results. We are aware that in some circles (most notably ESL in the U.S. and Canada) that TI may not be prevalent and that focus on form may be entirely meaning-oriented. But we are also aware that TI is still used around the world in a number of FL contexts and that a good deal of practitioners believe passionately in the use of drills and mechanically-oriented activities.

According to Allen, her study differs from VanPatten and Cadierno in three ways: the grammatical structure, the open-ended production task, and a much larger sample size (Allen, 2000, p. 72). The results of her study differed from those of VanPatten and Cadierno (1993) as well as Cadierno (1995). In the original studies, PI subjects improved on interpretation tasks while TI subjects did not. On production tasks, PI and TI subjects improved but not differentially. In Allen's study, the TI and PI subjects both improved on the interpretation task and on the production task, however on the production tasks, TI subjects improved more than did PI subjects.

Polio and Gass (1997) had this to say about conceptual replications with different outcomes from original studies:

> A problem may arise in the interpretation of the results: If the results are not the same in the replication as those in the original, one needs detailed information on the original study to determine why. Were the original results merely spurious or is there something in the methodology or subject population that differed significantly? (p. 502)

As we pondered the differences between Allen's results and those of previous research, we doubted that population was the source of the differences, although VanPatten and Cadierno's participants were university students and Allen's were high school students (VanPatten & Oikennon, 1996, used high school students as participants in their study). We thus look to methodological differences to explore why the results may be different. On a close comparison of the studies, our conclusion is that the differential results between the two studies are due to differences in the materials. Because authors of research generally cannot append an entire treatment or treatments to their study, they generally must offer only examples of what they have done. Such was the case in VanPatten and Cadierno (1993)[2] as well as Allen (2000). We thus asked Allen to share with us her materials and we were struck by several aspects in the materials that we feel led to the different results she obtained.[3]

The first aspect of the materials concerns the assessment instrument and some of the items in the instructional treatments. As has been shown in the literature and has been captured in VanPatten's model, lexical semantics or event probabilities may help learners to determine who does what (to whom). Some of the items in Allen's study are problematic in that they do not take into account event probability. For example, when confronted with an input string such as *Le professeur fait étudier le verbe "être" `a l'élève* (The instructor gets the student to study the verb "to be"), the learner can rely on event probabilities to interpret the string. The learner may ask himself "Why would the teacher study the verb? Shouldn't the student study the verb?" During instructional treatments, such sentences do not allow for the treatment to push learners away from the First-Noun strategy; during assessment, learners may respond correctly but not because they have learned or know anything about the structure in question.

A second aspect of the materials that caught our attention is that in the assessment tasks, the interpretation and production structures were different. In the interpretation task, Allen limited the sentences to third-person singular as in (5) above. However, for the production task, she used the structure with first-person singular object pronoun as in (6) above. The reason is not clear for the change and does not allow for direct comparison between interpretation task results and production task results. In VanPatten and Cadierno, all testing was limited to third-person singular since this was the most problematic aspect of the grammatical feature under study and word order was held constant. Recall that with the French causative structure, with full nouns the subject of the second verb appears postverbally but with pronouns the subject/agent of the second verb appears preverbally and is "closer" to the English structure (*Mes parents me font étudier* 'My parents make me study').

The third and most important aspect of Allen's materials that we noticed is the blurring between processing and traditional instruction that occurs during the initial phase of the lesson, that is, prior to practice. Recall that TI is defined as the move from mechanical to meaningful to communicative practice. However, during the explicit phase of TI in Allen's study, learners were engaged in processing input strings much in the same way they would if they were part of the processing group. In fact, in Allen's materials learners reviewed and processed a total of 23 sentences (13 with third-person, 10 with *me* as in sample

---

[2]The complete treatment materials for the VanPatten and Cadierno study are found in Cadierno (1992) and are reviewed in detail in VanPatten (1996) chap. 3.

[3]We thank Allen for generously sharing her materials with us.

sentence (6) from above) before practice began. At the same time, learners in the processing group did not receive any practice in production (mechanical or otherwise), holding true to the nature of PI. In short, we feel that the results that Allen received in her study are at least partly due to the differences in the content of the assessment tasks and in the TI treatment between the two studies.[4]

We thus set out to replicate the results of VanPatten and Cadierno (1993) using materials and assessments instruments that address the issues we note above. Although we describe our treatments below, we summarize here that (1) we controlled for lexical semantics and event probability both in treatment and assessment, (2) limited testing to third-person (the more problematic structure due to word order), and (3) created instructional treatments following the materials used in VanPatten and Cadierno.

METHOD

Participants

Participants were undergraduate students from two universities in the Midwest, three classes from University 1 and four classes from University 2. In order to get an adequate number of subjects for this study, it was necessary to conduct the study at two institutions. Participants from University 1 were enrolled in a fourth quarter French course and those from University 2 were enrolled in a third semester French course (equivalent to a fourth quarter course). The participants would not have received any formal instruction on the French causative prior to treatment because in French textbooks this structure is not taught until sometime late in the second year of university study. Even if some participants had been exposed to the structure via formal instruction, all were tested for knowledge of this structure prior to treatment (see assessment tasks below as well as the results of the pretests in Table 5.1). Students were familiar with the verb *faire* ("to do" or "to make"), a verb used in the French causative construction as well as in noncausative structures. For example, to say "to ski" in French one says *faire du ski*. This verb is taught early in the first year of university study and is a frequent and highly useful verb in classroom talk (e.g., *Qu'est-ce que tu fais?* What are you doing? *Qu'est-ce que tu as fait hier soir?* What did you do last night?).

---

[4]There is another aspect of Allen's materials that merits a note. Her initial activities during the PI treatment in which learners process the causative and indicate a correct interpretation do not force them to do so. All stimulus sentences were causative; students did not have to distinguish, for example, between causative *faire* and non-causative *faire*. Following VanPatten and Cadierno's materials in which learners had to distinguish between SVO and OVS structures, we mixed together causative and non-causative *faire* in the activities so that learners would actually have to pay attention in order to respond.

As in VanPatten and Cadierno (1993), the seven classes were assigned to one of three instructional groups: processing instruction, traditional instruction and a (no instruction) control group. One class from each institution was assigned to the processing instruction group and one to the traditional instruction group. The control group was comprised of one class from University 1 and two classes from University 2. In order to be admitted to the final data pool, participants had to have been present for the pretest, full treatment and posttest. Additionally, they had to have scored below 60% on the pretest following the criteria in VanPatten and Cadierno for inclusion. The final n sizes were the following: Processing U1 n = 18, Processing U2 n = 11; Traditional U1 n = 11, Traditional U2 = 9; Control U1 n = 14, Control U2 n = 14.

Materials

Instructional materials. Two separate instructional packets were designed for this study, one for the processing group and one for the traditional group. Both packets were balanced for (1) vocabulary, (2) number of activities, (3) and practice time. Additionally, care was taken to ensure that practice items in the processing packet did not allow students to rely on event probabilities to interpret input strings. This was done so that they would be pushed to rely instead on processing sentence structure to interpret meaning. As in VanPatten and Cadierno (1993), the first page of both packets contained explicit grammar explanation about the causative construction (see Appendix A). In regards to the explicit information that the two groups received, the difference was that the processing group also received information about the word order problem that learners of French are confronted with when they must interpret sentences that contain the causative construction. The traditional group was not given this information since it is not part of traditional approaches to grammar instruction and most FL instructors in the U.S. do not treat processing problems during explicit instruction.[5]

Five activities followed this explicit information page (Activities A through E). In the processing packet, the activities were comprised of structured input activities that consisted of both referential and affective activities. Referential activities are those meaning-based activities with right or wrong answers; for example, students hear a sentence and match it to one of two pictures. Affective activities are those in which students offer a reaction to a statement or sentence by indicating whether or not it's true for them, who in their family does that, and so on (see Lee & VanPatten, 1995, chap. 5 and VanPatten, 1996, chap. 3 for

---

[5]Although we do not have data on this, we do not believe this is an overstatement. Both researchers are involved in teacher education and training and regularly observe classes. Neither of us has seen processing issues be addressed by instructors. No textbook that we have examined includes matters of processing.

additional information and guidelines concerning structured input activities.) As in the VanPatten and Cadierno study, activities in the traditional packet followed the pattern of moving from mechanical, to meaningful and to communicative practice. The differences between the activities in the processing and traditional group can be summarized as follows: structured input activities in the processing group required participants to attend to both meaning and form to successfully complete the activities but they were never required to produce the target structures; activities in the traditional packet always required participants to produce the target forms; the initial mechanical activities did not require participants to attend to meaning to successfully complete the activity (see also Wong, chap. 2, this volume). Sample activities appear in Appendix B.

After completing five activities, participants again received explicit information about the target structure, this time focusing on the causative construction that uses preverbal pronouns. This explicit information was followed by three more activities (F through H); structured input activities in the processing group and mechanical and communicative activities in the traditional group.

Assessment tasks. Two versions of the assessment task were created, one was used as the pretest and the other the posttest. Following VanPatten and Cadierno (1993), this task consisted of an interpretation task and a production task. The interpretation task required participants to listen to a series of sentences about people doing various activities and to determine who was doing a particular action in each sentence. For example, participants hear:

Andrée fait promener le chien à Phillipe.
(Andrée makes to walk the dog to Phillipe)

On their answer sheet, participants were asked, "Who walks the dog?" Participants had to write down a name, "nobody" or "someone else" as appropriate for each sentence. The correct answer for the above sample item is "Phillipe."

There were 14 sentences on the interpretation task, seven contained the causative construction and seven were distracter items. Five of the target items followed the pattern *Jean-Paul fait lire le journal à Henri* (Jean-Paul makes to read the newspaper to Henri/Jean-Paul makes Henri read the newspaper). The correct response to the question "Who reads the paper?" would be "Henri." Two of the target items followed the pattern *Jean-Phillipe fait laver la voiture* (Jean-Phillipe makes to wash the car/Jean-Phillipe is having the car washed). A correct response to the question "Who washes the car?" would be "someone else" because the person is not specified in the utterance. Five out of the seven distracter items contained the verb *faire* that was not in the causative construction (e.g., *Barbara fait du bateau mais pas Claudette* 'Barbara goes boating but Claudette does not').

In the production task, learners were shown a series of 10 pictures on an overhead projector. They were required to write a sentence to describe each picture. The first part of each sentence was started for them. For example, in one picture Mark is telling Richard to buy milk. On their answer sheets learners would see

      Marc fait _____

and they would have to answer *Marc fait acheter du lait à Richard.*

Five of these items were target items that required participants to use the causative structure. The five remaining items were distracter items that also required them to use the verb *faire*, but not in the causative construction. Distracter items that required non-causative *faire* were used because we wanted to see if participants actually learned something from instruction or if they were applying a test-taking strategy, that is to say, making all sentences causative constructions because that is what they were learning. All test items on both the interpretation and production task maintained third-person structure.

Procedure

Participants from both institutions completed an informed consent and were given the pretest one week before treatment.   Treatment time required approximately 45 minutes and the posttest required 10 minutes. Because classes at University 1 were 78 minutes long, the entire treatment and posttest were done on the same day. Because classes at University 2 were only 50 minutes long, treatment was broken up into two days, with the posttest taking place after the last activity on the second day. Because of scheduling conflicts, we were forced to restrict a delayed posttest to only one site, the second posttest was administered to the University 2 groups five weeks after instruction. University 1 did not participate in the second posttest.

The same person who was also one of the researchers of this study carried out instruction for both treatment groups at both institutions. Participants in both groups were first given explicit information about the French causative construction. At University 1, participants (from both processing and traditional groups) then went on to complete activities A through E, received explicit information about the causative structure that uses preverbal pronouns, and then completed activities F through H. They were given the posttest immediately after activity H. At University 2, following explicit instruction, participants (from both processing and traditional groups) completed activities A through E and then turned their packets in to the researcher. The next day, packets were returned to participants and treatment began with instruction about the causative structure that uses preverbal pronouns. Following this instruction, participants completed activities F through H and then completed the posttest. The control group was given distracter activities to work on and then completed the posttest.

At University 1, distracter activities and posttest were done on the same day. At University 2, distracter activities were given over two days with the posttest following the activities on the second day.

Scoring

Only the target items were scored on the posttest. The maximum possible score for the interpretation task was seven. One point was awarded for each correct response. No partial credit was given on this task. For the production task, the maximum score was 10. 2 points (full credit) were awarded for each correct response. Points were not deducted for vocabulary errors, spelling of people's names or for code-switching due to lack of vocabulary. For example, if a participant wrote "*Marie fait faire les dishes à Sylvie*" for 'Marie has Sylvie do the dishes,' full credit was still given. Partial credit (1 point) was awarded if (a) a participant had a verb in the infinitive following *faire* but did not have the preposition *à* followed by a name, and (b) if a participant had the preposition *à* plus a name but did not have a verb in the infinitive following *faire*. The following are examples of items that were awarded 1 point:

> Claudine fait promener le chien.
> [Correct answer: Claudine fait promener le chien à Diane.]
> Sylvie fait la cuisine à Marie.
> [Correct answer: Sylvie fait nettoyer la cuisine à Marie.]

RESULTS

Two ANOVAs were conducted on the pretests, one for the interpretation task and one for the production task. Treatment and University were entered as independent variables. No main effect was obtained for Treatment on the interpretation pretest, $F(2, 71) = 2.62$, $p = .08$, and no main effect for University, $F(1, 71) = 2.53$, $p = .12$. There was no interaction, $F(2, 71) = 2.92$, $p = .06$. Means are reported in Table 5.1. Because there were trends toward a main effect for Treatment, we ran a post hoc Fisher's test and a post hoc Scheffé (the latter being more stringent) with Treatment as the independent variable. The Fisher's yielded one difference: Control better than Processing, $p = .03$. The Scheffé did not, $p = .12$. Although normally one would be disconcerted about these pretreatment findings, for the present study they are actually good news. Given that overall the Control group was better than the Processing group from the outset, if the Processing group made gains and surpassed the Control group and if the Control group did not make gains, then this would speak to the effect of processing instruction. If there were a pretreatment difference such as Processing better than Control or Traditional, then we could not make such claims.

For the production test, there was no main effect for Treatment, $F(2, 71) =$ .64, $p = .53$, but there was a main effect for University, $F(1, 71) = 6.30, p = .01$. There was no interaction, $F(2, 71) = .07, p = .93$. Means are reported in Table 5.1. The post hoc Scheffé conducted on the effect for University revealed that U1 had better scores than U2 on the production test, $p = .01$. Because of the effect for University, we did not collapse the data but entered University into the repeated measures ANOVAs reported below. However, we did not consider this to be a problem. If, after treatment, the differences between Universities disappeared, we could take this as further evidence of the impact of Processing Instruction (or Traditional, for that matter).

Interpretation Test

A repeated measures ANOVA revealed a main effect for Treatment, $F(2, 71) =$ 29.81, $p = .00$, and no main effect for University, $F(1, 71) = .24, p = .63$. There was a main effect for Time, $F(1, 71) = 230.79, p = .00$, meaning that there was improvement from pretest to posttest for the two experimental groups (see Table 5.1). There was an interaction between Treatment and Time, $F(2, 71) = 86.11, p$ = .00, and a post-hoc Scheffé revealed that this interaction was due to a significant difference between the processing group and the traditional group, p = .01, a significant difference between the processing and control group, $p = .00$, and a significant difference between the traditional and control group, $p = .00$. There was no interaction between Time and University, $F(1, 71) = 1.23, p = .27$. An interaction bar plot for all results appears in Fig. 5.1. (Fig. 5.1 includes bars for the delayed posttest that are reported later.)

We note here that there seemed to be a ceiling of five points on the interpretation test; that is, only several subjects received a perfect score of seven after treatment. In reviewing the data, we found that most subjects consistently missed the two sentences that had someone else perform the action. For some reason, these sentences proved to be difficult even after instruction.

To summarize, both the processing and traditional groups improved from pre- to posttest, but the processing group improved more and the differential gains between the two groups were significant. The control group did not improve.

Production Test

A repeated measures ANOVA revealed a main effect for Treatment, $F(2, 71) =$ 9.701, $p = .00$, and no main effect for University, $F(1, 71) = 1.84, p = .18$. There was a main effect for Time, $F(1, 71) = 166.73, p = .00$, meaning that there was improvement from pretest to posttest for the two experimental groups (see Table 5.1). There was an interaction between Treatment and Time, $F(2, 71) = 37.35, p$ < .0001, and a posthoc Scheffé revealed that this interaction was due to a significant difference between the processing and control groups, $p = .00$, and a significant difference between the traditional and control groups, $p = .03$. There was no difference between the processing and traditional groups, $p = .40$. There was no interaction between Time and University, $F(1, 71) = 3.03, p = .09$. An interaction bar plot for production results appears in Fig. 5.2.

As we scored the production data, we noticed that some subjects seemed to be applying a test-taking strategy. These subjects, mostly from the traditional groups, completed *all sentences* whether causative or not by adding verbs and a second person preceded by the object marker *à*; one could not tell whether they had actually learned what a causative was. We thus conducted a second ANOVA on the data pulling out these subjects. Two subjects were eliminated from the Traditional U1 group, three from the Traditional U2 group, and one from the Processing U2 group. The results were the same as on the original ANOVA conducted on all subjects. There was a main effect for Treatment $F(2, 65) = 8.52, p = .00$, and no main effect for University $F(1, 65) = 1.37, p = .25$. There was a main effect for Time $F(1, 65) = 135.56, p = .00$. There was an interaction between Time and Treatment $F(2, 71) = 33.68, p = .00$, and a posthoc Scheffé revealed that this interaction was due to a significant difference between the processing and control group, $p = .00$. There was no difference between the processing and traditional groups, $p = .28$. However, unlike in the original ANOVA, there was no difference between the traditional and control groups, $p = .13$. There was no interaction between Time and University $F(1, 65) = 3.09, p = .08$.

To summarize, for the production test both experimental groups improved with no difference between their improvements. The control group did not improve. When the test-taking strategy was taken into account in the second analysis, there was no difference between the traditional and control groups.

Longer-Term Effects

As we said previously, we were unable to enlist the University 1 participants for a delayed posttest due to scheduling conflicts related to the syllabus that governed the course. We administered the delayed posttest at University 2. However, attrition in the participant pool took its toll (see also VanPatten & Fernández, this volume). When scoring the data for participants who completed all sections of the study and also after removing subjects who clearly did not do the tasks as we expected, the final n sizes were TI = 6, PI = 8, C = 11. We considered these sizes to be too small for a statistical procedure on a variable as important as longer-term effects. We therefore decided to eliminate our research question regarding the longer-term effects.

TABLE 5.1
Scores for interpretation and production tests

Variables		n	Pretest Mean	SD	Posttest Mean	SD
Interpretation[a]						
TI,	U1	11	.09	.30	2.73	2.49
	U2	9	.22	.44	3.44	2.35
PI,	U1	18	.11	.32	4.94	.99
	U2	11	.00	.00	5.09	.54
C,	U1	14	1.00	1.79	.71	1.82
	U2	14	.07	.27	.07	.26
Production[b]						
TI,	U1	11	1.73	1.56	6.64	2.84
	U2	15	.44	1.33	6.89	2.98
PI,	U1	18	2.06	2.10	8.29	3.01
	U2	14	.46	1.51	8.36	3.08
C,	U1	14	2.36	3.34	2.71	3.71
	U2	30	1.21	2.64	1.93	3.29

[a] range = 0 - 7,   [b] range = 0 – 10

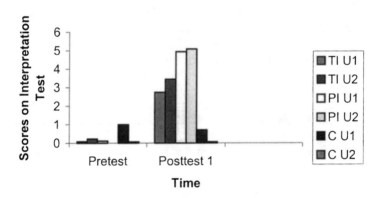

Fig.5. 1. Interaction Bar Plot for Interpretation Results.

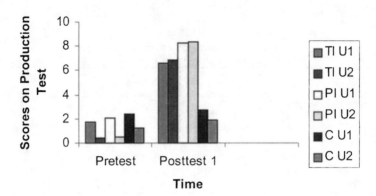

FIG. 5. 2   Interaction Bar Plot for Production Results.

Summary of Results

Based on the results presented above, the answers to our research questions are these:

1. Yes, there is a difference between how learners who receive processing, traditional, and no instruction perform on an interpretation test after treatment. The processing group was superior compared to the traditional group, which was in turn superior to the control group.

2. No, there is no difference between how learners who receive processing and traditional instruction perform on a production test after treatment. However, both groups were superior to the no instruction group except when a test-taking strategy is taken into account. When this strategy is taken into account, then those who receive processing instruction are better than those who receive traditional and these in turn are better than those who receive no instruction.

3. Question three was eliminated as per the discussion above.

DISCUSSION AND CONCLUSION

We begin this discussion by recognizing the limited cell sizes for our study. Because of the initial differences in performance between the two university populations on the production pretest, we could not collapse the data into one pool. However, we would also like to point out that this difference disappeared after treatment so that perhaps the post-treatment results may not be so limited after all. We also remind the reader that there were trends toward a difference in groups before treatment, with the control group scoring significantly better than the PI group. Our results clearly show that this initial potential problem disappeared as the PI group made significant gains and the control group did not. Therefore, the treatment offered by PI did indeed have a strong positive effect.

It is clear that our results differ from Allen's. In her study, she found no difference between traditional and processing instruction on her interpretation test either immediately after treatment (we ignore the matter of delayed test results due to our elimination of research question 3). For the production test, she found an initial superior post-treatment performance for the traditional group. Our results suggest superior performance by the PI group after treatment for interpretation.

For production, there is no difference between PI and TI after treatment, but it is interesting to note that when test-taking strategy is taken into account there is no difference between the TI and Control groups. Allen reports no such test-taking strategy with her TI group largely because she had no means of ascertaining such a strategy. The reader is reminded that Allen's production posttest did not include items with noncausative *faire* (it also switched the focus from third-person to first-person) and thus her test would not have revealed whether learners actually learned the contrasts. A summary of the differences in results between the two studies and the VanPatten and Cadierno study appears in Table 5.2.

TABLE 5.2
Summary Comparison of Results from Allen (2000), VanPatten and Cadierno (1993), and the Present Study

	Allen (2000)	The Present Study	VanPatten & Cadierno (1993)
Interpretation			
Posttest 1	TI = PI > Control (?)	PI > TI > Control	PI > TI = Control
Posttest 2	TI = PI > Control (?)	n.a.	PI > TI = Control
Posttest 3	TI = PI > Control (?)	n.a	PI > TI = Control
Production			
Posttest 1	TI > PI > Control (?)	PI = TI > Control Results 2[a]: PI = TI, PI > Control, TI = Control,	PI = TI > Control
Posttest 2	TI = PI > Control (?)	n.a.	PI = TI > Control
Posttest 3	TI > PI > Control (?)	n.a.	PI = TI > Control

[a]With participants removed who demonstrate a test-taking strategy.

As suggested earlier, the difference in results is most likely due to the nature of the instructional treatments in both studies as well as the nature of the assessment tasks. We argued that there was a blurring of the processing and traditional treatments in Allen's study that is only apparent if one reads through the instructional treatments carefully. If subjects in a traditional group are given the chance to process before practice as in Allen's study, one might expect no difference between the two groups on the interpretation test after treatment. This is what happened. In our instructional groups, however, we maintained strict fidelity to the materials in VanPatten and Cadierno so that there was a clear distinction between processing and traditional instruction.

We believe that the differences between the two studies on the production task are due to the nature of the structure used. Recall that Allen switched from third-person to first-person from the interpretation to the production test. The result was a difference in word order. We maintained third-person sentence structure across both tests, as did VanPatten and Cadierno in their study. In addition, in Allen's test, subjects were instructed to write five sentences involving X *me font* Y as the base structure. In our test, subjects had to discriminate between causative and non-causative *faire* in order to complete each sentence. We could thus tell to what extent the subjects had truly learned something from the instructional formats. As we reported above, it was clear that five subjects in the traditional groups (only one in the PI groups) were applying a test-taking strategy. Thus, we believe our test provides for better discrimination of treatment effects.

That five TI subjects and only one PI subject used this strategy to perform the production tasks after treatment would suggest that there may be an unnoticed negative effect for traditional grammar instructional formats; namely, that students are more likely to not learn and to "go through the motions" than if they were exposed to other instructional formats. We can only speculate here about the TI students' learning in Allen's study since she did not maintain third person across her two assessment tasks and they also received incidental processing practice before instruction. More important, however, is the speculation of what might be going on in the many foreign language classrooms across the U.S. where TI is alive and well. Just what are students learning? And what are they learning how to do?[6] One reviewer remarked that TI doesn't exist in the form in which it does in the present study. Coming from an ESL perspective, the reviewer offered that communicative approaches have encouraged the connections between meaning and form since the mid-1980s and that if our representation of foreign language instruction is correct, then "this is a

---

[6]Lightbown (1983) reports the problems of overlearning in classrooms in which rote practice is a dominant teaching/learning behavior. She, too, suggests negative effects in that such learning creates barriers for a true interlanguage system to develop.

sad comment on the state of foreign language teaching in the U.S." This particular reviewer's concern is not unfounded. Not only can this approach to instruction in formal features of language be seen in just about every FL textbook published in this country, as late as the fall of 2001 both researchers sat in on different workshops at different universities in which they heard the workshop leaders discuss the importance of explicit information plus mechanical practice (any practice devoid of meaning) *as a necessary step in the learning component of languages* (see also Wong & VanPatten, in press). As SLA researchers looking at instructed SLA within the context of foreign languages in the U.S., we believe that research studies such as the present one are important for (1) demonstrating the limits of TI and (2) demonstrating that input *can* if not *does* play a fundamental role in acquisition regardless of context. We suggest, however, that future research on PI turn its attention away from comparisons with TI and examine it within the context of other meaning-based approaches to focus on form or grammar instruction.

To be clear, we also point out that we did not replicate the results of VanPatten and Cadierno's study exactly. Although the results on the production test were the same, on the interpretation test, the TI group in the present study did improve and our analyses revealed a significant difference between its scores and those of the control group. However, our analyses also showed that the PI group outperformed the TI group after treatment. In a sense, the basic conclusion of VanPatten and Cadierno's study still holds; namely, that PI is superior to TI.

The present study demonstrates the importance of replication studies in SLA research. In this particular study we have been able to offer important differences in two studies' treatments and assessments that are not obvious to readers without access to the materials. In addition, not only do we demonstrate results that are different from the study we replicated, but our results also differ somewhat from the original study (i.e., VanPatten & Cadierno, 1993). The present results for interpretation start out resembling VanPatten and Cadierno's but differ on the delayed posttest. Our hypothesis is that this difference is due to certain high-scoring subjects not taking the delayed posttest as well as two subjects' scores dipping. Given the small n sizes we would expect a change in outcome on the statistical analyses. For the production results, the present results resemble those of VanPatten and Cadierno. When test-taking strategy is taken into account, the results change and suggest that PI is actually superior to TI. However, we once again offer this result with caution given the n sizes involved. We thus believe that our results speak to the generalizability of PI to other structures as well as its overall superiority over TI and is in line not only with the original VanPatten and Cadierno study but also with Benati (2000), Cadierno (1995) and others cited earlier. Although it may be the case that the effects of PI will be shown not to be generalizable to all structures in all contexts, it is equally reasonable that as we examine such results we keep in mind Polio and Gass's suggestions about examining methodological issues when results differ.

We end by stating that although our interpretations and conclusions about Allen's results are different from hers, we do not wish to diminish the importance of any attempt at replication. Indeed, Allen's study underscores the need not only to replicate but also to replicate again. Our knowledge of SLA is, in many respects, still in its infancy. Replication studies may help us better interpret what we think we do know and/or confirm our understanding of what we observe.

REFERENCES

Benati, A. (2000). Processing instruction: Un tipo di grammatica comunicativa per la classe di lingua straniera. Il caso del futuro italiano. *Italica, 77,* 471–494.

Cadierno, T. (1995). Formal instruction from a processing perspective: An investigation into the Spanish past tense. *The Modern Language Journal, 79,* 179–193.

Lee, J., & VanPatten, B. (1995). *Making communicative language teaching happen.* New York: McGraw-Hill.

Lightbown, P. (1983). Exploring relationships between developmental and instructional sequences in L2 acquisition. In H. W. Seliger & M. H. Long (Eds.), *Classroom oriented research in second language acquisition* (pp. 217–243). Rowley, MA: Newbury House.

MacDonald, J. L., & Heilenman, L. K. (1992). Changes in sentence processing as second language proficiency increases. In R. J. Harris (Ed.), *Cognitive processing in bilinguals* (pp. 325–336). New York: Elsevier Science.

Polio, C., & Gass, S. M. (1997). Replication and reporting: A commentary. *Studies in Second Language Acquisition, 19,* 499–508.

VanPatten, B. (1997). On the relevance of input processing to second language acquisition theory and second language instruction. In A. T. Pérez-Leroux & W. R. Glass (Eds.), *Contemporary perspectives on the acquisition of Spanish: Vol. 2. Production, processing, and comprehension* (pp. 93–108). Somerville, MA: Cascadilla Press.

VanPatten, B., & Cadierno, T. (1993). Explicit instruction and input processing. *Studies in Second Language Acquisition, 15,* 225–243.

VanPatten, B., & Oikkenon, S. (1996). Explanation vs. structured input in processing instruction. *Studies in Second Language Acquisition, 18,* 495–510.

Wong, W., & VanPatten, B. (in press). The evidence is IN: drills are OUT. *Foreign Language Annals.*

APPENDIX A

Explicit Information Used in the Instructional Packets

We often ask or get people to do things for us by telling them to do something.

Paul says, "John, would you mind doing the dishes?"

If you and I were to describe what is happening we might say:

"Paul gets John to do the dishes."

or

"Paul makes John do the dishes."

This is called a causative construction (because someone is causing a behavior in someone else.) French has a similar structure using the verb *faire*. Let's repeat our examples from above.

Paul says, "Jean, pourrais-tu faire la vaisselle?"

We report on this saying, "Paul fait faire la vaisselle à Jean."

How would we describe the following scenario?

Wynne says, "Sara, pourrais-tu promener le chien?"

We would describe Wynne getting Sara to do it like this.

We say, "Wynne fait promener le chien à Sara."

Often we don't mention who we get to do something; we might simply say we have something done.

"Paul fait nettoyer la chambre."

In this case, Paul has the room cleaned, but we don't know who or how.

[The following additional information was for PI only.]

One of the problems the *faire causatif* presents is in listening comprehension. Second language learners of French often misinterpret what they hear because the word order is different from English. For example, it is not uncommon for learners of French to make the following mistake:

They hear: "Jean fait faire la vaisselle à Paul."
They incorrectly think: John is doing the dishes for Paul.

or

They hear: "Marc fait couper les cheveux.
They incorrectly think: Marc cuts hair.

In the activities that follow, we will practice hearing and interpreting the *faire causatif.*

APPENDIX B

Example of Referential Activity in PI

Activité B. Listen to each sentence then indicate what it means in English.

1. a. Lucie paints the walls.   b. Lucie has the walls painted.
2. a. Robert builds a house.   b. Robert has a house built.
3. a. Marie does chores.   b. Marie has the chores done.
4. a. Donnie is making the cake.   b. Donnie is having the cake made.
5. a. Sabine corrects the mistakes.   b. Sabine has the mistakes corrected.
6. a. George washes the dishes.   b. George has the dishes washed.

Activity B. Teachers script:

Read each sentence only once. Review the answer after each question; do not wait until the end to review answers. Students do not repeat or otherwise produce the structure.

1. Lucie fait peindre les murs.
2. Robert fait construire une maison.
3. Marie fait le ménage.
4. Donnie fait préparer le gâteau.
5. Sabine fait corriger les fautes.
6. Georges fait la vaisselle.

Example of Affective Activity in PI

Activité C. Read each sentence then decide whether or not it is typical of a parent-child relationship. Imagine the child is 10 years old.

Un parent. . .	C'EST TYPIQUE	CE N'EST PAS TYPIQUE
1. fait faire les devoirs à son enfant.	☐	☐
2. fait étudier chaque soir à son enfant.	☐	☐
3. fait faire de l'exercice à son enfant.	☐	☐
4. fait nettoyer la salle de bain à son enfant.	☐	☐
5. fait garder la soeur de 5 ans à son enfant.	☐	☐
6. fait se coucher à une certaine heure à son enfant.	☐	☐
7. fait regarder les nouvelles à son enfant.	☐	☐

Now, repeat the above but this time imagine that the child is 18 and still lives at home. Do any answers change? (Note: activity continues with 7 more items as per above.)

Example of Initial Mechanical Activity for TI

Activité B. For each situation, create a result.

MODEL   Ma mère ne veut pas nettoyer la maison. →
            Ma mère fait nettoyer la maison.

1. Lucie ne veut pas peindre les murs.
2. Robert ne veut pas construire la maison.
3. Marie ne veut pas faire le ménage.
4. Donnie ne veut pas préparer le gâteau.
5. Sabine ne veut pas corriger les fautes.
6. Georges ne veut pas faire la vaisselle.

Example of a Meaning-based Activity for TI

Activité C. Fill in the blank with what you think the parent must be making a 10 year-old child do. Use the following verbs.

faire, garder, se coucher, regarder, étudier, nettoyer, donner

Un parent ...
1. _____ les devoirs à son enfant.
2. _____ la leçon à son enfant.
3. _____ de l'exercise à son enfant.
4. _____ la salle de bain à son enfant.
5. _____ à manger au chien à son enfant.
6. _____ à une certaine heure à son enfant.
7. _____ les nouvelles à son enfant.

Now, repeat the above but this time imagine that the child is 18 and still lives at home. (Note: activity continues with 7 more items as per above.)

Chapter 6

Processing Instruction and Spanish *Ser* and *Estar:* Forms With Semantic-Aspectual Values

An Chung Cheng
University of Toledo

The purpose of the present study[1] is to see if the results of VanPatten and Cadierno (1993) are generalizable to a semantic-aspectual feature of language, in this case the Spanish copular verb *estar*. Given the complexities in the use of this verb plus its rather late acquisition by L2 learners, it is an ideal candidate to test the extent to which processing instruction (PI) is a useful intervention for helping the acquisition of all structures in a language. As we will see, form-meaning mapping with *estar* is not nearly as neat and transparent as that of NVN being either SVO or OVS as in the case of the VanPatten and Cadierno study. This copular verb in Spanish has rather subtle properties that are in evidence at the surface level by different classes of lexical items that co-occur with it. We will compare the effects of PI with traditional instruction (TI) to see if the overall superior results of PI in previous research (as well as in this volume) obtain in this study as well.

BACKGROUND

Theoretical Classifications of Spanish *Ser* and *Estar* Selection

Following a number of studies in sociolinguistics, language contact (Gutiérrez, 1992) and SLA (Geeslin, 2000a, 2000b, 2002a, 2002b; Ramírez-Gelpi, 1995),

---

[1]The author would like to thank Kimberly Geeslin for her input in data coding and Bill VanPatten for his helpful and useful comments during the drafting of this manuscript. They are, of course, not responsible for all remaining errors and shortcomings.

the present study adopts an analysis of the use of the verb *estar* (and its counterpart, *ser*) based on Silva-Corvalán (1986, 1994) and Geeslin (2000a, 2002a). The Spanish copula, which has a dual usage, *ser* and *estar,* is a connector to link grammatical categories and carries little or no lexical meaning in comparison to other verbs. However, given the opposition between *ser* and *estar*, these forms do carry some semantic value. *Ser* and *estar* contrast semantically and pragmatically in a number of syntactic contexts, with differences in meaning according to the reference of the subject and what is attributed to the subject by the predicate element. The two verbs do not occur in complete complementary distribution and share a variety of structural environments. For example, both are acceptable with a large number of adjectives, whereas some adjectives can occur only with *estar* (e.g., *lleno*/full) while others can occur only with *ser* (e.g., *responsable*/responsible) under normal conditions. That is, Spanish predicate adjectives fall into three groups: (1) those that allow only *ser*, (2) those that allow only *estar*, (3) those that allow both *ser* and *estar*.

It is the third category that has generated most debates in Spanish linguistics and requires an understanding of some subtle semantic distinctions. As a general rule, the uses of *ser/estar* with adjectives are usually based on dichotomies such as permanent vs. temporary/transitory or essential/inherent vs. accidental/ circumstantial (Falk, 1979; Navas Ruiz, 1963; Vañó-Cerdá, 1982). The use of *estar* with an attribute often indicates a state that results from a change or is potentially modifiable. Furthermore, the differences between the use of *ser* and *estar* do not depend only on syntactic or lexical constraints; the extended discourse and shared knowledge among the speakers must be considered as well. In her concept of semantic transparency, Silva-Corvalán (1986, 1994) distinguished between *ser* and *estar* by using such binary parameters as (1) inherent vs. circumstantial, (2) imperfect vs. perfective, (3) permanent vs. temporary, (4) defining vs. dependent on concrete experiences, (5) susceptible vs. not susceptible to change, and (6) class vs. individual frame of reference. She proposed that the meaning of *estar* as opposed to *ser* includes at least two elements: state of being and perfectivity. This permits the selection of *estar* in three semantic and pragmatic contexts: individual frame, susceptibility to change, and circumstantial attribute.

The contrast between *ser* and *estar* is transparent with types of adjectives that have different meanings associated with the copula selection. Table 6.1 lists the contextual features of *ser* and *estar* with examples for each category. The copula choice is less apparent in the context "modality contrast," in which the *estar* usage results in a change in modality depending on the aforementioned six parameters. Modality contrast accounts for the largest group of adjectives in referent + copula + adjective combinations. In the final category (the lowest degree of transparency), the adjectives of "near synonymy" do allow both *ser/estar* but the copular verbs do not seem to carry any semantic value.

TABLE 6.1
Categories, Variables and Examples of Spanish in Ser/Estar + Adjective Constructs

Variables	*Examples*
Semantic Transparency	
Ser required	*Las imágenes son similares.*
	The images are similar.
Estar required	*Pepito está arrepentido.*
	Pepito appears repentant.
Modality contrast	*La vida es/está demasiado tranquila.*
	The life is/becomes too quiet.
	El florero es/está roto.
	The flower vase is broken.
Meaning change	*Juan es callado.*
	Juan is shy.
	Juan está callado.
	Juan seems silent.
Near Synonymy	*Juan es/está casado.*
	Juan is married.
Frame of Reference	
Class frame	*Javier es tímido.*
	Javier is shy.
Individual frame	*Javier está tímido ahora.*
	Javier seems shy now.
Aspect	
Perfective (completed)	*Javier está nervioso.*
	Javier seems nervous.
Imperfective (on going)	*Javier es nervioso.*
	Javier is nervous.
Adjective Class	
Age	*Los hijos son/están mayores.*
	The children are/look older.
Physical appearance	*El pelo de la chica es/está rizado.*
	The girl's hair is/ looks curly.
Description/evaluation	*Todo es/está horrible.*
(non-animate)	Everything is/looks horrible.
Mental state	*Estela está disgustada.*
	Estela seems upset.

Considering the frame of reference, a clearer basis for copula choice would depend upon the type of implied comparison that the sentence expresses (Falk, 1979; Franco and Steinmetz, 1983, 1986). *Ser* is used to classify the referent (i.e., subject) as one type among several. For example, the proposition *María es bonita* ("Mary is pretty") expresses the idea that María is pretty in the sense that her beauty is greater than that of average girls. In contrast, *estar* is used to present the referent within an individual frame of reference; that is, the subject is compared with itself under different conditions. This implies that the relationship between the referent (i.e., subject) and the attribute (e.g., adjective) is susceptible to change. For example, the proposition *María está bonita ahora* ("María is pretty now") asserts that María looks pretty in the sense that her appearance is prettier than what it usually is.

Temporal aspects also denote the difference between the two verbs, especially in constructs using past participles (Luján, 1981). *Ser* is used when the attributes (i.e., past participle) refer to imperfective states. *Estar* is used when the attributes refer to perfective states; therefore *estar* constructs must be interpreted as inherently referring to a period of time whose beginning or end is assumed. For instance, *la carta está escrita* (the letter is written) denotes a process with a terminal phase. In contrast, *manejar el coche* (to drive the car) denotes an activity with no finishing point. Hence predicates like *manejar el coche* are imperfective and thereby cannot be used with *estar*.

In addition, adjectives are also categorized into such classes as age, size, sensory character, physical appearance, description (non-animate), evaluation, color, mental state, physical state, moral value (see Silva-Corvalán, 1986, 1994; Gutiérrez, 1992).

Acquisition of Spanish *Ser* and *Estar* and Processing Strategies

The complexity of the uses of Spanish *ser/estar* causes a great deal of difficulty for second language learners. Even though *ser* and *estar* are generally introduced in the first few chapters of most beginning level Spanish textbooks and are used very frequently in the classroom, they are not acquired as early nor as accurately as expected. The choice of *ser* and *estar* is difficult because learners first have to acquire the distinction between adjective types (e.g. inherent vs. accidental) and between aspectual types (i.e., perfective vs. imperfective) before they can acquire a specific copula for each type.

Previous studies on the acquisition of beginning and intermediate English learners of Spanish have found similar transitional stages in the development of copula choice. VanPatten (1985, 1987) proposed five transitional stages for the acquisition of *ser* and *estar* by adult speakers of English:

Stage 1. Absence of copula in learner speech. (**Juan alto*/John is tall.)
Stage 2. Selection of *ser* to perform most of copula functions.
          (**Juan es enfermo*/ John is sick.)
Stage 3. Appearance of *estar* with progressive.
          (*Juan está estudiando*/ John is studying.)
Stage 4. Appearance of *estar* with locatives.
          (*Juan está en la clase*/ John es in the classroom.)
Stage 5. Appearance of *estar* with adjective of condition.
          (*Juan está enfermo*.)

VanPatten argued that these stages in the acquisition of *ser* and *estar* by adult speakers of English cannot be attributed to classroom teaching approaches or sequence of instruction. The process of acquiring the use of *ser* and *estar* involves the interaction of such factors as simplification, communicative value, frequency in input, and first language transfer. However, the acquisition sequences with locatives and adjectives of condition appear different in an immersion context. In contrast to classroom learners, the participants in a study abroad program acquired the locative function of *estar* after the conditional (Ryan & Lafford, 1992). Nevertheless, investigating the accuracy in using *ser* and *estar* in a variety of settings, studies by Briscoe (1995), Finnemann (1990), Geeslin (2000a), Guntermann (1992), and Ramírez-Gelpi (1995) all confirmed the transitional stages of the development of *ser* and *estar* acquisition proposed by VanPatten. In addition, Guntermann (1992) indicated *ser* + past participle combinations (passive) appeared latest among the Peace Corps volunteers living abroad for almost one year. Examining the oral production of 77 college students ranging from first semester to fourth year, Briscoe also indicated that the acquisition of *estar* with adjectives of condition and *ser* with past participles, locative (event) and time was not achieved until beyond the fourth year of study. Interestingly, Briscoe found a drop in the accuracy rate for *ser* with adjectives of characteristics during the third semester, which might be an indication of learners' awareness of the *ser/estar* opposition in copula + adjectives combinations. However, as criticized by Geeslin (2000a) the data categorization of *ser*/characteristics and *estar*/condition in the aforementioned studies fell short in providing explanations of learners' behavior in the syntactic contexts where *ser* and *estar* contrast.

In an effort to avoid the problem of error-analysis design as in all previous research (when speaker's intentions were unknown), Geeslin (2000a) coded data by contextual features from semi-structured interviews, a picture-description task, and contextualized questionnaire by seventy-seven high school learners. In the investigation of the overall distribution of copula, she found a number of predictors for the usage of *estar* in the progress across four levels of instruction in terms of grammatical accuracy, adjective class, semantic transparency, animacy, susceptibility to change, dependence on experience, directionality, dynamicity, perfectivity, frame of reference, task and telicity. Her study was especially significant in that she investigated the interactions among these various contextual features in copula choice by Spanish learners and stressed the importance of incorporating sociolinguistic research in SLA studies.

Not satisfied with the inconsistency of some contextual features (e.g., animacy, dependence on experience) in predicting usage of *estar* as participants' proficiency improved, Geeslin's subsequent studies re-examined the overall distribution of copula from perspectives of contextual features in various theoretical supports. Within the parameter of aspect, Geeslin (2000b) indicated that perfectivity, telicity and dynamicity were all significant predictors of the usage of *estar* by learners but not sufficient to describe the differences between participants at various levels of ability, nor the process of change. In the contexts of *ser* and *estar* based on semantic transparency, Geeslin (2002a) found that contexts in which only one copula is allowed ("*ser* required," "*estar* required") and those in which copula contrast results in a shift in modality were significant predictors of learners' improvement across time, whereas the contexts where the *ser* and *estar* opposition produces a clear meaning change or no apparent meaning difference ("near synonymous") were not. In an effort to link the stages of language loss in sociolinguistics and stages of acquisition of Spanish copula, Geeslin (2002b) proposed a mirror-image hypothesis in which the frame of reference was acquired later in SLA, whereas it was lost earlier in the process of language change. In addition, L2 learners acquired earlier the feature "susceptible to change" (e.g., *Juan es inteligente*, inherent characteristic, not changing vs. *Juan está alegre*/Juan appears happy, changing), but it was lost later among the third generation. In addition, Geeslin suggested that adjective class (e.g., mental state, physical state, color), dependency on experience, and aspect are significant predictors of *estar* use, although no developmental pattern of acquisition was found. In summary, the two contextual features, frame of reference and semantic transparency, are the contexts in which learners' *estar* use appeared later in the development of the copula acquisition, while adjective class and aspect are also significant predictors.

Regarding input processing, Spanish copula omission in the earliest stage can be explained by its lack of communicative value (Bransdorfer, 1991). Because the Spanish copula is a connector that carries little or no lexical meaning for English learners, very often sentences containing these verbs are interpretable via the content lexical items and the context; therefore the copulas bear little communicative value (see VanPatten's Lexical Preference Principle, this volume, chap. 1). The finding that learners omit the copula in the early stages implies that they allow copula forms to slip by unprocessed because the meaning is retrievable from contextual information such as referent and adjective. In addition, the overuse of *ser* may be attributed to frequency in the input; *ser* is three times more frequent than *estar* (VanPatten, 1987). It is hypothesized, then, that early stage learners are less capable of processing oral messages for meaning while attending to the copula *estar*. Finally, the analogy between *es* in Spanish (*ser* in third person singular form) and *is* in English might reinforce the use of *ser* as default in the copula + adjective combinations. In teaching the Spanish *ser* and *estar* distinction, the challenge is to make the learner perceive the subtle distinctions between the two in constructs in which they share the same linguistic context. Given that learners tend to generalize the use of *ser* early on and *estar* is slower to emerge, it is the acquisition of *estar* that is of interest and ought to be the target of instruction. Thus, the purpose of PI in the present study was to push learners away from the Lexical Preference Strategy and to have them actually process *estar* and connect appropriate meanings to it.

Motivation for the Present Study

Cheng (2002) found that the performance of students who received traditional instruction (TI) improved only on sentence production and guided composition tests, while that of the PI group improved on both interpretation and production tests when only the *estar* data was analyzed. The results of this research with second-year college students of Spanish partially corroborate earlier findings by VanPatten and his fellow researchers. However, the data from guided composition assessment presented a unique problem. Although the PI and the TI groups performed equally well, both groups performed significantly better than the control group on the first posttest. The problem arose in that the control group, like those who received instructional treatments, improved by the second posttest. Given this finding, one is left only with the qualitative aspect of improvement. That is, in the original study, the error rate of *estar* in the analysis of the composition data revealed little about the copula choices in general. A detailed analysis of the categories of improvement may shed light on the effects of instruction.

Because there are no clear-cut rules of Spanish copula choice in referent + copula + attribute combinations, any judgment of the appropriateness of a token would have to be determined on the semantic and pragmatic constraints. This is especially problematic when participants' intentions were uncertain, as in the composition tasks. As a consequence, in Cheng's study the tokens of *ser* or *estar* were not counted toward data analysis if there was a discrepancy regarding accuracy of token use between two raters who are native Spanish speakers, which might obscure the results of data analysis. Therefore, a different approach to investigating learners' copula choice in reference to variables such as frame of reference, semantic transparency and adjective class may bring about revealing information for the production of target forms at the discourse level. Rather than considering the accuracy rate of *estar* uses, this study examined the emergence of *estar* + adjective with the aforementioned contextual features.

The study addresses the following research questions: (1) Will there be any statistical differences in how learners who receive processing instruction, learners who receive traditional instruction, and learners who receive no instruction on the Spanish *ser* and *estar* with adjective and past participle produce discourse containing the target forms in reference to contextual features as semantic transparency, frame of reference, or adjective class? (2) If an effect for instruction is found, will it hold on a delayed posttest?

METHOD

The current study compares two types of instruction: traditional instruction and processing instruction. The participants were divided into three groups: (1) a traditional instruction (TI) group, (2) a processing instruction (PI) group, and (3) a control group, which did not receive any explicit instruction on *ser* and *estar*. The pretest, administered one week before instructional treatments, ensured comparability between groups and served as a baseline for determining the effects of instruction. The first posttest was conducted immediately after the experimental treatments to examine the immediate effects of instruction. The second posttest was administered three weeks after instruction to evaluate the retention of knowledge. In each test, the participants completed three types of tasks: sentence interpretation, sentence production, and guided composition. For the purpose of this chapter, we only look at the data from the composition task in the three tests (see Cheng, 2002 for the overall results.)

Participants

The study initially involved 197 students in fourth-semester Spanish university courses. To be included in the final data pool, the participants had to complete all stages of the experiment (tests and treatment) and had to have English as their first language without any frequent exposure to Spanish outside the classroom (assessed via a background questionnaire). In addition, any participant who scored above 60% on the *estar* items of the pretests was removed from the pool to account for previous knowledge and to ensure no ceiling effect for learners already at some demonstrably high level of knowledge and ability with the copular verbs. Because this study investigated the overall distribution of the *estar* tokens, the participants who did not complete all compositions by describing all four pictures in the three tests were also removed from the data pool. However, if participants' compositions demonstrated over generalization of *ser* (exclusive use of *ser* + adjective combinations only) in the pretest, they were included in data analysis, even though they scored higher than 60% correct in the pretest. Based on these criteria, the final data pool consisted of 83 participants. There were 29, 28, and 26 participants in the PI, TI, and control groups, respectively.

Materials

Instructional packages. Separate instructional packets for the PI and TI groups were developed to reflect the two different approaches to focusing on *ser* and *estar* followed by adjectives and past participles.

Traditional instruction involved explicit grammar explanation of the usage of *ser* in contrast to *estar* in terms of semantics and aspectual information and exercises to emphasize the production of the target features. The package of materials given to participants in this group was derived from the intermediate Spanish textbook *Pasajes: Lengua* and its companion workbook in slightly modified form to accommodate this study. There were two sections in the course packet: The first involved an explanation of the usage of *ser/estar* with an adjective and the second involved an explanation of *ser/estar* followed by a past participle. In each section, the contrast between *ser* and *estar* was introduced, as were activities providing opportunities to produce these forms immediately after the explanation by moving from typical controlled mechanical drills to meaningful and communicative open-ended questions. It should be noted that the mechanical drills are limited to verb conjugation regarding subject-verb agreement and most activities are meaning bearing because of the subtle properties of the copular verbs. This departs somewhat from the way mechanical drills are used when the issue is sentence structure (see, e.g., VanPatten & Cadierno, 1993 as well as VanPatten & Wong, this volume). I return to the potential effects of this difference later in the discussion of the results.

The guidelines proposed by Lee and VanPatten (1995) served as the basis for the instructional materials for processing instruction. The explanation in the processing package deliberately directed the learners' attention to the functions of *ser* and *estar*, reminding them not to overlook *ser* and *estar* because these verbs might help provide clues to sentence meaning. The sequence of the presentation of explanation and activities was slightly different in the two PI and TI packages. In the PI package, the uses of *ser* and *estar* were presented sequentially, followed by activities focusing on one target structure at a time, whereas in the TI package the uses of *ser* and *estar* were presented simultaneously. The activities manipulated input to push-learners to get meaning from target forms. In general, the study used four types of exercises in processing instruction, featuring both referentially- and affectively-oriented activities. Participants in the PI group were not required to produce target forms in any activities; they only had to participate in interpretation practices. Sample activities are presented in the Appendix.

Despite the different formats used in the two instructional approaches, efforts were made to balance the two instructional packages for vocabulary, the number of tokens for each construct, and the number of practice and activity types. Care was also taken to check the tokens of each instructional package against those of the testing materials to avoid a teaching-testing bias. That is, no token was repeated in both teaching and testing materials.

Assessment Tools. Only the composition data will be analyzed in this study as the interpretation and sentence production results are reported in Cheng (2002). The guided composition task asked participants to describe a series of drawings that narrated a story. To control for the use of target structures in the participants' writing, 12 key adjectives were provided beside each drawing, and participants were instructed to use all of the words given while writing their stories. Key words included targeted adjectives as well as other vocabulary helpful to talk about the people, objects, and events in the drawings. The participants were free to add details to make the story interesting.

Procedure

The participants' normal class periods in their regular classrooms were used for all of the instructional treatments and tests, and all of the oral and written instructions were given in English. The regular instructors were not involved in teaching during the tests and were replaced by a third-party neutral and experienced instructor who was not the researcher.

The participants in each class were randomly assigned to take one version of the measurement during the pretest. To rule out the possible effects of test item familiarity and test order, a split-block design was used in the arrangement of three versions of the tests. To ensure internal consistency and stability among the pre- and posttests, three pilot studies on the test items were conducted for the discriminability analysis and normality of data distribution.

Data Coding

Rather than using an error-analysis approach, the present study examined the overall distribution of the use of *estar* in guided compositions in each test. Each instance of the syntactic structure copula + adjective/past participles that appeared in compositions was analyzed as an individual token. All tokens were coded for response type: *ser*, *estar*, omission. As discussed earlier, because *estar* is an indicator of progress in Spanish copula acquisition, it is the contextual features that predict its emergence that are of interest. Each token of *estar* + adjective/past participle was also coded for the frame of reference and the semantic transparency variable (the two features that appeared later among the four levels of participants as shown in Geeslin's studies). The semantic transparency category includes five variables: *ser* required, *estar* required, modality contrast, meaning change, and near synonymy. The coding system of modality contrast followed Silva-Corvalán's use of the six binary parameters: inherent vs. circumstantial, imperfect vs. perfective, permanent vs. temporary, defining vs. dependent on concrete experiences, susceptible vs. not susceptible to change, and class vs. individual frame of reference. The decision about semantic transparency was made at the sentence level to be consistent with previous studies. In addition, to investigate participants' copula choice on aspectual values, perfectivity was coded as one variable. Based on the class of adjective appearing in the compositions, the following variables were coded: age, description/evaluation, physical appearance, and mental state. Therefore, each *estar* token in the compositions was coded in terms of these eleven contextual features.

RESULTS

To ensure that no differences between groups existed prior to treatment, separate one-way ANOVAs on *ser* and *estar* uses by the three experimental groups in the pretest were conducted. The results indicated that there was no significant difference[2] on each variable of contextual feature among the three groups in the composition task. Therefore, any comparative effects attributed to types of instruction will not be attributed to the prior knowledge of any of these groups.

The composition task in the three tests generated a total of 2,138 tokens among three instructional groups. Table 6.2 shows the overall distribution of *ser* and *estar* with no categorical distinctions. The total number of tokens in each instructional group within each test is shown along with the percentage of the total that this number represents. As shown in the distribution of Table 6.2, the use of *estar* increased gradually across time regardless of group. This is consistent with previous findings that show a decrease of overgeneralization of *ser* in contexts where *estar* is required. The increases appeared more evident in the PI and TI groups across time, which suggest positive instructional effects. Although the percentage of the *estar* token in the TI group is higher than the PI group in the first posttest, the rate of *estar* token used in the TI group dropped in the second posttest in contrast to the steady performance of the PI group in the two posttests. A two-way ANOVA revealed a main effect for Instruction type, $F(2, 80) = 6.49$, $p = .002$, and for Time, $F(2, 80) = 19.78$, $p = .00$, meaning that there was improvement from pretest to posttests for the instructional groups. There was no significant interaction, $F(2, 80) = 1.65$, $p = .16$. Given the significant main effect for instruction, a post hoc Scheffé revealed that the effect was due to the significant differences between the PI and Control groups, $p = .01$, and between the TI and control groups, $p = .006$. Results of one-way ANOVAs showed that in the first posttest there was a main effect for Instruction, $F(2, 80) = 6.57$, $p = .002$, which was due to significant differences between the PI and control groups and between the TI and control groups, $p = .02$, $p = .004$, respectively, as shown in the post hoc Scheffé. Only a marginally significant main effect, $F = 2.57$, $p = .08$, for Instruction was obtained in the second posttest. Therefore, both the PI and TI groups produced more *estar* tokens than the control group overall, which demonstrates positive instructional effects over control group immediately after treatments. However, the difference among the three groups was not evident three weeks later, which explains in part

---

[2] The F and p values for each variable are: Total use of *ser*, $F(2, 80) = .160$, $p = .863$; Total use of *estar*, $F(2, 80) = .147$, $p = .853$; *Estar* Required, $F(2, 80) = .216$, $p = .806$; *Ser* Required $F(2, 80) = .449$, $p = .640$; Modality $F(2, 80) = .984$, $p = .378$; Meaning Change, $F(2, 80) = 2.076$, $p = .132$; Near Synonym (not applicable), Frame of Reference, $F(2, 80) = .557$ $p = .575$; Perfectivity, $F(2, 80) = .126$ $p = .882$); Age, $F(2, 80) = .257$, $p = .774$; Description/Evaluation, $F(2, 80) = .405$, $p = .668$; Physical appearance, $F(2, 80) = 1.804$, $p = .171$; Mental State, $F(2, 80) = .135$ $p = .874$.

the findings of Cheng (2002) that the control group also improved over time similar to the treatment groups.

Table 6.3 summarizes the results of two-way ANOVAs on each variable in which *estar* is used with adjectives in the two composition posttests. Considering the semantic transparency, the results indicated significant main effects for Instruction and for Time on the contexts: where the predicate adjective must be used with *estar* only (*estar* required) and where the *estar* usage resulted in the change in modality. In addition, there was a significant interaction between Instruction and Time on the contextual feature "*estar* required," and a post hoc Scheffé revealed that this interaction was due to a significant difference between the PI and the control groups, $p = .002$, a significant difference between the TI and control groups, $p = .015$, and significant differences between the pre- and posttest 1, $p = .000$, and between the pre- and posttest 2, $p = .002$. In a closer examination on each posttest, a one-way ANOVA results indicated a significant main effect for Instruction on "*estar* required," $F(2, 80) = 10.43$, $p = .00$, and it was due to the significantly higher mean of the PI group than that of the control group, $p = .00$, and to the significantly higher mean of the TI group than of that of the control group, $p = .004$. In the second posttest, the ANOVA results showed no main effect for Instruction in contexts where *estar* must be used, $F = .794$, $p = .455$. Therefore, the instructional effects were not evident in the delayed posttest when only *estar* must be used with certain adjectives. Table 6.4 shows summary report of the post hoc Scheffé for *estar* use with contextual features on each posttest.

Considering the modality constraint, two-way ANOVAs revealed significant main effects for Instruction and for Time as shown in Table 6.3. The post hoc Scheffé revealed that the mean of the PI group was significantly higher than that of the control group, $p = .025$, and the mean of the TI group was higher than that of the control group, $p = .022$. No significant difference was found between the TI and PI groups, $p = .998$. Although there was no main effect for Instruction in the first posttest, $F(2, 80) = 2.035$ $p = .137$, one-way ANOVA results revealed a significant main effect for Instruction only in the second posttest, $F(2, 80) = 4.33$, $p = .016$, and the main effect was due to the significantly higher mean of the PI group than that of the control group, $p = .018$. This suggests a delayed effect for the PI group.

As shown in Table 6.3, although there was no main effect for Instruction on the variable "meaning change," there was a main effect for Time, meaning that there was improvement from pre- to posttests. It should be noted that there was only one token with the adjective *interesada* in the compositions generated by participants under the variable where *estar* use favored a change in meaning of the sentence. Therefore, results on the contextual feature "meaning change" are not conclusive in this study. Because there was no token used in the context of "near synonym," no statistical analysis was performed.

TABLE 6.2
Responses for all Groups Across Time

Tests		Tokens of ser		Tokens of estar		Total
		Number		Number		
Pretest	PI	163	(75.8%)	52	(24.2%)	215
	TI	161	(73.5%)	58	(26.5%)	219
	Control	157	(77.7%)	45	(22.3%)	202
Posttest 1	PI	132	(50.0%)	132	(50.0%)	264
	TI	122	(46.7%)	139	(53.3%)	261
	Control	172	(72.0%)	67	(28.0%)	239
Posttest 2	PI	119	(47.6%)	131	(52.4%)	250
	TI	130	(53.1%)	115	(46.9%)	245
	Control	164	(67.5%)	79	(32.5%)	243

With the contextual feature "frame of reference," the two-way ANOVA results (see Table 6.3) indicated significant main effects for Instruction and for Time, and there was no significant interaction. The post hoc Scheffé revealed that the mean of PI was significantly higher than that of the control group, $p = .000$, the mean of TI was higher than that of the control group, $p = .001$, and there was no significant difference between the PI and TI groups, $p = .65$. Also, the instructional effects remained over time. The one-way ANOVA on each posttest revealed significant main effects on Instruction, $F(2, 80) = 6.02$, $p = .004$, which were due to the contrasts in which both PI and TI were superior to the control group on each posttest as shown in Table 6.4. Although the mean of PI is slightly higher than that of TI, there was no significant difference between the two.

Looking at the aspectual feature, the ANOVA results on "perfectivity" indicated significant main effects for Instruction and for Time, and there was no significant interaction as shown in Table 6.3. The post hoc Scheffé revealed that the mean of PI was significantly higher than that of the control group, $p = .002$, the mean of TI was higher than that of the control group, $p = .019$, and no significant difference was found between the PI and TI groups, $p = .748$. The instructional effects remained over time as evident in the significant difference between pre- and posttest 1, $p = .000$, and between pre- and posttest 2, $p = .000$. The one-way ANOVAs showed that there was no main effect on Instruction in the first posttest. There was a significant main effect for Instruction in the second posttest, $F(2, 80) = 4.68$, $p = .012$, and it was due to the significantly higher mean of PI than that of the control group, $p = .017$, as shown in post hoc Scheffé (see Table 6.4).

TABLE 6.3
Summary of Two-Way ANOVAs of *Estar* Usage in Reference to Contextual Features in
the Posttests

Source	df	SS	MS	F	p
***Estar* Required** Instruction	2	22.187	11.089	7.031	.001**
Time	2	40.735	20.367	12.913	.000**
Instruction x Time	4	18.751	4.688	2.972	.020*
Modality Instruction	2	24.190	12.095	4.990	.008**
Time	2	74.796	37.398	15.428	.000**
Instruction x Time	4	17.246	4.312	1.779	.134
Meaning Change Instruction	2	.730	.365	1.674	.190
Time	2	4.350	2.175	9.976	.000**
Instruction x Time	4	1.479	.370	1.696	.152
Frame of Reference Instruction	2	87.589	43.795	12.850	.000**
Time	2	160.078	80.329	9.778	.000**
Instruction x Time	4	23.973	5.993	1.758	.138
Perfectivity Instruction	2	42.420	21.210	7.101	.001**
Time	2	114.187	57.094	19.194	.000**
Instruction x Time	4	16.487	4.122	1.386	.240
Age Instruction	2	.009	.004	.383	.682
Time	2	.614	.307	2.586	.077
Instruction x Time	4	.652	.163	1.372	.244

TABLE 6.3 (*cont'*)

Source	df	SS	MS	F	p
Description					
Instruction	2	3.577	1.789	1.528	.219
Time	2	23.602	11.801	10.080	.000**
Instruction x Time	4	4.677	1.169	.999	.409
Physical Appearance					
Instruction	2	.175	.008	.186	.830
Time	2	2.040	1.020	2.170	.116
Instruction x Time	4	2.537	.634	1.349	.252
Mental State					
Instruction	2	31.256	15.628	6.949	.001**
Time	2	68.983	34.492	15.336	.000**
Instruction x Time	4	20.221	5.055	2.248	.065

With regard to contextual features of adjective class, separate ANOVAs were conducted on variables such as age, description, physical appearance and mental state. As shown in Table 6.3, no significant main effect for Instruction was obtained in these variables except for the adjectives of mental state. There were significant main effects for Instruction and for Time but no significant interaction regarding the variable "mental state." The post hoc Scheffé revealed that the mean of PI was significantly higher than that of the control group, $p = .004$, and the mean of TI was higher than that of the control group, $p = .009$. The instructional effects remained over time, as evident in the significant difference between pre- and posttest 1, $p = .00$, and between pre- and posttest 2, $p = .00$. The one-way ANOVAs showed a main effect for Instruction, $F = 3.74$, $p = .028$, in the first posttest but the post hoc Scheffé revealed that marginally significant differences existed between the PI and control groups, $p = .071$, and between the TI and the control groups, $p = .058$. There was no significant difference between the PI and TI groups, $p = .994$. In the second posttest, there was a significant main effect for Instruction, $F = 5.46$, $p = .006$, and it was due to the significantly higher mean of the PI group than that of the control group, $p = .015$, and the significantly higher mean of the TI group than that of the control group, $p = .025$ as shown in post hoc Scheffé. Regarding adjectives of description/evaluation,

TABLE 6.4
Summary of *post-hoc Scheffé* of *Estar* Usage in Reference to
Contextual Features in Posttests

Constraints	Posttest 1	Posttest 2
Estar required	PI > Control (p = .021) TI > Control (p = .004) PI = TI (p = .833)	(F = .794, p = .455)
Ser required	(F = .283, p = .754)	(F = .772, p = .466)
Modality	(F = 2.035, p = .137)	PI > Control (p = .018) TI = Control (p = .197) PI = TI (p = .545)
Meaning Change	(F = 4.101, p = .020)	(F = .518, p = .598)
Near Synonym	n.a.	n.a.
Frame of Reference	PI > Control (p = .009) TI > Control (p = .019) PI = TI (p = .971)	PI > Control (p = .001) TI > Control (p = .018) PI = TI (p = .689)
Perfectivity	(F = 3.232, p = .045)	PI > Control (p = .017) TI = Control (p = .080) PI = TI (p = .814)
Age	(F = 1.833, p = .167)	(F = .746, p = .477)
Description/evaluation	(F = 2.250, p = .112)	(F = .097, p = .907)
Physical appearance	(F = .239, p = .788)	(F = 1.438, p = .244)
Mental State	(F = .3.742, p = .028)	PI > Control (p = .015) TI > Control (p = .025) PI = TI (p = .983)

Note: > denotes significant difference between groups

although there was no main effect for Instruction, there was a main effect for Time, meaning that there was improvement from pre- to posttests.

In summary, based on the results presented above, the answers to the research questions are:

1. There were differences between how learners who received processing, traditional, and no instruction perform on *estar* use in composition tasks after treatment regarding the contextual features: "*estar* required," and "frame of reference." Both the processing and traditional groups

were superior to the control group but no difference was found between the processing and traditional groups.

2. The instructional effects remained in delayed posttest in the contextual features "frame of reference" and "adjectives of mental state,"[3] but not "*estar* required." There were also delayed effects of the processing group for *estar* usage in contexts of modality contrast and perfective aspect.

DISCUSSION AND CONCLUSION

The purpose of this study is to investigate the relative effects of types of instruction on Spanish learners' copula choice in reference to various contextual features while producing the target forms at discourse level. Different from the findings in Cheng (2002) in composition tests, the PI group outperformed the control group in the delayed posttest in contexts where *estar* use favored (1) modality contrast, and (2) perfective aspect, whereas the TI group did not differ significantly from the control group on either posttest. The reader is reminded that the contexts where *estar* use results in modality shift (e.g., *La habitación es/está bonita*; *El florero es/está roto*) account for the largest number of *ser/estar* + adjective contrast in meaning and is a predictor that emerges later in the development of copula acquisition. The better performance of the PI group in these two variables demonstrates that PI effectively encouraged more production of *estar* tokens at discourse level, which is one step further away from the over-generalization of *ser*. In turn, PI promotes the intake of *estar* usage toward the next stage in the development of copula acquisition.

Although this study revealed the delayed effect of PI on *estar* + adjective with certain lexical properties, it did not replicate exactly the original study of VanPatten and Cadierno (1993). There was no significant difference between the PI and TI groups on any of the contextual features of *estar* use. A closer examination of the instructional materials reveals that the TI materials in this

---

[3]It should be noted that ANOVA results yielded a significant main effect for Instruction on the contextual feature, adjective of "mental state" in the first posttest and marginally significant effects in the contrasts between the PI and control groups and between the TI and control groups as shown in the post hoc Scheffé (a more stringent statistic procedure). Thus, the immediate instructional effects on this feature should not be overlooked either.

[4]It should be noted that ANOVA results yielded a significant main effect for Instruction on the contextual feature, adjective of "mental state" in the first posttest and marginally significant effects in the contrasts between the PI and control groups and between the TI and control groups as shown in the post hoc Scheffé (a more stringent statistic procedure). Thus, the immediate instructional effects on this feature should not be overlooked either.

study included mechanical drills (in terms of verb conjugation only), but also provided substantially more meaningful exercises than those included in the TI of VanPatten and Cadierno (1993). The meaningful practice in the present study might have encouraged more form-meaning mapping during activities if learners were attending to the instructor and other learners' output as input. This is a potential problem of ecologically valid classroom-based research as noted in Farley (2001, and this volume). A largely meaning-based output treatment such as the one in this study may well provide incidental structured input to learners, as Farley suggests. The results are a meaning-based treatment that is both output and input oriented in nature and it is not surprising when the meaning-based group performs as well as the PI group (see also VanPatten & Wong's criticism, this volume, of the traditional treatment in Allen, 2000). However, the present study is clearly in line with other studies of PI and TI comparison in that learners who received PI never perform worse than those who receive TI (or MOI as in Farley's case). Thus, the beneficial effects of PI are generalizable to something as difficult as the *ser* and *estar* contrast in Spanish even if the exact results of VanPatten and Cadierno do not obtain.

Previous studies (except Geeslin's) on the acquisition of Spanish copula looked at learning outcomes from the perspective of error analysis, in which the accuracy of the copula choice is the only indicator. However, this line of research tended to overlook the qualitative perspective of the *estar* use by learners and clustered copula + adjective combinations all together without considering the interaction of the discourse context and the linguistic features of the sentence. By re-examining contextual features of *estar*, the current research underlines the importance of multiple approaches to data analysis in investigating grammar instruction on forms with multiple functions and semantic values, such as the temporal aspect or the subjunctive.

Another significant contribution of this study is that it identified the constraints that favored *estar* use in which pedagogical efforts would make greater impact on learners' development of copula acquisition. To acquire Spanish *ser* and *estar* learners must map the appropriate meanings with each copula and identify the contextual features that trigger the use of each copula. In the microanalysis of lexical items that co-occurred with *estar*, the results of this study suggest positive instructional effects on Spanish copula in contexts in which: (1) only *estar* is required (e.g., *El perro está solo*/The dog is alone); (2) *estar* denotes an individual frame of reference (e.g. *Javier está nervioso*/Javier looks nervous); (3) *estar is* used with adjectives of mental state (e.g., *Los padres están tristes*/The parents appear sad). Most importantly, delayed effects were found in contexts in which (4) *estar* usage results in modality shift and (5) *estar* entails perfective aspect. Therefore, instruction should direct learners' attention to input containing these contextual features and discourse situations in order to enhance the form-meaning mapping during comprehension and in turn accelerate acquisition processes. In the PI materials of this study, structured input activities included the use of *ser* and *estar* with a variety of contextual features. Future studies should focus on particular predictors of *estar* usage or only on contextual features emerging later in the development of copula acquisition. Future SLA studies should also identify those contextual features that are most difficult for learners to acquire.

One major limitation of this study is that there was only one type of assessment task. The majority of participants used the vocabulary items suggested in the composition task beside picture drawings without including additional adjectives. Different tasks provide learners with opportunities to produce different types of output as determined by discourse context. Other types of assessment tasks (e.g., oral interviews) might push participants to generate tokens in less processing time or to use more common adjectives in the target structure. Also, it is necessary to investigate PI not only with various assessment tasks beyond the guided composition task, but also on learners of different proficiency levels. Beginning learners may be less capable of generating tokens with a variety of contextual features, whereas intermediate learners may benefit more from instruction on *estar* in later acquired contexts.

REFERENCES

Bransdorfer, R. (1991). *Communicative value and linguistic knowledge in second language oral input processing.* Unpublished doctoral dissertation, University of Illinois, Urbana–Champaign.

Briscoe, G. (1995). *The acquisition of ser and estar by non-native speakers of Spanish,* Unpublished doctoral dissertation, University of Pennsylvania.

Cheng, A. C. (2002). The effects of processing instruction on the acquisition of *ser* and *estar. Hispania, 85,* 308–323.

Falk, J. (1979). *Ser y estar con atributos adjetivales.* Uppsala: Alqvist & Wiksell.

Farley, A. P. (2001). Authentic processing instruction and the Spanish subjunctive. *Hispania,* 84, 289–299.

Finnemann, M. D. (1990). Markedness and learner strategy: Form- and meaning-oriented learners in the foreign language context. *The Modern Language Journal, 74,* 176–187.

Franco, F., & Steinmetz, D. (1983). *Ser* and *estar* + adjective calificative. *Hispania, 66,* 176–184.

Franco, F., & Steinmetz, D. (1986). Taming *ser* and *estar* with predicate adjectives. *Hispania, 69,* 377–386.

Geeslin, K. (2000a). A new approach to the second language acquisition of copula choice in Spanish. In R. Leow & C. Sanz (Eds.), *Spanish applied linguistics at the turn of the millennium: Papers from the 1999 conference on the L1 & L2 acquisition of Spanish and Portuguese,* (pp. 50–66). Somerville, MA: Cascadilla Press.

Geeslin, K. (2000b). The parameter of aspect: Evidence from the second language acquisition of Spanish. In V. Swierzbin, F. Morris, M. Anderson, C. A. Klee & E. Tarone (Eds.), *Social and cognitive factors in second language acquisition: Selected proceedings of the 1999 second language research forum*, (pp. 185–203). Somerville, MA: Cascadilla Press.

Geeslin, K. (2002a). Semantic transparency as a predictor of copula choice in second language acquisition. *Linguistics: An Interdisciplinary Journal of the Language Sciences, 40*, 439–468.

Geeslin, K. (2002b). The second language acquisition of copula choice and its relationship to language change. *Studies in Second Language Acquisition, 24*, 419–450.

Gunterman, G. (1992). An analysis of interlanguage development over time: Part II, *ser* and *estar*. *Hispania, 75*, 1294–1303.

Gutiérrez, M. (1992). The extension of *estar*: A linguistic change in progress in the Spanish of Morelia, Mexico. *Hispanic Linguistics, 5*, 109–141.

Lee, J. F., & VanPatten, B. (1995). *Making communicative language teaching happen*. New York: McGraw-Hill.

Luján, M. (1981). Spanish copulas as aspectual indicators. *Lingua, 54*, 165–209.

Navas Ruiz, R. (1963). *Ser y estar: El estudio del sistema atributivo del español*. Salamanca: Acta Salmanticensia.

Pica, T. (1983). Adult acquisition of English as a second language in different language contexts. *Language Learning, 33*, 465–497.

Ramírez-Gelpi, A. (1995). The acquisition of *ser* and *estar* among adult native English speakers learning Spanish as a second language. Unpublished doctoral dissertation, University of Southern California.

Ryan, J., & Lafford, B. (1992). The acquisition of lexical meaning in a study abroad environment: *Ser* + *estar* and the Granada experience. *Hispania, 75*, 714–722.

Silva-Corvalán, C. (1986). Bilingualism and language change: The extension of estar in Los Angeles Spanish. *Language, 62*, 587–608.

Silva-Corvalán, C. (1994). *Language contact and change: Spanish in Los Angeles*. Oxford: Clarendon Press.

VanPatten, B. (1985). The acquisition of *ser* and *estar* in adult second language learners: A preliminary investigation of transitional stages of competence. *Hispania, 68*, 399–406.

VanPatten, B. (1987). Classroom learners' acquisition of *ser* and *estar*: Accounting for developmental patterns. In B. VanPatten, T. R. Dvorak & J. F. Lee (Eds.), *Foreign language learning: A research perspective* (pp. 61–75). Rowley, MA: Newbury House.

VanPatten, B., & Cadierno, T. (1993). Explicit instruction and input processing. *Studies in Second Language Acquisition, 15*, 225–243.

Vañó-Cerdá, A. (1982). *Ser y estar + adjetivos: Un estudio sincrónico y diacrónico*. Tubingen: Narr.

APPENDIX

Example of Grammatical Explanation in Processing Instruction.

English **to be** has several equivalents in Spanish: among them are **ser** and **estar**. In general, we use **ser** to tell who or what the subject is, or what it is really like. For example:

La nena **es** mona.

In the example above, the speaker believes the child to be cute. That is, cuteness is a defining trait. It is a characteristic that the speaker believes the child to normally possess. Thus, the speaker uses **ser** with the adjective to describe the child.

In contrast with **ser**, **estar** is used with adjectives to describe a condition or state that a subject is in. This condition or states is viewed by the speaker to not be one of the subjects defining traits. For example:

La nena **está** muy mona.

In the above example, the speaker does not believe that the child is typically cute. The speaker may even believe the opposite! On this particular occasion, the speaker perceives that cuteness is out of the ordinary for this child and thus uses **estar** with the adjective in order to convey this.

With the above information in mind, what do you think is the difference between the two statements below? Match each with the possible thoughts that a speaker might have when making them.

1. María **es** alegre.
2. María **está** alegre.
   a. "I don't know if María is a happy individual or not. She doesn't really strike me as such. She does, however, seem to be in a good mood."
   b. "My impression of María is that she is cheerful and happy with life. I wouldn't describe her as a sullen individual at all."

If you matched **1** with **b** and **2** with **a** then you are right!

!OJO! Many learners of Spanish "gloss over" **ser** and **estar** when listening to or even reading Spanish. They think that the meaning of a sentence can be obtained by simply paying attention to the "important" words. Note how you might miss out on a speaker's intended description of someone if you gloss over or skip **ser** and **estar** when listening or reading:

La chica _____ seria.

In this example, if you didn't catch **ser** or **estar** while the speaker was talking, you wouldn't know if that speaker was commenting on the girl's personality or on some state or condition she is in! Keep this in mind when doing the following activities.

Sample Activities for Processing Instruction[5]

(1) Directions: Indicate whether the speaker considers the underlined adjective to be an inherent or defining characteristic of the entity described.

	Sí	No
1. El ex-presidente Bush es <u>conservador</u>. (Ex-president Bush is conservative.) [other items follow]	☐	☐

(2 A) Directions: You will hear a series of sentences in Spanish, which describe the people or things around a student. Match each sentence you hear with one of the situations below.

(Participants heard: *El sillón de mi cuarto está viejo* /The armchair in my room looks old.)

1.___   a.   I bought the armchair 10 years ago, but it is still cozy and in good condition.
         b.   I bought the armchair last year. Since then it became my pet's playground.
              There are stains and scratches all over the chair.
[other items follow]

(2 B) Directions: Select the best way to complete each sentence.
         Mi hermans está raro_____./ My brother is strange _____.
         a.   *esta tarde/* this afternoon
         b.   *como sus amigos/* like his friends
[items follow]

(3)   Directions: What of the following are true for you? Check any that applies to your situation and then compare with your classmate.

___ 1. Mi clase de español es mejor este semestre en comparación con la del semestre pasado.
___ 2. La comida de la cafetería es mejor en comparación con el año pasado.
___ 3. Mi clase de español está mejor ya que ahora la serie Destinos se pone más interesante.
___ 4. La comida de la cafetería está mejor cuando se sirve caliente.

(4) Directions: Read the following passage. Then answer the questions that follow.

Juanito nunca se baña porque dice que no es necesario, que eso no es cosa de mayor. Su madre le obligó a ducharse porque tiene que ir a la Misa de Pascua hoy. --¡Qué limpio está Juanito! -- dice la madre, al verlo salir del baño.

Paso 1:   Find the phrase that includes ser/estar + adjective and underline it.

Paso 2: Based on the information you have just found, complete the following sentence

Juanito is clean compared with _____

Chapter 7

The Relative Effects of Processing Instruction and Meaning-Based Output Instruction

Andrew P. Farley
University of Notre Dame

As summarized in VanPatten (2002) and as we see from some of the research in this volume (e.g., VanPatten & Wong, Cheng), comparative research on PI and what VanPatten and Cadierno (1993) call traditional instruction (TI) has generally yielded overall superior effects for PI. PI consistently yields significant gains after treatment, while TI generally does not.

One limitation of previous studies on processing instruction is that the comparative instruction type in all cases was a traditional output-based instruction that included mechanical practice. Although it is valuable to compare PI with an instruction type widely used in language classrooms (see Wong & VanPatten, forthcoming), a comparison with a more meaning-based output instruction that does not have any mechanical component could provide new insight. Such a comparison would address the question of whether the results obtained in previous PI vs. TI research was due merely to the fact that PI is completely meaning based while TI is not. The general research question that guides the present study, then, is the following: Do the results of VanPatten and Cadierno (1993) as well as Cadierno (1995) obtain when a meaning-based output approach is the comparative treatment? However, as will be discussed in the present study, the answer to this question may be difficult to obtain in classroom-based research.

At the same time, this study also investigateS whether the consistently positive results of PI evidenced in the research to date can be obtained with a more complex and difficult structure, in this case, the Spanish subjunctive. This particular structure is notoriously difficult for L1 speakers of English as discussed in Collentine (1998). By offering yet another structure to research the efficacy of PI, we are in a better position to test its limits or potential for effecting change in learner knowledge and ability.

BACKGROUND

The Problem of Meaning

One criticism of the PI vs. TI research is that PI is completely meaning-based while TI is not. DeKeyser and Sokalski (1996), for example, state the following: "The problem [with the internal validity of the study] is not that the exercises [in the TI group] were not communicative; the treatment for the two groups differed more fundamentally: attention to form and meaning in one case, and attention to form only in the other" (p. 620). Although this statement is not quite accurate in that the TI materials in VanPatten and Cadierno did contain some if not about one-half meaning-based exercises, the point is well taken. One cannot be sure of the results of the VanPatten and Cadierno study because of the qualitatively different nature of the treatments. Although I agree with VanPatten (2002) that TI as operationalized in his studies is ubiquitous in the United States in classrooms and textbooks, from a theoretical perspective one cannot rule out the possibility that it is the fundamentally different amount of simultaneous attention to meaning and form in the groups that is causing the results.

However, I disagree with the solution to the issue in the DeKeyser and Sokalski study. Their study compared input and output groups by making sure that the input and output groups both had equal amounts of form-only and form + meaning exercises. The problem with this is two-fold. First, such a solution does not address the matter at hand, namely whether the results of the PI experiments are due to the consistent form + meaning nature of the activities. Second, such a solution destroys the very nature of PI, which has been well described in various places (Lee & VanPatten, 1995; VanPatten, 1993, 1996). The solution I propose to the problem at hand is to leave PI as is and to compare it to a completely meaning-based output approach. If indeed TI is not as good as PI, what about other output-based approaches? Thus, in the present study, I will compare PI as one treatment with an output treatment that is devoid of mechanical drills.

The Subjunctive in Spanish SLA

The subjunctive is a problematic structure for L1 speakers of English. Known for his work with the Spanish subjunctive, Collentine (1993) asserted that time dedicated by beginning-level instructors to teaching the subjunctive should be reduced, because the learners are not ready to acquire mood selection. Pereira (1996) compared a group that received processing instruction on marked subjunctive forms with a control group that received no instruction, finding only a very small effect for instruction. Her results lend support to Collentine's claim that low-level learners of Spanish are not ready to acquire Spanish mood. Collentine (1995) also suggested that instruction on mood selection in Spanish may not be very beneficial to intermediate-level learners. Collentine (1997) speculated that L2 learners' success with the acquisition of the Spanish subjunctive not only depends on their ability to process subjunctive morphology but also on their ability to process complex syntactic structures and assess discourse-pragmatic relationships. However, in this study I suggest that low-level learners possess certain interpretation strategies that hinder their ability to process the Spanish subjunctive after clauses of doubt.

Problems in the L2 acquisition of the Spanish subjunctive in nominal clauses after expressions of doubt can be explained using VanPatten's model of input processing (see Chapter 1, this volume). Of particular interest here is the Lexical Preference Principle, which states that lexical form is weighted more heavily than grammatical form in its importance to the learner's input processor. In sentences like *No pienso que viaje mucho* ('I don't think that he/she travels much'), the nonaffirmative phrase *No pienso* ('I don't think') communicates doubt to the learner. There is no reason for a learner to attend to the subjunctive verb ending (-*e* in *viaje*) in the subordinate clause, because it simply re-communicates the non-affirmation already expressed by lexical units in the main clause. However, the subjunctive may be affected by an additional processing problem as well. The Sentence Location Principle states that learners process items in sentence initial position first, then items in sentence final position, and finally items which are in the middle of the sentence. In the majority of Spanish utterances that include a subjunctive form (except direct commands), the subjunctive form is located in medial position—where it is least likely to be processed. For example, in the utterance *No creo que entienda el problema* ('I don't believe he/she understands the problem'), the subjunctive inflection (the -*a* of *entienda*) is found in the middle of the sentence. P4 predicts that learners will tend to overlook the subjunctive inflection because it is not in one of the more salient positions (sentence initial or sentence final).

Due to these learner difficulties in processing subjunctives in nominal clauses after expressions of doubt, this use of the subjunctive is a prime candidate for study on the effects of instruction type and the effects of processing instruction in particular. It could be argued that Collentine (1998) has already concluded that output-oriented instruction and processing instruction are equally effective in tasks involving the Spanish subjunctive. Collentine investigated the effects of instruction type on the acquisition of the Spanish subjunctive in adjectival clauses. Collentine divided learners into three groups: an output-oriented group, a processing instruction group, and a control group. The means of assessment were one comprehension task and one production task that were administered prior to treatment and immediately following treatment.

Collentine found that both the output-oriented group and the PI group made gains on the two tasks, and there was no significant difference in improvement between groups. From these results, Collentine concluded that output-oriented instruction is equally effective in tasks where the subjunctive has communicative value. However, it is not clear to what extent Collentine kept any processing principles in mind while developing his activities.

As mentioned above, learner difficulties with the subjunctive are predicated on two particular processing issues in VanPatten's model of Input Processing. Collentine does not cite these nor discuss them in his article. The subjunctive forms in his treatment materials consistently appeared in sentence-medial position, the least salient position for perception and subsequent processing. In addition, as VanPatten (2002) noted, some of the activities are "heavy" and require that the learner hold a great deal of information in working memory before indicating an answer. Ideally, as VanPatten recently pointed out, stimuli in PI activities ought to be short. Nonetheless, the participants in the PI group in Collentine's study did improve from pre- to posttest. The PI activities he created did bring about a statistically significant effect. On average, his participants improved about 4 points (out of 10), well below the gains made in previous research on PI. The question now remains whether another version of PI materials for the subjunctive might yield greater gains when taking into consideration some of the observed shortcomings.

In Farley (2001), 29 participants enrolled in a fourth-semester Spanish course were assigned to one of two treatments: PI and meaning-based output instruction (MOI). The MOI treatment was different from traditional output-oriented instruction types in that there was no mechanical component. The MOI activities were all meaning-based and required learners to use both meaning and form at some level during production. The tasks typically involved communicating one's opinions, beliefs, or feelings about a designated topic. The MOI group received the same explicit information as the PI group, but instead of structured input activities, they received activities that were designed so that the subjunctive forms were produced in utterance-initial position. The results indicated that processing instruction had an overall greater effect than meaning-based output instruction on how learners interpreted and produced the Spanish subjunctive of doubt. The output-oriented treatment and processing instruction were equally effective in a task involving production of subjunctive forms, but PI resulted in a greater effect than MOI on the interpretation task. Although PI in Farley (2001) was developed according to the guidelines put forth in VanPatten (1993, 1997—see also Wong, this volume, chap. 2—one limitation of the study was the size of the subject pool, which contained only 29 participants from a fourth-semester Spanish language course.

Yet another issue regarding research in PI is that no study reports on the effects of instruction at the microlevel, particularly whether instruction impacts regular and irregular forms equally and whether there is transfer of knowledge from exemplars in the treatment to novel test items. For example, it remains to be seen whether learners who receive PI have a capacity to generalize (by analogy) to process and produce subjunctive *forms* themselves (in contrast to *uses*) that are not presented during the PI treatment. The present study, then, will not only address the issue of the generalizability of the effects of PI to a new structure as well as whether the superiority of PI obtains when compared with MOI, it will also report on the effects of instruction at the microlevel.

RESEARCH QUESTIONS

The present study proposes the following research questions:

1. Do PI and MOI bring about improved performance on sentence-level tasks involving...
    a.   the interpretation of regular subjunctive forms?
    b.   the production of regular subjunctive forms?

2. Do PI and MOI bring about improved performance on sentence-level tasks involving...
    a.   the interpretation of irregular subjunctive forms?
    b.   the production of irregular subjunctive forms?

3. Do PI and MOI bring about improved performance on sentence-level tasks involving...
    a.   the interpretation of novel subjunctive forms?
    b.   the production of novel subjunctive forms?

4. Do PI and MOI bring about equal improved performance on all item types of...
    a.   the interpretation task?
    b.   the production task?

METHOD

Participants

The participants consisted of 129 university students from ten different sections of a fourth-semester Spanish grammar review course designed for those who had progressed through an intensive track. The 10 intact course sections were randomly assigned to two treatment groups: meaning-based output instruction and processing instruction. Students enrolled in the course did not receive explicit instruction or homework assignments on the Spanish subjunctive of doubt during previous weeks of the course. However, the students were accustomed to both input-based and output-based activities, both inclass and for homework. Following previous PI research design, only a subset of the participants who scored less than 60% on the pretest were used in the statistical analyses. In this way, ceiling effects were avoided.

Background information was gathered from the participants using a written survey. Participants who knew more than one second language or had contact with Spanish outside of class were excluded from the study. In addition, those who sought any additional explanation or practice outside of class during the treatment period were excluded. All participants who were not native speakers of English or reported any learning disabilities or hearing impairments were removed from the data pool. Finally, all participants who had placed directly into the fourth-semester course were removed from the study. After taking into account the information provided by the survey and those who had placed directly into the course, 67 participants were removed from the total of 129 possible, leaving 62 potential participants. This was reduced to 50 upon exlcusion of those who scored higher than 60% on both the interpretation and the production tasks of the pretest.

Materials

There were two instructional packets for the treatment. Each packet was designed to reflect a different approach to teaching the Spanish subjunctive in nominal clauses after expressions of doubt. The PI packet consisted of ten structured-input activities, and the MOI packet consisted of ten meaning-based output activities. Both instructional packets contained identical subject matter, vocabulary, and number of tokens. For both groups, the same one-page handout was distributed on the first day of instruction. This handout contained explicit information about the following:

1. How the subjunctive is formed;
2. Where the subjunctive is located within a sentence;
3. When the subjunctive is used (only its use with doubt was mentioned) and
4. How to process the subjunctive.

The last section told participants that the subjunctive verb ending is redundant because it simply expresses doubt a second time. They were encouraged to pay attention to the verb ending despite its redundancy. Although the information about processing is characteristic of PI, it finds relevance within MOI as well. Learners might tend to overlook the need to *produce* a subjunctive form when it simply expresses doubt a second time. Finally, one subordinate (nominal) clause was given as an example, and participants were required to choose between an indicative trigger and a subjunctive trigger. The answer was given to them at the bottom of the handout. After the participants read through the handout with the instructor, they began the activities. Participants in both groups were given identical explicit information so that the difference between types of treatment was limited to the nature of the activities themselves. The handout was collected on the second day of instruction to inhibit further study/review outside of class. As prescribed in VanPatten (1996) and Wong (this volume, chap. 2), both referential activities and affective activities were included in both oral and written modes.

The structuring of the PI activity involved a deliberate attempt to alter the strategy described in the Lexical Preference Principle. In addition, the Sentence Location Principle was also taken into account in that the main clause was separated from the subordinate clause whenever possible to take advantage of primacy effects that cause a phrase-initial subjunctive form to be processed more easily than a sentence-medial subjunctive form. With the referential activities, because the subordinate clause was separated from the matrix clause, participants were not able to rely on the lexical items (subjunctive triggers) to determine that doubt was being expressed. Instead, they were forced to attend to the subjunctive or indicative forms themselves to determine whether or not doubt was expressed and select the corresponding trigger. Finally, in each activity, meaning was kept in focus and only one grammatical point was presented: third-person present tense subjunctives in nominal clauses after expressions of doubt. The participants were required to not only read or listen to the input, but to make a decision concerning what they read or heard. For the referential activities, the participants were required to select the correct trigger (matrix clause) or subordinate clause to complete each sentence. For the affective activities, the participants were required to select the pre-formed statements that expressed their opinion or belief.

After completing each referential activity, the participants were given feedback as to what the right answers were. This feedback was given in order to ensure that participants made early connections between form and meaning and so that the treatment might better reflect a typical language classroom in which learner responses are not left unanswered by the instructor. During this time, none of the information on the handout was repeated and no further grammatical explanation was given. In addition, no feedback or justification was supplied when the correct answers to the activities were given. In other words, the participants were told the correct answer, but they were not told why it was correct. Five activities (three referential, two affective) were completed on the first day of instruction and five activities (three referential, two affective) were completed on the second day of instruction. Examples of referential and affective PI activity items are provided in the Appendix.

MOI consists of a grammar explanation and production-oriented language activities but does not contain a mechanical component. The MOI activities required participants to produce either subjunctive or indicative verb forms based on the triggers that they heard or read. These subordinate phrases usually expressed an opinion or belief that they had about the activity topic. Sometimes participants were required to guess what a famous person's opinion might be and to complete their statements accordingly. Meaning was kept in focus, and often vocabulary was provided to guide the participants' responses.

All referential MOI activities were structured such that the participants had to produce the correct subordinate verb or clause based on the trigger matrix clause. For these referential activities, an infinitive verb or phrase was given to use for each item. In the affective MOI activities, participants also had to produce a correct subordinate verb or clause based on the trigger matrix clause, but they could choose from suggested phrases. In these activities, responses were affective in nature in that they reflected the participants' opinions or beliefs. Examples of each MOI activity type are provided in the Appendix.

Both instructional packets were balanced to provide an equal number of referential and affective items. After completing each activity, the instructor called on participants to give their answers, and told them whether their answers were right or wrong. During this time, none of the information on the handout was repeated, and no further grammatical explanation was given. In addition, no feedback or justification was supplied when the correct answers to the activities were given. In other words, the participants were told the correct answer, but they were not told why it was correct. When a wrong answer was given by a participant, the instructor called on other participants until the correct answer was given.

Assessment

There were three versions (A, B, C) of the interpretation test and the production test. Having three versions of each test allowed for six possible orderings (ABC, BCA, etc.). Of the six possible orderings, five were used in this experiment; one of the five test sequences was randomly assigned to each of the five intact classes within each treatment group. That is, the PI group was comprised of five different course sections and each course section was administered a different test version ordering. Likewise, the MOI group consisted of five different course sections and each section received a different sequence of test versions. An ANOVA performed on pretest scores later revealed no effect for test version.

The interpretation task required a response to a series of aural utterances in which the main clause was omitted. Participants heard each pre-recorded utterance twice with a 10-second interval between each test item. The interpretation task required that participants complete each sentence by choosing between two main clauses that were written on the participants' answer sheet. For each subordinate clause, there were two main clauses to choose from—one that triggered the indicative and one that triggered the subjunctive. For example, participants heard ... *hable mucho* ('_____ [third person sing.] talks [subj] a lot') and had to circle either (a) *Yo creo que...* ('I think that ...') or (b) *No es verdad que* ... ('It is not true that ...'). At the end of the test, participants transferred their answers to a scantron answer sheet that required them to fill in the bubbles containing the letter of each correct answer. There were a total of 24 items on the test, consisting of:

- nine target items requiring subjunctive triggers which included:
  - three items containing regular subjunctive forms in the subordinate clause;
  - three items containing irregular subjunctive forms in the subordinate clause;
  - three items containing novel subjunctive forms (not seen during instruction) in the subordinate clause;
- three utterances requiring indicative triggers and
- twelve distractors unrelated to the indicative/subjunctive contrast.

The interpretation task was limited to 24 test items due to time constraints. The language used in the interpretation task consisted of high-frequency vocabulary that the participants had already covered in previous language courses. Those who placed directly into the fourth-semester course and did not take any of the previous Spanish courses were eliminated from the data pool. All three versions of the interpretation test were balanced for vocabulary and overall content.

The production task consisted of a sentence-completion task in which there were the following types of items:

- six target items of doubt that required subjunctives;
  - two items requiring regular subjunctive forms;
  - two items requiring irregular subjunctive forms;
  - two items requiring novel subjunctive forms;
- three items of certainty that required indicatives and
- twelve distractors unrelated to the doubt/certainty contrast .

Participants were instructed to change the verb form in parenthesis (if necessary) to complete each sentence correctly. Six items contained subjunctive triggers in the matrix clause and required a subjunctive to be produced to complete each sentence correctly. The purpose of the three items that required indicatives was to determine if overextension would occur. If participants produced a subjunctive in the subordinate clause on the items where the matrix trigger clause only allowed for an indicative subordinate, this would provide evidence for overextension. The distractors were unrelated to mood selection and required participants to use the preterite, the imperfect, the present indicative, or the infinitive.

Procedure

The pretest, consisting of an interpretation task and a production task, was administered one class day before treatment. All experimentation took place in the participants' regular classroom during their regular class periods. After the pretest was administered, the classes were randomly assigned to the two instructional conditions: MOI and PI. All instruction took place during two class days within the same week and no homework was given. Instructional materials were collected from the participants after the treatment.

The two days of experimental instruction were carried out by five instructors who were not the participants' regular instructors, and had never taught them before this study. These particular instructors were selected because they had experience teaching within a curriculum that incorporates both structured input activities and meaning-based output activities. That is, they were accustomed to both types of treatment and had used both activity types frequently in the classes they taught. Four of the instructors had near-native fluency and their L1 was English, and one instructor was a native speaker from Spain. An effect for instructor was avoided by using all five instructors for both conditions; that is, each instructor was responsible for teaching one section of each treatment. Both groups completed five activities on the first day of instruction and five activities on the second day.

Scoring

For the statistical analyses, raw scores were calculated on the subjunctive items in the following manner. For the interpretation portion, each correct answer received a score of one, each incorrect or blank response received a score of zero, and the total points possible were nine. A correct response involved selecting the main clause that corresponded with each subordinate clause containing a verb form in the subjunctive mood. The three indicative items were scored separately in the same manner, that is, zero versus one point for a total of three points.

For the production portion, one point was given for each correct use of the subjunctive if the verb form was correct in person/number and mood and contained no spelling error. Hence, the maximum score possible was six. If the participant used the subjunctive form but the verb did not agree in person or number or was spelled incorrectly (for example, if *trabejen* were written instead of *trabaje*), one-half point was awarded. In other words, if a clear attempt was made to produce a subjunctive (a vowel switch or stem change toward the subjunctive form), then one-half point was given. Each blank response received a score of zero and no points were given if a subjunctive form was not attempted when it was obligatory. As in the case of the interpretation test, the three indicative items were scored and analyzed separately using the same procedure as for production of subjunctive items. A score of zero was awarded for an indicative item if it was left blank or if a subjunctive form was incorrectly used. In this way, it was possible to examine to what extent participants were overgeneralizing or using a test-taking strategy (i.e., "Just make everything subjunctive").

RESULTS

Table 7.1 provides the mean test scores and standard deviations for both the PI and the MOI group on the subjunctive test items. This table shows that for the interpretation data, both the PI and MOI groups improved from pretest to posttest 1 and sustained that improvement from posttest 1 to posttest 2. The standard deviations did not increase or decrease dramatically on any of the tests for either group. Similarly, with regard to the production data in Table 7.1, the lower means on the pretest together with the higher means on both posttests indicate improvement for both PI and MOI groups. Again, the standard deviations did not differ dramatically between groups on any of the tests, and the results were sustained over time.

TABLE 7.1
Descriptive Statistics for Main Analyses

Task	Test	Instruc.	N	Mean	SD	Range
Interpr.	Pretest	PI	24	3.21	1.14	4
		MOI	26	3.58	1.24	4
	Post 1	PI	24	6.54	1.74	6
		MOI	26	7.04	1.82	6
	Post 2	PI	24	6.83	1.90	6
		MOI	26	6.69	2.00	6
Produc.	Pretest	PI	24	0.17	0.46	2
		MOI	26	0.33	0.66	2.5
	Post 1	PI	24	4.29	1.68	6
		MOI	26	4.12	1.73	6
	Post 2	PI	24	3.63	1.67	6
		MOI	26	3.81	1.74	5.5

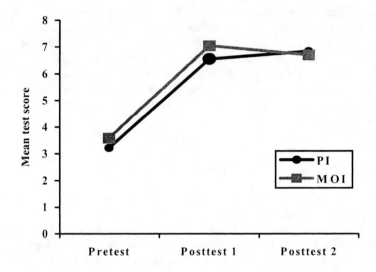

FIG. 7.1. Interaction Plot for Instruction Type and Time for Interpretation Data.

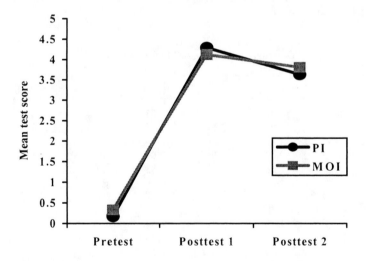

FIG. 7.2. Interaction Plot for Instruction Type and Time for Production Data.

Interpretation Data

Raw scores of the interpretation pretest and posttests were tabulated and a two-way analysis of variance (ANOVA) with repeated measures was performed. Instruction Type was the between-subjects factor, whereas Time (pretest, posttest 1, posttest 2) was the within-subjects factor.

The results reveal a significant main effect for Time $F(1, 50) = 84.31, p = .00$. There was no significant effect for Instruction Type, $F(1, 50) = .56, p = .46$, and no significant interaction between Instruction Type and Time, $F(1, 50) = .63, p = .54$. Figure 7.1 provides a visual representation of the gains made by both groups on the interpretation task.

In summary, the results of the analysis of the interpretation data suggest that both PI and MOI resulted in some type of knowledge gain. Both PI and MOI had a positive effect on the participants' interpretation of the Spanish subjunctive of doubt, and the effects of both PI and MOI were retained over time.

Production Data

Raw scores of the production pretest and posttests were tabulated and a two-way analysis of variance (ANOVA) with repeated measures was performed. Instruction Type was the between-subjects factor, whereas Time (pretest, posttest 1, posttest 2) was the within-subjects factor. The results reveal a significant effect for Time, $F(1, 50) = 148.47, p = .00$. There was no significant effect for Instruction Type, $F(1, 50) = .04, p = .85$, and no significant interaction between Instruction Type and Time, $F(1, 50) = .32, p = .73$. Figure 7.2 gives a visual representation of the gains made by each treatment group.

In summary, the results of the analysis of the production data suggest that both PI and MOI resulted in some type of knowledge gain. Both PI and MOI brought about improved performance on sentence-level tasks involving the production of the Spanish subjunctive of doubt. These effects proved durable two weeks after instruction.

Item Type Analyses

Table 7.2 shows the scores and standard deviations for the PI group and the MOI group for regular, irregular, and novel subjunctive items. This table indicates that, for the interpretation data, both the PI and MOI groups improved from pretest to posttest 1 on all three of the item types and sustained that improvement through the second posttest. Similarly, with regard to the production data, the lower means on the pretest together with the higher means on both posttests indicate improvement for the PI group and the MOI group on

TABLE 7.2
Descriptive Statistics for Item Type Analyses

Item Type	Task	Test	Group	N	Mean	SD	Range
Regulars	Interpretation	Pretest	PI	24	1.08	.83	3
			MOI	26	1.46	.90	3
		Post 1	PI	24	2.50	.66	3
			MOI	26	2.35	.85	3
		Post 2	PI	24	2.33	.87	3
			MOI	26	2.27	1.04	3
	Production	Pretest	PI	24	.08	.28	2
			MOI	26	.08	.27	2
		Post 1	PI	24	1.71	.69	2
			MOI	26	1.56	.75	2
		Post 2	PI	24	1.40	.77	2
			MOI	26	1.50	.81	2
Irregulars	Interpretation	Pretest	PI	24	1.33	.87	3
			MOI	26	1.23	.91	3
		Post 1	PI	24	2.17	.87	3
			MOI	26	2.35	.89	3
		Post 2	PI	24	2.17	.92	3
			MOI	26	2.42	.95	3
	Production	Pretest	PI	24	.02	.10	2
			MOI	26	.07	.23	2
		Post 1	PI	24	.92	.75	2
			MOI	26	1.17	.58	2
		Post 2	PI	24	.73	.66	2
			MOI	26	.94	.70	2
Novels	Interpretation	Pretest	PI	24	.79	.83	3
			MOI	26	.88	.86	3
		Post 1	PI	24	1.88	.99	3
			MOI	26	2.31	.84	3
		Post 2	PI	24	2.33	.64	3
			MOI	26	2.00	1.02	3
	Production	Pretest	PI	24	.06	.22	2
			MOI	26	.17	.42	2
		Post 1	PI	24	1.52	.65	2
			MOI	26	1.38	.75	2
		Post 2	PI	24	1.46	.79	2
			MOI	26	1.37	.74	2

TABLE 7.3
Results of ANOVAs Performed for Item Type Analyses

Task	Item Type	Instruction Type			Time			Instruction Type x Time		
		df	F	p	df	F	p	df	F	p
Interpretation	Regular	1	.11	.74	2	30.52	.00	2	1.55	.22
	Irregular	1	.68	.41	2	18.71	.00	2	.51	.60
	Novel	1	.18	.68	2	39.19	.00	2	2.59	.08
Production	Regular	1	.02	.89	2	107.53	.00	2	.61	.55
	Irregular	1	2.40	.13	2	59.85	.00	2	.60	.55
	Novel	1	.12	.73	2	78.94	.00	2	.60	.55

Note: PI: n = 24; MOI: n = 26.

all three item types—that is, items requiring the production of regular, irregular, and novel subjunctives.

Three separate ANOVAs were performed for the item type analyses of each task (interpretation and production)—one on regular verb data, one on irregular verb data, and one on novel verb data. In all three cases, for both the interpretation data and the production data, there was a significant main effect for Time. This indicates that both instruction types had a significant effect on the how participants performed on all three item types of both the interpretation task and the production task. In addition, in all six analyses (three for interpretation, three for production), there was no significant effect for Instruction Type and no significant interaction between Instruction Type and Time. This means that, although both groups improved after treatment, they performed similarly on all three item types of the interpretation task and on all three item types of the production task. Table 7.3 reports the results for each of the six ANOVAs performed.

In summary, for each of the three item types (regular verbs, irregular verbs, and novel verbs), both PI and MOI resulted in immediate effects and effects over time. This initial and sustained improvement was evident on all three item types of both the interpretation task and production task. Finally, no statistical difference with any item type was found between the performance of the two groups. It should also be noted that participants in both groups were able to maintain their performance on the *indicative* items after treatment. The two-way analyses of variance (ANOVA) with repeated measures performed on the indicative item data for both the interpretation task and the production task reveal a significant effect for test. This indicates that both instruction types had a significant effect on indicative item performance. However, there was no significant effect for instruction type and no significant interaction between instruction type and test. This means that although both groups improved after treatment on indicative items, there was no significant difference between the improvement of the MOI and PI groups. For the interpretation task, participants in both groups tended to select fewer clauses of doubt in the presence of indicative tokens after the treatment. For the production task, participants were producing fewer subjunctives (or incorrect forms) after a clause expressing assertion. These results indicate that there was no significant overuse of the subjunctive as a result of the treatment.

In addition to the comparative effects already discussed, ANOVAs were also performed on the item type data within PI and within MOI. These were carried out in order to investigate whether or not the mean scores within one treatment group would differ based on item type. The results revealed that there was no effect for item type for either group on the interpretation task. This indicates that, within both treatments, participant ability to interpret irregular subjunctives improved as much as their ability to interpret regular forms. In addition, the results indicate that the presence of novel forms (forms not seen during instruction) did not affect participant ability to interpret utterances in the assessment task. However, for both treatment groups, there was an effect for item type on the production task. Figures 7.3 and 7.4 provide a visual representation of the effects for morphology type that occurred within each instruction type on the production task. (Because the interpretation data did not yield significant effects for morphology type within PI or within MOI, interaction plots are not presented here for the interpretation task.) On the production task, participants in both treatment groups improved more on items containing regular morphology than on items containing irregular subjunctives. In addition, they produced novel verbs (also regular in form) just as well as the regular subjunctive forms that were seen and heard during the treatment. Table 7.4 summarizes the interpretation and production results of the ANOVAs performed on the item type data within each treatment group.

For the production data, post-hoc Scheffé analyses revealed statistically significant differences within the PI group between regular and irregular items, and between novel and irregular items. Within the MOI group, the only statistically significant difference was between the regular and irregular items. Table 7.5 summarizes the results of the two post-hoc Scheffé analyses.

Within both groups, participants improved more on regular items than on irregular items on the production task. Also, within the PI group, participants improved more with verbs not seen during treatment (but regular in form) than on irregular verbs that were presented in the treatment. Overall, these findings lend support to the notion that the irregularity of a form does have an effect on L2 learners' ability to produce subjunctives after expressions of uncertainty regardless of treatment.

DISCUSSION

The results of the present study differ from those of previous research that has compared processing instruction with traditional instruction (VanPatten & Cadierno, 1993; Cadierno, 1995; Cheng, 1995) in that PI does not appear to have been more beneficial to learners than the MOI group. In fact, the results of this experiment show that PI and MOI had very similar effects on how learners interpreted and produced regular, irregular, and novel subjunctives, as well as subjunctive forms in general. These results mirror those of Collentine (1998). Although the production-oriented materials were different (traditional TI versus MOI), the gains were similar for the production groups in both studies. In addition, although Collentine's PI materials were different from the PI materials designed for the present study, the gains for both processing groups were similar. Finally, the results were similar for both studies with regard to the relative effects of the two instruction types. In light of these similarities, it appears less defensible to claim that the design of Collentine's PI materials contributed to the processing group only equaling the production group. Although this position seemed plausible in light of the results of Farley (2001), it is no longer tenable. Two possibilities emerge here: the first, that the TI group in Collentine did not contain mechanical activities to the same degree and type as in VanPatten and Cadierno (thus being more MOI-like), the second, that there is something about the nature of the subjunctive that causes the results in our two studies to be different from those of other PI-oriented studies. The first possibility would require an examination of Collentine's TI materials, something that is beyond the scope of the present discussion. As VanPatten and Wong (chap 5, this volume) point out, it is clear that any comparative study involving different researchers is bound to lead to either subtle and perhaps profound differences in the operationalization of treatments and assessments that could affect the outcome of a study. In the present study, the MOI was purposefully constructed to be different from TI and so the outcomes are not so surprising. Because of the similarity in results across the various PI studies conducted by VanPatten and his colleagues in which TI was a point of comparison, Collentine's findings would lead one to conclude that there must be something about the how the treatments or assessments were realized. Again, one would need to examine the materials in detail to support such a claim.

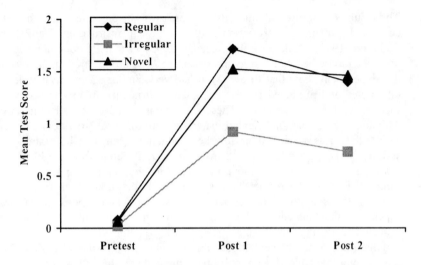

FIG. 7.3. Interaction Plot for Verb Type and Time *Within* PI.

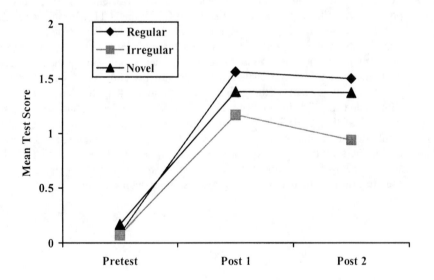

FIG. 7.4. Interaction Plot for Verb Type and Time *Within* MOI.

TABLE 7.4
Results of ANOVAS Performed *Within* Each Treatment

Treatment	N	Task	Verb Type			Time			Verb Type x Time		
			df	F	p	df	F	p	df	F	p
PI	24	Interpr	2	2.15	.13	2	51.26	.00	4	2.00	.10
	24	Produc	2	11.19	.00	2	128.10	.00	4	4.18	.00
MOI	26	Interpr	2	2.49	.09	2	36.46	.00	4	.77	.55
	26	Produc	2	4.21	.02	2	117.04	.00	4	1.72	.15

TABLE 7.5
Results of Post-hoc Scheffe for Verb Types in Production Task

Treatment	Verb Type (+)	Verb Type (-)	Mean Difference	Standard Error	Significance
PI	regular	irregular	.507	.1182	.00
	regular	novel	.049	.1182	.92
	novel	irregular	.458	.1182	.00
MOI	regular	irregular	.314	.1136	.03
	regular	novel	.071	.1136	.83
	novel	irregular	.244	.1136	.11

As for the subjunctive being different from other structures and thus having some kind of effect, it is not clear just what this difference might be. The variety of structures researched in the various PI studies so far would not readily suggest that structure type would make a difference. However, there is one thing different about the structure in the present study (as well as Collentine's) from those used in other PI research: as complex and difficult as the subjunctive actually is, we have centered research on just one use, and a very easy one to grasp at that: if one wishes to express disbelief or some kind of doubt, use the subjunctive. (In Collentine's case, the use of the subjunctive was with antecedents and relative clauses: If the antecedent is not known to actually exist, use the subjunctive.) Indeed, such simple rules are fairly easy to monitor for under the present task conditions. If we compare this to the issues surrounding word order and case marking, copula choice in Spanish, causative and non-causative structures, and so on, perhaps the structure—or better yet the reduction in use—is affecting the results of the present study compared to those of others. The only possible argument against this is the results of Cadierno (1995) and Benati (2001). These studies compared PI and TI with simple past and future tense, respectively. Although the simple past in Spanish does involve a complex morphological paradigm, both it and the future involve simple uses that are not novel to English speakers (something is either past or it isn't; something is either future or it isn't). Yet the results of both those studies are almost identical to those in the original VanPatten and Cadierno study. Thus, the two studies provide a counter example to our arguments about the subjunctive as a formal feature affecting the outcomes. In short, we are back to the issue of operationalization of constructs within a study and there must be something in the Collentine materials that are causing the results to appear like those of the present study, and not those of previous PI research.

Another interesting result of the present study was that, although the interpretation data yielded no effect for irregular morphology within either group, an analysis of the production data did reveal statistically lower means for the production of irregular forms. From this finding, logical questions arise. Why would performance on irregular items be any different than performance on regular items? Does the acquisition of regular morphology occur any differently from the acquisition of irregular morphology? To briefly address these questions, I turn to a number of neurobiological studies that have investigated how regular and irregular inflectional morphology is processed by the human brain.

Neurobiological research on first language processing lends support to the notion that the processing of regular and irregular morphology occurs via two brain processes that are anatomically, physiologically, and psycholinguistically distinct. For example, Marcus et al. (1992) proposed that both children and adult monolinguals mark past tense by making use of memory for irregular forms. In contrast, for regular forms, Marcus et al. claimed that learners adhere to an affixation rule by which, given any root, they can produce a regular form. Clahsen et al. (1992) point out that even impaired children make a distinction between regular and irregular plural markers for nouns during online processing of their native language. Penke et al. (1997) concluded that the monolingual brain processes regularly inflected words differently from irregular inflected words. To be specific, Penke et al. purported that regular morphology is processed via a computation that analyzes roots and inflectional affixes separately, whereas each irregular form is stored and accessed as an individual full-form entry in the lexicon. Finally, in Weyerts et al. (1997), an examination of the participants' brain negativities when reading L1 utterances led the researchers to conclude that regularly inflected plural nouns are processed in a manner different from plurals with irregular inflection.

Referring only to L1 acquisition, all of the aforementioned studies suggest that the processes involved in producing regular morphology are different from those involved in producing irregular morphology. In the present study, there was an effect for morphology type within both treatment groups on the production task. This result lends support (although not physiological in nature) to the notion that, like L1 learners, L2 learners also produce regulars and irregulars via two different sets of processes.

The discussion now turns to the question of why the PI group and the MOI group in the present experiment performed similarly and why the present results differ from the majority of research comparing PI with traditional instruction. One might suggest that the Spanish subjunctive does not lend itself well to PI. However, the results show that the PI group's mean score more than doubled from pre- to posttest for the interpretation task. In addition, the PI mean increased more than 21 times from pre- to posttest for the production task. In light of these improvements, it can be argued it was the efficacy of MOI, and not an ineffective PI treatment, that caused both groups to be statistically similar.

A distinction can be made between the MOI treatment used in the present experiment and the traditional instruction used in studies such as VanPatten and Cadierno (1993), Cadierno (1995), Cheng (1995), and VanPatten and Wong (this volume). In contrast to the aforementioned studies, the output-oriented treatment in this experiment had no mechanical component. There was no traditional practice of form or movement from more mechanical to more meaningful drills. Each MOI activity pushed learners to express opinions and beliefs using the subjunctive. Although the more meaningful nature of MOI may have been a factor influencing the equal performance between groups, it is by no means the only difference between MOI and traditional output-oriented instruction. In the MOI treatment, the learners responded by producing subjunctives in utterance-initial position. Therefore, when learners gave a correct answer to a particular activity item, their answer might have served as incidental structured input for other participants in the treatment. Indeed, MOI provided incidental input as would any output-oriented instruction type involving oral responses, but the structure of the incidental input provided by MOI mirrors the structure of input contained in a typical PI activity. This additional input may have carried some incidental effects similar to the intended effects of PI. Coupled with the explicit information regarding processing strategies, the MOI group may have been more PI-like than intended (see VanPatten & Wong, this volume, for a similar observation on the study by Allen, 2000).

One might argue that the results of the present study lend support to the idea that output practice itself (and not incidental input received during output practice) directly contributes to second language acquisition. However, the fact remains that no model or theory of SLA has been able to posit a learning mechanism that directly links output with the developing system. Input Processing, Universal Grammar, Connectionism, the Competition Model, and other current theories of SLA all link input with the development of the learner's internal system. Even The Output Hypothesis never makes the claim that output leads directly to acquisition; rather it argues that output stimulates the interaction of other processes that promote acquisition (Swain, 1998).

It has already been noted that the interpretation data for the MOI group in the present study differs from the interpretation data for the traditional groups in VanPatten & Cadierno (1993), Cadierno (1995), and Cheng (1995). However, Farley (2001) also found that the PI group outperformed the MOI group on the interpretation task. Recall that, due to time constraints, the learners in Farley (2001) completed a total of only eight activities. One might speculate that more exposure to the subjunctive and more practice with the forms (10 activities, all of equal or more content) in the present study could explain the different result. In other words, the fact that the MOI group received more incidental input in this MOI treatment than in the Farley (2001) treatment may account for the MOI group equaling the processing group on the interpretation task.

CONCLUSION

The roles of input and output in second language acquisition remain a point of contention among SLA theorists and practitioners. A number of contemporary studies provide evidence that input is the most important factor in SLA. However, as this study has shown, further research is needed to determine what differential and complimentary effects processing instruction and meaning-based output instruction have on L2 acquisition of a variety of linguistic forms and structures. In addition, research is needed to fully understand what factors may have caused the MOI group in the present experiment to perform as well as the PI group on the interpretation task. A comparison of the effects of input-free MOI, delivered via isolated computer terminals, with the effects of processing instruction, delivered via the same medium, might offer a better picture of which variables within MOI work to promote acquisition of the Spanish subjunctive (see Sanz, this volume, for an example of a PI study conducted with CALL). Identification of these variables could lead to the development of foreign language teaching curricula that combine the beneficial components of both PI and MOI in a single technology enhanced instruction type. With the current pedagogical trend toward computer-assisted language learning, this vein of research now becomes indispensable. Finally, it is important to note that PI has never failed to yield significant improvement on both interpretation and production tasks. The fact that MOI yielded results similar to those of PI in the present study does not obviate what has been shown, for example, in the rest of this volume and in previous research. PI consistently yields significant gains in both interpretation and production tasks. It is not clear that the same can be said of any output approach, including MOI, as operationalized in this study. What remains to be seen is whether MOI has a consistently strong impact on how learners interpret and produce various target language features and if it can consistently bring about effects similar to those of PI.

REFERENCES

Cadierno, T. (1995). Formal instruction from a processing perspective: An investigation into the Spanish past tense. *The Modern Language Journal, 79,* 179–193.

Cheng, A. (1995). *Grammar instruction and input processing: The acquisition of Spanish ser and estar.* Unpublished doctoral dissertation, University of Illinois, Urbana–Champaign.

Clahsen, H., Rothweiler, M., Woest, A., & Marcus, G. (1992). Regular and irregular inflection in the acquisition of German noun plurals. *Cognition, 45,* 225–255.

Collentine, J. G. (1993). *The development of complex syntax and the selection of mood by foreign language learners of Spanish.* Unpublished doctoral dissertation, University of Texas, Austin.

Collentine, J. G. (1995). The development of complex syntax and mood-selection abilities by intermediate-level learners of Spanish. *Hispania, 78,* 122–136.

Collentine, J. G. (1997). Irregular verbs and noticing the Spanish subjunctive. *Spanish Applied Linguistics, 1,* 3–23.

Collentine, J. G. (1998). Processing instruction and the subjunctive. *Hispania, 81,* 576–587.

DeKeyser, R., & Sokalski, K. (1996). The differential role of comprehension and production practice. *Language Learning, 46,* 613–642.

Farley, A. P. (2001). Authentic processing instruction and the Spanish subjunctive. *Hispania, 84,* 289–299.

Lee, J., & VanPatten, B. (1995). *Making communicative language teaching happen.* New York: McGraw-Hill.

Marcus, G., Pinker, S., Ullman, M., Hollander, M., & Rosen, T. (1992). Overregularization in language acquisition. *Monographs of the Society for Research in Child Development, 57,* R5–R65.

Penke M., Weyerts, H., Gross, M., Zander, E., Munte, T., & Clahsen, H. (1997). How the brain processes complex words: An event-related potential study of German verb inflections. *Cognitive Brain Research, 6,* 37–52.

Pereira, I. (1996). *Markedness and instructed SLA: An experiment in teaching the Spanish subjunctive.* Unpublished doctoral dissertation, University of Illinois, Urbana–Champaign.

Swain, M. (1998). The output hypothesis, second language learning and immersion education. In J. Arnau & J. Artigal (Eds.), *Immersion programs: A European perspective* (pp. 127–140). Barcelona, Spain: Publicacions de la Universitat de Barcelona.

VanPatten, B. (1993). Grammar teaching for the acquisition-rich classroom. *Foreign Language Annals, 26,* 435–450.

VanPatten, B. (1996). *Input processing and grammar instruction: Theory and research.* Norwood, NJ: Ablex.

VanPatten, B. (1997). The relevance of input processing to second language acquisition theory and second language instruction. In A. T. Pérez-Leroux & W. R. Glass (Eds.), *Contemporary perspectives on the acquisition of Spanish: Vol. 2. Production, processing, and comprehension* (pp. 93–108). Somerville, MA: Cascadilla Press.

VanPatten, B. (2002). Processing instruction: An update. *Language Learning, 52,* 755–803.

VanPatten, B., & Cadierno, T. (1993). Input processing and second language acquisition: A role for instruction. *The Modern Language Journal, 77,* 45–57.

Weyerts, H., Penke, M., Dohrn, U., Clahsen, H., & Munte, T. (1997). Brain potentials indicate differences between regular and irregular German plurals. *NeuroReport, 8,* 957–962.

APPENDIX

Referential PI Activity: Tu instructor(a)

You will hear the second half of a statement that someone recently made about your instructor. Circle the opinion phrase that correctly fits with each statement.

      1.   Yo sé que…
             No creo que…
      2.   Es obvio que…
             Dudo que…
      3.   Estoy seguro que…
             No es verdad que…

(7 more activity items of identical structure)

INSTRUCTOR'S SCRIPT
      1.   …coma en casa mucho.
      2.   …baile mucho en las discotecas.
      3.   …hace su tarea por la noche.

(7 more script items of identical structure)

Affective PI Activity: La "Enquirer"

Below are some opinions about *The National Enquirer*. Check off the opinions that you agree with.

No creo que la revista "Enquirer"…

       ___   haga buenas investigaciones.
       ___   cueste mucho dinero.
       ___   ponga la verdad en los artículos.
       ___   sea publicada en español.
       ___   tenga dinero de personas en esta clase.

(more activity items of same format)

Referential MOI Activity: Los animales domésticos

Paso 1: Are pets really like us? You will hear the first part of a sentence about a pet. Change the verb in parenthesis to correctly complete each sentence.

      1. _____ (ser) muy inteligente.
      2. _____ (tener) emociones.
      3. _____ (hablar) una lengua inteligente.
      4. _____ (necesitar) amigos.

INSTRUCTOR'S SCRIPT

    1.   No creo que el perro…
    2.   Es dudoso que el pez…
    3.   Es posible que el gato…
    4.   Es improbable que el serpiente…
(more activity items of same format)

Affective MOI Activity: Michael Jordan

Choose phrases from List B at the bottom of the page and match them with phrases from List A which express your opinion about Michael Jordan. Make sure to change the verbs in List B so that they make sense in each sentence.

LISTA A

    1. No creo que…_____
    2. Es dudoso que…_____
    3. Estoy seguro que…_____
(six more items of same format)

LISTA B

    1. escuchar música mientras levanta pesas.
    2. ser un hombre perezoso.
    3. ser el mejor jugador del mundo.
(six more choices of the same format)

Chapter 8

Commentary: Where PI Research Has Been and Where It Should Be Going

Joseph Collentine
Northern Arizona University

In this commentary, I first begin by couching Processing Instruction's importance as an instructional strategy within the larger debate on the efficacy of so-called Focus-on-Form(s) strategies for affecting grammatical development. I argue that the merits of Processing Instruction are found largely outside of this debate, and suggest that Processing Instruction's association with this debate has left an important question unanswered even after 10 years of research: What happens to grammatical development after Processing Instruction treatments? I then argue that continuing to contextualize Processing Instruction's merits within the Focus-on-Form(s) debate may ultimately be validating traditional approaches to grammar instruction. I conclude by discussing why we still do not know if Processing Instruction can achieve its ultimate goal of training learners to process input in ways that they would otherwise not do.

PROCESSING INSTRUCTION WITHIN THE FOCUS-ON-FORM, FOCUS-ON-FORMS, AND FOCUS-ON-MEANING DEBATE

The adoption of principles of communicative language instruction in foreign-language (FL) and second-language (L2) contexts in the 1980s shifted the perspectives of many researchers and instructors in terms of the importance of listening and reading. Up to that point, speaking and writing abilities were considered "active" skills whereas listening and reading were considered "passive" skills. Morley (1990) reminds researchers that learners are anything but idle when engaging in listening-comprehension activities. She argues that

listening comprehension is an active process rather than a passive state: "...
listening is no passive experience in two-way communication, or in one-way
communication, or in self-generated communication. All are highly active
participatory experiences" (p. 330). Krashen's Monitor Model (1982) and its
instructional manifestation known as the Natural Approach (Krashen & Terrell,
1983) validated the importance of the active nature of input-rich instructional
environments. Indeed, Larsen-Freeman and Long (1991) imply that input is the
most important means by which learners obtain data with which to build an
accurate representation of the target language, affirming that there are no known
cases of successful language acquisition without exposure to some form of
comprehensible input.

At the same time empirical studies were raising doubts about the ability of
comprehensible input to affect grammatical development. Canadian immersion
programs were reporting that learners' grammars were deficient (see Sanz,
2000). Even Terrell (1991) acknowledged that comprehensible input was not
sufficient for the acquisition of many structures. VanPatten (1993) subsequently
posed a quite simple question that has proven difficult to answer: "What kind of
grammar instruction fits with our newer context and input-rich communicative
classrooms?" (p. 435).

Two principal approaches to this dilemma arose in the study of second-
language acquisition (SLA). On the one hand, instruction could take a "Focus
on Form" (FonF) approach to grammar instruction, providing reactive
interventions to breakdowns in comprehension that encourage learners to focus
on some linguistic feature (e.g., an inflection or a functor) present in input that
learners are processing for meaning (Long, 1991). This approach was seen as a
compromise between the two dominant strategies of grammar instruction: (1)
The more traditional "Focus of Forms" (FonFS) instruction, in which language
curricula carefully sequence the introduction of grammatical phenomena to
learners according to the relative linguistic complexity of the phenomena to be
taught, such as the Grammar-Translation approach. In FonFS, activities are
mechanical in nature, asking learners to manipulate and alter structures without
being mindful of whether students are making form-meaning connections; (2)
"Focus on Meaning" (FonM), where learners either concentrate on the message
that they are to communicate or that they are to extract from input, which was
proving to be less-than-adequate for affecting grammatical development (e.g.,
the Natural Approach).

VanPatten, on the other hand, appears not to have concluded that the
shortcomings of FonM approaches could best be solved by pure FonF
approaches, which effectively required that instructors who provided
comprehensible input change their reactions to breakdowns in comprehension—
that is, by stopping to help learners see which form(s) is/are causing the
breakdown and what the form(s) mean(s) (See Figure 8.1). VanPatten (1993)
proposed that instruction change the behaviors of learners' cognitive
mechanisms that extract meaning from input. VanPatten and his colleagues

demonstrated that learners' input-processing mechanisms often interpret input incorrectly or they process it in ways that make it impossible to extract linguistic information (e.g., the phonological properties of inflections and the abstract meanings that they connote) that they could use to continue to develop a representation of the target language's grammar. Consequently, VanPatten (1993, 1996; VanPatten & Cadierno, 1993) posited that learners' grammatical development would be advanced with comprehensible input if they were trained to process input in different ways:

> It would seem reasonable, then, to suggest that rather than manipulate learner output to effect change in the developing system, instruction might seek to change the way that input is perceived and processed by the learner. (VanPatten & Cadierno, 1993, p. 227).

Nonetheless, the key difference between pure FonF approaches and that of VanPatten's Processing Instruction is what each attempts to alter within the mind of the learner: Whereas FonF is concerned with altering the elements of language that reside in the learner's developing system (e.g., particular inflections, their interrelationships, particular lexemes), Processing Instruction is concerned with the cognition that supports development (e.g., general principles for interpreting words and inflections when they reside in working memory).

In a sense, the merits of Processing Instruction should be considered outside of the Focus-on-X debate because its primary purpose appears not to be to make direct changes to the developing system, which advocates of FonF, FonFS, and FonM believe occurs within each of these three strategies. Processing Instruction attempts to alter the processing mechanisms so that the grammatical system might be better ready to respond to comprehensible input and therefore grow. In fact, all of the studies in this section show that this novel approach to grammar instruction is effective. This association of Processing Instruction with the Focus-on-X debate has produced two consequences. First, the primary difference between pure FonF and Processing Instruction has not been obvious to many researchers assessing the potential merits of Processing Instruction. Most efforts to replicate (e.g., Collentine, 1998; DeKeyser & Sokalski, 1996; Salaberry, 1997) the findings of VanPatten and his colleagues have not adequately focused on changing some processing mechanism relevant to a given grammatical structure. Instead they have probably provided learners with opportunities to notice forms to which they would not otherwise adhere, like pure FonF.

Focus on Form: Draw attention to forms causing comprehension breakdowns.

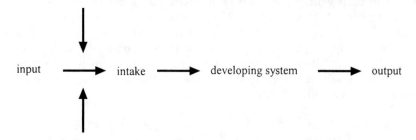

Processing Instruction: Focused practice to alter processing mechanisms.

FIG. 8.1. The Relationship Between Focus-on-Form, Processing Instruction, and Grammatical Development (adapted from VanPatten & Cadierno, 1993).

Second, and as a result of the first consequence, VanPatten and his colleagues have concentrated their efforts on testing the efficacy of Processing Instruction by continuing to compare its merits to FonFS, which has left a basic question unanswered after almost 10 years of research. As the chapters in this section reveal, much effort continues to be invested in comparing the relative benefits of Processing Instruction to so-called traditional grammar instruction, which is essentially FonFS. Research efforts would be more productive if investigators were now to simply assert that Processing Instruction is a proven beneficial strategy for promoting grammatical development in an input-rich environment. Given the research on Processing Instruction's efficacy to date, such an assumption would be quite reasonable (see VanPatten, 2002). With such an approach, the following pressing question might begin to be addressed in earnest:

> What is it that Processing Instruction trains students to do? Make form-meaning connections during Processing Instruction treatments and/or afterwards (i.e., in the input they encounter after Processing Instruction treatments)?

Before commenting further on the need and on the how to address this, it is important to discuss further why it might be time to abandon comparisons between the efficacy of Processing Instruction and traditional methods of grammar instruction.

PROCESSING INSTRUCTION VERSUS TRADITIONAL GRAMMAR INSTRUCTION

In a sense, a good deal of Processing Instruction research has served to validate FonFS approaches to grammar instruction. VanPatten and Wong (this volume) provide a clear motive for examining Processing Instruction's efficacy relative to traditional grammar instruction:

> Our reason for the selection of TI (traditional grammar instruction) for the experiments was (and still is) that TI is the *dominant form of grammar instruction in foreign languages in the U.S.* We were thus exploring PI vs. TI in order to couch our research within some kind of ecological validity. In this way, we could speak to researchers as well as practicing instructors regarding our results. We are aware that in some circles (most notably ESL in the U.S. and Canada) that TI may not be prevalent and that focus on form may be entirely meaning-oriented. But we are also aware that TI is still used around the world in a number of FL contexts and that a good deal of practitioners believe passionately in the use of drills and mechanically-oriented activities. (this volume, p. 104)

It is reasonable to assume that many L2 and FL educators will not retreat from the use of explanation plus output practice. It is my suspicion, however, that, in an important yet subtle way, the research agenda to investigate whether Processing Instruction is superior to traditional grammar instruction has served to validate the latter as much as the former. I show here that, while the so-called "effect size" (a *standardized* statistical measurement of a group's improvement within some treatment) of Processing Instruction treatments has been large, the effect size of traditional grammar instruction has been large as well, indicating that students learn much from such traditional approaches to grammar instruction. The consequence of this pattern may be that teachers and curriculum designers are yet to be convinced that their traditional practices will not adequately meet their objectives.

According to VanPatten, traditional instruction is defined as "explanation plus output practice that moves learners from mechanical to communicative drills" (VanPatten, 2000, p. 54; see also VanPatten & Cadierno, 1993, p. 498). The fact that this particular approach is careful to focus students' attention on the properties of individual forms, how those forms might change paradigmatically, and that this approach does not emphasize the need to make form-meaning connections suggests that traditional instruction is a type of FonFS. Processing Instruction, on the other hand, is constantly attentive to the need to make form-meaning connections and students make such connections in the context of meaningful communicative acts. Structured input exercises force students to make form-meaning connections with respect to a given grammatical phenomenon so that they can comprehend the message of the input they receive. Thus, Processing Instruction is a type of FonF, which VanPatten acknowledges: "It is important to note that Processing Instruction is not just another comprehension-based approach to language instruction [i.e., FonM] such as TPR or immersion; Processing Instruction is a focus on form that serves as a supplement to existing communicative and acquisition-oriented approaches..." (VanPatten, 2000, p. 52).

In the larger context of SLA, both FonF and FonFS approaches in general have proven to be effective agents of learning and neither proven to be more effective than the other in the short term. Norris and Ortega (2000) examine the relative benefits of FonF and FonFS approaches in a meta-analysis of 77 research studies conducted between 1980 and 1998, concluding:

> ...although both FonF and FonFS instructional approaches result in large and probabilistically trustworthy gains over the course of an investigation, the magnitude of these gains differs very little between the two instructional categories. (p. 210)

Norris and Ortega calculate the benefits of any particular treatment with an assessment of the treatment's effect size, which represents the magnitude of a treatment's impact (or lack thereof) on learning. Mathematically speaking, Norris and Ortega calculate effect size with a statistic know as Cohen's (1988) d, which indicates the effect of a treatment on a scale of standard deviations (e.g., a treatment producing an effect size of 2.0 indicates that the learners' average improvement was two standard deviations based on the study's assessment measured).

$$\text{Cohen's } d = (\text{mean}_{\text{pretest}} - \text{mean}_{\text{posttest}}) \div \text{pooled standard deviation}$$

This formula allows a researcher to compare the effect sizes for a number of treatments across studies without having to resort to "vote-counting" procedures for comparing the overall relative effectiveness of different treatments.

Two of the four studies reported in this section lend themselves to a comparison of the overall effect size of Processing Instruction and traditional instruction. VanPatten and Wong (this volume) provide data from two different universities. VanPatten and Cadierno (1993) provide another data set that compares Processing Instruction and traditional instruction. To increase the size of the data set, I have included the results reported in Cadierno (1995), who examines Processing Instruction's efficacy with the Spanish preterite as compared to the efficacy of traditional instruction. A comparison of the pretest-posttest data sets from these studies (disregarding delayed posttest effects) appears in Table 8.1.Two important patterns emerge from this analysis. First, Processing Instruction obviously has a greater overall effect size than traditional instruction, and its efficacy is particularly obvious in interpretation tasks. An analysis of variance (ANOVA) examining the main effect for group (i.e., Processing Instruction versus more traditional strategies) indicated that the greater effect for Processing Instruction approached significance, $F(1, 12) = 3.29, p = 0.095$. The ANOVA found no effect for task type (interpretation versus

TABLE 8.1.
Average Effect Sizes of PI and TI Based on Cadierno (1995), VanPatten & Cadierno (1993), and VanPatten & Wong (2003).

Task and Group	n	Mean	SD
Interpretation			
PI	4	8.04	7.51
TI	4	1.56	.69
Production			
PI	4	3.15	.67
TI	4	2.74	.58
Total			
PI	8	5.59	5.59
TI	8	2.15	.86

production task), $F(1, 12) = 0.96, p = 0.347$ and no interaction between group and task, $F(1, 12) = 2.55, p = 0.136$, which is more than likely due to the fact that Processing-Instruction interpretation tasks varied greatly (M = 8.04; SD = 7.51). Clearly, Processing Instruction affords learners a significant advantage in adhering to grammatical phenomena that they might otherwise overlook in listening and reading tasks.

Second, Norris and Ortega report from their meta-analysis that the overage effect size for FonF treatments is about one standard deviation. The analysis presented here speaks well for Processing Instruction, since its effect size seems to be about six standard deviations. Note, however, that the traditional grammar instruction groups have effect sizes that are double what Norris and Ortega report for FonF studies. To be sure, Norris and Ortega explain that FonF is not overall more effective than FonFS because both produce an average effect size of 1.0. Thus, it is even more interesting to note that traditional instruction treatments of Cadierno (1995), VanPatten and Cadierno (1993), and VanPatten and Wong (2003) have an average effect size of about two standard deviations.[1]

---

[1]The Farley study (this volume, chap. 7) was not included because the modified output group is most likely a FonF rather than a FonFS: the Farley modified output treatment appears to keep learners focused on meaning at all times. Still, to verify the trend reported in Table 8.1, I ran another analysis including the Farley groups, producing a

This limited analysis indicates the Processing Instruction produces very large effect sizes, and so it is inarguably a powerful instructional strategy for affecting grammatical development. However, given that non-Processing-Instruction treatments have consistently produced large effect sizes in and of themselves, it is not surprising that some researchers question the "superior" nature of Processing Instruction. The data unequivocally indicate that both Processing Instruction and traditional grammar instruction do a better than adequate job at helping learners to internalize new grammatical information, which is consistent with Norris and Ortega's (2000) finding that FonFS may be equally as effective as FonF. The reasons with which Norris and Ortega conjecture to explain this finding largely relate to the effect of individual learner differences. They posit that the 77 studies that they surveyed do not adequately consider factors such as language aptitude in general, age, learning style, and developmental readiness as well as the structural complexity of the targeted grammatical phenomenon (e.g., What is the relative effectiveness of Processing Instruction with grammatical phenomenon X at stages A, B, C, D, etc.?).

The stakes in conducting psychometric research are very high. If a carefully designed study does not control for the effects of an agent that could have sufficient importance on the outcome so as to compromise the goal of obtaining a sample that adequately represents the target population, the results are questionable regardless of whether the null hypothesis is accepted or rejected. For instance, if a researcher controlled for general language aptitude and learning style, we might see the overall effect size for Processing Instruction increase. It is my opinion that the incorporation of such considerations requires students of SLA to retool themselves by considering research methodologies and statistical tools allowing for multivariate analyses. The analysis of variance (ANOVA) tool is appropriate for highly controlled experiments. However, multivariate tools, such as discriminant analysis, regression analysis (and other structural equation modeling techniques), allow a researcher to isolate the effects of a given treatment while partialing out the effects of other potential mitigating factors, such as a whole set of individual variables (e.g., aptitude, age, L1 literacy, etc.) and curricular factors (e.g., number of reading/listening activities versus production activities across a semester, contact with the L2 outside of class, etc.). These sorts of techniques have been considered for a long time in the social sciences. The field of SLA has not reached this level of maturity, and to have important effects on curricular design researchers and FL educators may need to explore acquisition from a broader perspective.

---

comparison of Processing Instruction and other types of instruction. The results were very similar, with Processing Instruction having an average effect size of 5.1 and the other treatments an average effect size of 2.2. Again the difference approached significance $F(1, 16) = 3.26; p = .090$.

THE GOAL(S) OF PROCESSING INSTRUCTION

Of course, VanPatten and colleagues would take issue with the statement above that both Processing Instruction and traditional grammar instruction do a better than adequate job at helping learners to internalize new grammatical information. They would counter that Processing Instruction does not intend to help learners to internalize new grammatical information; rather, its purpose is to affect changes in the cognitive tools with which the learner filters out what is and what is not important in the input with respect to the comprehension of messages and with respect to acquisition. In other words, referring again to Figure 8.1, Processing Instruction seeks primarily to alter the *processing mechanisms* relevant to grammatical structure X and secondarily to draw attention to forms and inflections that might enhance comprehension (and so advance acquisition).

Two general principles regarding how learners process input predict the types of strategies learners will use when processing input (VanPatten, 1996, 1997, 2000, this volume). The first principle relates to the interaction between grammar and communicative value, and it leads to a number of corollaries. First, there is the *Primacy of Meaning Principle*: Learners process input for meaning before they process it for form. As mentioned in chapter 1 of the this volume, this principle entails corollaries such as the *Primacy of Content Words Principle*, the *Lexical Preference Principle*, the *Preference for Non-Redundancy Principle*, the *Meaning-Before-Nonmeaning Principle*, the *Availability of Resources Principle*, and the *Sentence Location Principle*. All told, the *Primacy of Meaning Principle* predicts that if a form does not present a targeted grammatical phenomenon in such a way that its meaning (however concrete or abstract) is not important to interpreting a sentence's meaning or if the form is not locationally salient, learners will not intake that form and its grammatical properties.

The second principle relates to grammar and propositional arguments (i.e., Who did what to whom?), a notion that is best captured by the *First Noun Principle*: learners tend to process the first noun or pronoun they encounter in a sentence as the subject/agent. Its corollaries are the *Lexical Semantics Principle*, the *Event Probabilities Principle*, and the *Contextual Constraint Principle*. The implication of this principle is that learners do not tend to look at grammatical cues to interpret the roles of arguments (e.g., agent, patient, beneficiary) when processing input, which can have important implications for how students process and learn from input representing languages whose basic word order is different from that of their first language.

With these principles in mind, processing instruction employs *structured-input tasks*, which are sequences of carefully crafted input sentences that, coupled with a given task demand (i.e., the information that learners must extrapolate from that input), attempt to cause learners' processing mechanisms to fail to interpret a sentence, to cause the learner to become cognizant of such a failure, and finally to encourage the learner to adopt a processing strategy that does not affect such a failure. These tasks help learners make form-meaning connections in one of two ways: by raising the communicative value of a targeted structure or by raising its acoustic salience. In either case, processing instruction's goal is "to *train* the nonnative ear to perceive and utilize the target forms during on-line processing" (Lee, 2000, p. 36, emphasis mine). The key implication is: *after working with structured-input tasks, learners should be able to discern more readily the semantic/pragmatic information that a grammatical phenomenon provides (however abstract) when they encounter the phenomenon in authentic input.* To understand the importance of this statement, a distinction must be made: learner response during an experimental treatment and learner response after an experimental treatment. Processing Instruction purports to have an effect on the learner not only during Processing Instruction treatments but also after such treatments. After all, the goal is to alter the underlying processing mechanisms (relating to some grammatical phenomenon) so that intake (of forms and inflections representing that phenomenon) will occur as the learner continues to learn the target language in an input-rich curriculum (e.g., a classroom setting) or environment (e.g., study abroad).

> During carefully crafted structured input activities, learners receive feedback early on that their processing is incorrect. They realize that what they thought they understood does not match the intended meaning of the speaker. Their internal mechanisms, then, are literally forced to adopt a new strategy and/or abandon the old one. The result is that the accommodation and restructuring mechanisms receive better (in this case, correct) data for internalization. (VanPatten & Fernández, this volume, p. 277)

For heuristic purposes, we could simplify this relationship by distinguishing between two types of input (see Fig. 8.2). Input type A is the structured input that students receive during a Processing Instruction treatment. In various ways, learners are sensitized to the semantic/pragmatic importance of the targeted grammatical phenomenon or to why learners might not attend to the phenomenon. Consequently, input type A (and all of the task demands associated with it) ultimately modifies the underlying processing mechanisms relevant to the phenomenon. It is my assumption, at least, that what is secondary in importance is the effect of Input type A on the developing system. Naturally, there should be some positive effect, but VanPatten and his colleagues appear to be more concerned with the cognitive abilities that learners walk away with after a Processing Instruction intervention, namely, the processing strategies that they adopt as a result of Processing Instruction. If so, input type B—the authentic input that learners process after input type A—should have a strong effect on the status of the targeted grammatical phenomenon within the learner's underlying

Bolded items have a strong response to input. *Italicized items* have a weaker (although potentially significant) response to input.

Input Type A → **Processing mechanisms** → *Developing system*
(specialized
intervention)

Input Type B → *Processing mechanisms* → **Developing system**
(authentic
input)

FIG. 8.2. Predicted Outcomes of PI.

developing system: input type A has served to alter the processing mechanisms relevant to the phenomenon and so intake of the phenomenon when it is present in Input type B should increase thereafter. It is the effects of input type B that have not been investigated to date in the research on Processing Instruction. In other words, we do not know if learners respond to forms constituting the targeted grammatical phenomenon in normal input conditions (i.e., authentic input) once they have left the Processing Instruction laboratory. Using an analogy from the field of genetics, the "expression" of the processing mechanisms should be significantly different after some Processing Instruction under normal environmental pressures than would be their "expression" in the absence of Processing Instruction.

It is possible to retort that Processing Instruction research has addressed this generalizability issue since astute researchers have examined the long-term effects of Processing Instruction. However, at the most, the delayed posttests that these investigators have administered only reveal whether learners' processing mechanisms remain altered as a result of the Processing Instruction intervention; delayed posttests do not reveal whether the learner's developing system is responding differently to authentic input. This should be a key challenge for researchers in the future.

VanPatten and Fernández (this volume) is a first attempt at seriously evaluating whether Processing Instruction truly meets its goal of providing learners with new strategies for processing input. They report that Processing Instruction can cause learners to interpret sentence-initial pronouns correctly up to eight months after treatment time. Indeed, a calculation of the effect sizes of the VanPatten and Fernández experiment indicates that, although the immediate posttest effect sizes for the interpretation and production tasks were low as Processing Instruction goes, d(interpretation) = 2.34; d(production) = 1.57, these effect sizes were still quite respectable eight months later, d(interpretation) = 0.70; d(production) = 0.76. Nevertheless, it is still important to note that

VanPatten and Fernández do not indicate whether the new processing strategy helped learners to properly interpret instances of object pronouns in Input B in their d ay-to-day c urriculum.[2] O ne way to d etermine whether t he students h ad adopted a new strategy would be to examine whether the amount of Input B that individual learners engaged (which presumably contained instances of object pronouns, such as dialogues) in and outside of class was a predictor of gains (or maintenance of gains) at that eight-month post-posttest.

CONCLUSION

Processing Instruction is a unique solution to the conundrum that VanPatten raised in 1993: In an absolutely input-rich environment, how can we remain attentive to learners' grammatical development? Processing Instruction is a powerful solution, with impressive effects on learning. Structured-input tasks challenge learners to make form-meaning connections that they might not otherwise make when they process authentic input whose grammatical information they have not been properly trained to extrapolate. It may be time to abandon comparisons between Processing Instruction and traditional approaches to grammar instruction perhaps until we learn whether it can meet its ultimate objective of retraining the learner's input processing mechanisms.

REFERENCES

Cadierno, T. (1995). Formal instruction from a processing perspective: An investigation into the Spanish past tense. *The Modern Language Journal, 79,*179–193.

Cohen, J. (1988). Statistical power analysis for the behavioral sciences. Hillsdale, NJ: Lawrence Erlbaum Associates.

Collentine, J. (1998). Processing instruction and the subjunctive. *Hispania, 81,* 576–587.

DeKeyser, R., & Sokalski, K. (1996). The differential role of comprehension and production practice. *Language Learning, 46,* 613–642.

Krashen, S. (1982). *Principles and practice in second language acquisition.* Oxford: Pergamon Press.

Krashen, S., & Terrell, T. D. (1983). *The natural approach: Language acquisition in the classroom.* Hayward, CA: Alemany Press.

---

[2]The reader is reminded that for the purposes of their study, VanPatten and Fernández "sanitized" the curriculum and removed as much exposure to object pronouns and OVS order as possible during the eight-month lag between treatment and final posttest. Thus, learners may not have had much opportunity to use new processing strategies while engaged with authentic input.

Larsen-Freeman, D., & Long, M. (1991). *An introduction to second language acquisition research*. London: Longman.

Lee, J. (2000). Five types of input and the various relationships between form and meaning. In J. Lee & A. Valdman (Eds.), *Form and meaning: Multiple perspectives* (pp. 25–42). Boston: Heinle & Heinle.

Long, M. H. (1991). Focus on form: A design feature in language teaching methodology. In K. de Bot, R. Ginsberg & C. Kramsch (Eds.), *Foreign language research in cross-cultural perspective* (pp. 39–52). Amsterdam: John Benjamins.

Morley, J. (1990). Trends and developments in listening comprehension: Theory and practice. In J. E. Atlis (Ed.), *Georgetown University roundtable on language and linguistics 1990* (pp. 317–337). Washington, DC: Georgetown University Press.

Norris, J. M., & Ortega, L. (2000). Does type of instruction make a difference? Substantive findings from a meta-analytic review. *Language Learning, 50,* 157–213.

Salaberry, R. (1997). The role of input and output practice in second language acquisition. *The Canadian Modern Language Review, 53,* 422–451.

Sanz, C. (2000). What form to focus on? Linguistics, language awareness, and education of L2 teachers. In J. Lee & A. Valdman (Eds.), *Form and meaning: Multiple perspectives* (pp. 3–24). Boston, MA: Heinle & Heinle.

Terrell, T. D. (1991). The role of grammar instruction in a communicative approach. *The Modern Language Journal, 75,* 52–63.

VanPatten, B. (1993). Grammar teaching for the acquisition rich classroom. *Foreign Language Annals, 26,* 435–450.

VanPatten, B. (1996). *Input processing and grammar instruction: Theory and research.* Norwood, NJ: Ablex.

VanPatten, B. (1997). The Relevance of input processing to second language theory and second language teaching. In W. R. Glass & A. T. Pérez-Leroux (Eds.), *Contemporary perspectives on the acquisition of Spanish* (pp. 93–108). Sommerville, MA: Cascadilla Press.

VanPatten, B. (2000). Processing instruction as form-meaning connections: Issues in theory and research. In J. Lee & A. Valdman (Eds.), *Form and meaning: Multiple perspectives* (pp. 43–68). Boston, MA: Heinle & Heinle.

VanPatten, B. (2002). Processing instruction: An Update. *Language Learning, 52,* 755–803.

VanPatten, B., & Cadierno, T. (1993). Explicit instruction and input processing. *Studies in Second Language Acquisition, 15,* 225–244.

Part III

The Roles of Structured Input and Explicit Information

The question of whether explicit information provided to learners about a target form is useful has been the focus of research in a number of studies in instructed SLA. In the collection by Schmidt (1995), for example, a number of studies suggest that explicit information is useful if not necessary for noticing and acquiring some grammatical features of language (e.g., Alanen, 1995; Robinson, 1995; outside of the Schmidt volume see also Scott, 1989, as well as the classic study conducted by Doughty, 1991). In these studies and others like them, the overall pattern that emerged is that subjects who receive explicit information tend to outperform both control groups and groups that receive "practice" only.

Are these previous findings generalizable to PI? In VanPatten and Oikkenon (1996), we set out to answer this question. We examined three groups: one that received regular PI from the VanPatten and Cadierno study; one that received structured input only from the PI package of materials; and one that received the explicit information only with no structured input. We set out to answer the following questions:

1. Which is responsible for improved performance on an interpretation test: explicit information, structured input activities, or a combination of the two?
2. Which is responsible for improved performance on a production test: explicit information, structured input activities, or a combination of the two?

If our results were like those of other researchers, we should see that the regular PI group and perhaps the explicit information group should perform better than the group that received structured input only.

Our groups contained the following numbers of subjects: PI = 17; SI only = 20; EI only = 22. The treatments were culled from the VanPatten and Cadierno materials with the processing problem again being the *First-Noun Principle* and OVS word order and clitic object pronouns in Spanish. For the PI group, the

183

subjects received the exact same materials as those in the VanPatten and Cadierno group. For the SI group, the subjects received only the structured input activities. That is, the instructor began the lesson with the first activity (a picture-based activity in which subjects had to determine which picture matched the sentence they heard) but did not tell the subjects what they were learning and did not provide them with prior explicit information. If subjects selected an incorrect picture, the instructor merely said the selection was incorrect, that the other picture was the correct one. No explicit information was provided as feedback on these errors. For the EI group, the subjects only received the explicit information and the examples contained in it. The instructor reviewed the information with them (it was on a handout) and then answered any questions they had. Because the PI and SI treatments lasted several days, the EI group reviewed the information each day.

The exact same assessment tasks used in VanPatten and Cadierno were used: a sentence-level interpretation test and a sentence-level production test. These were administered as a pretest and an immediate posttest with A and B versions of each. To review, the interpretation test consisted of 10 target items and 10 distracters; the production test consisted of five items with five distracters. The interpretation test was based on a referential activity performed by the processing group (e.g., "select the picture that best goes with what you hear") whereas the production test was based on an activity from VanPatten and Cadierno's traditional instructional package (e.g., "complete the sentence based on the pictures you see"). The interpretation test was scored as right or wrong answers for one point each (total = 10 points) and the production test was scored as two points each (2 points if correct use of object pronoun with correct word order, 0 points for no object pronoun, 1 point for incorrect use of object pronoun or problem with word order).

The ANOVAs conducted on the scores revealed that both the PI and SI groups made significant gains on the interpretation test whereas the EI group made no gains at all. The PI and SI gains were identical. On the production test, all three groups made gains. However, the differences between the scores of the PI and the EI group were significantly different while they were not different for the PI and SI groups, although the PI group did make more gains than the SI group. At the same time, the scores between the SI and EI groups were not significantly different on the production test even though the SI group's gains were greater. In short, the results on the production test were: PI = SI, PI > EI, and SI = EI.

We interpreted these findings to mean the following. First, EI is not necessary for PI to be successful. SI alone can cause gains equal to regular PI on both interpretation and production. At the same time, EI alone is insufficient given that PI was better than EI. Second, EI is not necessarily beneficial, either. On the interpretation test, the EI group made literally no improvement while the SI group's scores matched those of the PI group. This finding suggested to us that the EI component contributed nothing to PI and that SI alone was sufficient.

As for production, EI appears to be beneficial given that the SI group's scores on the production test were not significantly greater than those of the EI group although the SI mean score was much higher. However, because there were no statistical differences between the PI and SI scores after treatment but there were between the PI and EI groups' scores, a better conclusion is that SI alone is again sufficient and EI does not play a beneficial or causative role.

These results clearly contrast with those of other researchers. Why the difference? The most obvious one is that the nature of SI activities is quite different from that of other treatments used. Scott (1989) used embeddings in oral narratives (something like an input flood) and Alanen (1995) and Robinson (1995) both used versions of text enhancement. (Other research not cited here but cited in VanPatten and Oikkenon used variations on these two treatments.) PI is markedly different because of the nature of SI; it is the only treatment that identifies a processing problem and then manipulates the input such that learners are pushed away from a faulty or less-than-optimal strategy (see Wong, this volume, chap. 2). Input floods, text enhancement, and other similar treatments merely attempt to make grammatical features salient and/or increase their frequency in the input; they do not force the learner to make form-meaning connections the way PI and SI do.

To be absolutely clear, the point of the VanPatten and Oikkenon study was not to research explicit versus implicit learning, a quite problematic investigative endeavor. The point of the study was simply to see if EI made a difference. It did not. Those who would use the results to suggest that the results of SI only cannot be used to argue for implicit learning or implicit teaching would be incorrect. For me, all intervention in a classroom is explicit in some way. The way to interpret these results is this: SI activities, when created appropriately, do not need the services of EI; EI needs the services of SI activities.

The chapters in Part III present replications of the VanPatten and Oikkenon study using target forms that vary in transparency of meaning, acoustic salience, and morpho-syntactic role. In one study, the focus is not so much on explicit information presented *a priori* but rather the role of explicit information during the feedback used with activities. We will see that overall, SI activities that attempt to address a processing principle tend to be sufficient to cause changes in performance. However, we do find in the studies presented in this section that there is some variation from the original VanPatten and Oikkenon findings, although SI alone consistently appears to result in significant improvement after treatment. What the studies suggest is that the type of linguistic structure may make a difference in terms of whether EI is beneficial and in at least one case that perhaps what EI does is allow learners to monitor on the tasks used in the research. All studies, however, when considered along side VanPatten and Oikkenon's original research, lead to the same conclusion: EI is not necessary as part of PI. SI alone can push along acquisition, although with some structures it may take more SI activities to help them make form-meaning connections.

REFERENCES

Alanen, R. (1995). Input enhancement and rule presentation in second language acquisition. In R. W. Schmidt (Ed.), *Attention and awareness in foreign language learning* (pp. 259–302). Honolulu: University of Hawaii Press.

Doughty, C. (1991). Second language instruction does make a difference: Evidence from an empirical study of ESL relativization. *Studies in Second Language Acquisition, 13,* 431–469.

Robinson, P. (1995). Aptitude, awareness, and the fundamental similarity of implicit and explicit second language learning. In R. W. Schmidt (Ed.), *Attention and awareness in foreign language learning* (pp. 303–349). Honolulu: University of Hawaii Press.

Schmidt, R. W. (1995). Consciousness and foreign language learning: a tutorial on the role of attention and awareness in learning. In R.W. Schmidt (Ed.) *Attention and awareness in foreign language learning* (pp. 1–63). Honolulu: University of Hawaii Press.

Scott, V. (1989). An empircal study of explicit and implicit teaching strategies in French. *The Modern Language Journal, 73,* 14–22.

VanPatten, B., & Oikkenon, S. (1996). Explanation vs. structured input in processing instruction. *Studies in Second Language Acquisition, 18,* 495–510.

Chapter 9

Processing Instruction in French: The Roles of Explicit Information and Structured Input

Wynne Wong
The Ohio State University

VanPatten and Oikkenon (1996) set out to investigate whether it was the EI or SI activities that were responsible for the superior results reported in the empirical studies on PI. The researchers found that SI activities were the causative factor and that EI was not necessary or even beneficial for learners to make significant gains on sentence level tests that measured their acquisition of word order and object pronouns in Spanish. In other words, whether learners had EI or not did not have an impact on the results.

To date, this is the only published study that has separated out the effects of EI and SI activities in PI. Whether the results of VanPatten and Oikkenon could be generalized to other linguistic structures remains to be empirically tested. The purpose of the present study is to further investigate the roles of EI and SI activities in PI to determine if the results from VanPatten and Oikkenon could be generalized to other linguistic forms, specifically, forms of little meaning or communicative value.

BACKGROUND AND MOTIVATION FOR THE PRESENT STUDY

In the VanPatten and Oikkenon (1996) study the target structure was word order and clitic object pronouns. As in the original VanPatten and Cadierno study from which they culled the treatment materials, the particular processing problem the treatment was attempting to affect was the First-Noun Principle. One possibility in the outcome of the VanPatten and Oikkenon study is that word order is such an important cue that once learners receive feedback that they are making incorrect choices about who did what to whom, they quickly tune into word order. The processors engage in sort of an "Ah! The first word is not the subject!" eureka statement and they immediately begin to adjust themselves. In short, the particular structure has important consequences for meaning; if you don't get who did what to whom, you've missed the basic syntactic boat, so to speak. Thus, structured input can easily make a difference because of the relatively high communicative value that word order has once the processing problem is corrected.

But what about structures that don't communicate much or don't communicate new information? One such structure involves a change in article use in French that depends on when a statement is negative or affirmative. In French, the verb *avoir* means "to have." In simple affirmative statements of ownership or in simple statements of existence, the indefinite article is used.

(1) *Marie a un chat.*
   Marie has a cat.
(2) *Bill a un oiseau.*
   Bill has a bird.

When such statements are negative or nonaffirmative, (marked by *ne… pas* around the verb), *de* is used before nouns beginning with a consonant or *d'* before nouns beginning with a vowel. The regular indefinite articles are ungrammatical.

(4) *Marie n'a pas de chat./*Marie n'a pas un chat.*
   Marie does not have a cat.
(5) *Bill n'a pas d'oiseau./ *Bill n'a pas un oiseau.*
   Bill does not have a bird.

Following the Lexical Preference Principle (this volume, chap. 1) learners of French tend to rely on *ne … pas* to get the meaning of negation instead of *de* or *d'* and thus fail to apprehend the *un(e)* vs *de* distinction. The form *de/d'* can be characterized as a form that has no inherent semantic value, that is to say, the form has no meaning in and of itself. The idea of negation is already expressed by *ne … pas,* which is a content word. Using *un/une* or *de/d'* does not communicate any new information. The goal of PI in this case then would be to push learners to pay attention to the *de/un* distinction in order to determine whether the sentence/utterance is negative or affirmative. Given that this structure is quite different from that used in VanPatten and Oikkenon and is affected by a much different processing problem, can learners apprehend the structure in the absence of explicit information?

The purpose of the present study is to examine the generalizability of the findings of VanPatten and Oikkenon. If their results are replicated in the present study, then we will have additional data to support that EI is not necessary in PI.

If, however, the results are not replicated, we will have data to suggest that the results of VanPatten and Oikkenon are limited to the target structure that the researchers investigated.

Research Questions

The research questions for this study are similar to those asked by VanPatten and Oikkenon:
1. Which component of PI is responsible for improved performance on a sentence level interpretation task: EI, SI or a combination of the two?
2. Which component of PI is responsible for improved performance on a sentence level production task: EI, SI or a combination of the two?

METHOD

Participants

Participants for this study were undergraduate students from six sections of a first quarter French course at a Midwestern university. All participants were native speakers of English and had not received any formal instruction on the target structure prior to treatment. Each section was randomly assigned to one of four groups: (1) full PI, (2) EI only, (3) SI only, and (4) a no instruction control group.[1] One hundred and eight participants initially participated in the study. However, to be included in the final data pool, participants had to have been present for the pretest, full treatment, and posttest. Additionally, they had to have scored 60% or lower on the pretest following the criteria in VanPatten and Cadierno (1993) for inclusion. Fourteen subjects failed to meet full criteria for inclusion in the study and were removed. The final n sizes were PI = 26, EI = 22; SI = 25, Control = 21.

Materials

Treatment materials. Three separate treatment packets were designed for this study, one for the PI group, one for the SI group, and one for the EI group. The first page of the packet for the PI group contained EI about the meaning and the function of the target structure. To alert learners to the processing problem, they were told that learners of French tend to skip over the *de/un* distinction and rely instead on *ne … pas* to interpret sentences (see Appendix A). A series of eight SI activities followed the EI. Following the guidelines for creating SI

---

[1]VanPatten and Oikkenon did not include a control group that had no instruction in their study. They used the full PI group as their comparison group.

activities in Lee and VanPatten (1995) and Wong (this volume), these activities pushed participants to rely on the *de/un* distinction to get the meaning of negation (see Appendix B). For example, in Activity A, participants must determine whether or not the couple, the LeBlancs, has the household items listed by filling in the blanks with either "*Nous avons*" (we have) or "*Nous n'avons pas*" (We don't have). Notice that the *ne ... pas* is removed from the phrases so that learners must rely on the articles to determine whether the sentence should be affirmative or negative. By removing *ne ... pas*, participants are forced to pay attention to *de/d'* vs. *un/une/des* to get meaning. To ensure that participants are also keeping meaning in focus as they do this activity, the directions require them to form a conclusion about this couple's economic status at the end of the activity. Another example of an SI activity used in this study is Activity B in Appendix C. This is an affective activity that does not have a right or wrong answer. Participants are instead asked to give their opinions. Notice that the input is additionally structured following VanPatten's P4 so that the target form is in the most salient position.

The packet for the SI group contained the eight SI activities only. They did not get the page with the EI. The packet for the EI group contained only the page with the EI. This packet did not include any practice activities. The Control group did not receive any instruction. They only took the pretests and the posttests.

Assessment tasks. Following VanPatten and Oikkenon (1996), the assessment tasks were a sentence level interpretation task and a production task. The interpretation task contained 20 items: 10 items were target items and 10 items were distracters. The production had 12 items: six items were targets and six items were distracters. Two versions of each assessment task were created, one was used as the pretest and the other the posttest. In the interpretation task, subjects listened to the second part of a series of sentences and had to choose the correct phrase that began each sentence (see Appendix D). For example, if participants heard "*... de camarade de chambre*", the correct response would be "*Luc n'a pas ...*" The production task required subjects to complete sentences with the appropriate articles with the corresponding English translation underneath each sentence. For example, if subjects saw,

Roland n'a pas _____ *balcon.*
(Roland does not have a balcony)

they should have filled in the blank with *de* (see Appendix E for more sample items).

Procedure

All testing and treatment were conducted in participants' regular classrooms by the researcher. All participants completed an informed consent and were pretested two weeks before treatment. Treatment lasted one day.

On the treatment day, participants in the PI group first read the EI with the researcher and then completed the SI activities. During the activity phase, participants were told whether their responses were correct or incorrect but were not given any explanation as to why. After completing the last SI activity, they were immediately given the interpretation posttest followed by the production posttest.

Participants in the SI group worked on the SI activities only. They were not given the EI. During the SI activities, they were told whether their responses were correct or incorrect but they were not given any information as to why. After completing the activities, they were immediately given the interpretation posttest followed by the production posttest.

Participants in the EI group read the EI with the researcher and then worked on activities unrelated to the target structure for the remainder of the class period. At the end of these distracter activities, they were given the interpretation posttest followed by the production posttest.

The control group received no instruction. They were given the pretests and posttests only.

Scoring

Only the target items were scored on the posttests. The maximum possible score for the interpretation task was 10. One point was awarded for each correct response. No partial credit was given. For the production task, the maximum score was six. One point was awarded for correctly choosing between the *un/une* vs *de/d'* distinction. Points were not deducted for gender errors. For example, if participants wrote *un* for the item "*Christine a _____ maison à New York*," instead of *une* (correct response), full credit was still given because the participants still showed they understood that an indefinite article was the correct response. However, if they wrote *de* in the blank, they would get no credit.

Raw scores for each task were submitted to a repeated measures analysis of variance. Group was entered as the independent variable. The dependent variable was the scores on either the interpretation or the production task.

RESULTS

Two ANOVAs were conducted on the pretest scores, one on the scores for the interpretation task and one on the scores for the production task. The analyses revealed no significant differences between groups before treatment on either the interpretation pretest, $F(3, 94) = .925$, $p = .4321$, or the production pretest, $F(3, 94) = 1.532$, $p = .2117$. This means that any gains made on the posttests are due to the treatments and not to differences of existing knowledge between groups before treatment. Means are reported in Table 9.1 and Table 9.2.

Interpretation Task

A repeated measures ANOVA conducted on the interpretation task revealed a main effect for Treatment, $F(3, 94) = 23.944$, $p < .0001$, and a main effect for Time, $F(3, 94) = 128.448$, $p < .0001$. There was an interaction between Treatment and Time, $F(3, 94) = 26.517$, $p < .0001$. An interaction bar plot for this analysis appears in Figure 9.1.

TABLE 9.1
Mean Scores and Standard Deviations for Interpretation Task

		Pretest		Posttest	
	n	M	SD	M	SD
PI	26	0.692	1.320	8.538	2.249
EI	22	0.682	0.945	3.273	3.425
SI	25	1.240	1.786	5.480	3.676
C	21	0.952	1.161	0.905	1.221

Note: Range = 0-10

TABLE 9.2
Mean Scores and Standard Deviations for Production Task

		Pretest		Posttest	
	n	M	SD	M	SD
PI	26	1.231	0.908	4.846	1.690
EI	22	0.955	0.999	2.409	2.108
SI	25	1.600	1.118	3.360	2.177
C	21	1.238	1.136	1.238	1.261

Note: Range = 0-6

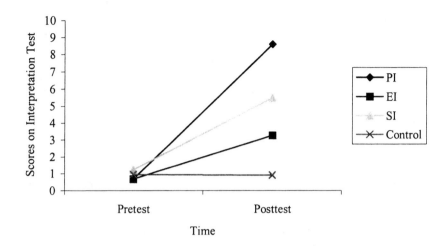

FIG. 9.1. Interaction Line Graph for Interpretation Results.

This visual representation suggests that all three treatment groups improved from the pretest to the posttest. Results of paired T-tests confirmed that the PI group made significant gains (t = -13.891, p < .0001), the SI group made significant gains (t = -5.439, p < .0001), and the EI group made significant gains (t = -3.332, p = .0032. The control group did not improve.

Looking at this visual representation, it appears that the PI group made the most gains followed by the SI group and then finally the EI group (see Fig. 9.1). However, a post-hoc Scheffé revealed that only the following contrasts were significant: (a) between the PI and the EI group (p < .0001); (b) between the PI and the control group (p < .0001); (c) between the SI and the EI group (p = .0371); and (d) between the SI and the control group (p < .0001). No other significant contrasts were found for the interpretation task

In short, although the PI group and the SI group were significantly better than the EI group and the control group, the gains made by the PI group and the SI group were not significantly different from each other. The EI group and the control group were also not significantly different from each other.

Production Task

A repeated measures ANOVA conducted on the production task revealed a main effect for Treatment, $F(3, 94)$ = 9.941, p < .0001, and a main effect for Time $F(3, 94)$ = 91.953, p < .0001. There was an interaction between Treatment and

Time, $F(3, 94) = 17.626$, $p < .0001$. A graphic representation of these results is displayed in Figure 9.2.

This graph suggests that all three treatment groups improved from the production pretest to posttest. Paired t-tests performed on each group confirmed that the gains made by the PI group were significant ($t = -13.568$, $p < .0001$), the gains made by the SI group were significant ($t = -4.176$, $p = .0003$), and the gains made by the EI group were significant ($t = -3.167$, $p = .0046$). The control group did not make any gains. The visual representation suggests that the greatest gains were made by the PI group, followed by the SI group and the EI group. However, a post-hoc Scheffé revealed that only the following contrasts were significantly different: (a) between the PI group and the EI group ($p = .0038$); (b) between the PI group and the control group ($p < .0001$); and (c) between the SI and the control group ($p = .0122$). No other significant contrasts were found for the production task. To summarize, the PI group and the SI group were significantly better than the control group but these two treatment groups were not different from each other. The PI group was also significantly better than the EI group. There was no significant difference between the SI group and the EI group. There was also no significant difference between the EI group and the control group.

DISCUSSION

Our first research question was the following: Which component of PI is responsible for improved performance on a sentence level interpretation task: EI, SI or a combination of the two? Our results suggest that significant improvement on the interpretation task is due to the presence of the SI activities. EI does not appear to be necessary in this type of focus on form instruction. Only the groups that received the SI activities, that is to say, the PI group and the SI group, performed significantly better than the control group who made no gains. The EI group who did not receive the SI activities was not significantly better than the control group. Consistent with the results of VanPatten and Oikkenon, the fact that there was no significant difference between the PI group and the SI group further supports the conclusion that SI is the most important component of PI. If EI were more important, then the PI group should have been significantly better than the SI group since the PI group had the EI while the SI group did not. That the participants who had only SI activities did as well as those who had both EI and SI shows that the EI did not have a significant effect

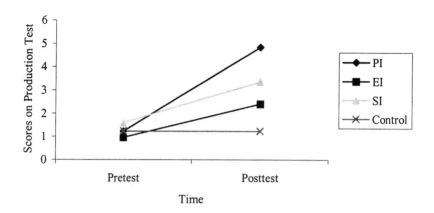

FIG. 9.2.   Interaction Line Graph for Production Results.

on the results. Unlike the results of VanPatten and Oikkenon, the EI group also made some improvement on the interpretation posttest (although they were minimal) in this study (as shown in the visual representation of results). This suggests that for this particular target structure, learners may be able to rely on EI to help them make gains on this type of task. The fact that the EI group was not better than the control group, however, also suggests that the impact of this information was minimal. In other words, the EI had enough of an impact to help participants in the EI group make some improvement on the interpretation posttest but it was not enough to enable them to perform better than the no instruction control group. In short, the learners could not successfully monitor their performance on this task with the knowledge they gained from the EI alone.

Our second research question was the following: Which component of PI is responsible for improved performance on a sentence level production task: EI, SI or a combination of the two? Our results show that once again, the SI activities appear to be the causative factor because only those participants who received SI activities, that is to say, those in the PI and SI groups, performed significantly better than those in the no instruction control group. Like in VanPatten and Oikkenon, the fact that the PI group (who got both EI and SI) was not significantly better than the SI group (who did not get EI) suggests that EI was not necessary. Had EI been more important, we should have seen a significant difference between the PI and SI groups, with the PI group performing significantly better. Instead, our results show that participants who got SI activities only were able to perform as well as those who got both SI and EI on the production task.

As in VanPatten and Oikkenon, the results of our production task also show that the EI group was able to improve from the pretest to the posttest (although again the gains were small compared to the other two treatment groups). Thus, we may also conclude that for this target structure, it is possible for learners to use EI to make some improvement on the production task. However, the fact that the EI group was not significantly better than the control group also suggests that the ability to use this information was minimal.

A summary of the results of VanPatten and Oikkenon (1996) and of this study are presented in Table 9.3. As this table illustrates, it is clear that the SI activities are the causative factor for the improved performance found in PI in both studies and for both types of assessment tasks. Therefore, we have evidence to conclude that the results of VanPatten and Oikkenon (1996) may be generalized to other target structures, specifically in this case, the use of *de* with *avoir* in French.

In an effort to avoid misinterpretation, I would like to reiterate the purpose of this study. As in VanPatten and Oikkenon (1996), the purpose of this experiment was to isolate the effects of SI and EI in PI in order to better understand which component of this type of focus on form instruction is responsible for the positive results found in PI studies. This point needs to be underscored because some recent criticisms of PI reveal that some SLA scholars may have misunderstood the purpose of the VanPatten and Oikkenon study (i.e., DeKeyser, Salaberry, Robinson, & Harrington, 2002), that is to say, that they apparently believe the purpose of this study was to compare explicit and implicit instruction.[2] However, as clearly stated in VanPatten and Oikkenon and in this study, the purpose here is to isolate the effects of the different components of PI, not to compare an explicit and an implicit mode of instruction. For this reason, it

---

[2]In their review of VanPatten and Oikkenon, DeKeyser, Salaberry, Robinson, and Harrington (2002) imply that the purpose of VanPatten and Oikkenon (1996) was to compare explicit vs. implicit instruction. They argue that because the EI group in VanPatten and Oikkenon did not have any opportunities to practice and because the SI group received feedback as to whether their responses were correct or incorrect, the treatment groups in this study should have been classified as a "good explicit-deductive" group (the full PI group), a "good explicit-inductive" group (the SI group), and a "poor explicit-deductive" group (the EI only group) "instead of an explicit and an implicit treatment" (p. 813). It needs to be noted that VanPatten and Oikkenon never state that they set out to compare explicit vs. implicit instruction. Their research design would have to have been very different had this been their intent. To reiterate, the purpose of VanPatten and Oikkenon was to research the effects of EI alone, SI alone, and PI (EI + SI) to see which component was responsible for the favorable results found in PI studies.

TABLE 9.3
Summary of Results from VanPatten and Oikkenon (1996) and the Present Study

	VP & Oikkenon (1996) (SP object pronouns)	Present Study (FR *de* with *avoir*)
Interpretation	PI=SI>EI	PI=SI>EI=C
Production	PI=SI>EI	PI=SI>C PI>EI EI=SI EI=C

Note: PI = Processing Instruction; SI = Structured Input; EI = Explicit Info; C = Control

was not necessary (and certainly not advisable) to control for time on task in the EI group or to give these participants any practice activities. To be sure, no researcher would ever suggest to instructors that they give learners only explicit information about a structure without any subsequent activities and then test them to see if they have acquired the structure. However, it was necessary to operationalize the EI treatment in this way because this study wanted to see what effect (if any) this information was having as a component of PI. The results reveal that it does not have an impact on PI.

The finding that the SI activities alone were sufficient to allow participants to make significant gains deserves some attention. Overall, empirical studies that have compared treatment conditions that involved the provision of EI with conditions that did not tend to show an advantage for EI. Alanen (1995), for example, examined the effects of textual enhancement and explicit rule presentation on adult learners' acquisition of semi-artificial Finnish locative suffixes and consonant gradation. Her subjects were randomly assigned to four groups: (1) a group that received textual enhancement, (2) a group that received explicit rule instruction, (3) a group that got both textual enhancement and rules and (4) a control group that did not receive either textual enhancement or rules. Results of a sentence completion task revealed that while all treatment groups made gains, the groups who received rules had an overall advantage over those who did not get the rules.

Using a pretest–posttest design, Scott (1989) investigated the effects of an explicit and implicit instructional treatment on L2 French learners' acquisition of relative pronouns and the French subjunctive. Participants in the explicit condition were given explicit information about the target structures followed by oral modeling of five example sentences containing the target structure for 15 minutes each day for six consecutive class days. Participants in the implicit condition were not given this explicit information. Instead, they heard stories that contained the target structure for the same amount of time. A paper and pencil posttest (multiple choice/fill-in-the-blank/short answer) showed that participants in the explicit condition performed significantly better than those in the implicit condition.

Other studies that have shown beneficial effects for EI include de Graaff (1997), Ellis (1993), Herman and Olsen Flannigan (1995), Robinson (1996), Rosa and O'Neill (1999), and Scott (1990) among others. Why is it then, that EI did not play a significant role in the present study? Why didn't the PI group that received both EI and SI activities do better than the group that received only SI activities? The answer may lie in the nature of the SI activities. Recall that the purpose of PI is to preempt inefficient processing strategies. The SI activities require learners to process form correctly in order to get meaning. Because the activities in PI are designed to ensure that learners are indeed making the proper form-meaning connections, the provision of EI may consequently be unnecessary. In other words, if the activities alone can result in form-meaning connections, then EI does not have much of a chance to have an impact on that process. On the other hand, in learning conditions where form-meaning connections may not necessarily be happening, learners may consequently rely more on EI. For example, in Alanen's (1995) textual enhancement condition, highlighting the target forms in the input may not have been sufficient for learners to see the form-meaning connection. In such a case, learners may need something more, perhaps EI, to help them make those connections. Because SI activities by nature push learners to make correct form-meaning connections, there will consequently be little or no use for EI.

Recently, some SLA scholars remarked that among the focus on form techniques that are in the literature, PI appears to yield some of the most promising results (e.g., Carroll, 2001; Doughty, 2002; Ellis, 2002; Norris & Ortega, 2000). These researchers attribute the positive results of this focus on form technique to the fact that PI is specifically targeted at altering learners' processing strategies. According to these scholars, in L2 learning situations where input alone may not be sufficient, the best kind of intervention may be one in which input is structured so that learners can perceive and parse L2 stimuli more effectively to make accurate form-meaning connections (Doughty, 2002; Ellis, 2002).

FUTURE RESEARCH

Other research on PI shows that the effects of PI are also observed on less controlled tasks (Sanz, this volume; VanPatten & Sanz, 1995) and are durable for up to at least eight months (VanPatten & Fernández, this volume). An area of research that has not yet been explored are learner perceptions of SI activities. Although I have shown along with other research that EI is not necessary for promoting acquisition if SI activities are used as a teaching technique, this does not mean EI is not useful—especially from a learner's perspective. It may be that EI works early on in a sequence of SI activities to focus attention, even though in the end it is not necessary. Having some kind of EI early on could potentially make things seem clearer and to the point. This may be particularly true for those learners who get frustrated easily. Future study should investigate this possibility.

SUMMARY AND CONCLUSION

The purpose of this study was to isolate the effects of SI and EI in a type of focus on form instruction called Processing Instruction in order to determine which component was responsible for the beneficial effects of PI. The results indicate that SI was the causative factor and not EI, lending support to VanPatten and Oikkenon's conclusions. Only those participants who had SI activities were able to perform significantly better than the control group. Whether learners had EI or not did not make a difference in the results.

Overall, empirical studies that include EI as a component in research designs tend to show that EI is at least beneficial in instructed SLA (e.g., Alanen, 1995; Ellis, 1993; Herman & Olson Flannigan, 1995, Robinson, 1996; Rosa & O'Neill, 1999; Scott, 1989, 1990). Results of the present study are not consistent with these findings. The present study showed no significant effect from EI (as evidenced by the lack of significant difference between the PI and SI groups). It was proposed that this was due to the nature of SI activities: When input is structured so that form-meaning connections are privileged, EI is not necessary or even beneficial. This suggests that the type of input that learners receive can have an impact on how they process input. The results of this study (as well as those of previous PI studies) suggest that optimal input processing may take place when the input in activities is structured with learners' processing strategies in mind so that form-meaning connections are maximized. In light of these results, instructors may want to re-examine the type of input and activities that they provide to learners in the L2 classroom.

REFERENCES

Alanen, R. (1995). Input enhancement and rule presentation in second language acquisition. In R. Schmidt (Ed.), *Attention and awareness in foreign language acquisition* (pp. 259–302). Honolulu: University of Hawaii Press.

Carroll, S. (2001). *Input and evidence: The raw material of second language acquisition.* Philadelphia: John Benjamins.

de Graaff, R. (1997). The eXperanto experiment: Effects of explicit instruction on second language acquisition. *Studies in Second Language Acquisition, 19,* 24–276.

DeKeyser, R., Salaberry, R., Robinson, P., & Harrington, M. (2002). What gets processed in processing instruction? A commentary on Bill VanPatten's "Update." *Language Learning, 52,* 805–823.

Doughty, C. (2002, March). *Effects of instruction on second language acquisition.* Paper presented at the Conference on Form-Meaning Connections in SLA, Chicago, IL.

Ellis, N. (1993). Rules and instances in foreign language learning: Interactions of explicit and implicit knowledge. *European Journal of Cognitive Psychology, 5,* 289–318.

Ellis, N. (2002, March). *The processes of second language acquisition.* Paper presented at the Conference on Form-Meaning Connections in SLA, Chicago, IL.

Herman, R. L., & Olsen Flannigan, B. (1995). Adding grammar in a communicative based ESL program for children: Theory in practice. *TESL Canada Journal, 13,* 1–16.

Lee, J., & VanPatten, B. (1995). *Making communicative language teaching happen.* New York: McGraw Hill.

Norris, J., & Ortega, L. (2000). Effectiveness of L2 instruction: A research synthesis and quantitative meta-analysis. *Language Learning, 50,* 417–528.

Robinson, P. (1996). Learning simple and complex second language rules under implicit, incidental, rule-search, and instructed conditions. *Studies in Second Language Acquisition, 18,* 27-67.

Rosa, E., & O'Neill, M. O. (1999). Explicitness, intake and the issue of awareness: Another piece to the puzzle. *Studies in Second Language Acquisition, 21,* 511–556.

Scott, V. M. (1989). An empirical study of explicit and implicit teaching strategies in French. *The Modern Language Journal, 73,* 14–22.

Scott, V. M. (1990). Explicit and implicit grammar teaching strategies: New empirical data. *French Review, 63,* 779–789.

VanPatten, B., & Cadierno, T. (1993). Explicit instruction and input processing. *Studies in Second Language Acquisition, 15,* 225–243.

VanPatten, B., & Oikkenon, S. (1996). Explanation vs. structured input in processing instruction. *Studies in Second Language Acquisition, 18,* 495–510.

VanPatten, B., & Sanz, C. (1995). From input to output: Processing instruction and communicative tasks. In F. Eckman, D. Highland, P. Lee, J. Mileham & R. Rutkowski Weber (Eds.), *Second language acquisition theory and pedagogy* (pp. 169–185). Mahwah, NJ: Lawrence Erlbaum Associates.

APPENDIX A

Explicit Information

The verb *avoir* means "to have."

Avoir

---

j'ai	nous avons
tu as	vous avez
il/elle/on a	ils/elles ont

Henri a deux voitures.	*Henri has two cars.*
Anne a une moto.	*Anne has a motorcycle.*
M. et Mme Leblanc ont trois maisons.	*Mr. & Mrs. Leblanc have three houses.*

When the verb *avoir* is used in the negative, any indefinite article (*un, une, des*) that follows it becomes *de* or *d'* (before a vowel).

Il a un stylo.	Il n'a pas de stylo.
Ils ont une moto.	Ils n'ont pas de moto.
Elle a des amis.	Elle n'a pas d'amis.

CAUTION:
Learners of French often skip over the *de/d'* vs. *un/une/des* distinction when listening and rely instead on the negation markers *ne...pas* to understand the sentence. In the activities that follow, you will practice listening for *de/d'* vs. *un/une/des* as clues to meaning.

APPENDIX B

Activity A. Chez les LeBlanc

Étape 1:
Pierre and Lise LeBlanc are talking about things they have and don't have in their house. Pay attention to the articles to determine whether they have or do not have the things mentioned. Complete each sentence with either "**Nous avons** ..." or "**Nous n'avons pas** ..."

_____ **une** salle de séjour.
_____ **de** télévision.
_____ **de** lit.
_____ **un** fauteuil.
_____ **une** cuisinière.
_____ **de** réfrigérateur.
_____ **une** table.
_____ **une** toilette.
_____ **une** douche.
_____ **de** baignoire.
_____ **de** lampes.
_____ **de** chaises.
_____ **des** souris (*mice*).

Étape 2: Based on these descriptions, decide with a partner how rich or poor this couple is and explain why.

Pierre et Lise sont....*très riches/ riches/ assez riches/ assez pauvres/ pauvres/ très pauvres* (circle one) parce que....

INSTRUCTOR'S SCRIPT
Give students a few minutes to work on step one on their own. Then, go over each answer with them. Go on to step two. Have them discuss their answers with a partner and then share with whole class to see if everyone wrote the same thing.

APPENDIX C

Activité B. The following sentences describe what is in and not in a college dorm room today. Read each sentence and decide whether each description is typical or not typical of a college dorm room today.

Aujourd'hui, une chambre d'étudiant a ...

une chaîne stéréo (*stereo*).	C'est typique	/ Ce n'est pas typique
une télévision.	C'est typique	/ Ce n'est pas typique
un lecteur de DVD (*DVD player*).	C'est typique	/ Ce n'est pas typique
un four à micro-ondes (*microwave*).	C'est typique	/ Ce n'est pas typique

Aujourd'hui, une chambre d'étudiant n' a pas...

de lavabo (*sink*).	C'est typique	/ Ce n'est pas typique
de cuisine (*kitchen*).	C'est typique	/ Ce n'est pas typique
de réfrigérateur.	C'est typique	/ Ce n'est pas typique
de radio.	C'est typique	/ Ce n'est pas typique

Now, repeat the above activity but this time imagine a college dorm room from the 1960s. Do any of your answers change?

En 1960, une chambre d'étudiant avait ...

une chaîne stéréo (*stereo*).	C'est typique	/ Ce n'est pas typique
une télévision.	C'est typique	/ Ce n'est pas typique
un lecteur de DVD (*DVD player*)	C'est typique	/ Ce n'est pas typique
un four à micro-ondes (*microwave*)	C'est typique	/ Ce n'est pas typique

En 1960, une chambre d'étudiant n' avait pas ...

de lavabo (*sink*)	C'est typique	/ Ce n'est pas typique
de cuisine (*kitchen*)	C'est typique	/ Ce n'est pas typique
de réfrigérateur	C'est typique	/ Ce n'est pas typique
de radio	C'est typique	/ Ce n'est pas typique

APPENDIX D

Sample Items for Interpretation Task

You will hear the last part of a series of sentences. Listen carefully and select the appropriate phrase that correctly completes each sentence. You will have 6 seconds to select a response after hearing the phrase.

(1)
  A. Laurent n'a pas ...
  B. Laurent n'aime pas ...
  C. Neither A or B
  D. Both A and B

(4)
  A. Elise aime ...
  B. Elise n'aime pas ...
  C. Neither A or B
  D. Both A and B

(2)
  A. Luc a ...
  B. Luc n'a pas ...
  C. Neither A or B
  D. Both A and B

(5)
  A. Claire n'a pas ...
  B. Claire a ...
  C. Neither A or B
  D. Both A and B

(3)
  A. Marie n'aime pas ...
  B. Marie n'a pas ...
  C. Neither A or B
  D. Both A and B

(6)
  A. Nadine a ...
  B. Nadine n'a pas...
  C. Neither A or B
  D. Both A and B

INSTRUCTOR'S SCRIPT

  1.   ... le vin français.
  2.   ... de camarade de chambre. *
  3.   ...les sandwichs au fromage.
  4.   ...le chocolat.
  5.   ...une grande fen☐tre. *
  6.   ...les amis.

*target items

APPENDIX E

Production Task

Fill in the blanks with the appropriate article.

1. Roland n'a pas _____ balcon (balcony).*
   (*Roland does not have a balcony.*)

2. Caroline n'aime pas _____ chats.
   (*Caroline does not like cats.*)

3. Christine a _____ maison à New York.*
   (*Christine has a house in New York.*)

4. Vincent n'a pas _____ télévision.*
   (*Vincent does not have a TV.*)

5. Clarice aime _____ poissons.
   (*Clarice likes fish.*)

6. Yvette n'a pas _____ chien.*
   (*Yvette does not have a dog.*)

7. Arnold aime _____ petites maisons.
   (*Arnold likes small houses.*)

8. _____ chambre de Nancy est grande.
   (*Nancy's room is big.*)

9. Annalisa n'a pas _____ voiture (car).*
   (*Annalisa does not have a car.*)

10. Julie préfère habiter dans _____ petite ville.
    (*Julie prefers to live in a small city.*)

11. Alice va acheter _____ nouvelle voiture.
    (*Alice is going to buy a new car.*)

12. Mireille a _____ petit garage.*
    (*Mireille has a small garage.*)

*target items

Chapter 10

The Effects of Structured Input Activities and Explicit Information on The Acquisition of The Italian Future Tense

Alessandro Benati
University of Greenwich

This study addresses the question of whether or not explicit information plays a significant role in instructed SLA within the framework of processing instruction.[1] Explicit information here is meant as "explanation about properties of language provided by an instructor, teaching materials or some other external sources" (VanPatten & Oikkenon, 1996, p. 6). Despite a growing body of research that has investigated the role of explicit information in instructed SLA, the role of explicit information in fostering SLA is unclear. On the one hand, some research seems to indicate that explicit information is beneficial (Alanen, 1995; de Graaff, 1997; among others). On the other hand, one study suggests that explicit information is neither beneficial nor necessary (VanPatten & Oikennon, 1996). The question is "Why are there differences in the outcomes of these studies?" One possibility is that results of VanPatten and Oikkenon's study, being the only one that clearly showed no effect for EI in the treatments administered, are a fluke. That is, they are spurious and only replication would determine whether the results are generalizable. Another possibility is that the type of treatment used in VanPatten and Oikkenon—namely processing

[1] First, I would like to express my special gratitude to Bill VanPatten for his review of this paper. I would also like to thank Wynne Wong and Richard Dove for their valuable feedback and suggestions. Last but not least, I thank my students at the undergraduate and postgraduate level for their help in carrying out this study. I am, of course, responsible for the ideas contained in this chapter.

instruction—does not require EI because of the effect of the structured input activities contained in the treatment.

As indicated by VanPatten (2002), "the aim of PI is in line with claims of those researchers who assert that acquisition is a failure-driven process (e.g., Carroll, 1999)" (p. 768). That is, for acquisition to happen, processing mechanisms must note that the parsing procedure is not getting the listener/learner the right information about the events (e.g., who did what to whom) and must therefore seek alternative procedures for successful interpretation. When these new procedures are successful, they replace the procedures that are not (or exist along with them). PI is designed to cause failure in interpretation at the beginning stages of activities so that the processors can begin to readjust. (See Carroll, 1999, for additional discussion, as well as VanPatten & Wong, this volume.)

Wong (this volume, chap. 2) provides a detailed account of PI and structured input activities in particular so I will not review PI here. However, as one examines the sample activities she offers, one can see just how structured input works. With the first-noun strategy, for example, learners tend to assign subject/agent status to the first noun they encounter in the sentence. Structured input activities would present learners a mix of sentences in which the first noun strategy works in some cases and in others it doesn't. When asked to pick which picture or rendition of a sentence matches what they hear, if learners pick the wrong one by relying on the first noun strategy, they are informed that this is incorrect (but not necessarily told why). What this does is cause the learners' processing mechanisms to rethink how they are assigning roles to nouns and pronouns and as the processing mechanisms adjust themselves, learners receive feedback that they are now interpreting sentences correctly.

MOTIVATION FOR THE PRESENT STUDY

VanPatten and Oikkenon (1996) and Sanz and Morgan-Short (forthcoming) lend support to the view that within the processing instruction approach, explicit information plays no role in the acquisition process. Their research suggests that carefully structured input activities are sufficient to push learners to make correct sentence interpretations when the problem is the first-noun strategy. The present study attempts to replicate these findings by addressing a different processing problem in a different language and structure. In the previous two studies, the processing problem was the first noun strategy. In the present study, the processing problem is the lexical strategy by which learners rely on lexical cues as opposed to grammatical markers for certain kinds of meanings (see the Lexical Preference Principle, this volume, chap. 1). In addition, this study included a delayed posttest to determine if the effects hold over a period of time. The main purpose of the present study is to address these issues by attempting to replicate VanPatten and Oikkenon's results with a different language and a different structure. If replication cannot be achieved, the results of VanPatten and Oikennon could be considered non-generalizable. If replication is achieved, then we have evidence that indeed the nature of structured input is such that it alone can cause changes in learner knowledge and/or performance.

The specific research questions for this study are:

1. Will structured input alone cause improved performance on an interpretation task equivalent to that of a full PI group? Will explicit information alone cause the same improved performance?

2. Will structured input alone cause improved performance on a production task equivalent to that of a full PI group? Will explicit information alone cause the same improved performance?

3. Will the improved performance on all tasks be retained over one month?

METHOD AND PROCEDURE

Participants

An experimental study was carried at the University of Greenwich among undergraduate students of Italian in their second semester of study to answer the research questions. Three groups were formed using a matching procedure as participants could not be randomly assigned.

The three criteria used for inclusion of participants in the final experiment were:

1. subjects' learning was limited to classroom instruction;

2. subjects who had previous experience or linguistic knowledge of the target language were excluded from the study; and

3. all the subjects had to be native English speakers.

In the end, 38 subjects took part in this experiment and were distributed as follows: processing instruction (n = 14), structured input only (n = 12), explicit information only (n = 12). The small size of the subjects involved in the experiment is due to the relative number of students who actually study Italian.

For the purpose of this experiment (see Fig. 10.1) the three groups were taught twice (3 hours each time) during the instructional treatments over a period of two consecutive days of instruction (6 hours total).

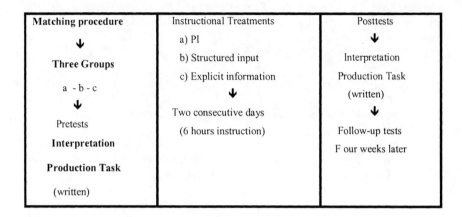

FIG. 10.1. Overview of the Experiment.

The Grammatical Feature

The future tense in Italian was chosen for two main reasons. First, the processing problem is different from that in the VanPatten and Oikkenon and the Sanz and Morgan-Short studies. VanPatten (1996) has stated that "learners prefer processing lexical items to grammatical items for semantic information" (p. 21). Musumeci (1989) conducted a cross-linguistic study in which she examined the ability to assign tenses in Italian (present, future, past) at sentence level under different conditions. Musumeci's study supported VanPatten's hypothesis and revealed that early stage learners of Italian use mainly lexical items in order to assign tense.

A second reason the future tense was selected is that it is low in frequency. As pointed out by VanPatten (2002), "low frequency in the input and other aspects of language may be factors that along with communicative value may doom a form to never get picked up by a learner" (p. 760). As such, the future tense lends itself to instructional treatment because early stage learners are likely to not have encountered much of it in the input and certainly not in their instructional materials.

Materials

PI Group. The instructional material used was the same as in the study carried out by Benati (2001) on the effects of PI on the acquisition of Italian future tense. (See Appendix A for examples.)

The instructional approach called PI involves three focus on form components: (1) explicit information about the structure/form; (2) explicit information about the processing problem; and (3) structured input activities. The presentation and information (see Appendix A) about the future verb forms involved providing learners with some information about the grammatical form and at the same time linking form and meaning. Individual forms (e.g., first person singular, second person singular) were presented one at a time (see Wong, this volume). The forms were contrasted with the present tense verb forms. Two things were especially emphasized: (1) the differences in acoustic stress between future and present verb forms; (2) the fact that although temporal adverbs generally indicate that the action of the verb occurs at the moment or will occur in the future, these adverbs are not always present in the input. Therefore, it was extremely important for the students to recognize future tense forms without relying on adverbs.

As part of the structured input component two main types of structured input activities (see Appendix B) were used: *referential activities* where learners have to identify at sentence level the time when the action had happened and the subject of the sentence; *affective activities* where learners respond to input sentences with opinions, conclusions, and so on.

In all activities, lexical items and discourse that would indicate a time frame were not present. Only the verb ending encoded tense in the input sentences. This was done in order to encourage learners to attend to the grammatical markers. Thus, the input was "structured" so that the grammatical form carried a meaning and the learner had to attend to the form to complete the task. Processing instruction aims at making learners interpret and comprehend the linguistic feature in oral and written form and not producing it. During treatment, learners did not produce the forms in question.

SI Only Group. In the case of the structured input only group (experimental group), participants received the same type and amount of structured input activities as in the case of the PI group but did not receive any explanation or explicit information about the Italian future tense. Treatment began immediately with structured input activities. Because the referential activities had right/wrong answers, the participants were told whether their answers were correct or not but were not told why. At no time during instruction were participants belonging to this group ever asked to produce a sentence with the future tense. They were, however, engaged in processing input sentences in a controlled situation so that they could make better form-meaning connections. At no time did the participants receive either explanation or feedback about the way the future tense is formed in Italian.

EI Only Group. The explicit information only group received the same type and amount of explanation and explicit information about the target feature as the PI group. This group, however, did not receive any practice with structured input activities. There were no practices of any kind.

For the EI group, the explicit explanation of the Italian future tense was spread out over two consecutive days and participants were invited to ask any questions related to the target structure. At the end of the instructional period, the time left over was used for practice not related to the target structure.

The researcher taught all groups during the regular period of instruction. The instructor acted as a facilitator during the experiment and made all possible efforts to pay the same amount of attention and show the same enthusiasm across the different treatment conditions. I point out again that given the nature of PI, neither the PI group nor the SI only group engaged in any production activities. That is, not once during the treatment period were participants called on to produce future tense forms in Italian.

Assessment Measures and Scoring

To assess the effects of the three treatments, a pretest and posttest procedure was adopted. Two tests were developed with three versions each: one interpretation task and one written production task (see Appendix B).

The three versions of the interpretation task were used as a measure of interpreting future tense at the sentence level. The test consisted of twenty aural sentences (10 in the present which served as distractors and 10 in the future) in which temporal adverbs and subject nouns or pronouns were removed, so that the participants could not rely on those elements to assign tense. The verb was never placed at the beginning of the sentence. The tests were recorded by a native speaker of Italian and played to the participants on a cassette player. No repetition was provided so that participants heard each sentence only once. The three versions were balanced in terms of difficulty and vocabulary during a pilot experiment. One version served as the pretest and the others served as the post-tests.

The written production task was developed and used to measure learner's ability to produce verbs in the future tense. The written production task (see Appendix C) consisted of a short text with five blanks where verbs should be. Participants had to put the correct future tense form in each blank. Only regular verbs were included. As in the case of the interpretation task, the three versions were balanced and pilot tested. In the present study, one served as the pretest and the others served as the posttests.

Scoring

For the interpretation task a correct response was scored as 1 point and an incorrect response was scored as 0. Only the future sentences were counted for a maximum score of 10.

For the written production test the raw scores were calculated as follows:

- fully correct future tense = 2 points;

- partially correct (wrong spelling but right ending, such as for the third-person singular *parlarà* instead of *parlerà*) = 1 point; and
- incorrect = 0 point.

Given that there were five verb forms the participants had to produce, the maximum score possible was 10.

RESULTS

The Interpretation Task

An ANOVA was carried out on the pretest scores for the interpretation task. The ANOVA revealed that there were no statistical differences among the three groups, $F(2) = 1.204$, $p = .312$. Therefore the groups could be considered comparable and any observed treatment effects would be due to the treatments and not to initial differences among groups.

As the means in Table 10.1 suggest, all groups seemed to improve with treatment. A repeated measures ANOVA carried out on the raw scores of the interpretation task revealed a significant main effect for Treatment, $F(2, 38) = 21.56$, $p = .000$, a significant main effect for Time, $F(1, 38) = 304.79$, $p = .001$, and a significant interaction between Treatment and Time, $F(2, 38) = 36.43$, $p = .000$. Figure 10.2 displays these results graphically.

A post-hoc Sheffé Test conducted on interaction yielded the following contrasts: The PI group performed better than the EI group ($p = .000$); there was no difference between the PI group and the SI group ($p = .592$); the SI group was also significantly better than the EI group ($p = .000$). Thus, although all groups improved, the PI and SI groups improved much more but were not different from each other.

To address the question of delayed effects, a second ANOVA was used on the raw scores of the two post-tests. The results revealed a significant main effect for Treatment, $F(2, 38) = 18.858$, $p = .000$, no difference for Time, $F(1, 38) = 1.680$, $p = .201$, and no interaction between Treatment and Time, $F(2, 38) = .759$, $p = .477$. The repeated measures ANOVA showed that there was no difference for Time between the first and the second posttest, therefore we conclude that the gains for both instructional treatments were maintained. A Post-hoc test conducted on instruction revealed the following contrasts: the PI group performed better than the EI group ($p = .000$); the PI group and the SI group were not significantly different from each other ($p = .784$); the structured input activities group was significantly better than the EI group ($p = .000$).

TABLE 10.1
Means and Standard Deviations for Interpretation
Task Pretest and Posttests

Group	n	Pretest		Posttest 1		Posttest 2	
		Mean	SD	Mean	SD	Mean	SD
PI	14	2.70	.91	8.30	1.00	7.7	1.19
SI	12	2.10	.94	7.80	1.27	7.5	1.38
EI	12	2.60	1.07	4.60	2.02	3.8	1.28

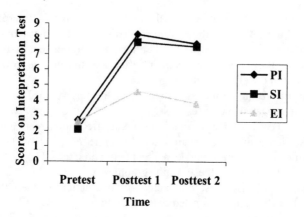

FIG. 10.2. Interaction Line Graph for Interpretation Task.

The Written Production Task

The ANOVA conducted on the pretest for the production task revealed no difference between the three groups, $F(2) = .743$, $p = .483$. As in the case of the interpretation task, these results indicate the groups were not different from each other before treatment and thus any effects would be attributable to treatment.

The means in Table 10.2 suggest again that all groups improved. A repeated measures ANOVA conducted on the raw scores of the written production task revealed a significant main effect for Treatment, $F(2, 38) = 30.38$, $p = .000$, a significant main effect for Time, $F(1,38) = 318.18$, $p = .002$, and a significant interaction between Treatment and Time, $F(2, 38) = 21.20$, $p = .002$. These results are displayed graphically in Figure 10.3.

TABLE 10.2
Means and Standard Deviations for Production
Task Pretest and Posttests

		Pretest		Posttest 1		Posttest 2	
Group	n	Mean	SD	Mean	SD	Mean	SD
PI	14	2.20	.80	7.30	1.34	6.50	.94
SI	12	1.90	.90	6.50	1.47	4.80	.92
EI	12	1.80	.83	3.10	.91	2.50	.97

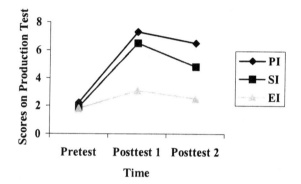

FIG. 10.3. Interaction Bar Plot for Written Production Task.

A post-hoc Scheffé Test conducted on the raw scores for the interaction yielded the following contrasts: the PI group performed statistically better in the production posttest than the EI group (p =.000) but not better than the SI group (p = .357); however, there was a difference between the SI group and the EI group (p = .003). Thus, although all groups improved, the PI and structured input-only groups made significantly more gains that the explicit information only group but were not different from each other.

The results of the second ANOVA carried out to address the question of the delayed effects, confirmed the previous finding of the interpretation task. The results showed a significant main effect for Treatment, $F(2, 29.531) = 59.774$, $p = .000$, no difference for Time, $F(1, 1.571) = 3.180$, $p = .154$, and no interaction between Treatment and Time, $F(2, .494) = 1.96$, $p = .615$. The repeated measures ANOVA revealed no difference for the Time variable between the first and the second posttest, therefore the gains for both instructional treatment were maintained. The Post-hoc test carried out for the interaction in the three groups showed the following contrasts: The PI group was better than the EI group (p = .000); no difference between the PI group and the SI group (p = .013); the SI group was better than the EI group (p = .000).

Summary of Results

The first question of this study was: Will structured input alone cause improved performance on an interpretation task equivalent to that of a full PI group? Will explicit information alone cause the same improved performance? The findings from the interpretation task clearly reveal that the structured input-only group made gains similar to those of the PI group. However, the explicit information-only group did not. Its gains were minimal.

The second question of the present study was: Will structured input alone cause improved performance on a production task equivalent to that of a full PI group? Will explicit information alone cause the same improved performance? The findings from the production task clearly reveal that the structured input-only group made gains similar to those of the PI group. However, once again, the explicit information-only group did not. Its gains were minimal.

The third question of the present study was the following: Will the improved performance on all tasks be retained over one month? Scores on the second posttest for the three groups did not differ statistically from the first posttest. In short, the treatment effects held one month later.

DISCUSSION AND CONCLUSION

The finding from the present study considered alongside the results of VanPatten and Oikkenon (1996) and Sanz and Morgan-Short (forthcoming) indicate that the main variable responsible for the effects of processing instruction on an interpretation and written production task is the structured input activities component. In both interpretation and production, the PI and SI groups made the same gains. What they had in common were the structured input activities. The explicit information group did not make the same gains, and what it did not share with the other experimental treatments were the structured input activities.

The results of the present study provide additional evidence that manipulating input to push processing changes does seem to be an appropriate pedagogical intervention. Although the results suggest that the role of explicit information might be minimal and does not play a significant role, the information provided to the explanation-only group resulted in improved performance, although not nearly to the degree as that achieved by the other two groups. These results might be attributed to the rule in question in this study (future tense), which is a less complex rule than the word order problem studied in VanPatten and Oikkenon (1996).

The overall results, when also compared with those of other studies in this section, unequivocally provide evidence that the results of VanPatten and Oikkenon's (1996) study are generalizable to a different rule, another romance language and measurable in terms of longer-term effects. It seems, then, that within PI explicit information is not necessary or beneficial. The results of our studies contrast with those reviewed in the first section of this chapter. The evidence here suggests that the larger question in instructed SLA may not be "Does explicit information make a difference during explicit instruction?" but "What effects are the actual treatments attempting to cause in the learner?" Perhaps the explicit information is needed in the other kinds of treatments because their activities are not attempting to engage the processes that structured input does. If this is the case, then we must re-evaluate any conclusions that suggest that explicit information is necessary or beneficial. The more appropriate conclusion appears to be that explicit information is beneficial (maybe even necessary) for some treatments but certainly not for all.

The results of the present study should be interpreted in light of several limitations. First, the division of the population into three groups creates quite small n sizes. Nonetheless, when compared with the results of VanPatten and Oikkenon (1996), Sanz and Morgan-Short (in press), Sanz (this volume), Wong (this volume, chap. 9), and Farley (this volume, chap. 11), the results parallel the other studies that have larger n sizes. Perhaps, then, this limitation is not as critical as it might seem. When studies coalesce in terms of results, something clear is emerging. In this case, it is the effect that structured input has on acquisition during processing instruction.

Another limitation is that the assessment tasks used in the present study were very controlled. Further studies should be conducted including different forms of assessment (e.g., timed tasks) that would reduce the ability to monitor and require participants to produce much more than verb forms. Moreover, tests used in this study did not include a measure of communicative behavior. VanPatten and Sanz (1995) and Sanz and Morgan-Short (in press) show that learners undergoing PI can improve in video narration tasks after treatment. The question, then, is: Can learners who receive only structured input perform as well on these other tasks?

In terms of pedagogical interventions, the present study offers further support for the hypothesis that acquisition happens as learners make form-meaning connections in the input they receive.

REFERENCES

Alanen, R. (1995). Input enhancement and rule presentation in second language acquisition. In Schmidt, R. (Ed.), *Attention and awareness in foreign language learning and teaching* (pp. 259–302). Honolulu: University of Hawaii Press.

Benati, A. (2001). A comparative study of the effects of processing instruction and output-based instruction on the acquisition of the Italian future tense. *Language Teaching Research, 5,* 95–127.

Carroll, S. E. (1999). Putting input in its proper place. *Second Language Research, 15,* 337–388.

de Graaff, R. (1997). The eXperanto experiment: Effects of explicit instruction on second language acquisition. *Studies in Second Language Acquisition, 19,* 249–297.

Musumeci, D. (1989). *The ability of second language learners to assign tense at the sentence level: A cross-linguistic study.* Unpublished doctoral dissertation, University of Illinois, Urbana–Champaign.

Sanz, C., & Morgan-Short, K. (in press). Positive evidence vs. explicit rule presentation and explicit negative feedback: A computer assisted study. *Language Learning.*

VanPatten, B. (1996). *Input processing and grammar instruction: Theory and Research.* Norwood, NJ: Ablex.

VanPatten, B., & Sanz, C. (1995). From input to output: Processing instruction and communicative tasks. In F. Eckman, D. Highland, P. Lee, J. Mileham & R. Rutkowski (Eds.), *Second language acquisition theory and pedagogy* (pp. 169–185). Mahwah, NJ: Lawrence Erlbaum Associates.

VanPatten, B., & Oikkenon, S. (1996). Explanation versus structured input in processing instruction. *Studies in Second Language Acquisition, 18,* 495–510.

VanPatten, B. (2002). Processing instruction: An update. *Language Learning, 52,* 755–803.

APPENDIX A

Explicit information

Future Tense
Third person singular form

The future is used to to talk about an action that has not yet taken place or making plan (in the picture above the future is used to make predictions.... Cosa succederà nel futuro ...?) **Third person singular future forms are formed by adding the future ending à to the infinitive of the verb** (however the *are* verbs change the a of the infinitive ending to an e). Here you are presented with the third person singular form for regular verbs:

FUTURE

	Arrivare	Prendere	partire
lui\lei	arriv-er-<u>à</u>	prend-er-<u>à</u>	part-ir-<u>à</u>

Paolo arriver<u>à</u> la settimana prossima
(Paolo will arrive next week)

There are two clues that will help you to recognize future tense forms:

1. the future tense (third person) of regular verbs is formed by adding the ending <u>à</u> to the infinitive minus the final e. The future endings of verbs in *are ere* and *ire* are the same.
2. the spoken stress on 3rd persons singular is on the final accented vowel of the ending.

The second clue will be very useful in order to distinguish future forms from those forms of the present tense (a). An important difference is in the spoken stress of the final vowel of the future tense.

Future forms are usually accompanied by temporal adverbs that indicate that the action of the verboccured in the future. Here are some of these future temporal adverbs:-**domani-la settimana prossima-il mese prossimo**

However, although these adverbials are a good clue to know that an action has occured in the future they are not always present in the sentences you encounter. This is the reason why it will be important for you to recognize future tense forms.

Sample Referential Structured Input Activity

Activity 1. Listen to each sentence. First, decide if the sentences are in the present or in the future; then select who will probably perform them or where they will take place.

1. present	Andrew	☐
future	Charles	☐
	Camilla	☐
2. present	Bush	☐
future	Blair	☐
	Silvio Berlusconi	☐
3. present	Francia	☐
future	Italia	☐
	Inghilterra	☐
4. present	Ravanelli	☐
future	Zola	☐
	Vialli	☐
5. present	Il Papa	☐
future	Clinton	☐
	La Regina	☐
6. present	Italia	☐
future	Francia	☐
	Giappone	☐

INSTRUCTOR'S SCRIPT
1. Diventerà il nuovo re d'Inghilterra
2. Visiterà l'Irlanda del Nord
3. Celebrerà il Giubileo
4. Gioca per il Chelsea
5. Abita a Buckingam Palace
6. Ospita i campionati del mondo di calcio

Activity 2

Step 1. Indicate whether or not you agree or disagree with each of the predictions listed below. Some of them will probably happen in the next ten years. Compare your response with someone else.

	Sono d'accordo	Non sono d'accordo
1. Una donna diventerà presidente degli USA.	☐	☐
2. Si troverà il vaccino per l'AIDS.	☐	☐
3. L'Italiano diventerà la lingua più importante d' Europa.	☐	☐
4. L'uomo arriverà sul pianeta Marte.	☐	☐
5. L'Irlanda del Nord diventerà uno stato indipendente.	☐	☐

Step 2. Compare your answer with your partners. Sei pessimista o ottimista?

APPENDIX B

Interpretation Task

Indicate whether the speaker is relating information about the present or the future.

1.	present	could not tell	future
2.	present	could not tell	future
3.	present	could not tell	future
4.	present	could not tell	future
5.	present	could not tell	future
6.	present	could not tell	future
7.	present	could not tell	future
8.	present	could not tell	future
9.	present	could not tell	future
10.	present	could not tell	future
11.	present	could not tell	future
12.	present	could not tell	future
13.	present	could not tell	future
14.	present	could not tell	future
15.	present	could not tell	future
16.	present	could not tell	future
17.	present	could not tell	future
18.	present	could not tell	future
19.	present	could not tell	future
20.	present	could not tell	future

SCRIPT FOR INTERPRETATION TEST

1. Nella classe di italiano insegneranno la grammatical agli studenti.
2. Ad una amica carrissima comprano un regalo molto bello.
3. A casa di un amico caro ascolto la partita di calcio.
4. A Londra assisterò ad una Conferenza sul disarmamento nucleare.
5. Ad una compagna di scuola presto i libri di Italiano.
6. In una scuola privata di una città italiana studio italiano.
7. In una biblioteca dell'Università consulterà i libri di storia per l'esame.
8. Al caffe dell'Università aspetta l' amico per andare al cinema.
9. Con vari amici di scuola lavorerò in un bar.
10. A tutti gli amici dell'Università manderete una cartolina dalla Spagna.
11. Le vacanze d'estate in Florida costano molti soldi.
12. Alla porta di ingresso salutate tutti gli amici di scuola.
13. Nel parco vicino a casa troverà una sua vecchia amica.
14. In un ristorante cinese molto elegante invita una amica a cenare.
15. Per il compleanno riceveranno molti regali dalla famiglia e dagli amici.
16. In una festa a casa di amici cucinerò degli spaghetti al pomodoro buonissimi.
17. In casa di un amico dell'Università prenderà un caffe prima di tornare a casa.
18. Nel campo da tennis vicino a casa gioca a tennis con un amico.
19. In vari paesi d' Europa compro un souvenir da portare a casa.
20. In compagnia di altri amici pranzerà in un ristorante francese.

APPENDIX C

Written Production Task

Complete the text with the future tense form of the verbs in parentheses.

L'anno prossimo (io) _____ (studiare) in una scuola americana molto famosa. Anche Paola _____(partire) per l'America per fare un Master a New York. Francesco e Giovanna, invece_____ (restare) in Italia per finire gli studi. Anche voi mi _____(raggiungere) in agosto per passare le vacanze insieme. E tu come _____(passare) l'anno prossimo?

Chapter 11

Processing Instruction and the Spanish Subjunctive: Is Explicit Information Needed?

Andrew P. Farley
University of Notre Dame

A point of debate among SLA researchers and practitioners is the extent to which explicit information (EI) is beneficial in promoting form-meaning connections within instructed SLA. The results of some studies (Scott, 1989; Alanen, 1995; de Graaff, 1997; among others) seem to indicate that it is beneficial and perhaps necessary with some instruction types; others such as DeKeyser (1998) and Sharwood-Smith (1985) argue that EI is beneficial in that it focuses learner attention more quickly on the targeted feature and allows it to be processed sooner. In contrast, the results of VanPatten and Oikennon (1996) suggest that explicit information provides no added beneficial effects for classroom L2 learners when the instruction type involved is processing instruction (PI). In that study, the group that received structured input alone performed as well or better than all other treatments. However, it has not yet been determined whether or not the results of VanPatten and Oikkenon are generalizable to other structures with arguably different (read "more difficult") processing and production problems. The Spanish subjunctive, the targeted grammatical structure for the present study, is one such structure. (See Farley, this volume, chap. 7, for an overview of the particular use of the Spanish subjunctive targeted for this study as well as a discussion of why it may be considered more difficult than the structure used in VanPatten & Oikkenon's study.) If the results of the present study are similar to those of VanPatten and Oikkenon, then we will have important evidence regarding the role of explicit information in instructed SLA; namely, that explicit information may appear to be useful, perhaps even necessary, in some kinds of instruction (e.g., that used in Scott, Alanen, and other studies) but not in PI. If the results are not similar, then we may be seeing some limitations on the conclusions about PI offered by VanPatten (e.g., VanPatten, 2002) and others.

The purpose of the present study, then, is to partially replicate the work of VanPatten and Oikkenon. In addition to altering the target linguistic structure, this study differs in that only two groups are compared: a PI group and a structured input only (SI) group. The questions guiding the study are the following:

1. As in VanPatten and Oikkenon, does SI alone bring about improved performance on sentence-level tasks involving the interpretation and production of the Spanish subjunctive of doubt?
2. If so, is the improved performance the same as that for a group receiving regular PI that includes explicit information?

METHOD

The present study used the same materials, assessment tasks, and analyses as those described in Farley (this volume, chap. 7). I will therefore not repeat all the information here, but will provide that which will allow the reader to understand the method of the experiment in order to interpret the results. The reader may wish to (re)read Chapter 7 before reading the present study.

Participants

University students from a fourth-semester Spanish course were randomly assigned to two treatment groups: processing instruction (PI) and structured input (SI). Prior to the treatment, the participants had not received any formal exposure to the Spanish subjunctive and no instruction in its use after expressions of uncertainty at any time during the semester. Participants had been exposed to processing instruction in previous coursework; that is, they were familiar with structured input activities, and they were accustomed to receiving information about processing strategies on a regular basis. As standard with research on PI, only the data from participants who scored less than 60% on the pretest were analyzed in order to avoid ceiling effects. In addition, those who indicated on a survey that they knew more than one second language were excluded from the study. Finally, those who indicated that they had studied the subjunctive in any way outside of class during the treatment period were also excluded. All participants were native speakers of English, and none reported any disabilities or impairments of any kind. The final n size for the study was 54.

Materials

Both the PI group and the SI group received ten structured input activities of two principal types: referential and affective. The referential activities required learners to focus on form and to make a decision about meaning based on form for each activity item. In contrast to referential activities, the affective activities had more than one correct answer. The affective activity items asked for learners' opinions or beliefs or were based on the learners' world knowledge. The activities were structured such that the learners would need to rely on the subjunctive verb form to complete the task at hand. (See Farley, this volume, chap. 7, for a full description with examples of the activities and how they consider the processing problems in the Lexical Preference Principle and the Sentence Location Principle.)

Five activities (three referential and two affective) were completed on the first day of instruction and five activities (three referential and two affective) were completed on the second day of instruction. Of the ten activities, six involved reading utterances containing subjunctives or indicatives and four involved listening. Participants never produced any subjunctives during any portion of the treatment. The instruction was administered over two consecutive days for a total of approximately one hundred minutes. With regard to the *activities*, treatment was identical for the PI and SI groups.

A one-page (one-sided) handout was given to the PI group on the first day of instruction. The first five minutes of the treatment were devoted to reading aloud the explicit information contained on the handout. Following the nature of explicit information used in PI (see Wong, this volume, chap. 2), this handout contained the following information: an explanation of the relationship between subjunctive forms and the meaning of doubt they can convey; and information (appropriate for a layperson) about processing strategies, showing learners how the Lexical Preference Principle and the Sentence Location Principle may not work to learners' benefit with the Spanish subjunctive. Finally, one sample referential activity item was provided as a model for the activities that would follow. After the instructor had finished reading the handout with the PI group, they immediately began the activities. During the rest of the session, none of the explicit information was repeated or referred to, and no further grammatical explanation of any kind was given. The instructor did, however, indicate during referential activities whether an answer was correct or not, but did not explain why (e.g., "Sorry, the answer is *Creo que* ... OK. Let's move on to the next one.") The handout was retrieved at the end of the 50-minute class period in order to prevent exposure or study outside of the two treatment sessions. During the second 50-minute session on the following day, the PI group did not receive the handout and the instructor did not make reference to it.

The SI group, of course, did not receive any explicit information of any kind prior to engagement in activities. The treatment started immediately with the first activity. As with the PI group, participants in the SI group did not receive explicit feedback with explanation if they answered incorrectly on a referential activity; the instructor merely said what the correct answer was but did not offer explicit information as to why. Thus, from beginning to end of treatment, the SI group did not receive information about what they were learning, how it worked, or what the learning problems might be. They were simply plunged head first into activities.

Assessment

The interpretation task required a response to a series of aural utterances. Test items required that participants choose between two main clauses already provided on their answer sheets to complete each sentence correctly. All test items were pre-recorded and played from a cassette player, with appoximately ten seconds elapsing between each test item. For each binary option test item, one clause triggered the indicative and the other triggered the subjunctive. For example, subjects heard … *cueste mucho* ('… it costs a lot.') and had to circle either (a) *Pienso que…* ('I think that …') or (b), *Dudo que* … ('I doubt that …'). Participants recorded their responses to each item on a scantron answer sheet and all test sheets were graded using a scanner and scantron-compatible computer software. There were a total of twenty-four items on the test, consisting of the following: (1) nine items requiring the selection of a matrix clause of doubt; (2) three items requiring the selection of a matrix clause of certainty; and (3) twelve distractor items unrelated to mood selection. Utterances in the interpretation task contained high-frequency lexical items that participants had already seen in previous coursework at the university level. There were three versions (A, B, C) of the interpretation task; all three versions were balanced for vocabulary and overall content. Using a Latin square design, a different ordering of the interpretation task was randomly assigned to the intact course sections within each treatment group.

The production task consisted of a written sentence-completion task in which there were the following types of items: (a) six items requiring the production of a subjunctive; (b) three items requiring the production of an indicative; and (c) twelve distractor items unrelated to mood selection. For the production task, participants conjugated the verb forms provided in parenthesis in order to finish each sentence in a grammatically correct manner. As already mentioned, six items contained a matrix clause of uncertainty and, therefore, required a subjunctive. The purpose for including three items requiring the production of indicatives was to determine whether or not overgeneralization would occur. If learners produced subjunctives where test items only allowed for indicatives, this was evidence of overgeneralization. The distractor items simply required subjects to produce other verb forms such as the preterite, the imperfect, and the future. As with the interpretation task, utterances in the production task contained high-frequency lexical items with which participants were already familiar. Again, there were three versions of the task which were balanced for content, and task versions were randomly assigned to the course sections within each group.

Procedure

Intact course sections were randomly assigned to one of the following treatments: SI only or regular PI (explicit information plus structured input). The treatment was administered to both groups during two 50-minute class periods on two regularly scheduled class days. No homework of any kind was assigned. Instructional materials were retrieved from the learners at the end of each treatment session.

All experimentation took place in the subjects' regular classroom during their regular class periods. The pretests were administered one day before instruction began. After the pretest was given, experienced language instructors who were not the participants' regular instructors and had never taught them before the present study conducted the classes. Like the participants, the instructors were familiar with structured input activities and they were used to sharing explicit information about grammatical points and about processing strategies on a regular basis. All of the instructors had either native or near-native proficiency in Spanish. To avoid the instructor being a confounding variable, each instructor taught two intact course sections each—one SI section and one PI section.

Scoring

For the interpretation task, the maximum score possible was nine for the subjunctive items and three for the indicative items. Raw scores were calculated in the following manner: correct response = 1 point; incorrect and blank responses = 0 point.

For the production task, the maximum score possible was six for the subjunctive items and three for the indicative items. Raw scores were calculated in the following manner. One point was awarded for the subjunctive items when any clear attempt was made to produce a subjunctive verb form. A clear attempt was defined as a vowel switch or stem change toward the subjunctive form. Conversely, no credit was awarded if a subjunctive form was not attempted. For the indicative items, one point was attributed to each attempt to produce an indicative verb form. A clear attempt was defined as the absence of a vowel switch or stem change toward the subjunctive. There was no penalty for errors in person/number or spelling mistakes unrelated to the vowel or root required.

RESULTS

The pretest means for both groups were below chance on the interpretation task. In addition, the means for both groups on the production task were below one-half point out of the six possible. Thus, participants in neither group appeared to have any significant amount of familiarity with the subjunctive after expressions of uncertainty.

For the interpretation task, both groups improved from the pretest to the first posttest and both groups sustained their improvement through the second posttest. In addition, the standard deviations for both groups increased from pretest to posttest 1 and again from posttest 1 to posttest 2, with the PI group recording a slightly higher standard deviation than the SI group at all three phases. Similarly, a comparison of the pretest means on the production task with the means on both posttests shows an improvement for both groups. The standard deviations on the production task more than tripled for both groups after the treatment. This was probably due to the fact that learners had become aware of the subjunctive as a possible answer, resulting in more variation in response to test items. The standard deviations did not differ dramatically from posttest 1 to posttest 2, and they were similar between treatment groups as well. Finally, the improvement for both groups was sustained over time. Table 11.1 presents the descriptive statistics for both groups on the subjunctive test items.

Interpretation Data

Raw scores for the interpretation task were calculated and a two-way analysis of variance (ANOVA) with repeated measures was performed. Instruction Type (SI, PI) was the between-subjects factor, whereas Time (pretest, posttest 1, posttest 2) was the within-subjects factor. The results reveal a significant main effect for Time, $F(1, 54)$, $= 38.54$, $p = .00$. There was also a significant effect for Instruction Type, $F(1, 54) = 17.46$, $p = .00$, and a significant interaction between Instruction Type and Time $F(1, 54) = 14.83$, $p = .00$. Figure 11.1 is a visual representation of the gains made by both groups on the interpretation task. From the means table and the figure, it is clear that the significant interaction is due to the PI group making greater gains than the SI group.

Production Data

Raw scores for the production task were calculated and a two-way analysis of variance (ANOVA) with repeated measures was performed. Instruction Type (SI, PI) was the between-subjects factor, whereas Time (pretest, posttest 1, posttest 2) was the within-subjects factor. The results reveal a significant main effect for Time, $F(1, 54) = 70.96$, $p = .00$. There was also a significant effect for Instruction Type $F(1, 54) = 11.57$, $p = .00$, and a significant interaction between Instruction Type and Time, $F(1, 54) = 9.63$, $p = .00$. Figure 11.2 is a visual

TABLE 11.1
Descriptive Statistics for Subjunctive Items

Task	Test	Treatment	N	Mean	SD	Min	Max	Range
Interpr.	Pre	SI	31	3.90	1.01	0	5	5
		PI	23	3.13	1.10	0	5	5
	Post 1	SI	31	4.39	1.43	0	9	9
		PI	23	6.43	1.70	0	9	9
	Post 2	SI	31	5.00	1.63	0	9	9
		PI	23	6.74	1.89	0	9	9
Prod.	Pre	SI	31	.48	.77	0	3	3
		PI	23	.22	.52	0	3	3
	Post 1	SI	31	2.35	2.15	0	6	6
		PI	23	4.43	1.75	0	6	6
	Post 2	SI	31	2.26	2.13	0	6	6
		PI	23	3.74	1.66	0	6	6

representation of the gains made by both groups on the production task. Again, from the means table and the figure, it is clear that the significant interaction is due to the PI group making greater gains than the SI group.

To summarize so far, both SI and PI made significant gains due to their respective treatments. Thus, we can say that SI alone is sufficient to cause improved performance on both interpretation and production tasks within the present framework. However, unlike previous research, the PI group made even greater gains. SI, then, did not bring about the same improved performance on either the interpretation or production tasks.

Indicative Items

Analyses were conducted separately on the indicative items to test for either overgeneralization of the subjunctive or a test taking strategy by which participants might answer with more subjunctive responses simply because that is what they were learning. Table 11.2 presents the descriptive statistics for both groups on the indicative test items.

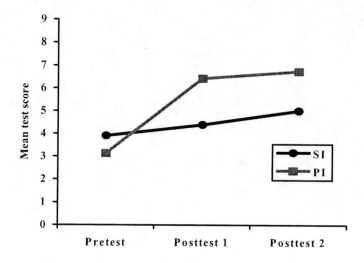

FIG. 11.1. Interpretation Data for Subjunctive Items.

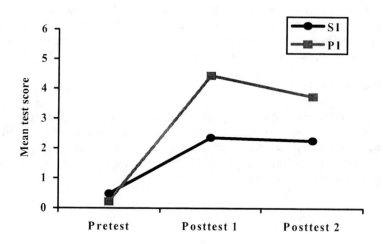

FIG. 11.2. Production Data for Subjunctive Items.

Raw scores for the indicative items of the interpretation task were calculated and a two-way analysis of variance (ANOVA) with repeated measures was performed. Instruction Type (SI, PI) was the between-subjects factor, whereas Time (pretest, posttest 1, posttest 2) was the within-subjects factor. The results did not reveal a significant main effect for Time, $F(1, 54) = 2.50$, $p = .09$. There was a significant effect for Instruction Type, $F(1, 54) = 9.96$, $p = .00$, and a significant interaction between Instruction Type and Time $F(1, 54) = 3.78$, $p = .03$. Figure 11.3 is a visual representation of the mean scores on the indicative items of the interpretation task for both groups. The means table and figure show that the significant interaction is due to the PI group's better performance.

Raw scores for the indicative items of the production task were calculated and a two-way analysis of variance (ANOVA) with repeated measures was performed. The results did not reveal a significant main effect for Time, $F(1, 54) = 1.53$, $p = .22$. There was no significant effect for Instruction Type, $F(1, 54) = 2.17$, $p = .15$, and no significant interaction between Instruction Type and Time, $F(1, 54) = .39$, $p = .68$. Figure 11.4 is a visual representation of the mean scores on the indicative items of the interpretation task for both groups.

The results, then, suggest that neither the PI nor the SI group overgeneralized the subjunctive in the present study or that they engaged in a test-taking strategy. In addition, the PI group improved on the interpretation task with indicative items while the SI group did not.

DISCUSSION

As expected, PI did bring about improved performance on sentence-level tasks involving the interpretation and production of the Spanish subjunctive of doubt. The SI group also improved on the sentence-level tasks involving the interpretation and the production of the Spanish subjunctive, although they did not receive any explicit information. Thus, in line with other research, SI alone appears to be sufficient to cause significant gains in scores after treatment (see, especially, Sanz, this volume, and Sanz & Morgan-Short, in press). However, different from related research is the finding that the two treatments did not bring about equal improved performance on the tasks. Both the interpretation data and the production data revealed that the PI group outperformed the SI group and the difference in mean scores for both tasks was found to be statistically significant. In addition, the PI group improved on the indicative items of the interpretation task, whereas the SI group did not perform as well after the treatment. The question before us, then, is why these results are different from other research in which PI and SI are compared? Even though the SI only group did make significant gains, why did PI fair better?

TABLE 11.2
Descriptive Statistics for Indicative Items

Task	Test	Treatment	N	Mean	SD	Min	Max	Range
Interpr.	Pre	SI	31	1.55	1.03	0	3	3
		PI	23	1.35	.88	0	3	3
	Post 1	SI	31	1.48	.72	0	3	3
		PI	23	2.13	.87	0	3	3
	Post 2	SI	31	1.45	.81	0	3	3
		PI	23	2.13	.92	0	3	3
Prod.	Pre	SI	31	2.84	.37	0	3	3
		PI	23	2.52	.79	0	3	3
	Post 1	SI	31	2.58	.67	0	3	3
		PI	23	2.39	.94	0	3	3
	Post 2	SI	31	2.65	.61	0	3	3
		PI	23	2.52	.79	0	3	3

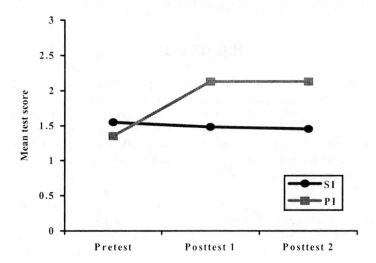

FIG. 11.3. Interpretation Data for Indicative Items.

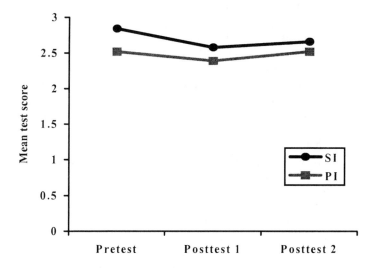

FIG. 11.4. Production Data for Indicative Items.

What is different in the present study, of course, is the target item. The nature of the subjunctive mood in contextualized language use is not readily transparent. Unlike tense (in which the difference between past, present and future is relatively clear and understandable to all adult learners) and agency (that subjects/agents and objects/patients play quite different roles), mood as a feature is not readily understandable or clear to learners. This is especially the case if the L1 does not have a particularly active or vibrant subjunctive mood. And because the subjunctive is triggered by a variety of semantic conditions, there is no simple one-to-one correspondence. In the present study, only one use of the subjunctive was selected. However, Although the triggers for the subjunctive in the structured input activities could all be grouped under the umbrella term "doubt," this categorical use of the subjunctive may not be readily transparent when the triggers range from *I doubt that*, to *I'm not sure that* to *It's possible that*. Contrast these with the triggers for a past tense inflection: *yesterday*, *last week*, *two days ago*, and so on. In this latter case, the triggers all readily connect to the concept of "pastness" without a problem. Better yet, compare the subjunctive mood with agency. "Who does what to whom?" is essential to sentence interpretation and it is easier to pick up on the cues to agency/patience once a person has clear feedback that a misinterpretation has occurred. Something like *It's impossible* or *It's highly likely*, both of which trigger the subjunctive in Spanish, does not readily connect to "doubt" as a category. What the subjunctive has, then, is a form that needs to be connected to multiple submeanings. More than likely, learners first begin subjunctive acquisition as item learning; that is, for them particular phrases and not semantic categories trigger the subjunctive verbal inflection. If this is the case, it would take longer for the SI group to make these connections. For the PI group, the added explicit information may have helped them see the form-meaning connections in the structured input activities more quickly and reduce the item-by-item analysis that the SI participants must have undertaken.

If the above interpretation is correct, then the conclusion of the present study is that explicit information may be *beneficial* in PI for some features of language; those that have opaque or semantically non-transparent form-meaning connections. However, because the SI group did make significant gains without explicit information, we cannot conclude that explicit information is necessary. Clearly, as in the case of all the other studies comparing SI and PI, SI is the necessary and sufficient ingredient of PI. For some structures, however, learners may need more SI than they would otherwise. To test this hypothesis, a researcher would need to deliver all instruction via computer that would also track response accuracies over time. In such an experiment, one would want to compare PI and SI with past tense forms and PI and SI with subjunctive forms. The prediction would be that learners in the SI past group would get to more accurate responses sooner than would those with SI with subjunctive.

CONCLUSIONS

Is explicit information beneficial in promoting form-meaning connections within instructed SLA? The present study suggests that explicit information is beneficial in helping learners notice and subsequently process the Spanish subjunctive after expressions of doubt. At the same time, the study also suggests that with SI alone learners can still acquire the subjunctive in the absence of explicit information. The interpretation of these results, then, is that explicit information can affect the *rate* of acquisition by affecting the onset of when learners actually begin to make accurate form-meaning connections. This is especially true for structures that are less transparent in terms of the type of meaning that is being connected with the form. In the final analysis, however, when all studies of PI and SI are considered together the conclusion must be this: Although explicit information may bring added benefits causing learners to notice the subjunctive sooner, structured input remains the *necessary and perhaps sufficient* component of PI that leads to form-meaning connections in instructed SLA.

REFERENCES

Alanen, R. (1995). Input enhancement and rule presentation in second language acquisition. In R. Schmidt (Ed.), *Attention and awareness in foreign language learning and teaching* (pp. 259–302). Honolulu: University of Hawaii Press.

de Graaff, R. (1997). The eXperanto experiment: Effects of explicit instruction on second language acquisition. *Studies in Second Language Acquisition, 19*, 249–297.

DeKeyser, R. (1998). Beyond focus on form: Cognitive perspectives on learning and practicing second language grammar. In C. Doughty & J. Williams (Eds.), *Focus on form in classroom second language acquisition* (pp. 42–63). Cambridge: Cambridge University Press.

Sanz, C., & Morgan-Short, K. (in press). Positive evidence vs. explicit rule presentation and explicit negative feedback: A computer assisted study. *Language Learning.*

Scott, V. (1989). An empirical study of explicit and implicit teaching strategies in French. *The Modern Language Journal, 73*, 14–22.

Sharwood Smith, M. (1985). From input to intake: An argumentation in second language acquisition. In S. Gass & G. Madden (Eds.), *Input in second language acquisition* (pp. 394–403). Rowley, MA: Newbury House.

VanPatten, B., & Oikennon, S. (1996). Explanation versus structured input in processing instruction. *Studies in Second Language Acquisition, 18*, 495–510.

VanPatten, B. (2002). Processing instruction: An update. *Language Learning, 52*, 755–803.

Chapter 12

Computer Delivered Implicit Vs. Explicit Feedback in Processing Instruction

Cristina Sanz
Georgetown University

Processing Instruction (PI) is an instructional technique that addresses both the learner's attentional resources and the target form's characteristics such as salience and communicative value (VanPatten, 1993, 1996).[1] It seeks to change the way input is processed by the learner through provision of a clever mix of raw positive evidence, that is, practice in decoding input, and information about how the language works in the form of explicit information involving explanation of the target form as well as information about wrong processing strategies. (Although others may prefer the term explicit information, I use the terms *explanation* and *explicit information* interchangeably in the present paper.) Its input-focused practice is crucially structured so that learners need to attend to the target grammatical form/structure to understand the meaning and complete the activity (that is, the input practice involves task-essentialness; see Loschky & Bley-Vroman, 1993). The input is also manipulated so as to make it more salient: Only one form is presented at a time, and the key forms appear at the beginning of the sentence, a position that has been identified as more salient (Rosa & O'Neill, 1998). Grammar explanation is based on both linguistic and psycholinguistic principles and is geared to make learners aware of the need to

---

[1]The study was made possible by a Georgetown University Graduate School grant-in-aid and by funding secured by Edward Dixon, Faculty Liaison for the Faculty of Languages and Linguistics at Georgetown University through a FIPSE grant. I would like to thank Kara Morgan with whom I have co-authored reports of a study of which this is part, Gorky Cruz for transferring to LIBRA the original Hypercard application, and the graduate students in Instructed SLA for their effort in data gathering. Many thanks also to Bill VanPatten for his comments. Any remaining errors are mine.

change specific processing strategies. Out of the three components of instruction—explanation, structured input, and feedback—PI research has focused on the first two, leaving aside feedback as an uncontrolled variable. In this sense, PI research is no different from general research on the effects of explicit instruction (e.g., Alanen, 1995; de Graaff, 1997; N. Ellis, 1993; Robinson, 1996; Rosa & O'Neill, 1999; Spada & Lightbown, 1993; White, 1991).

Partly in response to critiques of PI studies which claimed that the variables of explanation and structured input had been confounded, VanPatten and Oikkenon (1996) examined the isolated effects of explicit information and practice by dividing 59 participants into three experimental groups which included: (1) A group that received both grammatical explanation and structured input (that is, regular PI), (2) a group that received explanation only (EO), and (3) a group which received structured input only (SIO). They found that for the interpretation task both the full PI and the SIO groups outperformed the EO group. For the production task, all groups improved, but the PIs and SIOs improved more. Based on these findings, the authors suggested that structured input activities, as opposed to explanation, were primarily responsible for the benefits found in PI. The findings of this study would be stronger, however, if the methodological design had better controlled for the amount of time on task and the feedback offered during treatment. It seems that the EO group was at a distinct disadvantage since their treatment lasted less than a fourth of the amount of time of the other treatments. Also, the EO group did not have the opportunity to make mistakes related to the target structure and receive feedback on their errors, whereas the PI and SI did receive feedback. Although these limitations must be considered, the results taken together with other PI studies (see Wong, this volume, chap. 2, and VanPatten, 2002) suggest that PI with its structured explanation, practice, and feedback is conducive to SLA. Particularly, the element of structured input may be key.

BACKGROUND

Feedback in SLA

As mentioned earlier, studies that address the effects of grammatical explanation generally offer feedback as part of their operationalization of instruction. This use of feedback, when not clearly defined, becomes a confounding variable that may interact with explanation. Complicating matters further, the type of feedback offered with explanation varies widely among the studies. It ranges from feedback given to an entire class to that which is addressed to an individual in a classroom setting to that provided by a computer program only indicating the correctness of an individual's answer or offering additional explicit information. Although most researchers have not isolated feedback as a variable, others have aimed to explore the role of feedback in L2.

An initial question that empirical research has addressed is if feedback provided any beneficial effect on the SLA process. Doughty and Varela (1998) investigated the potential effects of feedback in a communicative classroom setting. Students receiving recasts improved on both the accuracy of their oral production and increased the number of attempts they made to produce the target form. A second question to be answered regarding feedback is how effective feedback is compared to other means of providing learners with similar information. Tomasello and Herron (1989) found that students given feedback acquire target forms better than those provided with models of the form. They suggested that if students formed a hypothesis and received immediate feedback giving them information on the correctness of that hypothesis, they would then be able to "cognitively compare" their interlanguage to that of the target language, a process that may lead to acquisition (p. 392). The next logical step in feedback research was to attempt to distinguish between effects of different types of feedback. Leeman (2000) examined if the positive effects of recasts identified in previous literature were due to the negative evidence component or to the enhanced saliency component of recasts. She found that groups exposed to recasts and enhanced saliency significantly outperformed a control group on a posttest, but only the enhanced saliency group maintained the effects on a delayed posttest.

Also attempting to distinguish between effects of different types of feedback, Carroll and Swain's (1993) study assigned 100 adult ESL learners to four experimental groups and a control group. Participants received training on the English dative alternation under one of four conditions: group (a) was provided with metalinguistic information; group (b) was told whether a response was right or wrong and was given a model; group (c) was told whether a response was right or wrong; and learners in group (d) were asked if they were sure about their response. The control group was given no feedback. All groups receiving feedback performed significantly better than the control group. Also, the group whose feedback included metalinguistic information outperformed all other groups. Carroll and Swain concluded from the results that both direct and indirect forms of feedback could aid L2 learners' learning of abstract linguistic generalizations, but that explicit feedback was most helpful.

Finally, Rosa's unpublished dissertation (Rosa, 1999) also investigated the issue of explicit and implicit feedback as part of a larger study on the relationship between an external variable (i.e., explicitness as grammatical explanation prior to and during practice) and an internal variable (i.e., awareness in L2 development). Her study adds to the debate on the role of implicit and explicit evidence in SLA, and investigates whether exposure to L2 input through problem-solving comprehension tasks (solving a puzzle) of varying degrees and types of explicitness have a differential effect on learner's intake and controlled written production of a Spanish structure. The study distinguished between differential effects on production of old and new examples of the key form, namely Spanish contrary-to-fact conditional sentences in the past. One-hundred fifth-semester Spanish students were equally divided into five treatment groups which resulted from combining the three independent variables: task-essentialness (problem-solving vs. simple exposure); explicit/implicit feedback, and grammar explanation. Feedback was operationalized as follows: explicit feedback provided information regarding the time reference of the sentence plus the appropriate verb form; and implicit feedback as in "OK" or "Try again"

Participants had to write down the sentence fragment that solved every puzzle on an answer sheet so as to establish that attention was paid to the target structure; they were asked to think aloud while solving the puzzle to establish levels of attention and to complete a questionnaire after treatment for further assessment of level of awareness. Based on her results, Rosa concluded that type and degree of explicitness have differential effects; specifically, she found that more explicit treatments lead to significantly higher levels of attainment and that explicit feedback is superior to explicit rule presentation. In her discussion, as in the title of her study, task-essentialness takes a second place to focus on explicitness and awareness. However, results from the experimental groups were consistently superior to those of the control group, leading to the obvious conclusion that task essentialness has a differential effect, and that meaningful practice, rather than mere exposure, is enough to promote a change in L2 behavior.

Feedback in CALL

Feedback offered in *CALL* (Computer Assisted Language Learning) programs has found some pedagogical support. It potentially can improve students' performance on written assignments (Warden, 1995) as well as on target linguistic forms and structures (McCarthy, 1996; McEnery, Baker, & Wilson, 1995). Although students' perceptions of different types of feedback may vary (Brandl, 1995), they are mostly positive (McEnery et al., 1995; Nagata 1993; Nagata & Swisher, 1995; Yang & Akahori, 1999).

Nagata (1993; Nagata & Swisher, 1995) reports one of the few empirical studies specifically addressing the effectiveness of feedback in CALL. Nagata suggested that because computers provide immediate feedback, they are more effective as they can draw learners' attention to problems in their developing grammars. She thus set out to examine if traditional or intelligent feedback, as operationalized below, served better as a "consciousness-raiser." She first designed the Nihongo-CALI system that included a morphological parser, a syntactic parser, and three databases, including a lexicon, morphological rules, and syntactic rules. The quasi-experimental study compared the effectiveness of the two different levels of computer feedback, traditional versus intelligent, on 32 students' production of Japanese passive structures. The students, who were enrolled in a second-year university Japanese course, were paired by results of a written test to assess knowledge of basic grammar and assigned randomly to two groups. The traditional group (T-CALI) received feedback indicating what was missing or not expected, and the intelligent group (I-CALI) received feedback that included the above plus detailed metalinguistic explanations. The analyses showed that after four computer treatment sessions, type of feedback did not affect production of verbal predicates, but the I-CALI group significantly outperformed the T-CALI group on production of particles. Also, the means were higher and the standard deviations were lower for the I-CALI group's responses on a questionnaire on students' preferences, indicating that the I-CALI system was uniformly preferred over the T-CALI system. Qualitative analysis of the questionnaire revealed that students in the T-CALI group experienced difficulty in understanding how to correct answers and carrying over the knowledge to other items. However, it was observed that even for the I-CALI group, too many error corrections may be "more information than [a student] can pay attention to at a time" (p. 345). Nagata concludes from the study that "when a grammatical system is nontrivially complex, metalinguistic feedback by means of computer-aided instruction involving natural language processing is more effective than traditional CALI feedback" (pp. 34 –355).

Nagata's results, taken together with research on the impact of feedback in SLA such as Carroll & Swain's work, suggest that explicit feedback, as opposed to feedback without grammar explanation, results in augmented acquisition of a complex structure. Contrary to this conclusion, work by Leeman (2000) and VanPatten and Oikkenon (1996) suggest that practice in decoding manipulated input (in their work enhanced and structured, respectively) rather than simple exposure in combination with negative or explicit evidence can lead to changes in L2 knowledge, a conclusion that Rosa's results on the task-essentialness variable also suggest. Obviously, the effects of explicit feedback depend on whether it is provided during production or during practice in decoding input, in combination with pure exposure or as part of tasks characterized by task essentialness, defined by Loschky and Bley-Vroman (1993, p. 132) as "the most extreme demand a task can place on a structure . . . the task cannot be successfully performed unless the structure is used." The present study contributes to this line of research on the impact of explicit information in the form of feedback and continues VanPatten and Oikkenon's work to further refine the design of PI studies and dissect the effects of practice in decoding structured input versus. the effects of explicit rule presentation.

For the first time, a study on PI will implement CALL in its design not only to test the effectiveness of PI outside the classroom but to provide feedback that is immediate, individualized, and focused on the key form. Based on the literature reviewed, the present study not only tests the hypothesis that exposure to structured input will lead to a change in L2 behavior, but also that immediate explicit feedback will further enhance those effects. The group receiving explicit feedback will significantly outperform the implicit feedback group in their ability to interpret and produce Spanish O-cliticpro V S and O-cliticropro V sentences.

THE STUDY

Participants

One hundred forty-two students enrolled in first- or second-year courses of Spanish language programs at Georgetown University volunteered to participate in the study in exchange for free tickets to one of the movie theaters in the university area; however, only 53 fulfilled the requirements needed to be part of the final sample. Sixteen of them were randomly assigned to the implicit feedback group, and 12 to the explicit feedback group.[2] Each group interacted with a different computer lesson. All participants were monolingual native speakers of English who scored at or below 60% on the interpretation pretest and had completed all treatment and testing sessions.

Instructional Materials

The computer lessons had been transferred to a Mac-based multimedia authoring system for educators called LIBRA[3] from a Hypercard application created by Sanz and colleagues in 1992. Participants interacted with two different lessons that resulted from combining [+/-feedback], but the lessons were identical in the type and amount of practice on processing O-clitic proV S and O-clitic pro V types of clauses. None of the treatments included explanation prior to practice. Following PI principles (see Wong, this volume, chap. 2), practice is characterized by not engaging participants in producing language but actively engaging them in processing meaningful input, by presenting one form (first, second, or third person) at a time, by combining both referential and affective activities and by combining different types of input: oral and written, sentential and discourse-level (i.e., articles, short biographies). Because the lessons were input-based, all participants needed to do was identify the correct visual cue (still frames) by clicking on them with a mouse, thus avoiding any typing errors. Practice decoding oral input was similar to these examples with the only difference that the input was an oral recording digitized for the purpose of delivery via computer.

Explicit feedback as it was operationalized in the experiment had a great potential to make a change in the participants' linguistic behavior because it was

---

[2]The present study was conducted as part of a project on the effects of amount and timing of explicit instruction vs. raw positive evidence. The other 25 participants were exposed to explicit discussion of grammar rules *prior* to engaging in practice. For a report, see Sanz & Morgan-Short (in press).

[3]For a review of LIBRA and further details on the lesson see Sanz (2000).

(1) immediate and could take advantage of what has been called 'the cognitive window of opportunity' (Doughty, 1998); (2) personalized and provided only when needed; and (3) focused on O-cliticpro V S and O-cliticpro V clauses and the source of error (incorrect use of the strategy or VanPatten's Principle 2, this volume). This was possible because in input-based activities such as those prescribed by PI guidelines there was only one possible source for each error and because limiting action to the click of the mouse would eliminate typing errors. An example of explicit feedback can be seen in Figure 12.1, which shows how the information provided as part of the feedback benefits from what we know about the way learners process O-cliticpro V S and O-cliticpro V sentences and the reason for the error.

Implicit feedback was operationalized as follows: The computer responded "OK" if the user's response was correct. "Sorry, try again" was displayed on the screen if the participant had chosen an incorrect response. This procedure respected the validity of the study, as CALL users expect computer lessons to provide feedback of some sort. In addition, the purpose of structured input activities is to push learners to a different processing strategy; this can only occur if they receive information that an interpretation is incorrect. Table 12.1 shows a summary of the treatments.

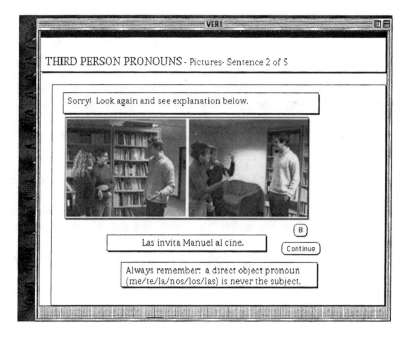

FIG. 12.1. Example of Practice at the Sentential Level With Explicit Feedback.

TABLE 12.1
Treatment Groups

Group	Practice	Explanation	Explicit Feedback
[-E, -F]	X	-	-
[-E +F]	X	-	X

Note: E = Explanation; F = Explicit Feedback

Testing Materials

The testing materials were the same as those used in Sanz's dissertation (1994), in VanPatten and Sanz (1995), and in Sanz (1997), but limited to the written mode. These studies showed that benefits of PI instruction extended beyond the sentential level and held true for more communicative tasks. They also concluded that, since learners performed differently on different tasks, the use of any one test to ascertain the effects of instruction may not be as reliable a method as would be the use of a variety of tests. Following this principle, the present study elicited two types of linguistic behavior, namely ability to interpret and ability to produce O-cliticpro V S and O-cliticpro V sentences, and included two different types of production tasks; one eliciting sentence-level production– in the nature of a sentence completion task and another discourse-level task that involved video retelling. The interpretation and sentence completion tasks are described in different sections of the present volume (see, for example, summaries of VanPatten & Cadierno, 1993, and VanPatten & Oikkenon, 1996, in this volume); therefore, I only provide details of the video-retelling task. This task required students to produce a connected short composition describing a story shown to them on a monitor. Two different stories were shown. Each story contained seven connected events. The participants were instructed to provide as much detail as possible so that students in other classes could pick out the video based on the description. These instructions provided both a communicative context for the task and maximized the amount of information elicited. Each video was shown twice. During the first viewing, the participants were instructed to do nothing but watch. During the second viewing, they were allowed to take notes, but they were not allowed to refer to them when they were writing their description. The descriptions were written only after the second viewing, and the monitor was turned off.

Different versions of each test were created as pretests and posttests in order to avoid test item effects. Given that we used the same tests as in previous research on PI with object pronouns in Spanish, which were balanced and tested for reliability, the present study assumed that there would be no effects due to test variation.

Procedure

Pretests were conducted in the participants' regular classes with the help of tape players and transparencies for the interpretation test, and VCRs for the video clips for the video-retelling task. After the pretest, participants were contacted to arrange individual times for the treatment phase of the experiment scheduled for not earlier than one week after the pretest. As participants came in for the treatment, they were randomly assigned to one of the two groups: implicit or explicit feedback. Group 1 (n = 12) received explicit feedback, whereas Group 2 (n = 16) received implicit feedback. Participants individually completed the posttest immediately after the treatment following a procedure identical to that used in whole classes. They recorded their answers in three separate packets distributed using a split-block design. In order to attempt to control for test effects, the order of the battery of tests (sentence interpretation, sentence completion, and video retelling) was different within each of the three packets. Distracting activities and a vocabulary familiarization list preceded each task. Scoring procedures also followed VanPatten and Cadierno; therefore, this section details only procedures for the Video Narration task (VanPatten & Sanz, 1995), which allowed for participant variation. Because each subject could produce a different number of sentences with preverbal object pronouns, the number of correct uses in the obligatory contexts created was counted for each participant and points were awarded in the same manner as in the sentence completion task. Adding the number of points awarded, and dividing that number by two times the number of obligatory contexts, created yielded a percentage score for the Video Narration task for each participant. For purposes of easy comparison, scores for the interpretation and sentence completion tasks were calculated as percentages as well.

RESULTS AND DISCUSSION

Results from a t-test showed no statistical differences between groups on the interpretation pretest, $t(27)$ = 0.015 , p = 0.988. Therefore, any between-group differences found on the posttests can be attributed to the treatment.

Results indicated that both groups increased in their comprehension and production of O-cliticpro V S and O-cliticpro V sentences as a consequence of exposure to the computer lessons. The average increase for both groups on the interpretation test was 32.20 points, for the sentence completion test it was 32.51 points, and for the video retelling test it was 29.93 points. The mean scores for each group by test are shown in Table 12.2.

A repeated measures ANOVA performed on the scores for the interpretation test yielded a significant main effect for Time, $F(1, 26)$ = 92.14, $p < .001$.

TABLE 12.2
Mean Scores for All Tasks: Learning Condition by Time

			Interpretation		Production: Sentence Completion		Production Video Retelling	
			Pre	Post	Pre	Post	Pre	Post
Group	N							
[-E -F]	16	Mean	26.25	62.50	42.44	66.00	31.38	55.75
		SD	18.57	22.06	35.84	30.59	33.38	30.80
[-E +F]	12	Mean	26.15	66.67	42.15	83.62	22.69	58.15
		SD	15.02	24.90	32.43	17.25	31.934	26.10

No effect was found for Group, $F(1, 26) = .25$, $p =.875$. No significant interaction was identified (Group x Time $F(1, 26) = .58$, $p =.45$). Both groups significantly increased their ability to interpret O-cliticV sentences, but no group significantly outperformed the other.

The same analysis was performed on the sentence completion test scores and similar results were obtained. Although there was a significant main effect for Time, $F(1, 26) = 27.03$, $p < .001$, no main effect was found for Group, $F(1, 26) = .847$, $p = .366$. No significant interaction was identified (Group x Time $F(1, 26) = 2.048$, $p = .164$). Scores from the video retelling were also analyzed. Again, similar results were obtained. A significant main effect was found for Time, $F(1, 26) = 5.94$, $p = .045$, but no effect was found for Group, $F(1, 26) = 2.63$, $p = .15$. No significant interaction was identified (Group x Time $F(1, 26) = 0.507$, $p = .50$). Results from the production data suggest that, similar to the interpretation findings, the structured input activities alone did result in a gain in ability to produce the target form. The type of feedback, whether implicit or explicit, produced no differential effects.

Results from the present study agree with those from VanPatten and Oikkenon, Leeman, and Rosa and O'Neill. All participants in this study, like Rosa and O'Neill's, learned as a result from practice in decoding input. Like Leeman's, these results show that it is enhanced input rather than negative evidence that is capable of leading to acquisition. And like VanPatten and Oikkenon's results, they show once more that it is practice in decoding structured input rather than provision of explicit evidence that is responsible for the effectiveness of PI.

These results run contrary to other studies on the effects of feedback, such as Nagata's and Carroll and Swain's. These two studies, like all previous research on instructional feedback, with the exception of Rosa (1999), are characterized by providing feedback on learner's production. The present study shows that explicit feedback provided on input-decoding performance during online sentence processing does not enhance the acquisition of morphosyntax as measured by interpretation and production tasks.

These results also run contrary to those from Rosa (1999), a study that, like ours, looked at the effects of explicit vs. implicit feedback in combination with practice in decoding input. Although the results of the present study show no significant differences between groups, Rosa found that the group that received only implicit feedback (the IFE group) performed significantly worse on the production of old items and the recognition and production of new items. Why should Rosa's IFE group have performed differently compared to the groups receiving at least one form of explicitness (prior to or during practice), whereas in the present study the group that received only implicit feedback ([-E, -F]) did not perform significantly different? A closer examination of the experimental treatments reveals underlying methodological differences that may account for these differential results.

Perhaps one of the most significant differences between Rosa's treatment and ours is the number of opportunities provided to learners, a key issue in the most implicit instructional techniques. In Rosa (1999), the practice provided to the learners consisted of 28 sentences, 18 of which contained the target forms. The present study, however, provided learners with 56 practice items, all of which required the use of the target form. A second difference in the practice was that my learners were presented with only two options for each item when participants in Rosa (1999) had to decide between four options. Consequently, Rosa's participants were required to eliminate three incorrect options to identify the correct choice as opposed to only having to eliminate one option in the present study. For groups given any amount of explicit information, the quantity of practice was sufficient so that significant differences did not occur between groups. However, without any explicit information, 18 practice items containing the target form supplied along with three incorrect options simply may not have been enough evidence to be conducive for noticing or internalizing the target form. Perhaps if the amount of practice had been greater, the IFE group would not have performed significantly different from the other groups.

A significant factor in Rosa's study is that the task-essentialness inherent to the puzzle task may have been lessened for groups not provided with some form of explicit information. For the groups receiving at least one form of explicit information, it was made apparent that the target-form was necessary to establish whether the hypothetical situation was relevant to the present or the past. With this information, learners were at one point or another directed to the tense (present or past) of the sentence provided as context for the puzzle sentence. Participants in the IFE group were never directed to distinguish between the present and past tense in the context sentence, and they might not have noticed the corresponding aspectual difference inherent in the target form. Without noticing the aspect of the form, making a form-meaning connection would not occur. Thus, while in the present study the task-essential practice did not vary between groups, Rosa's IFE group's practice may not have been task-essential as was the practice for the other groups. The non-essentialness of making form-meaning connections might be an explanation as to why the IFE group's performance differed from the other groups in her study.

Input processing research has identified the first-noun strategy as the one responsible for incorrect assignment of semantic functions to the NPs in a sentence. Spanish L2 studies show that a number of factors, among them transfer, salience, and frequency interact to delay the realization by learners that they are applying the wrong strategy. Processing Instruction has been designed to alter the L2 learner's processing strategy and combines various elements: explicit information about the strategy, its correct and incorrect use, practice in decoding structured input, and feedback. This study, together with VanPatten and Oikkennon and others, shows that it is structured input alone that works to force learners toward another processing path. In contrast with studies on the effects of explicitness combined with simple exposure, the present study concludes that simple exposure to input may not be sufficient and that practice is more effective; but not just any type of input or any type of practice. If acquisition is a failure-driven process (Carroll, 2001), PI sets learners up right from the start to make them fail and to make them realize that they have failed (see VanPatten, 2002). The input has been structured to increase the frequency of problematic utterances and meaningful activities are designed such that learners must interpret each sentence correctly in order to respond. Practice invites failure very early on thus causing learners to reevaluate their processing strategies and change them. A correct new strategy is reinforced by continuous provision of structured input. In conclusion, within PI it is positive evidence alone that leads to a change in processing and consequent L2 development.

CONCLUSIONS AND IMPLICATIONS

A series of studies has investigated the effects of Processing Instruction on a number of morphosyntactic and semantic features. This research has compared PI with production-based practice and has also dissected the explicit information component from the exposure-through-practice (structured input) component in an attempt to identify which of the two is responsible for the effectiveness of PI. The present study has added to this line of research by investigating the effects of explicitness in the form of feedback in PI to conclude, like VanPatten and Oikkenon (and others in the present volume), that it is practice in decoding structured input that leads to a change in processing strategies with positive consequences for acquisition.

Explicit feedback was operationalized in such a way as to make it the most effective possible: it was immediate, provided only when needed, individualized, and focused on the key form, the way computers can deliver feedback. As a matter of fact, my interest in conducting this study was as much theoretical as it was practical. CALL literature has for years discussed the most effective design of computer-generated feedback, including intelligent feedback. Perhaps because it is only loosely connected with SLA literature, the discussion has never questioned the effectiveness of feedback itself. That is, many in CALL have assumed that feedback was necessary and have worked toward making it as explicit as possible. However, this line of research has never asked an even more basic question: perhaps the feedback is required because the instruction and practice were not informed by SLA theory and research and the pedagogical tasks themselves were not optimal. Results from the present study suggest that some of the energy devoted to the design of the best possible feedback in CALL should instead be focused on the design of meaningful tasks that require attention to both meaning and form.

REFERENCES

Alanen, R. (1995). Input enhancement and rule presentation in second language acquisition. In R. Schmidt (Ed.), *Attention and awareness in foreign language learning* (pp. 259–302). Honolulu: University of Hawaii Press.

Brandl, K. K. (1995). Strong and weak students' preferences for error feedback options and responses. *The Modern Language Journal, 79,* 194–211.

Carroll, S. (2001). *Input and evidence: The raw material of second language acquisition.* Philadelphia: John Benjamins.

Carroll, S., & Swain, M. (1993). Explicit and implicit negative feedback: An empirical study of the learning of linguistic generalizations. *Studies in Second Language Acquisition, 15,* 357–386.

de Graaff, R. (1997). The eXperanto experiment: Effects of explicit instruction on second language acquisition. *Studies in Second Language Acquisition, 19,* 249–276.

Doughty, C. (1998). Keynote address at The Second Language Research Forum. Honoloulu: The University of Hawaii at Manoa.

Doughty, C., & Varela, E. (1998). Communicative focus on form. In C. Doughty and J. Williams (Eds.), *Focus on form in classroom second language acquisition* (pp. 114–138). Cambridge: Cambridge University Press.

Ellis, N. (1993). Rules and instances in foreign language learning: Interactions of explicit and implicit knowledge. *European Journal of Cognitive Psychology, 5,* 289–318.

Leeman, J. (2000). Towards a new classification of input: An empirical study of the effect of recasts, negative evidence, and enhanced salience of L2 development. Unpublished doctoral dissertation, Georgetown University, Washington, D.C.

Loschky, L., & Bley-Vroman, R. (1993). Grammar and task-based learning. In G. Crookes & S. Gass (Eds.), *Tasks and language learning: Integrating theory and practice* (pp. 123–167). Clevedon, Avon: Multilingual Matters.

McCarthy, B. (1996). Fully integrated CALL: Mission accomplished. *ReCALL, 8,* 17–34.

McEnery, T., Baker, J. P., & Wilson, A. (1995). A statistical analysis of corpus based computer vs. traditional human teaching methods of part of speech analysis. *Computer Assisted Language Learning, 8,* 259–274.

Nagata, N. (1993). Intelligent computer feedback for second language instruction. *The Modern Language Journal, 77,* 330–339.

Nagata, N., & Swisher, M. V. (1995). A study of consciousness-raising by computer: The effect of metalinguistic feedback on SLA. *Foreign Language Annals, 28,* 336–347

Robinson, P. (1996). Learning simple and complex second language rules under implicit, incidental, rule-search, and instructed conditions. *Studies in Second Language Acquisition, 18,* 27–67.

Rosa, E. (1999). A cognitive approach to task-based research: Explicitness, awareness and L2 development. Unpublished doctoral dissertation. Georgetown University, Washington, D.C.

Rosa, E., & O'Neill, M. (1998). Effects of stress and location on acoustic salience at the initial steps of Spanish L2 input processing. *Spanish Applied Linguistics, 2,* 24–52.

Rosa, E., & O'Neill, M. (1999). Explicitness, intake, and the issue of awareness: Another piece to the puzzle. *Studies in Second Language Acquisition, 21,* 511–556.

Sanz, C. (1994). Task, mode and the effects of input-based explicit instruction. Unpublished doctoral dissertation, University of Illinois, Urbana–Champaign.

Sanz, C. (1997). Experimental tasks in SLA research: Amount of production, modality, memory, and production processes. In A. T. Pérez-Lerroux & W. R. Glass (Eds.), *Contemporary perspectives on the acquisition of Spanish: Vol. 2. Production, processing, and comprehension* (pp. 41–56). Somerville, MA: Cascadilla Press.

Sanz, C. (2000). Implementing LIBRA for the design of experimental research in SLA. Language. *Learning and Technology Millennial, 13,* 27-31.

Sanz, C., & Morgan-Short, K. (in press). Positive Evidence vs. Explicit Rule Presentation and Explicit Negative Feedback: A Computer-Assisted Study. *Language Learning.*

Spada, N., & Lightbown, P. M. (1993). Instruction and the development of questions in L2 classrooms. *Studies in Second Language Acquisition, 15,* 205–224.

Tomasello, M., & Herron, C. (1989). Feedback for language transfer errors: The garden path technique. *Studies in Second Language Acquisition, 11,* 385–395.

VanPatten, B. (1993). Grammar instruction for the acquisition-rich classroom. *Foreign Language Annals, 26,* 433–450.

VanPatten, B. (1996). *Input processing and grammar instruction: Theory and research.* Norwood, NJ: Ablex.

VanPatten, B. (2002). Processing instruction: An update. *Language Learning, 52,* 755–803.

VanPatten, B., & Cadierno, T. (1993). Explicit instruction and input processing. *Studies in Second Language Acquisition, 15,* 225–243.

VanPatten, B., & Oikkenon, S. (1996). Explanation versus structured input in processing instruction. *Studies in Second Language Acquisition, 18,* 495–510.

VanPatten, B., & Sanz, C. (1995). From input to output: Processing instruction and communicative tasks. In F. Eckman, D. Highland, P. Lee, J. Mileham & R. Rutkowski (Eds.), *Second language acquisition: Theory and pedagogy* (pp. 169–185). Hillsdale, NJ: Lawrence Erlbaum Associates.

Warden, C. A. (1995). Expert system impact on writing errors in Taiwanese business English classes. *CALL Journal, 6,* 22–29.

White, L. (1991). Adverb placement in second language acquisition: Some effects of positive and negative evidence in the classroom. *Second Language Research, 7,* 133–161.

Yang, J. C., & Akahori, K. (1999). An evaluation of Japanese CALL systems on the WWW comparing a freely input approach with multiple selection. *Computer Assisted Language Learning, 12,* 59–79.

Chapter 13

Commentary: When PI is Focus on Form it is Very, Very good, but When it is Focus on Forms …

Catherine J. Doughty
University of Hawai'i

The Processing Instruction (PI) research program and the Input Processing (IP) model that underlies it have stimulated considerable interest in the applied SLA literature, a valuable discussion to which I take the opportunity to contribute briefly in my commentary on the chapters in this section.[1] Two major points of contention are whether the limited capacity memory model invoked in the IP model is valid, and whether various studies have operationalized PI in ways that are true to the original model and/or in ways that allow a valid comparison between PI and traditional instruction (TI) (Dekeyser, et al., 2002). While these issues have generated important debate concerning the nature of L2 processing, the former concerns large cognitive processing issues that will likely take many years to resolve, and the latter I think, in part, is a red herring. Therefore, I concentrate my discussion on the operationalization of PI, making three specific points concerning L2 learner attention, explicit L2 instruction, and measuring the effects of instruction on SLA.

First, the potential that I have always seen in PI lies in its aim to draw learner attention to form while meaning and function are evident to the learner, that is, focus on form (Doughty & Williams, 1998a & b; Long, 1991; Long & Robinson, 1998).[2] When maximally specified, however, PI often comprises more elements than are necessary for inducing the noticing of forms while processing meaning, and hence is either inefficient or, at times, may be counterproductive. My second point is that the discussions in the literature that persist on the topic of whether the explicit instruction in PI and traditional

---

[1] See *Language Learning 52,4* for a point-counterpoint discussion between Van Patten and DeKeyser, et. al.).

[2] Focus on form, a momentary processing phenomenon, need not always be entangled in the memory model debate to be examined in its own right.

instructional treatments are comparable in any one particular study, and/or are matched to the mode of outcome measures, are way off track. This is because it is precisely the explicit instruction component that appears to be an unnecessary element of PI. And, finally, as is the case with every other kind of effects-of-instruction research to date, most studies designed to assess PI have not paid careful attention to the validity of outcome measures. This is an aspect of research design that will have to improve if findings of PI—or concerning any other type of L2 instruction—are to be considered trustworthy (Doughty, 2003; Norris & Ortega, 2000).

Let us now turn to a more detailed discussion of each of these points, relying on the designs and outcomes of the four studies reported in this section to provide concrete examples of the issues. Each has intended in some way or another to extend the PI research paradigm that was launched in the early 1990s (VanPatten & Cadierno, 1993). That this line of research has proceeded in such an orderly fashion is certainly to be commended, and all of my comments in the section are intended to improve the design of this and other types of effects-of-instruction research. Taken together, the four PI studies address two research questions, the latter of which, is motivated by the findings of VanPatten & Oikkenon (1996) (as discussed in more detail by VanPatten at the outset of this section):

1.   Does PI alter any other inefficient L2 processing strategies, that is besides the first-noun strategy?

2.   What are the contributions of the individual components of PI (i.e., explanation, structured input processing, and feedback), or, put another way, which are necessary?

For convenience, I have summarized the designs and findings of the studies in Table 13.1. As shown in column two, all four researchers have clearly explicated an L2 processing problem. Furthermore, the study reports all include detailed descriptions plus examples of how the PI treatments were operationalized (or citations of other readily accessible sources where these may be found). This kind of exemplary study reporting is all too uncommon in the published literature (Norris & Ortega, 2000).

With respect to the frequently asked question concerning whether PI can solve other processing problems besides the first-noun strategy, the results of the three studies that address this (Wong, Benati, and Farley) appear, on the face of it, to be compatible with the logical assumption that PI should be generalizable. However, I suggest that caution is in order regarding the interpretation of the

TABLE 13.1
Extending PI to Other Learning Problems

Author	Learning Problem	Processing Aim	Pedagogic Technique	Results
Wong	L1 English L2 French learners do not notice the *de/un* distinction as the information provided by *de* (neg.)) is redundant with other forms (*ne ...pas*) *Lexical strategy*	Attract learner attention to a redundant and difficult to perceive form	Remove the *ne ... pas* so that learners must process *de/un*	Interpretation: all groups but controls improved *PI=SI>EI=control* Production: all groups but controls improved *PI=SI; SI=EI; EI=control*
Benati	L1 English L2 Italian learners are more apt to use lexical items (e.g., adverbs) than morphemes (e.g., inflections) to assign tense *Lexical strategy*	Attract learner attention to a redundant and difficult to perceive form	Remove the lexical items and force learners to process bound morphemes	Interpretation and production findings the same: all groups improved; no control group *PI=SI>EI*

Note: TABLE 13.1 continues on the next page

findings of these studies. On close examination of the structured processing activities employed in all three, it becomes evident that they often depart considerably from some SI activities used in earlier studies. As shown in Table 13.2, the activities are much more like language manipulation and metalinguistic activities (e.g., fill in the blank, label the sentence) than are many of the referential and affective processing activities in earlier studies. This is not a trivial departure because, in my view, the single most valuable component of PI has not been operationalized in these newer PI treatments. In other words, meaning and function are not made evident to learner at that time that they are

TABLE 13.1
Extending PI to Other Learning Problems (*cont'*)

Author	Learning Problem	Processing Aim	Pedagogic Technique	Results
Farley	L1 English L2 Spanish learners get the meaning of subjunctive mood from the trigger phases (like *Dudo que* ...) *Lexical strategy*	Attract learner attention to a redundant and difficult to perceive form	Require learners to match trigger clauses with appropriate mood	Interpretation and production findings the same: both groups gained; no control group; neither group overgeneralized *PI>SI*
Sanz	L1 English L2 Spanish learners attempt to assign the subject role to the first noun-like entity encountered *First-noun strategy*	Get learner to use the actual (more difficult to perceive) cues in the input rather than L1 word order expectation to assign grammatical roles	Match a picture to a sentence heard or respond to the meaning of an utterance.	Interpretation, S-level production, and video retelling findings the same: both groups improved; no control group; no differential effect of type of feedback *SI + metafb = SI +yes/nofb*

directed to process the target feature.[3] The reader can easily discern differences in activities by comparing Fig. 12.1 in Sanz, this volume, p. 247, with the activities that appear in the other studies listed in Table 13.2.

In the Sanz activity, as well as in other earlier studies (Cadierno, 1992; VanPatten & Cadierno, 1993; VanPatten & Oikkenon, 1996), and in the study reported by Sanz in this section, learners match an utterance to a visual representation (picture or video clip). The picture makes the meaning clear, and the learner then is required to allocate attentional resources to paying attention to the cues in the utterance so that it can be matched to the

---

[3]It could be argued that English translations provided ensure comprehension on the part of the learner. However, it is not at all evident what the connection between comprehending input in the L1 has to do with processing L2 input.

TABLE 13.2
Instructional Treatments

Author	Interpretation Activities - Referential	Interpretation Activities – Affective
Wong	Complete sentences of these types ___ *de* + noun or ___ *un* + noun or by filling in the blank with *Nous avons* or *Nous n'avons pas.*	Looking at lists of what college dorm rooms could have (some stated in affirmative, some negative) decide what is and is not typical today and in 1960.
Benati	Listen to a sentence and label it as future or present. Then select from a list of celebrities the one most likely to do the activity described in the sentence. Hear: *Diventerà il nuovo re d''Inghiliterra* Select: Present Andrew Future Charles Camill	Agree or disagree with predictions (expressed in future tense).
Farley	Listen to the subordinate clause of a sentence, and then choose the correct between two main clauses provided in writing. Hear: *...hace su tarea por la noche.* Select: *Yo sé que* *No creo que...*	On a list that begins with a clause that triggers subjunctive (*No creo que la revista "Enquirer"...*), check off items that you agree with
Sanz	Listen to a sentence and select the picture that goes with what you hear.	Read a list of sentences and indicate which ones apply to you.

meaning portrayed in the picture. This type of activity that genuinely fosters focus on form embodies, in my opinion, the real value of PI in that the intended aim of altering an unsuccessful strategy is achieved in the context of processing meaning. Including metalinguistic activities in a PI instructional sequence is likely to be superfluous, but when the essential activity that fosters forms-meaning-function mapping is missing, this constitutes a serious omission, and renders the PI like traditional instruction. VanPatten & Cadierno (1993) have themselves observed that whereas PI intends to lead to acquisition, TI results in a different knowledge system.

In considering what may have brought about the departure from the original PI treatment design, it became clear that the processing problems addressed in these studies are of a different nature than is the first noun strategy. Essentially, there are at least two types of processing problems that L2 learners experience: they may be processing according to a strategy that has been developed during L1 acquisition (such as the first-noun strategy), or they may be failing to notice something that is not salient in the input, either because it is difficult to perceive or because the information is available in some other more noticeable form, or both: For instance, the lexical strategy will get the learner information concerning tense. The details of these processing problems have been delineated in IP theory, and so need not be further elaborated here (see VanPatten, this volume). What is striking is the effect that the difference in learning problem has had on the design of the PI treatments in the studies under discussion.

In essence, the lack of meaningfulness of the forms has led to the omission of any component fostering meaningful processing in the instruction. More specifically, in addressing the failure-to-notice cases, two approaches have been taken in designing PI treatments: Wong and Benati have removed the more salient cue to try to force learners to process the less salient cue, and Farley requires learners to match the cues to the subjunctive, each of which appears in different clauses. The consequence of both approaches has been that the activities are focus on forms activities (i.e., language manipulation) rather than focus on form (i.e., mapping). One could ask whether focus on forms is ultimately necessary in cases when meaning is not available to be processed. Certainly the pedagogic procedures that have been implemented in these studies have led learners to be able to succeed on the test items in the outcome measures employed in the studies. However, as I argue later, the knowledge gained is not relevant to real SLA processes.

Thus, the question of how to draw learner attention to redundant or imperceptible forms in the input remains a thorny one and one that requires further investigation. It should be noted, however, that SLA research to date has demonstrated rather clearly that focus on forms results, at best, in only temporary influences on interlanguage development (Lightbown, 1983; and see Doughty, 2003, for discussion). What may be required is an emphasis on promoting the processing of chunks of meaningful language with only perceptual (not metacognitive) attention draw to redundant or hard-to-notice forms.

Close examination of the PI treatments in the approach taken by Wong and Benati also shows that the input has been simplified in a way that may potentially be detrimental to SLA. In other words, some of the data that is necessary for language acquisition has been removed from the processing. Because the L2 learner needs to be able to notice imperceptible cues when they occur along with the more readily perceptible ones, it would seem that, rather than simplification, input elaboration (Yano, Long, & Ross, 1994), perhaps in conjunction with input enhancement, would be a more effective pedagogic technique to draw learner attention to redundant elements. Another possible problem with their approach is a misunderstanding of the concept of task-essentialness, proposed by Loschky & Bley-Vroman (1993), that is, that learners must process the form in order to succeed at the task. What this means precisely is a requirement that learners must process the form correctly, otherwise the task completely fails. An example would be trying to build a machine and having parts leftover for not having understood that they needed to have been included. The consequence of this would be that the machine would not function. It would then (hopefully) be evident what was not understood (if the construction problem can be resolved, that is), and a subsequent attempt at the task might result in the correct processing of the critical input. In the SI activities in these studies, the only thing that happens if the form is not correctly processed is that the learner gets feedback that the answer is not correct. In other words, the task can be done, albeit inaccurately. To be sure, task essentialness is difficult to implement in any case, and difficult, if not impossible in the case of redundant features of language, or features of language that can be expressed by alternative means. Figuring out how to do so in PI or any other type of L2 instruction would make a valuable contribution to advancing the instructed SLA research agenda, but I suspect that only meaningful features of language are amenable to this design feature.

Next, we may consider the other major research question, addressed by Wong, Benati, and Sanz: What are the contributions of the individual components of PI (i.e., explanation, structured input processing, and feedback, in the case of Sanz)? The answer to this question will come from careful comparisons such as are already underway among studies carried out in the PI paradigm. PI in its original conceptualization entails at least two kinds of processing: focus on forms, or metalinguistic processing (the EI or metalinguistic explanation component), and focus on form (in the SI activities that make meaning evident to the learner) as depicted in the following scheme:

Metalinguistic explanation
↓

Structured input processing
↓

Implicit Feedback (correct/incorrect)

PI also provides the learner with feedback on decisions that, in some SI activities, are dependent on correct processing.

Which, then, are the effective components of PI? I believe that the original insight provided by IP theory, that is, that learner processing which goes awry needs to be altered, is correct (see Doughty, 2003, for more discussion). However, it is equally important that the new processing strategy be psycholinguistically valid. This view is well motivated by the Noticing Hypothesis, which, stated in general terms, is as follows: "SLA is largely driven by what learners pay attention to and notice in target language input and what they understand the significance of noticed input to be" (Schmidt, 2001, pp. 3-4; see also Robinson, 2003; Schmidt, 1990, 1992, 1993, 1995, 1998). In specifying the Noticing Hypothesis beyond its general formulation, Schmidt has claimed that learners must pay attention to what he terms "surface elements" in order to acquire them. Schmidt has not been explicit about what these surface elements are, but he has been clear about what they are not. Specifically, he states that "the objects of attention and noticing are elements of the surface structure of utterances in the input –instances of language—rather than any abstract rules or principles of which such instances may be exemplars (Schmidt, 2001, p. 5).

The key points to understand concerning L2 input processing are that metalinguistic awareness and noticing are to be considered different kinds of mental processes, and the real issue for me is how learners should be assisted through pedagogical procedures—such as the SI activities in PI—in effectively noticing the "surface elements." The explicit instruction evident in both PI and TI should be recognized for what it is—metalinguistic explanation that is known to lead to declarative knowledge about language rather than deployable language ability. As a matter of fact, a number of studies in the PI paradigm have now shown that, as was to be expected, the metalinguistic explanation that precedes structured processing activities is not a necessary component of PI (Van Patten & Oikkenon, 1996; Sanz & Morgan-Short, in press, and Sanz, this volume). However, it should be noted that a potentially crucial component of the explicit instruction is that it orients the learner to the processing problem. Without such orientation, are learners still able to alter their processing strategies? Apparently they are able to do so, since findings seem to converge on SI being equally as effective as PI. Given this, I carefully examined the SI in a number of the earlier studies. What I discovered was that the SI activities continue to orient the learner to the learning problem (for instance by reminding the learner that word order in English and Spanish differ). It remains an empirical question then whether this orientation is necessary or not, since it appears in both the EI and SI components of PI. (These comments were removed in the VanPatten & Oikkenon study).

The final element of PI, the feedback, is also now being systematically investigated in the PI research program. If the function of the metalinguistic explanation (EI) and structured input activities is to orient learners as to what to pay attention to, then the function of the feedback enables them to adjust whenever they are not processing appropriately. Sanz (this volume) and Sanz & Morgan-Short (in press) have compared types of feedback (metalinguistic, i.e., no and why wrong vs. implicit, i.e., yes/no feedback) and have shown that neither the metalinguistic explanation nor metalinguistic feedback are necessary. More specifically, groups with and without the explanation part of PI did equally well, and the type of feedback did not make a difference either. Given that the SI activities used in this study were based on those used in the original PI research (and thus do include the valuable focus on form activities), these are potentially credible findings.

Taking together the findings of PI studies to date, the minimal configuration for effective PI is represented by the uppermost shaded portion of Table 13.3. What remains to be investigated is whether the implicit feedback is a necessary component of PI (see the shaded and doubly bordered line of Table 13.3). I expect that feedback is necessary because, without any kind of feedback, learners would not know if they were processing incorrectly, and thus needed to change their approach to the input (see VanPatten, 2002c, for discussion of this). And, as has been noted before, when the processing problem involves a simple alternation, implicit feedback may be all that is necessary (DeKeyser & Sokalsi, 1996; Sanz, this volume), however, once the processing problem becomes more complex, the value of feedback is more difficult to ascertain.

The last point to make concerning the PI studies reported here and elsewhere is that it suffers from a research design problem that currently plagues all studies of the effects of different types of L2 instruction. The outcome measures that are typically used are not valid for testing whether the underlying system has been changed in any way (Doughty, 2003; Norris & Ortega, 2000).

TABLE 13.3
Comparisons of Possible Components of PI

Pre-processing	Processing[4]	Post-processing
Metalinguistic explanation	Structured input processing	Metalinguistic Feedback (why incorrect)
Metalinguistic explanation	Structured input processing	Implicit Feedback (correct/incorrect)
Ø	Structured input processing	Metalinguistic Feedback (why incorrect)
Ø	Structured input processing	Implicit Feedback (correct/incorrect)
Metalinguistic explanation	Ø	Ø
Ø	Structured input processing	Ø
Ø	Ø	Ø[5]

In other words, the kind of knowledge that they test is metalinguistic, declarative knowledge about language. This is a harsh criticism which is not unique to PI studies, and which must be made of practically all effects of instruction research. Table 13.4 displays the measures employed in the four studies reported in this section. Of these, only the video retelling task used by Sanz can be considered valid. Since the aim of PI is to assist learners in processing input so that it becomes intake for acquisition, then the ultimate test of the effectiveness of PI (or any other kind of instruction) has to include a valid measure (or measures) of SLA (Norris & Ortega, 2000). We must turn our attention in instructed SLA research to resolving this thorny problem. I hope that researchers in the PI paradigm will contribute to this effort.

---

[4] The PI paradigm includes two types of SI activities, referential (e.g., match picture to utterance) and affective (determine whether an utterance applies to you). To be complete, the comparisons would have to be expanded from what is depicted here.

[5] This condition constitutes a true control group, which should be, but often is not, included in all PI studies.

TABLE 13.4
Measures in PI Studies in This Section

Author	Interpretation Measure	Production Measure
Wong	Aural sentence completion. Hear ___ *de* + rest of sentence or ___ *un* + rest of sentence Fill in blank by choosing between *Elle a* or *Elle n'a pas.*	Fill in the blank with *de* or *un* A translation is available.
Benati	Listen to a sentence and label it as future or present.	Fill in the blank of a sentence by changing an infinitive verb into future
Farley	Listen to the subordinate clause of a sentence, and then choose the correct between two main clauses provided in writing.	Fill in the blank of a sentence by changing an infinitive verb into appropriate mood (indicative or subjunctive)
Sanz	Listen to a sentence and select the picture that goes with what you hear.	S-level: Complete the sentence based on what you see in the picture. Video retelling: write a short composition after watching a video twice.

The studies reported and discussed throughout this volume are part of substantive research paradigm. PI researchers are systematically investigating the applicability of PI to a range of L2 processing problems, and are trying to establish which components of PI instruction are responsible for learning outcomes. I have suggested in my commentary that a minimally specified version of PI consisting of those SI activities that facilitate focus on form (and excluding metalinguistic activities that encourage focus on forms) is likely to emerge as the only psycholinguistically valid operationalization of PI. This is because such activities remain true to the original insight from IP theory that when learners misanalyze the input, their input processing strategy must be altered. Whereas it is clear that the metalinguistic components of PI implemented either in the phase prior to SI activities (the EI) or in the feedback (explicit feedback) are not necessary, and the role of implicit feedback in altering learner processing requires further investigation. Finally, outcome measures that truly reveal the effects of PI instruction, that is to say show that input processing changes have led to L2 restructuring, must be developed.

REFERENCES

Cadierno, T. (1992). Explicit instruction in grammar: a comparison of input based and output based instruction in second language acquisition. Unpublished doctoral thesis, the University of Illinois at Urbana–Champaign.

DeKeyser, R., Salaberry, R., Robinson, P., & Harrington, M. (2002). What gets processed in processing instruction? A commentary on Bill VanPatten's 'Processing instruction: An update.' *Language Learning* 52, 805–223.

Doughty, C. (2003). Instructed SLA: Constraints, compensation, and enhancement. In C. Doughty, & M. H .Long (Eds.), *Handbook of second language acquisition* (pp. 256–310). Blackwell Handbooks in Linguistics. New York: Basil Blackwell.

Doughty, C. & Williams, J. (1998a). Issues and terminology. In C. Doughty & J. Williams (Eds.), *Focus on form in classroom second language acquisition* (pp. 1–11). Cambridge: Cambridge University Press.

Doughty, C. & Williams, J. (1998b). Pedagogical choices in focus on form. In C. Doughty & J. Williams (Eds.), *Focus on form in classroom second language acquisition* (pp. 197–261). Cambridge: Cambridge University Press.

Lightbown, P. (1983). Exploring relationships between developmental and instructional sequences in L2 acquisition. In H. W. Seliger & M. H. Long (Eds.), *Classroom-oriented research in second language acquisition* (pp. 217–43). Rowley, MA.: Newbury House, 1983.

Long, M. H. (1991). The design and psycholinguistic motivation of research on foreign language learning. In B. F. Freed (Ed.), *Foreign language acquisition research and the classroom* (pp. 309–320). Lexington, MA.: D. C. Heath.

Long, M .H. & Robinson, P. (1998). Focus on form: Theory, research, and practice. In C. Doughty & J Williams (Eds.), *Focus on form in classroom second language acquisition* (pp. 15–41). Cambridge: Cambridge University Press.

learning: Integrating theory and practice (pp. 1 23–167). C levedon, U K: Multilingual Matters.

Norris, J. M., & Ortega, L. (2000). Does type of instruction make a difference? Substantive findings from a meta-analytic review. *Language Learning, 50,* 157–213.

Robinson, P. (2003). Attention and memory during SLA. In C. Doughty & M. H. Long (Eds.), *Handbook of second language acquisition* (pp. 631–78). Blackwell Handbooks in Linguistics. New York: Basil Blackwell.

Sanz, C., & Morgan-Short, K. (in press). Positive evidence vs. explicit rule presentation and explicit negative feedback: A computer-assisted study. *Language Learning.*

Schmidt, R. (1990). The role of consciousness in second language learning. *Applied Linguistics, 112,* 17–46.

Schmidt, R. (1992). Psychological mechanisms underlying second language fluency. *Studies in Second Language Acquisition, 14,* 357–85.

Schmidt, R. (1993). Awareness and second language acquisition. *Annual Review of Applied Linguistics, 13,* 206–226.

Schmidt, R. (1995). Consciousness and foreign language learning: a tutorial on the role of attention and awareness in learning. In R. Schmidt (Ed.), *Attention and Awareness in Foreign Language Learning* (pp. 1–63). Honolulu: University of Hawaii Press.

Schmidt, R. W. (1998). The centrality of attention in SLA. *University of Hawaii Working Papers in ESL 16,* 1–34.

Schmidt. R. W. (2001). Attention. In P. Robinson (Ed.) *Cognition and second language instruction* (pp. 3–32). Cambridge: Cambridge University Press.

VanPatten, B. (2002a). Processing instruction: An update. *Language Learning, 52,* 755–803.

VanPatten, B. (2002b). Processing the content of Input Processing and Processing Instruction research: A response to DeKeyser, Salaberry, Robinson & Harrington. *Language Learning, 52,* 825–831.

VanPatten, B. (2000c). Processing instruction, prior awareness, and the nature of second language acquisition:A (partial) response to Batstone. *Language Awareness, 11,* 240-258.

VanPatten, B., & Cadierno, T. (1993). Explicit instruction and input processing instruction. *Studies in Second Language Acquisition, 15,* 225–243.

VanPatten, B ., & O ikkenon, S. (1996). E xplanation v ersus s tructured i nput i n processing i nstruction. *S tudies in Second Language Acquisition, 1 8,* 4 95–510.

VanPatten, B. & Oikkenon, S. (1996). Explanation versus structured input in processing i nstruction. *S tudies in Second Language Acquisition, 18,* 495–510.

VanPatten, B. & Sanz, C. (1995). From input to output: Processing instruction and communicative tasks. In F. Eckman, D. Highland, P. Lee, J. Mileham &

R. Rutkowski (Eds.), *Second language acquisition: Theory and pedagogy* (pp. 169–185). Hillsdale, NJ: Lawrence Erlbaum Associates.

Warden, C. A. (1995). Expert system impact on writing errors in Taiwanese business English classes. *CALL Journal, 6,* 22–29.

White, L. (1991). Adverb placement in second language acquisition: Some effects of positive and negative evidence in the classroom. *Second Language Research, 7,* 133–161.

Yang, J. C., & Akahori, K. (1999). An evaluation of Japanese CALL systems on the WWW comparing a freely input approach with multiple selection. *Computer Assisted Language Learning, 12,* 59–79.

Yano, Y., Long, M. H., & Ross, S. (1994). The effects of simplified and elaborated texts on foreign language reading comprehension. *Language Learning, 44,* 189-219.

Part IV

Long-Term Effects of PI

The matter of long-term effects of instruction has been recognized as a problem in most research on instructed SLA and focus on form. Although most scholars now believe that focus on form is beneficial to SLA, scholars also acknowledge that the research on whether instructional effects have any long-term effects is scant, at best—and the research that does exist is equivocal in terms of whether instruction has any lasting benefits.

The research on PI is but a decade old and during that time no study has researched the critical question of long-term effects of instruction. In this volume we have seen that along with previous research, PI appears to be an effective short-term treatment, although several studies report observed effects one-month after treatment. The sole study in this section presents the findings of an eight-month study on the long-term effects of PI. As such, it is not only unique within the context of PI research but it is also one of several studies in instructed SLA in general in which long-term effects are investigated. Because the authors have chosen to use the same materials as VanPatten & Cadierno, the study falls squarely in line with replication research that attempts to isolate a particular variable or issue. The results are encouraging yet sobering at the same time. The study also reports on problems inherent in conducting such long-term research within the context of a large American university.

Chapter 14

The Long-Term Effects of Processing Instruction

Bill VanPatten
Claudia Fernández
University of Illinois at Chicago

Research on the effects of instruction has revealed, overall, a positive effect for focusing learners' attention on form (Norris & Ortega, 2000). Of course, it is not clear that all instruction is equally beneficial or that all instruction works on the various processes involved in acquisition the same way (Doughty & Williams, 1998; VanPatten, 2002; also, see Collentine, this volume, for a discussion of effect sizes). It could be that some instructional efforts only develop explicit knowledge by which learners can perform some tasks (Doughty, 2003) or still that other efforts develop particular skills that don't transfer to other skills (e.g., DeKeyser & Sokalski, 1996). Nonetheless, there seems to be evidence that some types of formal focus, because they are derived from previous research about what we actually know about learner processing, actually do have some kind of significant effect.

Despite this rather rosy outlook on the beneficial effects of formal instruction on learners' knowledge and/or linguistic behavior, there remains the question of long-term effects. In short, the question is this: Do the beneficial effects observed in the research so far hold over the long run? Or are they short lived, the effects fading within weeks after experimental treatment? This is an important issue given claims about focus on form, grammar instruction, and intervention in instructed SLA in general. If the effects of intervention are short-lived, then as some have claimed (e.g., Krashen, 1982, and elsewhere), acquisition results from exposure to input and nothing else. If long-term effects can be found, then such a position is less tenable. In the present study, we address this issue within the framework of processing instruction (PI).

BACKGROUND

A review and meta-analysis of the studies on instructional effects appears in Norris and Ortega (2000). Surveying the field exhaustively, but eventually restricting their analysis to studies that met certain criteria for the reporting of research, they found that overall there is an effect for instruction and that this effect is observable regardless of instructional variables. That is, regardless of whether the instruction was explicit or implicit, whether the instruction consisted of a focus on form (form plus meaning to communicate something) or focus on forms (form without the intent to communicate meaning), and regardless of several other factors, there seem to be positive effects for instruction in general.

Doughty (2003), however, suggests that the conclusions of Norris and Ortega must be taken with some caution. In her examination of their analysis, she notes that there is a bias toward explicit learning and testing and concludes that the observed effects may actually be due to applying explicit knowledge to tests that allow learners to make use of explicit knowledge (see Doughty, this volume, for similar comments). In VanPatten and Oikennon (1996), Sanz and Morgan-Short (in press), and Sanz (this volume), however, there is clear evidence that at least in one type of instructional approach, explicit knowledge learned during the explicit phase of instruction is not responsible for outcomes.

Despite Doughty's well-taken cautionary remarks, we will take as our point of departure that in general, research on instruction demonstrates a positive outcome. That is, those who receive instruction generally do better than those who do not (see also, e.g., Long, 1983; Larsen-Freeman & Long, 1991; Lightbown, Spada, & White, 1993). What is overwhelmingly true of the research, however, are two points: the short-term nature of most studies and the actual type of instruction used and the processes it attempts to affect. We will deal with each point in turn.

Short-Term Effects

Most research on instructional effects examines only short-term gains. All experimental research, of course, would by definition contain some kind of immediate posttest measure to ascertain whether the treatment(s) had an effect. But a good deal of research includes "delayed" posttests, most of which occur anywhere from one-week to one-month after treatment (e.g., DeKeyser & Sokalski, 1996; Robinson, 1996; Scott, 1989; Trahey & White, 1993; VanPatten & Cadierno, 1993; J. White, 1998; and the collection in Schmidt, 1995; among others). Norris and Ortega note that in such studies, the effect of instruction appears durable, in spite of observable decreases in the effect size in their analysis.

Few studies examine longer-term effects. Striking examples to this exception are some observational studies and one empirical study conducted in

Canada. Lightbown (1983) reports that one year after intense drilling and practice on certain forms—which seemed to alter reported natural orders of acquisition (e.g., Krashen, 1982)—the effects of the instruction were not in evidence, and natural orders of acquisition reasserted themselves in learner output.

In another study, Spada and Lightbown (1993) report that five-months after an instructional intervention on WH-questions, learners appeared to maintain the gains made during the intervention (reported in White, Spada, Lightbown & Ranta, 1991). However, unlike experimental studies in which treatment is normally a "one shot" intervention, in the Spada and Lightbown study, learners continued to receive interaction and feedback that included the targeted structure. Thus, the long-term effects observed in this study are not attributable solely to the intervention but to the intervention plus the continued feedback.

In short, there are few studies that look at long-term gains beyond several weeks or a month. The few that have report conflicting findings; one offers evidence of instructional effects wearing off; the other that instructional effects hold but the treatment was sustained during the long-term nature of the study.

Why Might We Expect Something Different with PI?

In a series of studies, we have demonstrated the relative superior effects of PI to more traditional instruction that uses drills plus some meaning-based practice. In these studies, we find that participants who undergo processing instruction in which they never produce a structure do not only perform better on particular kinds of interpretation tests, but they also can access their newly created knowledge for production on a variety of tests. We have found this is true for word order and object pronoun placement in Spanish (VanPatten & Cadierno, 1993), for past tense in Spanish (Cadierno, 1995), for the future tense in Italian (Benati, 2001), for the French causative with *faire* (VanPatten & Wong, this volume) and for the copular verbs *ser* and *estar* in Spanish (Cheng, 1995, 2002). We have found that the effects of PI are observable in difficult discourse-oriented tests such as video story retelling (VanPatten & Sanz, 1995; Sanz & Morgan-Short, 2002). We have also found that the observed effects of PI are not due to explicit information provided to learners but apparently solely to the type of input activities the learners receive, called "structured input" (VanPatten & Oikennon, 1996; and see the various papers by Benati, Farley, Sanz, and Wong, this volume, on the relative roles of explicit information and structured input in PI). Since a detailed review of these studies and others is beyond the scope of this chapter, the reader is referred to VanPatten (2002).

To be sure, a few so-called replication studies report different findings, namely that an input-oriented instruction and an output-oriented instruction have differential effects with no superiority for the input group (DeKeyser & Sokalski, 1996; Salaberry, 1997) or that the effects of PI and TI are actually the same (Allen, 2000; Collentine, 1998). We have discussed these studies elsewhere (Sanz & VanPatten, 1998; VanPatten, 2000, 2002) but note here the following two points. The first point is that the studies may not be actual replications of PI vs. TI as in VanPatten and Cadierno (1993) and our other studies. Instead, these are more general input vs. output-based studies. This is particularly true of the first two studies, DeKeyser and Sokalski (1996) and Salaberry (1997). This point is important because PI has a particular underlying theory that is not evident in these studies and they do not attempt to cause the same type of change in acquisition that PI does, a point we return to shortly. The second point is that even when replication studies, however conceptually or methodologically flawed they may be (as pointed out in VanPatten, 2002, and VanPatten & Wong, this volume), obtain results in which PI is no better than TI, it is also true that PI is just as good as TI. Taken together with our other studies, the overall picture that emerges is that PI appears to be an effective focus on form with a variety of structures in different languages. Why is this the case?

PI is predicated upon a particular theory or model of input processing that identifies particular processing problems or processing "strategies" that may lead to partial or erroneous acquisition (VanPatten, 1996). The motivation for PI is this, then: if input is fundamental for acquisition, and if we can identify strategies that learners take to processing input, perhaps we can push learners to get better intake from the input if instruction actually attempted to alter their processing strategies. One such strategy is described in the *First-Noun Principle* (VanPatten, this volume). Learners begin the processing of sentences with a strategy that guides them to attach subject or agent status to the first noun or pronoun they encounter in an utterance/sentence. While this works fine for languages with only SVO or SOV sentences, this strategy does not work on passives in which the first noun is thematically the patient of the verb or for those languages with flexible word order where OVS may be a frequent structure. Such is the case in Spanish. English speakers of Spanish have been repeatedly shown to process sentences such as (1), (2) and (3) incorrectly as indicated by the translations marked with an asterisk.

(1) Al león lo mató el hombre.
    lion-ACC it-ACC killed the man-NOM.
    The man killed the lion.
    *The lion killed the man.
(2) La vio el chico.
    her-ACC saw the boy-NOM.
    The boy saw her.
    *She saw the boy.
(3) A Juan le gusta mucho María.
    Juan-DAT to him is pleasing Mary-NOM.
    *John likes Mary.

The result of this incorrect processing is that learners' input processing mechanisms deliver wrong data to the accommodation and restructuring mechanisms responsible for internalization and actual grammar building.

Learners blithely ignore case marking, gender agreements between object nouns and clitic object pronouns, mismatches between number marking on object pronouns and verbs, and their grammars erroneously conclude that Spanish is rigidly SVO.

Current thinking about acquisition includes the notion that the change of internal grammars is, in part, failure-driven at the level of input processing. Carroll (2001), for example, claims that when a parsing mechanism fails, that is when a learner is confronted with the fact that the way in which the sentence is parsed does not match the meaning as evidenced by the environmental context, the parser is forced to rethink what it is doing. Causing the parser to fail is precisely what PI does. During carefully crafted structured input activities, learners receive feedback early on that their processing is incorrect. They realize that what they thought they understood does not match the intended meaning of the speaker. Their internal mechanisms, then, are literally forced to adopt a new strategy or abandon the old one. The result is that the accommodation and restructuring mechanisms receive better (in this case, correct) data for internalization. (Because we provide examples of PI activities later, we will not show here how these activities work.)

To our knowledge, no other focus on form technique or approach attempts to do this (and this also explains the failure of some studies to replicate the findings from our other studies; the researchers did not grasp that PI was about causing processing failure and then correcting it). We believe, then, that PI is a good choice to test the possible long-term effects of instruction. Other approaches may cause temporary performance improvement and the subsequent decline in performance may be due to the fact that the instruction did not affect the mechanisms used for processing and acquisition (e.g., DeKeyser & Sokalski, 1996). PI, however, deliberately attempts to affect the processing mechanisms. If it does, we would expect that post-treatment gains should hold over time. That is the hypothesis that underlies the present study.

RESEARCH QUESTION

This study is a conceptual replication of VanPatten and Cadierno (1993). While the focus of that study was to compare traditional instruction with PI, the focus of the present study was to observe any effects of PI over a longer period of time. The following question guided our study:

> Do the observed effects of processing instruction in previous research, hold over time?

In this study, our participants were instructed on the Spanish OVS sentences and clitic pronouns. Their interpretation and production skills on these forms were measured right after instruction and eight months later.

METHOD

Participants

Nine third-semester Spanish as a foreign language classes at the University of Illinois–Chicago were used for this study. Although the total number of potential participants enrolled in these courses was 218, due to absenteeism and the elimination of non-native speakers of English, the total number of eligible participants who took the pretest, received the treatment, and took the immediate posttest was 163. Because our purpose was to observe the long time effect of a one-time treatment, three entire classes containing participants had to be eliminated. The instructors of these classes inadvertently reviewed and practiced object pronouns outside of the study (no other instructors did). The total number of participants then, who were included in the analysis of the pretest and immediate posttest data and who could be considered potential participants for the delayed posttest, was 94. Eight months later, only 54 of these participants registered in fourth semester Spanish. Due to mid-semester withdrawals and absenteeism, only 45 students took the delayed posttest. Thus, our final n size was 45.

Instruction

The instructional packets used were exactly the same as in VanPatten & Cadierno (1993). Following, VanPatten (1993), PI treatment consisted of three components: (1) explicit information about the target structure; (2) explicit information about wrong processing strategies; and (3) structured input activities.

Participants first received explanation contrasting the grammatical difference between the subject of a verb and the object of a verb. They then received information on Spanish subject pronouns and direct object pronouns followed by information about placement of object pronouns and word order. It was especially emphasized that, unlike English, Spanish has a flexible word order and that object pronouns may be placed in a pre-verbal position resulting in sentences of the OVS type and even the OV type. Participants' reliance on the first-noun strategy was then brought to their attention by explicitly telling them that as learners they would naturally rely on this strategy but that it often would lead to misinterpretation. Later in the treatment, participants learned that object nouns may be placed before the verb and that they were case marked with a.

A	la señora	la	saluda	el señor.
The woman –OBJ		her –OBJpro	greets	the man –SUBJ.
The man greets the woman.				

They were again reminded of the first-noun strategy.

Explicit information was followed by structured input activities consisting of two basic types. The first, called referential activities, push the learner to rely on the object pronoun or the *a* case marker to get the meaning of the sentence. Activities of this type have a right or wrong answer. Some involved selecting a picture to represent what was heard and others involved selecting an English rendition as in the examples that follow.

> ***Actividad.*** You are going to hear some sentences in Spanish. Match each sentence you hear with one of the statements below.

(Instructor reads aloud: "Me llama un hombre")
1.   □ A man is calling me.
       □ I am calling a man.
(Instructor reads aloud: "Visito a mis padres")
2.   □ My parents visit me.
       □ I visit my parents.
Etc.

> ***Actividad.*** *Select the best English rendition of each sentence.*
> 1.   A mi mamá la besa mucho mi papá.
>   a. My mother kisses my dad a lot.   b. My father kisses my mom a lot.
> Etc.

It is important to point out that participants had to interpret both SVO and OVS kinds of sentences in the same activity. This keeps participants from performing the activities mechanically without paying attention to meaning or what they are doing, a problem that has surfaced in certain replication studies and confounded those results (e.g., Allen, 2000).

The second type of structured input activities is called affective activities. These activities do not have a right or wrong answer; rather, participants express an opinion, belief, or some other response about the real world (e.g., "true for me /false for me," "I agree/I disagree,"). An example follows.

> ***Actividad.*** Indicate whether or not each statement applies to you and your parents. Share your response with a classmate.

Sí, se me aplica	No, no se me aplica	
□	□	1. Los llamo con frecuencia.
□	□	2. Los visito los fines de semana.

Etc.

It is important to point out that in PI participants are engaged in structured input activities, but are never asked to produce any sentences containing the target structure, in this case object pronouns. Although the reasons for this are discussed in detail elsewhere (e.g., Lee & VanPatten, 1995, in press; VanPatten, 1993, 1996, 2000, 2002), we point out here that PI is predicated on two important observations about second language acquisition. The first is that learners come to acquisition with certain processing strategies, such as the first-noun strategy that is the focus of the present and previous research. These strategies may impede or hinder acquisition since the learner is essentially getting the data wrong from the input. The second observation is neatly summarized in Carroll (2001); certain aspects of learning proceed when processing fails. That is, the learner's internal processors must notice[1] a mismatch between the meaning processed and the meaning intended. PI does this when learners see that they select the wrong picture, select the wrong English equivalent and so on. The point of these observations is that acquisition is not production dependent, at least not the acquisition of a grammar. Production may be beneficial and at times critical (Swain, 1998; VanPatten, forthcoming), but the bottom line is that the grammar changes when learners process something new or differently in the input.

Assessment Instruments

The same pretests and posttests used in VanPatten and Cadierno (1993) were used for the present study. There were two versions of these tests, A and B. Both versions consisted of an interpretation section, a distracter section, and a production section. During the interpretation test, participants would listen to an OVS sentence and had to choose between two pictures to represent what they heard. Five were critical OVS sentences with a noun as the O (e.g., *Al chico lo llama la chica*). Another five were critical OVS with a clitic object pronoun as the O (e.g., *Lo saluda la chica*). There were five distractors of SVO structure. The total test, then, consisted of 10 critical items and five distractors.

The production section consisted of five critical items and five distractors. Each item consisted of two pictures depicting two successive events that formed a "story." The task was to complete the story based on the visual by using the verb given in parentheses. As an example, one picture would depict a girl greeting a boy, and the next picture would depict the same girl kissing the boy. The sentence completion was *La niña saluda al niño y entonces* _____ *(besar)* ("The girl greets the boy and then _____ [to kiss]"). An expected correct answer would be *lo besa* ("[she] kisses him"). For the distractors, the visual cues were unrelated, for example, the first picture would be a woman waking up her husband and the second would be a dog chasing a cat. The sentence completion would be *La mujer despierta al marido y* _____ *(seguir)* with the expected response *el perro sigue al gato*.

---

[1]We use the term *notice* neutrally, without any claim about awareness. Processors, we believe, by definition perform their computations without awareness.

Although all vocabulary was checked against materials used in the courses, as in VanPatten and Cadierno (1993) a vocabulary familiarization sheet was handed to participants prior to testing. Participants did not report any problems with the basic vocabulary used in the study.

The distracter section appeared between the interpretation and the production sections and consisted of five open-ended questions in Spanish about personal information (e.g., What is your favorite hobby?). The idea behind the distracter section was to clear participants' working memory of items from the first section before proceeding to the next.

Procedure

Pretests, instruction, and immediate and delayed posttests were given during the participants' regular class time and in their regular classrooms. The first day participants took the pretest before receiving any instruction. The two versions of the tests (A and B) were randomly assigned to each of the nine groups. Those groups that received version A as the pretest, received version B as the immediate posttest. Those groups who received version B of the pretest received version A as the immediate posttest. For the delayed posttests all participants received version A of the test given that the participants were at that time mixed together in various classes. However, given the very long time between the immediate posttest and the delayed posttest, we did not see that test familiarity would be a problem.

After the pretest, participants received instruction via PI on Spanish preverbal direct object pronouns. The instruction lasted two consecutive days with no homework, and participants turned in their packets on the first day and received them again the next day. The posttest was administered immediately after instruction on the second day. The names of the participants were kept on record after the scoring phase in order to keep track of them for the delayed posttest. Because one of the researchers was the director of the language program in which the participants were students, the curriculum was controlled for no instruction on object pronouns and no feedback on object pronouns during the interval between the immediate and delayed posttest. As noted previously, three instructors were identified as having inadvertently worked explicitly with object pronouns incorrectly believing that this target structure would appear on the participants' final exam for the third-semester. All participants from these instructors were removed from the data pool as discussed previously.

Eight months later we tracked down those participants who had completed the pretest, treatment, and immediate posttest phases and identified the classes they attended. For practical reasons, the posttest was given to all of the students in these classes. However, only the tests for those participants who completed all phases of the study were scored. All others were discarded.

Scoring

The interpretation section of the test was scored by a simple correct/incorrect procedure. Correct answers were worth 1 point and incorrect answers were worth zero. The maximum possible score was ten. For the production section, we followed a 2, 1, 0 scoring procedure. We gave two points for any correct answer with an object pronoun (e.g., *lo besa,* "she kisses him"). A score of zero was given if an incorrect clitic pronoun was used indicating the use of the object pronoun as the subject (e.g., *la* instead of *lo*) if no pronoun was used, or if a subject pronoun was used in place of an object (e.g., *besa ella*). A score of 1 was assigned to all other cases. This scoring procedure followed VanPatten and Cadierno's idea that instruction could result in partial acquisition. For example, participants might pick up on object pronouns themselves but still have problems with word order.

RESULTS

As Table 14.1 depicts, participants improved from pretest to the immediate posttest on the interpretation task, the mean scores rising from 1.84 to 6.07. We also can also see, however, that there is a decline on the delayed 8-month posttest, from 6.07 to 3.31. A repeated measures ANOVA yielded a significant effect for time, meaning that there was improvement after the treatment, $F(44) = 57.63$, $p < .0001$. A post-hoc Scheffé test was conducted to determine the precise nature of this main effect. The Scheffé revealed that there was a significant difference between scores on the pretest and scores on the immediate posttest ($p < .0001$), a significant difference between scores on the pretest and scores on the delayed posttest ($p = .0019$), and a significant difference between scores on the immediate posttest and the delayed posttest ($p < .0001$). What this means, then, is that the learners improved significantly then declined, but were still significantly better compared to their performance on the pretest. Figure 14.1 is a visual representation of the scores on the interpretation task.

In Table 14.2 we see that on the production task, learners improved from the pretest (1.02) to the immediate posttest (5.87) but that once again the scores decline from the immediate posttest to the delayed posttest (3.36). A repeated measures ANOVA yielded a significant effect for time, meaning that once again there was improvement after treatment, $F(44) = 32.69$, $p < .0001$. As in the interpretation results, a post-hoc Scheffé test was conducted to determine the precise nature of this main effect. The Scheffé revealed that there was a significant difference between scores on the pretest and scores on the immediate posttest ($p < .0001$), a significant difference between scores on the pretest and scores on the delayed posttest ($p = .0009$), and a significant difference between scores on the immediate posttest and the delayed posttest ($p = .0003$). Exactly as in the case of the interpretation results, what the production results mean is that

TABLE 14.1
Mean Scores on the Interpretation Task

	n	*Mean*	*SD*	*SE*
Pretest	45	1.84	1.54	.23
Immediate Posttest	45	6.07	2.07	.31
Delayed Posttest	45	3.31	2.68	.40

TABLE 14.2
Mean Scores on the Production Task

	n	*Mean*	*SD*	*SE*
Pretest	45	1.02	2.17	.32
Immediate Posttest	45	5.87	4.02	.60
Delayed Posttest	45	3.36	4.02	.60

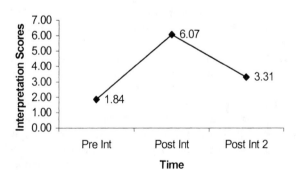

FIG. 14.1. Line Graph of Scores on the Interpretation Task.

the learners improved significantly then declined, but were still significantly better compared to their performance on the pretest. Figure 14.2 is a visual representation of the scores on the production task.

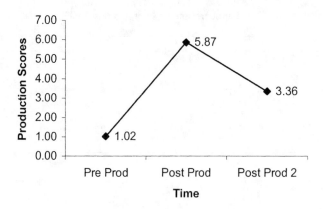

FIG. 14.2. Line Graph of Scores on the Production Task.

DISCUSSION AND CONCLUSION

The results of the present research are quite clear. Learners receiving processing instruction that attempts to alter the first-noun strategy make significant gains in knowledge and ability. Despite a decline in this knowledge and ability over an eight-month period, learners are still performing better than they did on the pretest. This result is impressive because at no point did learners receive additional instruction or feedback regarding object pronouns, OVS sentences or processing as in the case of the Lightbown and Spada (1983) study. The syllabi for the courses and the materials used in the present study had been "sanitized" so as not to draw any attention or invite any explicit work with object pronouns and word order during the eight-month period. Thus, the residual effects observed on the delayed posttest can be attributed to the effects that the one-time treatment had on the learners' developing grammars and processing strategies.

We are well aware of an important potential criticism of the present study; namely, that we had no control group that did not undergo instructional treatment yet took the tests. Due to practical concerns we could not have a control group. Previous attempts in our studies to conduct longitudinal studies of this type with various experimental groups and a control group resulted in so much attrition that the final n sizes became too small to seriously entertain any analyses of the data. For the present study, we opted to only look at a processing group. We included all sections of third-semester Spanish that were available to us and from these 218 participants, only 44 wound up in the final data pool. This represents an attrition rate of approximately 80%. If we had divided the initial participant pool into two equal groups, a control and a PI group, we would have run the risk of having one or both groups with not enough participants to perform the analyses we wanted.

Regardless of the practical matters in conducting a long-term study such as this, we believe that the lack of a control group still does not constitute a serious problem. We know from other PI studies with control groups that the control groups show no improvement up to the last delayed posttest one month after treatment (e.g., Benati, 2001; Cadierno, 1995; VanPatten & Cadierno, 1993; VanPatten & Wong, this volume) so they appear to be unaffected by test familiarity or any other potential intervening variables. Just as important, however, is that in the early descriptive research on the first-noun strategy, the majority of it was conducted with third- and fourth-semester learners of Spanish (Lee, 1987; LoCoco, 1987; VanPatten, 1984). This would suggest that under regular circumstances and without PI, learners may conclude two years of basic language study at the college level still relying on the first noun strategy. Since the participants in our study were at the same level (i.e., second year college study of Spanish), we believe a control group would reveal no change over time.

We would also like to address another important potential limitation, namely the one that Doughty (2003, this volume) claims is not isolated to PI research but to instructed SLA research in general. This limitation is the type of assessment tasks used. In the present study, we used the same tasks that VanPatten and Cadierno used. According to Doughty, these tasks run the risk of being metalinguistic in orientation and invite the use of explicit knowledge, thus potentially negating any claims we could make about the underlying grammatical system having been affected by the treatment. Doughty claims that in the Sanz study (this volume) the video retelling task, which pushed participants to produce language at the discourse level in a confined time period, is the best indicator that learners are tapping their underlying system and not a conscious knowledge source. We do not disagree with her assessment. We argue here that because our results on the other tasks are strikingly similar to those of Sanz (this volume) and VanPatten and Sanz (1995)—who also included a video retelling task—we would speculate that learners in our study could show improved performance on the video retelling task as well. Nonetheless, we acknowledge the limitation of the tasks we used and remind readers that future research needs to address Doughty's criticism regarding how instructional treatment effects are measured.

Before concluding we would like to draw the reader's attention to an important point regarding the scores in this study and those in previous PI studies. In the VanPatten and Cadierno studies, learners made great gains from pre- to posttests, usually starting around means of 1.5 or 2.0 and ending up somewhere between 8.0 to 9.0 on a possible range of 0-10. In this study, the initial immediate posttest gains are lower (around 6.0 on both tests). When the possible range is 0-10, a two-point difference in initial gains can be considered significant. In short, although there was significant improvement, the participants in the present study did not perform as well on the immediate posttests compared with participants from other related studies. This point is important considering that the same principal researcher is involved and the exact same treatment and testing materials are involved. We believe this suggests something important as researchers compare studies from different institutions and populations. Although our results are certainly comparable to those of previous PI research, why did the participants not perform to the same degree as in previous research? We can only speculate. Perhaps they were more disinterested than participants in our previous research and thus paid attention during treatment but not as much. Thus, they may have provided less effort. Perhaps there are cognitive or cultural differences between the participants in this study and those in our previous studies, although all were native speakers of English. Whatever the reason, the point is that what we see from our results is that anytime we get unexpected results, we must look to our population as a possible source of the difference. When researchers attempt replications and they are from different institutions with different participant populations, this must be factored into an explanation of results if they are different as well.

We conclude by suggesting that despite the observations made during our discussion, we believe we have found a long-term effect for PI, at least in the case of OVS/clitic object pronouns in Spanish and the first-noun strategy. To be sure, there was decline from the immediate posttest, but eight months later learners are still better with OVS and object pronouns than they were before treatment. The decline suggests that the effects are durable and the decline may simply be due to lack of continued evidence in the input (i.e., frequency may affect durability—see, e.g., Ellis, 2002; VanPatten, Williams, & Rott, forthcoming). The reader will recall that the curriculum was sanitized to prevent learner "engagement" with clitics, word order issues, and feedback during interactions regarding the target item. In other words, we denied them access to normal input and interaction that would provide the needed frequency that underlies strength of form–meaning connections. Despite the decline in performance, we believe we are on the right path in looking at instructional intervention that concentrates on learners' input processing mechanisms and strategies.

REFERENCES

Allen, L. Q. (2000). Form-meaning connections and the French causative: An experiment in processing instruction. *Studies in Second Language Acquisition, 22*, 69–84.

Benati, A. (2001). A comparative study of the effects of processing instruction and output-based instruction on the acquisition of the Italian future tense. *Language Teaching Research, 5*, 95–127.

Cadierno, T. (1995). Formal instruction from a processing perspective: An investigation into the Spanish past tense. *The Modern Language Journal, 79,* 179–93.

Carroll, S. E. (2001). *Input and evidence: The raw material of acquisition.* Philadelphia: John Benjamins.

Cheng, A. (1995). *Grammar instruction and input processing: The acquisition of Spanish Ser and Estar.* Unpublished doctoral dissertation, University of Illinois, Urbana-Champaign.

Cheng, A. C. (2002). The effects of processing instruction on the acquisition of s*er* and *estar. Hispania, 85,* 308–323

Collentine, J. (1998). Processing instruction and the subjunctive. *Hispania, 81,* 576–587.

DeKeyser, R., & Sokalski, K. (1996). The differential role of comprehension and production practice. *Language Learning, 46,* 613–642.

Doughty, C. (2003). Instructed SLA: Constraints, compensation, and enhancement. In C. Doughty & M. H. Long (Eds.), *The handbook of second language acquisition* (pp. 254–310). Oxford: Basil Blackwell.

Doughty, C., & Willliams, J, (Eds.). (1998). *Focus on form in classroom second language acquisition.* Cambridge, UK: Cambridge University Press.

Ellis, N. (2002). Frequency effects in language processing. *Studies in Second Language Acquisition, 24,* 143–188.

Krashen, S. D. (1982). *Principles and practice in second language acquisition.* Oxford: Pergamon Press.

Larsen-Freeman, D., & Long, M. H. (1991). *Introduction to second language acquisition research.* London: Longman.

Lee, J. F. (1987). Morphological factors influencing pronominal reference assignment by learners of Spanish. In T. A. Morgan, J. F. Lee & B. VanPatten (Eds.), *Language and language use: Studies in Spanish* (pp. 221–232). Lanham, MD: University Press of America.

Lee, J., & VanPatten, B. (1995). *Making communicative language teaching happen.* New York: McGraw-Hill.

Lee, J., & VanPatten, B. (2003). *Making communicative language teaching happen* (2nd ed.). New York: McGraw-Hill.

Lightbown, P. M. (1983). Exploring relationships between developmental and instructional sequences in L2 acquisition. In H. Seliger & M. Long (Eds.), *Classroom-oriented research in language acquisition* (pp. 217–243). Rowley MA: Newbury House

Lightbown, P. M., Spada, N., & White, L. (1993). The role of instruction in SLA: Introduction. [Special issue]. *Studies in Second Language Acquisition, 15,* 143-145.

LoCoco, V. (1987). Learner comprehension of oral and written sentences in German and Spanish: The importance of word order. In B. VanPatten, T. R. Dvorak & J. F. Lee (Eds.), *Foreign language learning: A research perspective* (pp. 119–129). Cambridge, MA: Newbury House.

Long, M. H. (1983). Does second language instruction make a difference? *TESOL Quarterly, 17*, 359–382.

Norris, J., & Ortega, L. (2000). Effectiveness of L2 instruction: A research synthesis and quantitative meta-analysis. *Language Learning, 50*, 417–528.

Robinson, P. (1996). Learning simple and complex second language rules under implicit, incidental, rule-search, and instructed conditions. *Studies in Second Language Acquisition, 18*, 27–67.

Salaberry, M. R. (1997). The role of input and output practice in second language acquisition. *The Canadian Modern Language Review, 53*, 422–451.

Sanz, C., & Morgan-Short, K. (in press). Positive evidence vs. explicit rule presentation and explicit negative feedback: A computer-assisted study. *Language Learning.*

Sanz, C., & VanPatten, B. (1998). On input processing, processing instruction, and the nature of replication tasks: A response to M. Rafael Salaberry. *The Canadian Modern Language Review, 54*, 263–273.

Schmidt, R. (Ed.) (1995). *Attention and awareness in foreign language learning.* Honolulu: University of Hawaii Press.

Scott, V. (1989). An empircal study of explicit and implicit teaching strategies in French. *The Modern Language Journal, 73*, 14–22.

Swain, M. (1998). Focus on form through conscious reflection. In C. Doughty & J. Williams (Eds.), *Focus on form in classroom second language acquisition* (pp. 64–81). Cambridge: Cambridge University Press.

Trahey, M., & White, L. (1993). Positive evidence and preemption in the second language classroom. *Studies in Second Language Acquisition, 15*, 181–204.

VanPatten, B. (1984). Learners' comprehension of clitic pronouns: More evidence for a word order strategy. *Hispanic Linguistics, 1*, 57–67.

VanPatten, B. (1993). Grammar instruction for the acquisition rich classroom. *Foreign Language Annals, 26*, 433–450.

VanPatten, B. (1996). *Input processing and grammar instruction: Theory and research.* Norwood, NJ: Ablex.

VanPatten, B. (2000). Processing instruction as form-meaning connections: Issues in theory and research. In J. F. Lee & A. Valdman (Eds.), *Form and meaning: multiple perspectives* (pp. 43–68). Boston: Heinle & Heinle.

VanPatten, B. (2002). Processing instruction: An update. *Language Learning, 52*, 755–803.

VanPatten, B. (forthcoming). Input and output in establishing form-meaning connections. In B. VanPatten, J. Williams, S. Rott & M. Overstreet (Eds.), *Form-meaning connections in Second Language Acquisition.* Mahwah, NJ: Lawrence Erlbaum Associates.

VanPatten, B., & Cadierno, T. (1993). Explicit instruction and input processing. *Studies in Second Language Acquisition, 15*, 225–243.

VanPatten, B., & Oikennon, S. (1996). Explanation vs. structured input in processing instruction. *Studies in Second Language Acquisition, 18,* 495–510.

VanPatten, B., & Sanz, C. (1995). From input to output: Processing instruction and communicative tasks. In F. R. Eckman, D. Highland, P. W. Lee, J. Mileham & R. R. Weber (Eds.), *Second language acquisition theory and pedagogy* (pp. 169–185). Mahwah, NJ: Lawrence Earlbaum Associates.

VanPatten, B., Williams, J., Rott, S. (forthcoming). In B. VanPatten, J. Williams, S. Rott, & M. Overstreet (Eds.), *Form-meaning connections in Second Language Acquisition.* Mahwah, NJ: Lawrence Erlbaum Associates.

White, J. (1998). Getting learners' attention: A typographical input enhancement study. In C. Doughty & J. Williams (Eds.), *Focus on form in classroom second language acquisition* (pp. 85–113). Cambridge: Cambridge University Press.

White, L., Spada, N., Lightbown, P. M., & Ranta, L. (1991). Input enhancement and L2 question formation. *Applied Linguistics, 12,* 416–432.

Part V

Final Commentaries

Parts I–III of this volume have concluded with commentaries by scholars in instructed SLA representing various perspectives. These commentaries have been useful because they point both to strengths and weaknesses in either the model of IP or the research on PI. Such commentary is necessary for advancement of any field or area within a field.

It is fitting to conclude the volume with some final observations and comments from several scholars whose task was to read all of the chapters in the volume and not just those in a particular section. One might think that to read all of the chapters and then to comment on the volume as a whole is a daunting task. Nonetheless, the scholars invited to offer final comments in this section completed their jobs with the usual timeliness and thoughtful insights for which they are known.

In the first commentary, Susanne Carroll comments critically on the model of IP (in the vein of Harrington in this volume) and at the same time comments that research on PI has much to offer. Going beyond Harrington, Carroll offers specific ways in which the principles of IP might be refined to offer greater explanatory or predictive power. James Lee critically reviews the gathered empirical research on PI in this volume and, adding his reading of previous PI research as well as research on instructed SLA in general, serves up a research agenda on PI of testable hypotheses.

In the final chapter in this section, I reflect on the comments and criticisms offered in the volume and also consider the results of the research presented. In agreement that the model of IP will most likely look considerably different five years from now, I argue that changes in the model do not invalidate the previous and present research on PI. In a certain sense, the three chapters in this section set a large part of the research agenda on IP and PI for a number of years to come.

Chapter 15

Commentary: Some General and Specific Comments on Input Processing and Processing Instruction

Susanne Carroll
Universität Potsdam

The chapters in this volume, along with previously published work by Bill VanPatten and his collaborators, constitute an important body of empirical and theoretical research. It is important in part because of its sheer size, now several books and many individual papers. It is important too because of the number of linguistic phenomena that have been investigated: semantic roles and their instantiation in word order or clitic and weak pronouns or the complex causative construction, present, past or future tense marking, mood (subjunctive marking), animacy marking, negative polarity items, or the choice of the correct Spanish copula *ser* or *estar*. It is important because what began as a mainly English L1– Spanish L2 enterprise has moved well beyond that group of learners to include other language pairs with different learning problems arising from unique form-meaning mappings. The collective evidence presented suggests, quite convincingly in my view, that Processing Instruction is a viable alternative to other foreign language instructional paradigms that either eschew a focus on form altogether or that resort to more traditional forms of metalinguistic instruction.[1] In my commentary, I focus on the model of Input Processing that

---

[1] I find it amusing, but also rather disturbing, that VanPatten would have to defend his decision to empirically demonstrate the superiority of Processing Instruction over explicit forms of grammatical instruction because EFL/ESL researchers in the USA find such approaches passé. I am amused because foreign language education has often been criticized for its "bandwagon" mentality whereby one fashion replaces another despite any demonstrated benefits of the new over the old. This mentality creates considerable cynicism among other researchers, parents, teachers, and the general public, which can hardly be to anyone's benefit. VanPatten's insistence on empirical validation of the utility

underlies the hypotheses of the Processing Instruction approach. VanPatten and his colleagues have insisted from the outset that modeling input processing and understanding why Processing Instruction works is just as important as demonstrating that it does. It is important that pedagogical activities be rooted in a viable psychology of language perception and learning. I fully agree with this logic. The essential point of my contribution is to argue the following point: We know far less about speech perception and language processing among second language learners than we need to know to meet this basic requirement. We know little indeed about the interaction of processing and learning mechanisms. And we know very little about how learning from input links to the behavior observable in learners through an analysis of their speech output and writing. Serious advances will have to be made on all these fronts to place the Processing Instruction approach on a solid footing.

ON THE SCOPE OF THE INPUT PROCESSING MODEL

One of the most important issues raised by the contents of this volume is the scope of the Input Processing Model. In his chapter *Input Processing in SLA* (this volume), VanPatten quite rightly begins with issues of terminology and definition. He is concerned with clarifying points of contention and eliminating misunderstandings that may have led to some of the criticisms of the Input Processing Model discussed throughout this volume (e.g., Harrington, 2001; Dekeyser, Salaberry, Robinson, & Harrington 2002). I have a certain sympathy for those who have not understood the point, for the scope of the Input Processing Model is not clear and it may turn out to be the case that it suffers from a serious case of mislabeling.

VanPatten points out that as he uses it, the term *processing* should not be construed as either perception, or noticing. It also does not refer to sentence parsing. He might have added that it is not a theory of how analyses of word and sentence meaning are integrated in real time into an interpretation of an utterance. Among psycholinguists investigating speech perception and sentence comprehension, the term *processing* can refer to any dynamic operation in real

---

of Processing Instruction is therefore to be loudly applauded. It speaks to a growing maturity in the field. I am disturbed because American researchers have great influence on the rest of the world, whether they know it or not. In the state of Brandenburg, Germany, where I work, the Ministry of Education has just introduced new program guidelines to improve English language instruction. The very traditional grammar teaching of the past is now "out." Implicit instruction of grammar is now "in." I am sure this will be shocking news to some of my colleagues who, like many linguists in Germany, choose the contents of their grammar courses to pre-service teacher trainees on the grounds that they will one day be teaching the same constructions and forms to their own students. In short, the impetus for the pedagogical innovation is not coming from us. Consequently, we can only hope that it is empirically well motivated.

time that converts a stimulus into a message or a message into a motor-articulatory plan.[2] Processing from this perspective is stage-like and includes everything from the subconscious detection of phonetic distinctions relevant to word recognition, through morphosyntactic parsing, and message integration (see, e.g., Forster, 1979). But the Input Processing Model is explicitly not a model of processing procedures. We shall see below that it is also not a model of the processing of input. One might be forgiven, then, for suggesting that perhaps the Input Processing Model has not been baptized in the most felicitous way and that some misunderstandings arise from the expectation that something termed the "Input Processing Model" ought to have something to do with how the learner analyses the signal and converts it into an understanding of a communicative intention. It is not obvious to me that the discussion in VanPatten's chapter or elsewhere in this volume will be enough to dispel further confusions.

VanPatten states that the model is not a model of parsing, meaning that it is not intended as a model of parsing algorithms that should capture what learners are doing in real time as they listen to a sentence. This observation strikes me as not only true but necessarily true, given the formulation of various principles of the model. The Sentence Location Principle, for example, appears to eschew a fundamental assumption of much work on parsing, namely that it is *incremental*. The assumption of incrementality is that words and morphemes are analyzed as they are heard–bit by bit. The Sentence Location Principle, in contrast, asserts that learners tend to process items at the beginning of a sentence before they process material at the end, which they process before they process material in the sentence medial position. As a claim about parsing-in-real-time, this assertion flies in the face of the fact that the material heard in sentence-medial position will be heard before the material in sentence final position and must, indeed, be parsed before it because, in right-branching languages in particular, parse decisions made in the middle of the utterance will often have profound consequences for the way in which successive material is analyzed. Compare in this regard *John believes the lie that Mary told him* versus *John believes that Jane said that Mary told him.* These utterances end with the same material but in the first case the embedded clause is embedded within an NP complement, headed by the semantically important word *lie* (which communicates that the speaker believes that some propositional content that corresponds to what Mary said is not true) but in the second case the sentence is embedded within the main verb phrase and John's belief is about what Jane said (and not about what Mary told him). A listener who parsed the end of the sentence before the middle would not be likely to arrive at the correct analysis. Moreover, although it is not impossible logically that a listener might hold all incoming material in working memory until the entire sentence has been heard and only then begin to analyze

---

[2]In what follows, I will simplify things by limiting my discussion to the perception-parsing-interpretation aspect of our behavior.

it, a great deal of research on sentence parsing suggests that we do indeed analyze speech as we hear it. The assumption of the incremental nature of parsing is thus well-supported (Kimball, 1973; Frazier, 1987; Gorrell, 1995). To abandon it as a constraint on second language processing would require empirical evidence of a sort not presented here, namely evidence showing how learners are processing stimuli in real time. There is nothing in VanPatten's discussion that would lead me to think he rejects incrementality. Ergo, Input Processing is not a theory of parsing.

VanPatten says that his principles are *constraints* on processing. It is less obvious to me that this statement must be true. Given what has just been said about the incremental nature of parsing, it strikes me that the Sentence Location Principle cannot be a constraint on parsing. It is not consistent with what we know about parsing to hypothesize that the ongoing semantic interpretation of a sentence is more likely to have an effect on a parse decision at the beginning of the sentence than at the end, which, in turn, will have more of an effect than at a point in the middle of the sentence. It seems to me that the literature on how meaning influences processing suggests that, once again, influence is exerted incrementally. Several processing options may be available after the first or second word of a sentence has been parsed; fewer will be available in the middle of the sentence and by the end the morphosyntactic and semantic contexts established by preceding material will lead the listener to be able to anticipate unique sentence endings.

To take another example, it strikes me that the *Availability of Resources Principle*, given the hypothesis that redundant or meaningless forms are processed after forms with meaning, is nothing more than the observation that language processing is constrained by available resources. This is a well-established fact, one in need of an explanation. The formulation of the principle may strike some as tautologous. It may strike others as superfluous because it could be argued that the processing of *any* novel form can take place only if the processing of other aspects of the utterance is not "draining" available processing resources.

Part of the problem of interpreting the model lies in the fact that VanPatten is vague about what he thinks processing involves. Constraining processes entails a definition of processes. This work remains to be done. It would also be helpful if VanPatten were clearer about the functional architecture of mind assumed. What assumptions are being made about the relationship between the sentence parser and the semantic component? Where and how can they interact? The discussion could also be considerably sharpened up, I suspect, by being more explicit about the kinds of data that the Input Processing Model is designed to explain. I wonder if some of the principles have not been formulated to account for data emerging from the developmental orders literature, viz. observations about what forms are used first in speech *production* as much as facts about how learners process the signal. The Primacy of Meaning Principle (and its subparts) is certainly compatible with the observation that roots and stems from the major lexical categories tend to be used in production before minor lexical and functional categories. Similarly, the First Noun Principle is compatible with the observation that certain learner groups tend to produce SVO orders before they produce other orders. Although one might assume that developmental orders in production reflect constraints on the processing of input, this is by no means a necessary assumption and would have to be carefully motivated.

To summarize this section: the Input Processing Model does not seek to be a model of input perception, parsing, or sentence interpretation. VanPatten says that it is a model of constraints on processing but defining constraints on processing pre-supposes that one knows what processing involves. The Input Processing Model qua constraints model needs a theory of perception and parsing and is difficult to interpret and evaluate without them. More clarity would emerge if the types of data that the model is trying to explain were discussed and an explicit commitment was made to a particular model of parsing and some functional architecture of the language faculty.

ON THE NOTION *INPUT* IN THE INPUT PROCESSING MODEL

Because manipulating input to make certain form-meaning relations more apparent is at the core of the success of Processing Instruction, understanding the *input* in Input Processing is essential. VanPatten makes use of both the Noticing Hypothesis and the input/intake distinction. It would appear, then, that by *input* he means visual or auditory stimuli in the learner's environment. This use would be consistent with terminological use in most of the field (cf. Carroll, 1999). However, if input processing consists of connecting forms with meaning then something needs to be said about how forms come to be mentally represented, that is, how forms emerge from stimuli that have been noticed. This is essential if the claim that "learners process input for meaning before they process it for form" is to have the status of something more than a tautology. I return to the problem of form segmentation below.

It is worth noting that VanPatten does not systematically follow his own terminology, treating *intake* as a subset of input, that is, as a subset of representations processed for meaning "in working memory and made available for further processing" (this volume, p. 7). The "further processing" referred to is accommodation and restructuring, that is., the processes of grammar acquisition. So processing is not just the analysis of (some undefined) representations for meaning, it is also those operations involved in encoding novel grammatical information. This slip is probably unavoidable since we just need a way of talking about mental operations of various sorts. Thus, the Processing Input Model would help us all out if it developed a typology of mental operations relevant to the processing of input.

PRINCIPLE 1: CAN THERE BE MEANING BEFORE THERE IS FORM?

Input Processing is about how learners map meanings to forms. Indeed the thrust of the focus-on-form activities is to draw the learners' attention to the fact that a given form is present when an utterance conveys a particular meaning. It is therefore more than surprising to see the formulation of the Primacy of Meaning Principle: learners process input for meaning *before* they process it for form. One needs to ask if learners *have* an input before they have a form. If the input is the signal, then it boggles the mind to think they are analyzing frequencies for meaning. Frequencies do not lend themselves to semantic interpretation. It is possible that VanPatten wants to say that content words are extracted from the signal before non-content words. This is, however, not very helpful because it merely recapitulates the problem to be explained: Why are the major lexical categories extracted from the signal and learned before the functional categories? In my view, the semantic properties of the forms in question are only partly implicated in the answer. The real story lies in a consideration of their phonetic and phonological properties.

The distinction between the major lexical categories ("content words") and functional or minor lexical categories cuts across several other distinctions in many languages, including the distinction between a *prosodic word* and a *clitic*. In English, a prosodic word is a unit of the phonology that can be uttered in isolation (i.e., with a pause at both the left and right edge of the form) because it has at least one stressed syllable. Stress in English is phonetically realized through a number of phonetic properties including pitch. The syllable of a prosodic word that instantiates the most prominent stress can be aligned with a pitch accent and bear a tone, meaning that it can also realize a tune (Beckman & Pierrehumbert, 1986; Beckman & Edwards, 1990; see also Bolinger, 1961, 1986; Brown, Currie, & Kenworthy, 1980; Ladd, 1996).[3] None of this is true of

---

[3] It is precisely these properties that make it possible for prosodic words to be repeated as single utterances in situations where a speaker has failed to make herself understood and believes that the learner has limited language abilities:

NS: The exercises are all on my homepage.
NNS: (…) <looks confused>
NS: EXERCISES… HOMEPAGE
NNS: oh…yes… EXERCISES

The research on negotiation for meaning (see Long, 1996 for a state-of-the-art review) asserts that word repetition facilitates comprehension. In discussions of word repetition, what is invariably meant is the repetition of the major lexical categories or the referential categories (N, V, Adverb, or Adjective) not repetition of the functional categories. Comprehension certainly depends in part on word recognition, so to the extent that focusing a lexical item facilitates word recognition, it ought to facilitate comprehension.

clitics, which I define as morphosyntactic, and semantic "words" that are not instantiated as prosodic words. This means that there are a number of distinct phonetic cues that might lead learners to segment and phonologically encode words from the major lexical classes of English precisely when they are realized as prosodic words, and that would lead them not to segment and encode clitics (determiners, auxiliaries, complementizers, tense morphemes, number morphemes, etc.). This is true despite the fact that many of the functional categories express important semantic distinctions. When we look at other languages we see similar sorts of phonetic and phonological properties coinciding with the major lexical categories.[4]

There is a connection between meaning and potential segmentability, although a rather indirect one. Lexical categories can be the locus of phonological prominence expressing informational focus (with a variety of phonetic cues signaling this such as syllable lengthening, an increase in amplitude, etc.).[5] Focused expressions are more likely to be expressed with a canonical articulation, meaning they are less variable (Bernstein Ratner, 1996). This means that the learner might have a better chance of encoding a more explicit phonological representation of the segments of the word on first or second (or third) hearing. The more detailed the representation of the segments of a word, the more likely it is that the learner's production will be target-like.[6]

This leads to an interesting prediction. On my story, a learner would be able to extract major lexical categories and functional categories equally well if they had exactly the same phonetic and phonological properties. Although my reading of the grammatical literature leads me to believe that there is no language where the full range of categories (lexical and functional) share all phonetic and phonological properties, there certainly are some languages where certain functional or minor categories share phonetic and phonological properties with the major lexical categories. These words ought to show up fairly early on or at least earlier than the clitic categories. I do not claim to have direct evidence to bear on this prediction but I note anecdotally that learners of German appear to be able to segment certain particles like *weg*, *auf*, or *wieder* fairly early on. These words can be stressed and prominent when they occur in sentence final position:

1) a. Geh weg!

---

[4]It is hardly a novel claim that some kinds of phonological units are acquired before others, cf., inter alia, the Free Form Strategy of Wode (1981). What has been lacking in the past has been the appropriate phonological theory (and the appropriate phonetic-phonology interface) that can explain why prosodic words (free forms) are acquired before clitics (bound forms).

[5]But this needs to be qualified. It is well known that nonmeaningful prosodic units can be made prosodically prominent too: "I said INtake not OUTtake."

[6]I should emphasize that this discussion is highly speculative. There is no solid empirical evidence about any of these hypotheses.

Go away
b. Der Zug fährt ein.
   The train drives in
   "The train is approaching"
c. Schreib mal wieder!
   Write again
   "Write more often!"

The fact that learners can extract these particles does not mean that they have acquired their meaning or mastered their use. Nonetheless having a form is the first step in mapping a meaning onto a form. Of course, it has frequently been asserted that content words are more "salient" (noticeable) in the signal than functional categories but I suspect that what is meant by this claim is that they have physically isolable properties that make them more perceptible independently of the competence grammar. My claim, in contrast, is a claim about the nature of linguistic representations. The relevant properties are in the mind/brain of the learner/listener, not in the signal per se. In other words, the listener has knowledge that makes certain features of the signal useful and informative for locating word boundaries and syllable edges. These features will be detected and encoded, making salience a *consequence* of language-specific phonetic and phonological parsing procedures. So we are left with a number of distinct problems related to the processing of forms. What are the phonetic features that the learner can detect and encode at the very initial stage? What happens to the system when features that are expected are not instantiated? In other words, can a lack of something in the input trigger acquisition?[7] Is transfer of knowledge something that we see only initially? Or are there major phases of transfer that correspond to major stages of processing? Are there correlations to be expected between referential items and prosodic properties like focus and prosodic prominence that occur across typologically unrelated languages and therefore might indeed turn out to be universal input processing principles?

It is possible that I have missed something fundamental in the discussion and misunderstand what VanPatten means by the term "form." I understand him to mean *formative* (some kind of phonetic, phonemic or phonological representation). In other words, I take him to be hypothesizing that learners are capable of extracting formatives from the speech signal and that formatives are to be analyzed for meaning before they are analyzed for *non-semantic morphosyntactic properties*. This, of course, is something quite different from the formulation of the Primacy of Meaning Principle as given. Let us reformulate it in the suggested way:

---

[7]In a connectionist paradigm, this situation is predicted to occur.

> *Revised Primacy of Meaning Principle (Version 1):*
> Learners process formatives for meaning before they process
> them for non-semantic morphosyntactic properties.

I speculate further and say that perhaps what is really intended is something like
the hypothesis in Version 2:

> *Revised Primacy of Meaning Principle (Version 2):*
> Learners process formatives using semantic information to
> establish morphosyntactic properties (like word class) before
> they process them using purely morphosyntactic
> distributional information.

This really would constitute a constraint on learning because it states that
learners tend to prefer meaning-form mappings to distributional properties at the
same level of analysis to establish the grammatical properties of new formatives.
According to this hypothesis, the learner would bootstrap into the syntax using
semantic properties such as semantic class. Thus, a learner would, for example,
understand that a THING is being referred to in some utterance and on the basis
of that interpretation classify the formative heard as a noun. This kind of
meaning-formative mapping would take place before the learner learns how to
identify formatives as nouns on the basis of the fact that they follow the
determiner *der, die or das.*[8] Or a learner would understand that *führen ... durch*
is an ACTIVITY and understand that what follows *führen* is a PATIENT, for
example, *Wir führen die Analyse durch* "We will carry out the analysis." It
seems to me that this, too, is compatible with much of what is said in chapter 1.
If this is a proper interpretation of VanPatten's intention, only he can say.

In this section I raised the issue of how forms are extracted from the speech
stream and suggested that this is a first and necessary step in processing input. In
short, I argued that there can be no processing of input for meaning before there
are forms onto which meanings can be mapped. I suspect that many of the
observations made about the types of words that learners use at different stages
of acquisition are ultimately to be explained in terms of those phonetic
properties that facilitate segmentation of a phonological unit from the signal,
although I note that there is no serious sustained research on this important
question. I observed that major lexical categories in many languages correspond
to prosodic words. Prosodic words are phonological units that are instantiated by

---

[8]This kind of bootstrapping has been proposed for first language acquisition. I suspect
that it is actually unlikely that it occurs with any frequency in SLA for the simple reason
that understanding the intended meaning of an utterance tends to activate the L1 words
for that meaning. This activation then makes the contents of the L1 lexical entry
available, including word class, argument structure, selectional properties, case
assignment features, and so on. Any and all of these properties might be transferred to the
analysis of the L2 formative.

phonetic properties that learners may be sensitive to from the earliest stages of acquisition. Functional categories tend not to correspond to prosodic words. This distinction has nothing to do with the semantic properties of the forms in question except insofar as the major lexical categories will be more readily focussed. I then attempted to reformulate the Primacy of Meaning Principle in such a way as to assume that formatives are simply available to the learner (however that might happen). This permitted me to zero in on what might be the true contrast that VanPatten wants to establish: not meaning vs. form but rather meaning versus morphosyntactic distinctions. This then led to a speculative question: Is the appropriate constraint to be formulated in terms of a preference for using semantic information to establish grammatical properties of formatives over distributional properties?

SOME COMMENTS ON THE NOTICING HYPOTHESIS

Developing a model of the segmentation of forms in SLA will force us, I suspect, to uncouple both processing and second language learning from the Noticing Hypothesis of Schmidt (1990) in its strongest version, for which there is little substantive evidence.[9] The Noticing Hypothesis is, of course, critical to Processing Instruction since the manipulations of the instruction are intended to cause the learners to notice the occurrence of particular forms in an utterance to mean certain things. If the Noticing Hypothesis is inadequate in some respects, it will seriously limit the applicability of the Processing Instruction Theory. I suspect that Processing Instruction will not extend to every acquisitional problem and certainly VanPatten and his collaborators have never claimed that it will. But it is important for all concerned to understand the kinds of limits the theory will have to contend with. Thus, Tomlin and Villa (1994) pointed out many years ago in a critical review of Schmidt's work that noticing should not be equated with the detection of features in the signal (what VanPatten here calls "signal registration"). All models of speech perception presuppose detection of signal features, as well as what Tomlin and Villa call *orientation to the signal* and *alertness*. There are certainly good empirical reasons to think that many aspects of the speech signal are detected well below the threshold of awareness in the processing of language (Boomer & Dittman, 1962; Scott, 1982; Nagel, Shapiro, Tuller, & Nawy, 1996; Shattuck-Hufnagel & Turk, 1996, in a monolingual context, see Henderson & Nelms, 1980, in an SLA context). There are independent reasons to think that language processing and language learning are not unique in this regard (Roediger, 1990; Blaxton, 1992).

---

[9]The strong version is the claim that Schmidt himself makes, namely, that no aspect of a second language can be learned unless it is first noticed in the input. The major claim of this section is that not all learning requires noticing. An equally important claim is that much of what we learn is not "in" the input (speech signal) to be noticed in the first place.

I believe that the acquisition of precisely those acoustic features that permit us to "hear" forms in the speech stream of a novel language involves acquisition without noticing. I also suspect that there is a great deal of acquisition that has to occur from the moment of first exposure to the moment when one can reliably "hear" new forms in an utterance and ask: "What does [...] mean?" It is a fascinating question as to what features of the signal L2 learners are actually sensitive to that permit them to extract some kind of phonetic information and begin building phonological representations. Anne Cutler, for example, has done extensive research over many years on the problem of whether word recognition is an automatic consequence of the activation of a lexical entry, in which case you get the left and right edges of the word "for free,"or whether there are "pre-lexical" segmentation processes that impose form boundaries on the signal. She makes a serious case that language acquisition could only be possible if we develop and apply pre-lexical segmentation processes that extract forms and present them to the word activation and word recognition processes (Cutler, 1996). She and her collaborators have argued that humans possess an a priori capacity to encode periodicity in the signal (Cutler & Mehler, 1993). This bias evolves into modes of language specific listening based on the phonetic patterns in the signal and statistical properties of the words that infants are exposed to in the first year of life (Cutler, Mehler, Norris, & Segui, 1986; Cutler, 1990, 1992, 1994; Cutler & Otake, 1994; Otake, Hatano, Cutler, & Mehler, 1993). Language specific listening is, in short, an acquired phenomenon. Moreover, it has been claimed that it is not something one can "turn off." Cutler, Mehler, Norris, and Segui (1992) have gathered empirical evidence that suggests that bilinguals apply the same language specific segmentation process to each of their languages. Thus, if a bilingual makes use of a segmentation process sensitive to sequences of strong-weak syllables, he will do so not only in English where the phonology of words makes this segmentation strategy useful, but also in French, where it isn't. What this suggests is that many of the formatives the learner will initially "hear" will not be forms in the sense that VanPatten appears to intend. They will be prosodic units, possibly units that correspond to minimal prosodic words in the L1.

It is equally questionable whether learners can attend to semantic distinctions per se in the input. Most individuals, when presented with the sentence *The horse raced past the barn fell* for the first time, fail to come up with a meaningful interpretation. On the contrary, their reading of the sentence is anomalous and no amount of staring at the sentence helps to come up with an alternative. When given the string *The horse ridden past the barn fell* and an explanation of the possible meaning of the first sentence, everyone has an "Oh I get it now" reaction. At which point, no amount of staring at the first sentence allows one to recover the impossible parse. From the moment when we understand how to parse the sentence, that parse emerges.

In this section, I argued that the Input Processing Model might want to rethink its commitment to the Noticing Hypothesis to take into consideration the fact that much of our phonetic and phonological knowledge occurs unconsciously and below the threshold of our awareness. I suspect that much of our syntactic and semantic acquisition will also not be consistent with the Noticing Hypothesis. Attention and attentional control are usually discussed in the context of the regulation of our behavior. It is unclear to what extent input processing can be characterized in these terms. Input processing may be better characterized as something that happens to us rather than something we do.

THE FIRST NOUN PRINCIPLE

The First Noun Principle states that learners tend to process the first noun they encounter in a sentence as the subject/agent. This principle as formulated is making two quite distinct claims. The first is that the first noun is processed as a grammatical subject. The second is that the first noun is processed as an agent. Let me deal with these predictions separately.

Grammatical functions are not directly encoded in the signal and must be assigned to discrete units as part of a morphosyntactic parse of a sentence. As is well known, there is considerable cross-linguistic variation exhibited among the languages of the world as to the cues that encode grammatical functions. Some languages are *topic prominent* in that topics are marked with grammatical functions and placed in sentence-initial position. Topics are involved in a number of grammatical relations. Chinese is said to be a language of this sort and many grammatical categories can play the function of topic in addition to noun phrases (Li & Thompson, 1976, 1981). Other languages are said to be *subject prominent*, in that verb agreement expresses a formal relationship between the verb and the subject of the sentence. It strikes me as unlikely, therefore, that the First Noun Principle will turn out to be a universal principle of input processing, rather than a strategy typical of English speakers or other speakers of subject-prominent languages. Xiao (2002) cites previous research by Rutherford (1983) showing transfer of topic marking strategies among Chinese learners and documents similar strategies among the child learners studied. Klein and Perdue (1992) argued that information structure plays an important role in the linearization of all learners telling narrative tales. Their Italian L1-German L2 learner Vito tends to map topics onto the first NP of a string in his spontaneous production. We must be cautious in extrapolating from production data to claims about input processing, but unless experiments are done that carefully distinguish between topics and non-topics, we cannot know how sensitive to topic status speakers of subject prominent languages are.[10]

Agent is a universal semantic category. We therefore ought to expect that all L2 learners will be sensitive to cues in the environment to agentivity (such as

---

[10]I note in this regard that in many English sentences the grammatical subject will simultaneously express the topic and the agent.

self-propulsion, force dynamics, intentionality, and so on). Research involving cross-linguistic comparisons of processing strategies have shown quite clearly that speakers are not all mapping the Agent semantic role onto the first noun phrase of the sentence (Bates, McNew, MacWhinney, Devescovi, & Smith 1982; MacWhinney, Bates, & Kliegl, 1984, the chapters in MacWhinney & Bates, 1989). This is what we ought to find given the variable word orders of many languages. One of the important results of this research is that it demonstrates quite clearly that processing depends on a weighting of a variety of cues to a particular analysis. Thus, in German, it might be the case that the first noun phrase is the topic, subject, and agent, but in many sentences these functions tease apart, in which case the listener relies on cues unrelated to position to analyze the sentence.

(2) a. Die Kuh frisst das Gras.
     The cow eats the grass.
  b. Das Gras frisst die Kuh.
  c. Die Kuh das Gras frisst.
  d. Das Gras die Kuh frisst.

All of the sentences of (2) are possible in German and all have the same propositional meaning, although they would not be used in exactly the same circumstances. This is because the variations in word order typically reflect differences in the information structure with focussed referents being put in the first position of the sentence. Only sentence (2a) exhibits informationally unmarked word order with wide scope focus.[11] The principles of P2 attempt to capture the fact that processes can constitute clusters but the model does not explain what happens when the cues do not cluster. In other words, in contrast to the Competition Model that has a worked-out set of principles for defining cue competition and making precise predictions as to which cue in the input will "win out," the various subprinciples of the First Noun Principle are offered as alternatives to word order but no predictions follow as to when a learner might invoke versions a, b or c. This strikes me as a weakness of the model in comparison to the Competition Model.

The Input Processing Model would be improved by an attempt to explicitly work out the way in which an explicit semantic representation would lead the learner to impute particular meanings to input utterances and to encode forms to carry precisely those meanings. This would require being much more explicit about the semantic theory that is assumed to underlie the principles than is available from a reading of the current papers. Serious discussion of semantic issues (reference, predication, quantification) is pretty sparse in SLA research,

---

[11]This means that the focus could be the direct object NP *das Gras* or the VP *frisst das Gras* or the entire sentence. All of the other examples have narrow scope focus on either *die Kuh* or *das Gras*.

and I don't want to be seen as singling out the Input Processing researchers for a general failing of the field. Still, it behooves those who think that meaning is somehow driving the acquisition of form to be clear as to what meanings are or are not. This is especially important when there is talk of some forms being "meaningful" and others not. Number is a meaningful semantic distinction. Mood is also a meaningful semantic distinction. I have already articulated my suspicion that if learners rely initially on adverbs to express, for example, notions of time and place, rather than functional categories, it is more a consequence of the phonetic properties of the latter than their semantic properties. I won't revisit this issue. I will simply say here that it still might turn out to be the case that learners exhibit particular semantic sensitivities, processing names before expressions denoting quantities, or action words before attributes. Investigating this issue might require that we look at languages that we do not see too much in the literature, such as Finnish or Turkish. Given the successful collaborative work that VanPatten and his colleagues have accomplished in the past, I have no doubt that they can extend their research in the appropriate direction.

CONCLUSIONS

In this chapter I raised questions about the exact scope of the theory of input processing, about the processing assumptions and the theory of meaning implicit in the work of VanPatten and his colleagues. I have done so in the belief that addressing these issues would add considerable clarity to the theory of constraints underpinning Processing Instruction. The idea of applying a set of Slobinian style Operating Principles to SLA is not novel (the ZISA project, for example, made a first stab in the same direction, see Clahsen, Meisel, & Pienemann, 1983). In my own research (Carroll, 2001), I have argued that Operating Principles constitute empirical observations in need of theoretical explanation. I have raised this criticism again here with respect to the constraints of Input Processing. I have also suggested a number of directions for future studies, in particular, with languages that have different typological properties from English, Spanish, and French, which have, so far, been the major languages involved either as the L1 or as the L2. All researchers with an interest in second language acquisition and language processing by learners and bilinguals would profit from such extensions. The careful and clever studies that have come to typify VanPatten's research are bound to provide interesting results. I certainly am eager to see more work on Input Processing and Processing Instruction.

REFERENCES

Bates, E., McNew, S., MacWhinney, B., Devescovi, A., & Smith, S. (1982). Functional constraints on sentence processing: A cross-linguistic study. *Cognition, 11*, 245–299.

Beckman, M. E., & Pierrehumbert, J. B. (1986). Intonational structure in Japanese and English. *Phonology Yearbook, 3*, 266–309.

Beckman, M. E., & Edwards, J. (1990). Lengthenings and shortenings and the nature of prosodic constituency. In J. Kingston & M. E. Beckman (Eds.), *Between the grammar and the physics of speech. Papers in laboratory phonology* (pp. 152–178). Cambridge: Cambridge University Press.

Bernstein Ratner, N. (1996). From 'signal to syntax': But what is the nature of the signal? In J. L. Morgan & K. Demuth (Eds.), *Signal to syntax: Bootstrapping from speech to grammar in early acquisition* (pp.135–150). Hillsdale, NJ: Lawrence Erlbaum Associates.

Blaxton, T. A. (1992). Dissociations among memory measures in memory-impaired subjects: Evidence for a processing account of memory. *Memory and Cogntion, 20*, 549–562.

Bolinger, D. L. (1961). Ambiguities in pitch accent. *Word, 17,* 309-317.

Bolinger, D. L. (1986). *Intonation and its parts: Melody in spoken English.* London: Edward Arnold.

Boomer, D. S., & Dittmann, A. T. (1962). Hesitation pauses and juncture pauses in speech. *Language and Speech, 5,* 215–220.

Brown, G., Currie, K., & Kenworthy, J. (1980). *Questions of intonation.* London: Croom Helm.

Carroll, S. (1999). Putting 'input' in its proper place. *Second Language Research, 15,* 337–388.

Carroll, S. (2001). *Input and evidence: The raw material of second language acquisition.* Amsterdam: Benjamins.

Clahsen, H., Meisel, J. M., & Pienemann, M. (1983). *Deutsch als Zweitsprache: der Erwerb ausländischer Arbeiter.* Tübingen: Narr.

Cutler, A. (1990). Exploiting prosodic possibilities in speech segmentation. In G. T. M. Altmann (Ed.), *Cognitive models of speech processing: Psycholinguistic and computational perspectives* (pp. 105–121). Cambridge, MA: MIT Press.

Cutler, A. (1992). The production and perception of word boundaries. In Y. Tohkura, E. Vatikiotis-Bateson & Y. Sagisaka, (Eds.), *Speech perception, production and linguistic structure* (pp. 419–425). Tokyo: IOS Press.

Cutler, A. (1994). Segmentation problems, rhythmic solutions. *Lingua, 92,* 81–104.

Cutler, A. (1996). Prosody and the word boundary problem. In J. L. Morgan & K. Demuth (Eds.), *Signal to syntax: Bootstrapping from speech to grammar in early acquisition* (pp. 87–99). Hillsdale, NJ: Lawrence Erlbaum Associates.

Cutler, A., & Mehler, J. (1993). The periodicity bias. *Journal of Phonetics, 21,* 103–108.

Cutler, A., Mehler, J., Norris, D., & Segui, J. (1986). The syllable's differing role in the segmentation of French and English. *Journal of Memory and Language, 25,* 385–400.

Cutler, A., Mehler, J., Norris, D., & Segui, J. (1992). The monolingual nature of speech segmentation by bilinguals. *Cognitive Psychology, 24,* 381–410.

Cutler, A., & Otake, T. (1994). Mora or phoneme? Further evidence for language-specific listening. *Journal of Memory and Language, 33,* 824–844.

DeKeyser, R. M., Salaberry, R., Robinson, P., & Harrington, M. (2002). What gets processed in processing instruction: A response to Bill VanPatten's "Update." *Language Learning, 52,* 805–823.

Forster, K. I. (1979). Levels of processing and the structure of the language processor. In W. E. Cooper & E. C. T. Walker (Eds.), *Sentence processing: Psycholinguistic studies presented to Merrill Garrett* (pp. 27–85). Hillsdale, NJ: Lawrence Erlbaum Associates.

Frazier, L. (1987). Sentence processing: A tutorial review. In M. Coltheart (Ed.), *Attention and performance XII* (pp. 601–681). Hillsdale, NJ: Lawrence Erlbaum Associates.

Gorrell, P. (1995). *Syntax and parsing.* Cambridge: Cambridge University Press.

Harrington, M. (2001). Sentence processing. In P. Robinson (Ed.), *Cognition and second language instruction* (pp. 91–124). Cambridge: Cambridge University Press.

Henderson, A. I., & Nelms, S. (1980). Relative salience of intonation fall and pause as cues to the perceptual segmentation of speech in an unfamiliar language. *Journal of Psycholinguistic Research, 9,* 147–159.

Kimball, J. (1973). Seven principles of surface structure parsing in natural language. *Cognition, 2,* 15–47.

Klein, W., & Perdue, C. (1992). Framework. In W. Klein & C. Perdue (Eds.), *Utterance structure: Developing grammars again* (pp. 11–59). Amsterdam: Benjamins.

Ladd, D. R. (1996). *Intonational phonology.* Cambridge: Cambridge University Press.

Li, C. N., & Thompson, S. A. (1976). Subject and topic: A new typology of language. In C. N. Li (Ed.), *Subject and topic* (pp. 457–490). New York: Academic Press.

Li, C. N., & Thompson, S. A. (1981). *Mandarin Chinese: A functional reference grammar.* Berkeley, CA: University of California Press.

Long, M. H. (1996). The role of the linguistic environment in second language acquisition. In W. C. Ritchie & T. K. Bhatia (Eds.), *Handbook of second language acquisition* (pp. 413–468). San Diego, CA: Academic Press.

MacWhinney, B., & Bates, E. (Eds.). (1989). *The crosslinguistic study of sentence processing*: Cambridge: Cambridge University Press.

MacWhinney, B., Bates, E., & Kliegl, R. (1984). Cue validity and sentence interpretation in English, German and Italian. *Journal of Verbal Learning and Verbal Behavior, 23,* 127–150.

Nagel, H. N., Shapiro, L. P., Tuller, B., & Nawy, R. (1996). Prosodic influences on the resolution of temporary ambiguity during on-line sentence processing. *Journal of Psycholinguistic Research, 25,* 319–344.

Otake, T., Hatano, G., Cutler, A., & Mehler, J. (1993). Mora or syllable? Speech segmentation in Japanese. *Journal of Memory and Language, 32,* 358–378.

Roediger, H. L. III (1990). Implicit memory: Retention without remembering. *American Psychologist, 45,* 1043–1056.

Rutherford, W. C. (1983). Language typology and language transfer. In S. M. Gass & L. Selinker (Eds.), *Language transfer in language learning* (pp. 358–370). Rowley, MA: Newbury House.

Schmidt, R. W. (1990). The role of consciousness in second language learning. *Applied Linguistics, 13,* 282–301.

Scott, D. R. (1982). Duration as a cue to the perception of a phrase boundary. *Journal of the Acoustic Society of America, 71,* 996–1007.

Shattuck-Hufnagel., S., & Turk, A. E. (1996). A prosody tutorial for investigators of auditory sentence processing. *Journal of Psycholinguistic Processing, 25,* 193–247.

Tomlin, R., & Villa, V. (1994). Attention in cognitive science and second language acquisition. *Studies in Second Language Acquisition, 16,* 183–203.

Wode, H. (1981). Language acquisitional universals: A unified view of language acquisition. In H. Winitz (Ed.), *Native and foreign language acquisition: Annals of the New York Academy of Sciences, 379,* 218–234.

Xiao, Y. (2002). The syntactic development of school-age Chinese-speaking children learning English. *IRAL, 40,* 235–271.

Chapter 16

On the Generalizability, Limits, and Potential Future Directions of Processing Instruction Research

James F. Lee
Indiana University

We know that children and adults can acquire a second language without the benefit of explicit instruction in grammatical form(s) as is the case with learners all over the world who acquire a second language in natural settings such as in contact situations, languages of commerce, and heritage languages spoken in homes or communities. We also know that instruction can accelerate acquisition as well as help learners ultimately attain greater proficiency. Instruction is, therefore, beneficial but not necessary for acquisition to take place. Within language teaching circles, a great debate arose around the issue of grammar teaching in a communicative or communication-oriented curriculum. The debate polarized as whether or not to teach grammar, that is, the presence or absence of explicit instruction in form. VanPatten (1988) redirected the debate from "do we or don't we?" by asking a better question, "how do we?." How do we teach grammar in a communicative framework? How do we teach grammar so that instruction works with acquisitional processes not against them? A partial answer to these questions is to teach aspects of a second language grammar through Processing Instruction (Lee & VanPatten, 1995, 2003; VanPatten, 1996, 2000a, 2000b, and elsewhere).

A synonym for instruction is *intervention* so that the difference between naturalistic acquisition and instructed acquisition is the difference between the absence or presence of intervention in the process. Processing Instruction is, therefore, a type of intervention and is an extremely well described intervention (e.g., Lee & VanPatten, 1995, 2003; VanPatten, 1996, and elsewhere). The purpose of PI is to intervene as learners process input rather than at the time they would formulate output. The intervention intends to affect learners' processing strategies so that they process input for both form and meaning and so that they process the input more accurately. By processing form-meaning connections in the input more accurately, learners eventually feed better data to their developing L2 systems. Processing instruction includes two features: explicit information regarding forms and processing strategies as well as a particular type of practice with forms, that is, structured input activities. To more bluntly paraphrase Wong (this volume, chap. 2), if the instruction does not address a processing problem by correcting an inappropriate processing strategy or by instilling an appropriate processing strategy, then the instruction is not Processing Instruction.

Research on Processing Instruction has been published since 1993. I can summarize the entirety of the database as follows: learners who receive processing instruction on syntactic, perceptual, and semantic processing strategies significantly improve on sentence interpretation tasks whereas learners who receive traditional instruction do not. Learners who receive processing instruction on syntactic and perceptual strategies significantly improve on sentence and discourse production tasks as do learners who receive traditional instruction. When instruction involves semantic processing strategies, the superior effects of processing instruction are less pronounced but in no case have learners who received processing instruction improved less than those who received other types of instruction. In other words, traditional and meaning-oriented instruction might yield equal results to Processing Instruction, but never yield superior results whereas Processing Instruction often does yield superior results.

The purpose of this chapter is to examine the depth and breadth of the Processing Instruction research to address the questions of, on the one hand, how generalizable the findings of the research are and, on the other, how limited they are. I do so by addressing a series of questions and addressing PI as its own entity as well as one contrasted to other types of instruction. I also offer suggestions for future research to augment the generalizability of the research base and, possibly, to open research on Processing Instruction to new avenues of investigation. These suggestions are framed as hypotheses concerning the effects of Processing Instruction.

WHAT PROCESSING STRATEGIES HAVE BEEN EXAMINED IN PI RESEARCH?

For a study to be considered as one on Processing Instruction, it must address a processing problem. The PI research is rich in the types of processing problems addressed; syntactic, perceptual, and semantic processing strategies have been taught to language learners who then employ them successfully on both interpretation and production tasks. Does PI do what it claims it will do? Yes, and it does so across different types of processing problems. It teaches learners to process input differently than when they are left to their own devices. Is PI more or equally effective as other types of instruction? As elaborated below, PI is more effective than other types of instruction when the processing strategy is syntactic or perceptual and equally effective when the processing strategy is semantic.

Syntactic Strategies: Word Order Phenomena

The most-researched processing strategy is that of inappropriately using the first-noun strategy to process OVS sentences in Spanish (Sanz, 1997, and this volume; VanPatten & Cadierno, 1993; VanPatten & Fernández, this volume; VanPatten & Oikennon, 1996; VanPatten & Sanz, 1995) and to process *faire causatif* sentences in French (VanPatten & Wong, this volume). By using this processing strategy learners inaccurately interpret the first noun or pronoun they encounter in a string as the agent. *Lo ve María*, is interpreted as 'He sees Maria' not as 'Maria sees him.' *Jacques fait laver le voiture à Jean*, is interpreted as 'Jacques washes Jean's car' not as 'Jacques makes Jean wash the car'. The processing problem is not only a misinterpretation of sentence meaning but the potential for inaccurate data being delivered to the developing system. *Lo*, for example, is not a subject pronoun in Spanish nor is *à Jean* a possessive construction in these French sentences.

This research has demonstrated, consistently and clearly, that learners of Spanish and French can be taught not to employ an inappropriate word order strategy. Learners who receive processing instruction interpret underlying agent/object relations more accurately than learners who receive traditional instruction and that processing instruction and traditional instruction are equally effective in having learners correctly produce sentences and, in Spanish, discourse using object pronouns. That different languages and different word orders have been investigated contributes to the generalizability of Processing Instruction as an intervention that effectively alters inappropriate processing strategies.

Perceptual Strategies: Forms Determine Semantically Appropriate Interpretations

In both Spanish and Italian, verb-final stress can be a distinctive feature for identifying different tenses. In Spanish, the difference between 'I speak' and 'he spoke' is signaled by the acoustic stress on the penultimate versus final syllable, *hablo* and *habló*, respectively (which are also marked orthographically). As Cadierno (1995) found for Spanish and Benati (2001) for Italian, learners can be taught to pay attention to the ends of verbs to interpret the time frame to which a sentence refers, present or past, present or future. Both find that learners who receive processing instruction interpret time frame more accurately than those who receive traditional instruction but that processing instruction and traditional instruction are equally effective in having learners correctly produce sentences using the past and future forms.

Cheng (2002, and this volume) examines the contrast between Spanish copular verbs *ser* and *estar* when used with past participles. When used with *ser*, a past participle denotes a passive sentence construction but when used with *estar* the past participle refers to the resultant state of an entity. Processing whether the copula is *ser* or *estar* leads to the correct interpretation of a sentence's meaning. In order to process the copula, learners must be taught to attend to a monosyllabic word versus a bisyllabic word, *es* versus *está*, respectively, so there is a perceptual element to this investigation. When she focuses her findings on *estar*, Cheng finds that learners who receive processing instruction interpret sentences with *estar* more accurately than learners who received traditional instruction. Learners who received processing instruction improve just as much as those who receive traditional instruction on sentence production and on guided compositions (Cheng, 2002). Cheng (this volume) examines the sentences in which learners used *estar* in the guided compositions to evaluate the effects of contextual variables on the use of *estar*. She found that learners who received processing instruction perform the same as those who received traditional instruction.

Farley (2001a, 2001b, and this volume, chap. 11) examines Spanish subjunctive and indicative verb forms in subordinate clauses as the key to triggering a semantically appropriate matrix clause. By processing a form as subjunctive, the appropriate matrix clause trigger would be an expression of doubt; by processing the form as indicative, the appropriate matrix clause trigger would be an expression of affirmation. In order to determine the correct matrix clause, learners must attend to vocalic alternations in unstressed syllables, *habla* versus *hable*, for example. Typical Spanish word order places the matrix clause first so that the semantic information (doubt/affirmation) is presented first and the subjunctive/indicative form is merely a reflex form. Farley changed the order of the elements in his instruction, placing the subordinate clause first so that learners would be forced to process the form. He compared the effects of processing instruction with meaning-based output instruction; the differences between the two exist only at the level of practice activities as learners in both groups received the same explicit information about subjunctive and indicative. When he examined 29 subjects in 2001, he found that learners who receive processing instruction interpret sentences more accurately than those who receive meaning-based output instruction. The two instructional groups perform equally well on a sentence production task. When Farley amplified his database to 50 subjects (this volume) he found equal effects on interpretation and production tests for processing and meaning-based output instruction. (My reservations about Cheng and Farley's research are presented in the section on subjects' characteristics.)

Wong (this volume, chap. 9) demonstrates that learners of French can be taught to pay attention to an indefinite article to determine affirmative sentence meaning and the definite article to determine negative sentence meaning. The form (type of article) signals affirmative or negative meaning. Given that negative sentence meaning is also semantically encoded pre- and post verbally (i.e., *ne... pas*), the definite article is redundant and of low communicative value. Wong's structured input practices remove the redundant element and focus learners' attention to the articles. Wong's purpose was not to compare processing instruction with traditional instruction but rather to determine what aspect of processing instruction (the explanation or practice with structured input) causes the improvement in learner performance. She found that the practice with structured input causes the significant change in learners' performance.

That different languages and different perceptual processing problems have been investigated contribute to the generalizability of Processing Instruction as an intervention that effectively instills in learners appropriate perceptual processing strategies. In other words, as a result of receiving PI, learners can be taught to use forms in the input to determine a semantic distinction: temporal framework, resultant state, affirmed propositions, and negative meanings. The clear superiority of PI to TI as demonstrated with syntactic strategies is not evident with all perceptual strategies; TI appears to be equally effective with regards to improving learner performance in some instances. Yet the important point that we cannot loose sight of in generalizing the findings is that learners who received PI significantly improved across two languages and three different semantic processing problems.

The above evaluations of syntactic, perceptual, and semantic processing strategies reveal that within each of these strategy types PI positively influences learners' processing strategies. The database is fairly robust representing findings from Spanish, French, and Italian. The database is quite robust in that we have positive results for PI with multiple examples of processing problems within each category of strategy. I can, therefore, conclude this evaluation of processing strategies by stating that the results of PI research are generalizable both within and across three types of processing strategies.

Processing Instruction data exist for syntactic strategies in Spanish and French, for perceptual strategies in Spanish and Italian, and for semantic strategies in Spanish and French. I am confident regarding the generalizability of Processing Instruction to Romance Languages but reasonable questions could be posed regarding the generalizability of Processing Instruction beyond Romance Languages. The current database is sufficient to support the following hypotheses:

- *Hypothesis 1.* PI can help learners of any L2 apply appropriate word order processing strategies.
- *Hypothesis 2.* PI can help learners of any L2 perceive and use acoustic stress when it is a distinctive feature of the language.

- *Hypothesis 3.* PI can help learners of any L2 to process a formal feature of that language to determine an appropriate semantic interpretation of a sentence.

ARE THE EFFECTS OF PI DURATIVE?

The question that any instructional treatment must address is whether the effects of instruction are found only on the day of instruction or whether the effects persist and endure one week, one month, one quarter, one semester, or one academic year later. VanPatten and Fernández (this volume) point out several challenges, difficulties, and obstacles in assessing long-term effects. One difficulty is subject availability/attrition but the most important obstacle is the curriculum itself. A valid assessment of long-term effects can only take place if learners/subjects receive no instruction of any kind on the target structure, which is a difficult demand for a language class. Some aspect of *ser* and *estar*, for example, appears every semester. Many books review preterit forms and object pronouns in subsequent chapters. Despite these difficulties many of the PI studies assessed the short-term durative effects of PI instruction. The results affirm that the effects of Processing Instruction persist one week (VanPatten & Cadierno, 1993; Cadierno, 1995), two weeks (Farley, 2001 a & b) and one month after instruction Cadierno, 1995; Benati, 2001). VanPatten and Fernández examine the long term durative effects of PI on a word-order strategy and find that significant effects on learner improvement can be seen after eight months. Learner performance is significantly better on the eight-month test than on the pretest but has significantly dropped from the one week post-test. One perspective to take on this one study is that the effects of PI are quite durative but not may not be permanent so that after fifteen months the learners' have regressed to their starting point. I believe we can take this perspective on most instruction. Obviously, a large lacuna in the research base supporting the effects of processing instruction is a determination of the long-term durative effects.

- *Hypothesis 4.* Evidence will be found to corroborate the long term durative effects of PI on word-order, perceptual, and semantic processing strategies.

WHAT CHARACTERIZES THE SUBJECTS WHO HAVE BEEN INVESTIGATED IN PI RESEARCH?

The original VanPatten and Cadierno (1993) study on Spanish object pronouns established the way in which subsequent research has been carried out. The effects of processing instruction have been examined using the standard and completely acceptable pretest/posttest repeated measures Analysis of Variance

(ANOVA). A pretest allows researchers to screen subjects for prior knowledge of the form or strategy under investigation by eliminating those who score too high; the ANOVA procedure assumes subject homogeneity, and a pretest is one method for establishing it. PI research typically examines subjects who performed less than 60% correct on the pretest. Logically, if a learner already knows the form or strategy then instruction will not make a difference. The pretest/posttest procedure allows researchers to make statements regarding the effects of instruction on improving performance; even a score of 60% indicates some prior knowledge, albeit incomplete prior knowledge. The pretest/posttest procedure has allowed researchers to implement their studies with second year learners whose vocabularies in the target language are greater than learners in their first semester of study. Only Wong (this volume, chap. 9), Benati (2001, and this volume), VanPatten and Wong (this volume) make a claim that their subjects are being taught the target form for the first time. This point should not influence our confidence in the research on syntactic and perceptual strategies, but it raises questions about Cheng and Farley's findings on the equal effectiveness of other instruction types to Processing Instruction with semantic processing strategies. Cheng's 83 subjects are all fourth semester learners of Spanish (who scored low on the pretest and should be included in the studies). Farley's 29 and 50 subjects are all fourth semester learners of Spanish (who scored low on the pretest and should be included in the studies). All these fourth semester learners received formal instruction on *ser* and *estar* beginning in the first semester of study and on the subjunctive of doubt (Farley's denomination) in the second semester of study. Neither uses a debriefing questionnaire to further screen subjects who, during instruction, might have recalled that they had learned this information previously; Leeser (2003) found that some of the subjects who scored low on the pretest indicated remembering the linguistic item he studied (Spanish future tense) and scored well on the posttest. Leeser eliminated these subjects from the data pool.

I reiterate for emphasis that the pretest/posttest repeated measures ANOVA is a standard means to measure change. But now that PI research has been with us for over a decade, we could also inquire about the effects of PI when PI is the *initial* instruction learners receive on a grammatical form, be they object pronouns, causative constructions, future tense and/or the past tense, copular verbs, the subjunctive/indicative contrast, and/or negative constructions. What are the effects of PI on establishing the form-meaning connection in the first place rather than improving the form-meaning connections? Are the effects of PI on language production related to their previous knowledge (although VanPatten and Wong, this volume, and Benati, 2001, suggest that previous knowledge is not a critical factor)?

- *Hypothesis 5.* PI will be equally effective as an intervention for establishing initial form-meaning connections as it is for improving learners' performance.

The pretest/posttest repeated measures ANOVA has certainly provided strong evidence that Processing Instruction improves learners' performance. All the research to date has presented results only in aggregate terms. A lacuna in the database is, therefore, a consideration of individual differences. What are the characteristics of the learners who benefit the most from PI? What are the characteristics of the learners who benefit the least, if indeed, there are learners who make no significant improvement after instruction? For those who benefit the least, would more practice items help them improve more (as the results of Sanz, this volume, suggest)? It is simply logical to hypothesize that PI may be differentially effective within a group of learners.

- *Hypothesis 6.* Some learners' benefit more from PI than do others.

The PI research has examined three target languages, Spanish, French, and Italian, but only one native language, English. The homogeneity of the overall database lends weight to arguments of generalizability but is at the same time a limitation. Is Processing Instruction equally effective across a variety of native languages? I will hypothesize that it is for the simple reason that the processing strategies taught are specific to the target language. No matter the L1, learners can be taught, for example, to use Spanish- or French-appropriate word order processing strategies, Spanish- or Italian-appropriate perceptual processing strategies, and Spanish- or French-appropriate semantic processing strategies.

- *Hypothesis 7.* PI will be effective for instilling target-language specific processing strategies, no matter the L1 of the learners.

WHAT EVALUATION INSTRUMENTS HAVE BEEN USED TO ESTABLISH THE EFFECTS OF PI ON LEARNERS' PROCESSING STRATEGIES?

VanPatten and Cadierno's founding research used two types of assessment tests, one biased toward the processing group and the other biased toward the traditional group so that the testing was balanced across treatments and assessed the direct affects of both types of instruction. Both tests were discrete point, sentence level tasks and were appropriate assessments for the type of instruction offered. This pattern of test-construction characterizes all subsequent PI research. The repeated finding that Processing Instruction leads to significant improvement on form production tests across all three categories of processing strategies investigated spurred discussion and debate that resulted in research using discourse-level production tasks including oral and written video narration (VanPatten & Sanz, 1995; Sanz, 1997, and this volume) and guided compositions (Cheng, 2002, and this volume). This research has shown that PI is also effective at improving learners' performance on discourse-based production tasks.

That different languages and different processing strategies have been investigated contribute to the generalizability of Processing Instruction as an intervention that effectively improves learners' performance on sentence interpretation tasks, sentence production tasks and discourse-level production tasks. In other words, as a result of receiving PI, learners can both interpret and produce accurate forms in a second language. One limit on the database is absence of discourse-level interpretation tasks that might confirm the broader effects of PI on interpretation and might demonstrate further limitations of traditional instruction. How effective is processing instruction for improving learners' performance not only on sentence- but also on discourse-level interpretation tasks? Because PI affects discourse-level production, I can hypothesize that it will also affect discourse-level interpretation.

- *Hypothesis 8.* PI will yield significant improvement on discourse level interpretation tasks.

The PI research, thus far, has taken the appropriately conservative approach of assessing the direct or primary effects of instruction, that is, does PI alter inappropriate processing strategies and/or instill appropriate ones? The answer to this question is so resoundingly affirmative that PI researchers might move one step away from assessing direct/primary effects and determine whether secondary effects develop in learners as a result of receiving PI. Do learners who receive PI transfer that training to other forms? Two examples follow. After receiving instruction on using acoustic stress to determine past versus present temporal reference in Spanish, can learners transfer/apply the strategy to other examples of acoustic stress such as the distinction between Spanish future tense and past subjunctive forms (*hablará* and *hablara*, respectively)? After receiving instruction on avoiding the use of the First Noun Strategy to interpret preverbal object pronouns in Spanish, can learners transfer/apply the strategy to other structures such as Spanish *gustar*-type verbs that place an indirect object pronoun preverbally and the subject postverbally or to Spanish causative constructions that parallel the VanPatten and Wong research on French (this volume)?

- *Hypothesis 9.* Learners who receive training on one type of processing strategy for one specific form will appropriately transfer the use of that strategy to other forms without further instruction in PI.

WHAT ARE THE LIMITS OF PI RESEARCH TO DATE?

I have in previous sections addressed limitations of PI research with regard to the languages on which we have established the effects of PI, long term durative effects, subject characteristics, tasks used to evaluate the effects of PI, and determining transfer-of-training effects. The hypotheses I have generated respond to very specific aspects of the database. In this section, I expand my perspective and conjecture a bit farther a field.

In his original treatise on the theoretical foundations of Processing Instruction, VanPatten hypothesized that the effects of PI might be greater than the direct effects of instruction on a processing strategy. He poses the question, "Does processing instruction actually affect the acquired system, what is called in the general model the developing system?" (VanPatten, 1996, p. 154). With regard the to impact that teaching learners an appropriate word-order strategy would have, VanPatten and Cadierno (1993) argue that the use of the First Noun Strategy might also account for other acquisition patterns, among them, the lack of fronted object-noun phrases in learners' speech, the difficulty in acquiring the case marker *a*, and the pervasive use of subject nouns and pronouns in contexts in which they would normally be omitted

I, too, believe that the theoretical foundations on which PI has been developed support the claim that PI would affects learners' developing systems in a way or ways that other types of instruction do not and can not. No one has taken up the challenge of determining the effects of PI on learners' developing systems in general or on the specific features VanPatten and Cadierno mention. The task would be difficult, but it could begin with assessing learners' intuitions about the L2, not only with regard to the specific form taught but other similar structures.

- *Hypothesis 10.* Learners who receive PI will develop better intuitions about the L2 than will learners who receive other types of instruction.

To further explore the effects of PI on learners' developing systems we would do well to address another limit of the database. To date, each PI intervention has been carried out in isolation, that is, one set of learners is taught a word-order processing strategy, another set a perceptual processing strategy, and yet another a semantic processing strategy. What are the cumulative effects of receiving PI instruction on the different types of strategies? For example, do learners pick up a second and third processing strategy more quickly and efficiently than they pick up the first one? If they do, then PI would affect the rate of L2 development. Do repeated PI interventions remove individual differences? Are the effects of PI on developing systems (e.g., the intuitions referred to in Hypothesis 11) only visible after repeated PI trainings?

- *Hypothesis 11.* The cumulative effects of PI will be greater than its isolated effects.

SUMMARY AND CONCLUSION

To address the generalizability of PI research, I used the following questions to organize the review of the database.

- What processing strategies have been examined in PI research?
- What characterizes the subjects that have been investigated in PI research?
- What types of evaluation instruments have been used to establish the effects of PI on learners' processing strategies?
- Are the effects of PI durative?

The review presented in this chapter clearly attests to the generalizability of PI to

- several types of processing strategies;
- Romance languages;
- morphological, syntactic and semantic features of languages;
- learners whose native language is English;
- discrete point, open ended, communicative, written and oral tests;
- extended time frames of one week, one month and eight months.

To address the limits of the current data base as well as to suggest avenues of further investigation, I offered the following testable hypotheses on the effects of PI.

- *Hypothesis 1.* PI can help learners of any L2 apply appropriate word order processing strategies.
- *Hypothesis 2.* PI can help learners of any L2 perceive and use acoustic stress when it is a distinctive feature of the language.
- *Hypothesis 3.* PI can help learners of any L2 to process a formal feature of that language in order to determine an appropriate semantic interpretation of a sentence.
- *Hypothesis 4.* Evidence will be found to corroborate the long-term durative effects of PI on word-order, perceptual, and semantic processing strategies.

- *Hypothesis 5.* PI will be equally effective as an intervention for establishing initial form-meaning connections as it is for improving learners' performance.
- *Hypothesis 6.* Some learners benefit more from PI than do others.
- *Hypothesis 7.* PI will be effective for instilling target-language specific processing strategies, no matter the L1 of the learners.
- *Hypothesis 8.* PI will yield significant improvement on discourse level interpretation tasks.
- *Hypothesis 9.* Learners who receive training on one type of processing strategy for one specific form will appropriately transfer the use of that strategy to other forms without further instruction in PI.
- *Hypothesis 10.* Learners who receive PI will develop better intuitions about the L2 than learners who receive other types of instruction.
- *Hypothesis 11.* The cumulative effects of PI will greater than its isolated effects.

These 11 hypotheses indicate a robust future for Processing Instruction research.

REFERENCES

Benati, A. (2001). A comparative study of the effects of processing instruction and output-based instruction on the acquisition of the Italian future tense. *Language Teaching Research, 5,* 95–127.

Cadierno, T. (1995). Formal instruction from a processing perspective: An investigation into the Spanish past tense. *The Modern Language Journal, 79,* 179–193.

Cheng, A. (2002). The effects of processing instruction on the acquisition of *ser* and *estar. Hispania, 85,* 308–323.

Farley, A. (2001a). The effects of processing instruction and meaning-based output instruction. *Spanish Applied Linguistics, 5,* 57–94.

Farley, A. (2001b). Authentic processing instruction and the Spanish subjunctive. *Hispania, 84,* 289–299.

Lee, J., & VanPatten, B. (1995). *Making Communicative Language Teaching Happen.* New York: McGraw-Hill.

Lee, J., & VanPatten, B. (2003). *Making Communicative Language Teaching Happen* (2nd ed.). New York: McGraw-Hill.

Leeser, M. J. (2003). Second language comprehension and processing grammatical form: The effects of topic familiarity, mode, and pausing. Unpublished Ph.D. thesis, University of Illinois at Urbana–Champaign.

Sanz, C. (1997). Experimental tasks in SLA research: Amount of production, modality, memory, and production processes. In W. R. Glass & A. T. Pérez-Leroux (Eds.), *Contemporary perspectives on the acquisition of Spanish:*

Vol. 2. Production, processing, and comprehension (pp. 41–56). Somerville: Cascadilla Press.

VanPatten, B. (1988). How juries get hung: Problems with the evidence for a focus on form. *Language Learning, 38,* 243–260.

VanPatten, B. (1996). *Input processing and grammar instruction: Theory and research.* Norwood, NJ: Ablex.

VanPatten, B. (2000a). Thirty years of input (or intake, the neglected sibling). In B. Swierzbin, F. Morris, M. E. Anderson, C. A. Klee & E. Tarone (Eds.), *Social and cognitive factors in second language acquisition* (pp. 287–311). Somerville, MA: Cascadilla Press.

VanPatten, B. (2000b). Processing instruction as form-meaning connections: issues in theory and research. In J. F. Lee & A. Valdman (Eds.), *Form and meaning: Multiple perspectives* (pp. 43–68). Boston: Heinle & Heinle.

VanPatten, B., & Cadierno, T. (1993). Explicit instruction and input processing. *Studies in Second Language Acquisition, 15,* 225–243.

VanPatten, B., & Oikennon, S. (1996). Explanation vs. structured input in processing instruction. *Studies in Second Language Acquisition, 18,* 495–510.

VanPatten, B., & Sanz, C. (1995). From input to output: Processing instruction and communicative tasks. In F. R. Eckman, D. Highland, P. W. Lee, J. Mileham & R. R. Weber (Eds.), *Second Language Acquisition Theory and Pedagogy* (pp.169–185). Mahwah, NJ: Laawrence Erlbaum Associates.

Chapter 17

Several Reflections on Why There is Good Reason to Continue Researching the Effects of Processing Instruction

Bill VanPatten
University of Illinois at Chicago

My first duty in these final comments is to thank my colleagues who have contributed to this volume. From my perspective, the volume makes a solid contribution to research on instructed SLA in that it brings together a number of focused empirical studies that carry built-in replication on a variety of questions related to PI. The additional critical commentaries in each section and the final commentaries make this volume unique and balanced. Inspired by both the research and commentaries, my job here is to point to directions for growth in research on PI. Before doing so, I touch on some ideas related to IP, given that it underlies the very nature of PI.

ON INPUT PROCESSING

It is clear that the model of IP is not a finished product but merely a starting point. In that sense I believe it has done its first job; to direct attention to a neglected area of SLA research. Although the model does adequately describe certain processing strategies, it is currently deficient as an actual theory as suggested by Harrington and Carroll. There are four major areas that need addressing:

- the nature of *meaning* and *meaningful* in the model;
- the nature of processing;
- the incremental nature of parsing/processing; and

- the need to relate parsing issues to the processing of particular forms.

All are related to the explanatory adequacy and predictive ability of the model.

I cannot address all of these issues here, so I take the liberty of focusing my discussion here. I would first like to examine the issue of incrementality. In *adult L1 sentence parsing*, the incremental nature of processing is a given. For example, in Pritchett's (1992) work that attempts to relate parsing to grammatical principles, incrementality is clearly implied as he develops his principle of Theta Attachment, that is, that the theta criterion needs to be satisfied at every point during processing.[1] Thus, every noun that a hearer /reader encounters must be assigned an appropriate theta role as soon as possible. Under this procedure, parsing is incremental and cumulative at the same time.

There is at least one problem with assuming the same incremental nature of parsing for SLA; namely, models of adult L1 parsing do not have to consider that hearers may not even have the lexical entries in their grammars with the associated lexical entry information. L1 parsing can be incremental because it is assumed that native speakers "know all the words" and parsing is merely a matter of structural representation and—in the cases studied by those working in L1 parsing—ambiguity resolution. Pritchett, for example makes the following observation:

At this point it may be useful to summarize the fundamental parsing algorithm, which may be informally but accurately characterized as follows:

a. Input a word.
b. Recover lexical information. . .[2]
c. Maximally satisfy the theta criterion. . .
d. If input 'ceases' affirm that the resulting structure satisfies
all relevant grammatical principles (success); . . . (1992, p. 96)

What I wish to point out here is that Pritchett correctly notes that parsing (satisfying grammatical principles during real time comprehension) is dependent on knowing words and, in some cases, formal features of words. In short, parsing requires some kind of established lexicon (in addition to a set of syntactic rules). Working memory in such models of parsing only comes into play when reanalysis of a parse is required. Otherwise, native speakers are assumed to automatically and unconsciously parse away until they hit an

---

[1]Pritchett is actually most concerned with problems of theta reanalysis during processing, which he deems to be costly to parsing. His goal is to demonstrate the inadequacy of lexical, computational, and semantic approaches to parsing, all of which assume some sort of incremental nature of processing. He eventually constructs a more general principle of attachment as well as what he calls an On-line Locality Constraint.

[2]Suspension points indicate deleted material not relevant to the present discussion.

ambiguity (e.g., a garden path) that requires them to hold part of the sentence in working memory while a different analysis of the sentential structure is performed.

Second language input processing, on the other hand, is concerned more with how learners *get words and grammatical forms to begin with* so that a grammar can be built. As such, it cannot make assumptions that learners incrementally parse the way native speakers do. The Sentence Location Principle, for example, captures that early stage learners *may actually miss whole parts of utterances.* An early stage learner may be performing computations and analyses on the beginning of the sentence that are costly because either accessing stored information from the lexicon and grammar may not be as speedy as it is for a native speaker or the learner doesn't know what "the thing" is that was just heard at the beginning. In this scenario, a logjam is created in working memory that keeps the learner from processing what comes next. Depending on sentence length, the learner may thus only hear and process the beginning of the sentence and, once the taxing computations of that processing have been completed, what is next to enter working memory is the end of the sentence. In short, as the learner struggles with the first part of the sentence the input[3] stream may whiz by. The learner's parser *may want to parse incrementally*, but cannot given the input load, problems in access, problems with novelty, and so on. My point here is that although we can assume incrementality in L1 parsing models, *incrementality must develop over time in L2 learners.*

The above description does not necessarily mean that the Sentence Location Principle is correct in its formulation. A better way to understand the principle may be to formulate it as a contingency, such as:

> Learners will process incrementally unless they experience a computational burden at the beginning of the sentence. In such cases, processing is costly and processing of the rest of the utterance may suffer.

The implication in such a principle is that learners will, of course, have more successful parses when they do not encounter problems at the outset of the utterance. However, they may encounter difficulties later on in the sentence for the exact same reasons they encounter difficulty at the beginning: unknown words, problems with access, and so on. Thus, the above principle would have to be formulated to capture an incremental procedure that may be interrupted at any point:

---

[3]I use input here as it is used in the general SLA literature (i.e., language the learner hears). Carroll (this volume and elsewhere) does not limit the meaning to language that is external to the learner but also to the outcomes of processing, even if these are nonlinguistic (e.g., 'this parse isn't working' could be input for learning in her scenario).

> (Revised) Learners will process incrementally unless they experience a computational burden. At that point, processing may either breakdown or the learner will complete the computation causing the problem and then pickup again where possible.

What such a principle captures is that processing can breakdown anywhere and that this may impede the processing of novel forms (or formatives, to use Carroll's terms).[4] The questions to ask are: What do we gain by this principle? What predictions does such a principle make? It is not clear that we gain much in terms of explanatory power given that we are once gain merely describing the problem and we come back to our basic questions about input processing: How do learners make initial form-meaning connections? Why do they make some and not others?

A more useful principle that implies incrementality of processing but also captures the idea of the importance of the initial elements of an utterance might be this:

> *The Early Constraint Principle.* The processing of the initial element(s) constrains the processing of the rest of the sentence.

This principle is a bit more promising in that it can subsume any processing difficulties such as those suggested by the principle outlined above, while at the same time also allowing for some predictions about constraints on processing novel forms (i.e., constraints on learners making new form-meaning connections). As one example, let's take the current First-Noun Principle. With this principle, learners commit early on to a sentence structure. Thus, when they hear *Juan no conoce a María bien* ('John does not know Mary well'), they first hear *Juan* and retrieve its lexical information (e.g., noun, proper name, male) and project an NP, which in turn is tagged as subject (e.g., along the lines of Pritchett's need for the parser to assign theta roles as soon as possible). As they hear *no* there is nothing to disconfirm their structural assignment of *Juan* as subject (which is actually a structural relationship of the NP to the V), and the parser expects a verb to be next. As they hear *conoce* they retrieve its lexical information, that is, a verb with a particular meaning that requires two arguments and they project the VP. The parser expects to encounter an object NP next. There is still nothing to tell them *Juan* is not the subject, and as they hear *María* they tag this noun as object after retrieving its lexical information.

---

[4] It is important to note here that processing is used to discuss *initial* connections that learners make between a form and its meaning; not connections during parsing that the learner already has.

The same process occurs with *bien,* and the sentence is successfully computed, with all aspects of parsing being satisfied.

Note that we have said nothing about the function word *a*, which is used in Spanish to mark objects that could be construed as possible subjects, that is, when lexical semantics allows for it. In this case, *María* is case marked with *a* because the verb *conoce* does not rule her out as a possible subject; either she or John is capable of knowing. This contrasts with *la materia* ('the subject matter') which cannot be a subject for a verb like *conoce,* and hence no case marking is needed: *Juan no conoce la materia bien.* Let's suppose that this particular form(ative) is the potential new form-meaning connection for the learner, that is, the learner does not know that *a* means "accusative." The learner does know, however, the lexical items *Juan, María, conoce* and *bien.* Because the learner commits to sentence structure early on and expectations are fulfilled along the way, the case marker *a* may not initially be processed (i.e., its form connected with its meaning/function). The information it conveys is redundant (the learner has already used word order to derive the relationships of nouns to the verb) and the parser, having no way to project it into the sentence, simply ignores it and it is dumped from working memory. This is a case where a form may get registered[5] but not processed (not connected with its meaning or function). In this scenario, parsing impedes the possible connection of form and meaning.

Another example comes from English. It is well known that learners have problems with the acquisition of *do*. As I have suggested elsewhere (VanPatten, 1996), it is possible that learners initially process *do* as a simple question marker, which is a possible surface feature in languages. Japanese has *wa* and French may use *est-ce que*, both of which allow the languages to maintain canonical ordering of elements (SOV and SVO, respectively). In addition, it seems that children learning English as a first language may pass through a stage where they initially process *is* as a question marker, producing sentences such as *Is Ben did go?* and *Is I can do that?* (Radford, 1997, pp. 11-12). In English yes/no questions with *do*, canonical order with lexical verbs is maintained, for example, as in *Do you like chocolate?* where *you like chocolate* represents canonical declarative word order. (Because of their rather distinct phonetic realizations, *does* and *did* may not be associated with *do* by the learner, and it would not be until the learner does process these forms—most likely for tense features—that connection to *do* will be made.) If learners process *do* as a particle, then they commit to a sentence structure early on in parsing that is not the actual structure of the sentence and subtle abstract properties of *do* as part of INFL (or whatever functional category it belongs to) do not make their way into the grammatical system. The result is erroneous acquisition that may evidence

---

[5]I am using the term *registered* here to avoid any implications of noticing that may involve awareness. Contra to Carroll's observations, there is no commitment of IP to the Noticing Hypothesis. In VanPatten (1996, chap. 2), I discuss why both IP and PI can ignore the controversy surrounding "noticing" and still make headway in a research agenda. See also Truscott (1998).

itself in learner speech, for example, *Do you can say this?* (see also, Hawkins, 2002). In this particular scenario, how learners initially connected a form to its meaning (and function) impacted the parsing of the sentence. It would not be until learners somehow note that *do* can carry person–number information as well as tense that the grammar reanalyzes the sentence structure and the parser is forced to commit to a different syntactic structure. In other words, only when learners make the form-meaning connections involving the inflections on *do* is parsing altered.

Moving away from the issue of incrementality, it is also likely that as we grapple with parsing matters that go beyond "who did what to whom", the role of L1 influence will surface. In ambiguity resolution, we have seen with E. Fernández (1999) that learners have L1 preferences that carry over to the L2. What other aspects of L1 processing are carried over into L2 processing? Despite the fact that I have argued previously for universality of the First-Noun Principle, a model/theory of IP could approach processing from a transfer point of view. In this case the first-noun strategy would be replaced by the following:

> ***The L1 Transfer Principle.*** Learners begin acquisition with
> L1 parsing procedures.

Under this scenario, the L1 English-speaking learner of Spanish begins L2 parsing with an SVO preference. Once the learner tags the first noun as the subject, the Early Constraint Principle would influence the rest of the parsing. These may not be the kinds of principles that would emerge from the comments made in this volume, but they illustrate that the model can evolve in fundamental (and perhaps, more succinct) ways. They also illustrate how parsing can interact with making form-meaning connections. Parsing may constrain the form-meaning connections at a certain point and likewise when the learner commits to a particular form-meaning connection, this may constrain the syntactic projections the parser could make.

Now let us suppose that under a Minimalist approach to parsing that certain checking procedures have to be satisfied during L1 parsing. That is, let's suppose that the feature-checking requirement of grammaticality applies to parsing following Pritchett's (and others') idea that parsing and grammatical principles are related. In such a case, the parser wants to check off features as the sentence is heard so that all matches are satisfied. If the parser hears "John" and it is assigned sentential subject role, then the parser expects to hear a verb that agrees with it, for example, "bites" and not "bite." What happens with the following sentences? How does the parser handle these?

> (1) Yesterday I heard a great story.
> (2) Yesterday I hear a great story.
> (3) I heard a great story yesterday.
> (4) I hear a great story yesterday.

Although in (1) and (3) the parser has no problems checking off subject-verb agreement, it does have difficulty checking off the pastness of the verb with the adverb that presumably has scope over the entire sentence in (2) and (4). It is not clear to me what native speakers would do with such sentences but let's imagine this from the perspective of an L2 learner. If the Early Constraint Principle is correct, then the parsing/comprehension of each sentence results in differential outcomes. For (1) and (2), as soon as the learner identifies the adverb and accesses its lexical information (e.g., <adverb: PAST>) pastness should permeate the sentence and both (1) and (2) should be understood as occurring in the past. For (3) and (4), however, the early parsing of the verb form should constrain each sentence such at (3) would be comprehended as a past situation but (4) would be understood as a present tense situation. This is empirically testable and if the Early Constraint Principle is correct, then our predictions will bear out. But what if the learner thinks that all four sentences refer to past events? What are we to make of our Early Constraint Principle? One conclusion could be that the Lexical Preference Principle overrides the Early Constraint Principle and is more "primitive" or "universal." That is, content words take precedence over grammatical form for providing semantic information. And if native speakers do the same, then this is even stronger evidence for the primacy of lexical items in retrieving meaning from utterances.[6]

Now, if we imagine that the learner *doesn't* know the past tense yet—precisely a case of having to make an *initial* form-meaning connection—but has just figured out what *yesterday* means, then we ask ourselves: how will the learner come to process past tense forms (i.e., connect the form to its meaning) during on line processing? Clearly, some kind of lexical knowledge precedes the processing of a grammatical form that expresses an overlapping semantic notion. In this case, the learner must process and learn lexical markers of tense before processing and learning grammatical markers of tense. If this is so, then our Lexical Preference Principle might be restated as a constraint in the following way:

> **(Revised) Lexical Preference Principle**. If grammatical forms express a meaning that can also be encoded lexically, then learners will not initially process those grammatical forms until they have lexical forms to which they can match them.[7]

---

[6]Note that native speakers must process these sentences when dealing with L2 speakers whose production lacks grammatical markers. My sense is that the lexical items win out (see, e.g., Sato, 1986).

[7]Such principles also help us to understand why instruction speeds up acquisition. If this principle constrains acquisition, learners who are taught words and their meanings (such as temporal adverbs) will get the requirements for processing grammatical form sooner than those who do not.

If we also maintain the L1 Transfer Principle, then we would predict that learners with L1 languages like English that mark tense will connect past tense markers (forms) to meaning (pastness) before learners with L1 languages that don't mark tense grammatically (e.g., Chinese). This scenario reflects the feature checking nature of parsing (if it is a true aspect of parsing) in that a Spanish speaker's L1 parser needs to check tense while a Chinese speaker's L1 parser does not—at least not in the way the Spanish L1 parser does. Thus, the intersection of these two new principles predicts the conditions under which learners will get form-meaning connections (if at all) and also which learners (i.e., from what L1 going into what L2) may get them sooner.[8]

What all of this suggests is that new principles may and most likely will emerge to replace the current ones as the profession attempts to grapple with the nature of input processing as a significant part of acquisition. Both Carroll and Harrington are interested in these matters and from an instructional viewpoint, we see concern for input processing being discussed from outside of the PI framework. For example, Doughty (2003) says "… the goal of L2 instruction should be to organize the processing space to enable adults to notice the cues *located in the input,* as they did when they were children … A guiding principle in this regard is to engage perceptual processes during implicit learning, rather than processes that promote metalinguistic awareness" (p. 298, emphasis original). No matter how a model handles parsing and its affects on input processing, researchers must continue to address the two fundamental questions that underlie the research. I repeat them here:

1. Under what conditions do learners make initial form-meaning/function connections?
2. Why, at a given moment in time, do they make some and not others?

We will welcome additional questions that emerge as research on input processing progresses and begins to address the criticisms in both Harrington and Carroll in this volume.

ON PROCESSING INSTRUCTION

I would like to begin here by commenting on the following question: If the model of IP needs (substantial) revision, then what does this do to PI and all the research on it to date? My answer is "relatively little." First, the research results of PI are robust enough (as Carroll, Lee, Collentine, and Lightbown underscore) to be taken as an indication that we are definitely on the right track in terms of

---

[8]Note that I am not addressing the issue of phonetic and phonological properties that Carroll discusses but one could assume that the these aspects of L1 parsing would also transfer into attempts to process L2 input.

one kind of pedagogical intervention. We should not toss out the baby with the bathwater. What I mean here is that the results of PI are clear and there is room for future research, but what is also clear is that as the model of IP is revised, we may see potentially different grammatical forms and structures emerge as candidates for pedagogical intervention and/or we may find alternative explanation for the observed benefits of PI.

Let's take the VanPatten and Cadierno study as our starting point. Currently, that study is predicated on the IP principle The First Noun Principle. The instructional intervention, by pushing learners away from that strategy, has been shown to be successful. Let's suppose the IP model is reformulated such that the principles of incrementality and position-initial processing are included as major organizing principles under the Early Constraint Principle suggested above. Let's also suppose that we work with something like the L1 Transfer Principle. Because processing is incremental and because position-initial processing can affect the rest of sentence processing, the effects of the first-noun principle would still obtain because of the interaction of the L1 Parsing Transfer Principle and the Early Constraint Principle.

Does this reformulation mean that the results of, for example, VanPatten and Cadierno are invalid? No. It would mean that the researchers did the right thing but for the wrong reason. We could still effectively construct PI using the same materials as in VanPatten and Cadierno. The materials would still serve to overcome the L1 transfer problem as well as the early constraint problem.

I would briefly like to touch upon an aspect of research design in PI. In the present volume, Doughty makes the observation that the PI studies she reviewed suffer from a problem of assessment tasks that may measure metalinguistic information or conscious knowledge of the grammar. She also correctly notes that this is not a problem of PI research but a problem of the larger field of instructed SLA in general. However, research on PI must continue to do something that other approaches to instructed SLA do not; measure to what extent a processing strategy has been altered. In VanPatten and Cadierno, we included both interpretation and production tasks because only the interpretation task could measure if learners could now interpret novel sentences correctly. Does this task rely on metalinguistic knowledge? Possibly. However, note that in the VanPatten and Oikkenon study as well as the three studies in Part III of the present volume, SI only groups do not get metalinguistic information. How, then, are they able to perform these tasks? Does metalinguistic knowledge "emerge" through the course of performing the activities? Possibly. One way out of this dilemma is to examine Lee's hypothesis regarding discourse tasks. One could, for example, embed target OVS structures into a longer speech stream and then test interpretation of that particular sentence. The burden of keeping information (i.e., content from the discourse) in working memory should mitigate against any use of metalinguistic knowledge during processing. There is danger in constructing such tasks, however. In VanPatten and Houston (1998), we demonstrated that certain kinds of context immediately preceding an OVS clause causes learners *not* to apply the first-noun strategy. Clearly, discourse tasks have to be structured carefully.[9]

CONCLUSION

I am optimistic about the future of theory and research on both IP and PI. The present volume clearly outlines the changes needed in a model of IP for it to be maximally useful, the points that Harrington and Carroll clearly make. As I have said before, the model may be deficient, but it has served its purpose in pointing researchers' attention to where I have thought we ought to be looking when it comes to processes in SLA. As Doughty (2003) points out, regardless of any shortcomings, PI is one approach that clearly focuses on processes and processing rather than language forms alone in instruction. This is all because of a focus on IP as a starting point. Theory revision or replacement is welcome when it is centered on accounting for observed phenomena.

As for PI, I think it is very clear that even within the current model of IP, we can continue to research its efficacy. Collentine's remarks are well taken; there is no longer a need to compare PI to TI. PI must be dealt with for what it is and the components within it. For example, three chapters in this volume clearly point to problems with some current perspectives on the role of explicit information in instructed SLA in that learners do not need it if input is manipulated so that learners have to readjust their processing and parsing strategies. The role of explicit information may really only be to alert learners to a form-meaning connection that subsequently might speed up the resolution of processing failure. In a current study, we are getting a glimpse of this (C. Fernández, in progress). In this study, learners undergo PI with and without explicit information. However, each learner is taught individually and responses to each activity item are tracked. What we are seeing is that those who get EI almost immediately begin to make correct processing decisions during the structured input activities; those who get structured input only do not. It seems that 3 to 4 failures are necessary before the processing mechanisms begin to adjust themselves toward a correct processing decision. Nonetheless, the structured input only group does catch up to the explicit information + structured input only group. If these results continue to obtain, this study may be the first to offer empirical evidence about what explicit information actually does in instructed SLA.

These directions in looking at intervention along with Lee's list of hypotheses for a continued research agenda on PI, suggest that there is indeed a continued future for this one type of pedagogical intervention. This is welcome if the field of instructed SLA is to make headway in terms of sustained research

---

[9]The issue of solid research design and instrumentality cannot be overemphasized, not just for PI research but for all research in instructed SLA.

efforts regarding the viability of claims regarding instructional effects. To be sure, PI is not the only intervention that needs continued research. Too often research in instructed SLA is a one-shot deal; once a study is concluded, the researcher does not follow up with research that addresses the limitations of and questions inspired by the study. My hope is that a sustained research agenda on both IP and PI can serve as a model in this regard.

REFERENCES

Doughty, C. (2003). Instructed SLA: Constraints, compensation, and enhancement. In C. Doughty & M. H. Long (Eds.), *The handbook of second language acquisition* (pp. 254–310). Oxford: Basil Blackwell.

Fernández, C. (in progress). The role of explicit knowledge in instructed SLA: evidence from a PI study. Doctoral dissertation, the University of Illinois at Chicago.

Fernández, E. (1999). Processing strategies in second language acquisition: Some preliminary results. In E. Klein & G. Martohardjono (Eds.), *The development of second language grammars: A generative approach* (pp. 217–239). Philadelphia: Benjamins.

Hawkins, R. (2002). *Second language syntax.* Oxford: Basil Blackwell.

Pritchett, B. L. (1992). *Grammatical competence and parsing performance.* Chicago: University of Chicago Press.

Radford, A. (1997). *Syntactic theory and the structure of English: A minimalist approach.* Cambridge: Cambridge University Press.

Sato, C. (1986). Conversation and interlanguage development: rethinking the connection. In R. R. Day (Ed.), *Talking to learn: Conversation in second language acquisition* (pp. 23–45). Rowley, MA: Newbury House.

Truscott, J. (1998) Noticing in second language acquisition: a critical review. *Second Language Research, 14,* 103-135.

VanPatten, B. (1996). *Input processing and grammar instruction: Theory and research.* Norwood, NJ: Ablex.

VanPatten, B. & Houston, T. (1998). Contextual effects in processing L2 input sentences. *Spanish Applied Linguistics, 2,* 53–70.

Author Index

A

Akahori, K., 244, *255, 270*
Alanen, R., 183, 185, *186,* 197, 198, *199,*
    199, 207, *217,* 227, *239,* 242,
    253
Allen, L. Q., 15, 23, *28,* 33, 56, 61, 97, 99,
    100, 101, 111, 136, 163, 275,
    279, *286*
Anderson, J. R., 27, *28, 61*
Andrade, M., 53, *62*
Atkins, W. B., 90, *91*

B

Baddeley, A. D., 22, *29,* 90, *91*
Baker, J. P., 244, *254*
Barcroft, J., 13, 23, *28,* 35, *61*
Bates, E., 82, *91,* 305, *307, 308, 309*
Batstone, R., 67, *76*
Beckman, M. E., 298, *307*
Benati, A., 52, *61,* 93, *96,* 113, *114,* 162,
    210, *218,* 275, 285, 286, 313,
    316, 317, *322*
Bernstein Ratner, N., 299, *307*
Bever, T. G., 1, *2*
Blau, E. K., 11, *28*
Blaxton, T. A., 302, *307*
Bley-Vroman, R., 241, 245, *253,* 263
Bolinger, D. L., 298, *307*
Boomer, D. S., 302, *307*
Brandl, K. K., 244, *253*
Bransdorfer, R., 124, *137*
Briscoe, G., 123, *137*
Brown, G., 298, *307*

C

Cadierno, T., x, 22, *30,* 34, 45, 52, 55, 56,
    58, *61, 62, 63,* 66, *78,* 79, 84, 88,
    91, 92, 93, *96,* 99, 100, 101, 102,
    103, 104, 111, 113, *114,* 119,
    127, 135, 136, *138,* 143, 144,
    159, 162, 163, 164, *165, 166,*
    171, 172, 173, 174, 175, *180,*
    181, 189, *200,* 248, *255,* 258,
    260, 262, *268, 269, 274,* 275,
    276, 277, 278, 280, 281, 285,
    287, 288, 313, 316, 320, *322, 323*
Calvo, M. G., 90, *91*
Caplan, D., *91*
Carpenter, P. A., 7, 22, *29,* 89, *92*
Carroll, S., 52, *61,* 67, *76,* 198, *199,* 243,
    252, *253,* 297, 306, *307*
Carroll, S. E., 208, *218,* 277, 280, *287*
Chaudron, C., 5, *28*
Cheng, A., 52, *62,* 143, 159, 163, 164, *165,*
    314, 318, *322*
Cheng, A. C., 125, 126, 127, 130, 135,
    137, 275, *287*
Clahsen, H., 66, *77,* 162, *165, 166,* 306,
    307
Clark, E. V., 79, *91*
Clifton, C. Jr., 20, *28*
Coakley, C. G., 6, *31*
Cohen, J., 174, *180*
Collentine, J. G., 143, 144, 145, 159, *165,*
    171, *180,* 273, 275, *287*
Conway, L., *28*
Corley, M. M. B., 20, *28*
Crain, S., *28*

Cuetos, F., 20, *28*
Currie, K., 298, *307*
Cutler, A., 303, *307, 308, 309*

D

Dale, P. S., 82, *91*
d'Anglejan, A., 65, *77*
de Graaff, R., 198, *199,* 207, *218,* 227,
    239, 242, *253*
DeKeyser, R. M., 2, *2,* 9, 19, 27, *28,* 33,
    51*n,* 53, 57, *62,* 79, 80, 81, 88,
    89, *91,* 94, *96,* 144, *165,* 171,
    180, 196, *200,* 227, *239,* 257,
    265, *268,* 273, 274, 275, 276,
    277, *287,* 294, *308*
Devescovi, A., 305, *307*
Dittmann, A. T., 302, *307*
Dohrn, U., 162, *166*
Doughty, C., 52, *62,* 72, *76,* 183, *186,* 198,
    200, 243, 247, *253,* 257, 258,
    262, 264, 265, *268,* 273, 274,
    285, *287,* 332, 334, *335*

E

Edwards, J., 298, *307*
Egasse, J., 53, *62*
Ellis, N., 19, *28,* 52, *62,* 66, *76,* 198, 199,
    200, 242, *253,* 287
Ellis, R., 79, *91*
Ervin-Tripp, S. M., 15, *29*
Estevez, A., 90, *91*

F

Faerch, C., 7, *29*
Falk, J., 120, 121, *137*
Farley, A. P., 136, *137,* 146, 159, 164, *165,*
    217, 314, 316, *322*
Fernández, C., 178, 179, 198, 334, *335*
Fernández, E., 24, *29,* 330, *335*
Finnemann, M. D., 123, *137*
Forster, K. I., 295, *308*
Franco, F., 121, *137*
Frazier, L., 20, *28,* 296, *308*
Friedman, N. P., 80, 89, 90, *92*

G

Gass, S. M., 6, 12, 16, *29,* 66, *76,* 81, *91,*
    99, 100, *114*

Gathercole, S. E., 22, *29*
Geeslin, K., 119, 120, 123, 124, *137, 138*
Glass, W. R., 22, *30,* 34, *62*
Goodman, J. C., 82, *92*
Gorrell, P., 296, *308*
Gregg, K. R., 90, *91*
Gross, M., 162, *165*
Gunterman, G., 123, 138
Gutiérrez, M., 119, 122, *138*

H

Halter, R., 65, *77*
Harrington, M., 2, *2,* 9, 19, 21, 24, *28, 29,*
    51*n, 62,* 80, 81, 86, 88, 89, 90,
    91, 92, 94, *96,* 196, *200,* 257,
    268, 294, *308*
Hatano, G., 303, *309*
Hatch, E., 11, *29*
Hawkins, R., 330, *335*
Heilenman, L. K., *114*
Henderson, A. I., 302, *308*
Herman, R. L., 198, 199, *200*
Herron, C., 243, *254*
Hollander, M., 162, *165*
Horst, M., 65, *77*
Houston, T., 17, *31,* 335

J

Juffs, A., 24, *29*
Just, M. A., 7, 22, *29,* 89, *92*

K

Kasper, G., 7, *29*
Kellerman, E., 66, *76*
Kenworthy, J., 298, *307*
Kimball, J., 296, *308*
Klein, W., 7, 13, 23, *29,* 304, *308*
Kliegl, R., 305, *309*
Krashen, S. D., 7, *29,* 66, *76,* 81, *92,* 170,
    180, 273, 275, *287*

L

Ladd, D. R., 298, *308*
Lafford, B., 123, *138*
Larsen-Freeman, D., 19, *29,* 170, *181,* 274,
    287
Lee, J. F., 1, *2,* 11, 15, 22, *29, 30,* 33, 34,
    37, 38, 40, 45*n,* 55, *62,* 103, *114,*

127, *138,* 144, *165,* 178, *181,*
190, *200,* 280, 285, *287,* 311,
322
Leeman, J., 243, 245, *253*
Leeser, M. J., 317, *322*
Li, C. N., 304, *308*
Lightbown, P. M., 65, 67, 68, 69, 71, 72,
73, 74, *76, 77, 78,* 112*n, 114,*
242, *254,* 262, *268,* 274, 275,
284, *287, 289*
LoCoco, V., 1, *2,* 16, *30,* 285, *287*
Long, M., 170, *181*
Long, M. H., 11, 13, 19, *29, 30,* 170, *181,*
257, 263, *268, 270,* 274, *287,*
288, 298*n, 308*
Loschky, L., 241, 245, *253,* 263
Luján, M., 122, *138*
Lyster, R., 67, 68*n,* 72, *77*

M

MacDonald, J. L., *114*
MacWhinney, B., 23, *30,* 82, 87, *92,* 305,
307, 308, 309
Mangubhai, F., 22, *30*
Marcus, G., 162, *165*
McCarthy, B., 244, *254*
McEnery, T., 244, *254*
McNew, S., 305, *307*
Mehler, J., 303, *308, 309*
Meisel, J. M., 66, *77,* 306, *307*
Mitchell, D. C., 20, *28*
Miyake, A., 80, 89, 90, *92*
Morgan-Short, K., 208, 216, 217, *218,*
235, *239,* 246*n, 254,* 264, 265,
269, 274, 275, *288*
Morley, J., 169, *181*
Morris, F., 72, *77*
Munoz, E. M., 53, *62*
Munte, T., 162, *165, 166*
Musumeci, D., 23, *30,* 34, *62,* 210, *218*

N

Nagata, N., 244, *254*
Nagel, H. N., 302, *309*
Nam, E., 1, *2*
Navas Ruiz, R., 120, *138*
Navon, D., 89, *92*
Nawy, R., 302, *309*
Nelms, S., 302, *308*
Nicholas, H., 72, *77*

Norris, D., 303, *308*
Norris, J. M., 52, *62,* 174, 176, *181,* 198,
200, 258, 265, 266, *269,* 273,
274, *288*
Nusbaum, H. C., 82, *92*

O

Oikkenon, S., 52, *63,* 73, *78,* 88, *92,* 100,
114, 183, *186,* 187, 190, 196,
197, *200,* 207, 208, 216, 217,
218, 227, *239,* 242, 245, 248,
255, 258, 260, 264, *269,* 274,
275, *289,* 313, *323*
Olson Flannigan, B., 198, 199, *200*
O'Neill, M. O., 23, *30,* 35, *62,* 198, 199,
200, 241, 242, *254*
Ortega, L., 13, *30,* 52, *62,* 174, 176, *181,*
198, *200,* 258, 265, 266, *269,*
273, 274, *288*
Otake, T., 303, *308, 309*

P

Pashler, H. E., 22, *30*
Paulston, C. B., 45, 51, *62,* 94, *96*
Penke, M., 162, *165, 166*
Perdue, C., 304, *308*
Pereira, I., 144, *166*
Peters, A. M., 7, 8, *30*
Pica, T., *138*
Picard, M., 69*n, 77*
Pienemann, M., 25, 27, *30,* 66, *77, 92,* 306,
307
Pierrehumbert, J. B., 298, *307*
Pinker, S., 162, *165*
Polio, C., 99, 100, *114*
Pondea, L., 23, *30*
Pritchett, B. L., 326, *335*

R

Radford, A., 329, *335*
Ramírez-Gelpi, A., 119, 123, *138*
Ranta, L., 69, 71, *78,* 275, *289*
Rayner, K., 20, *28*
Robinson, P. J., 2, *2,* 9, 19, *28,* 51*n, 62,* 80,
81, 88, *91,* 94, *96,* 183, 185, *186,*
196, 198, 199, *200,* 242, *254,*
257, 264, *268, 269,* 274, *288,*
294, *308*
Roediger, H. L. III, 302, *309*

Rosa, E., 23, *30,* 35, *62,* 198, 199, *200,*
        241, 242, 243, 250, 251, *254*
Rosen, T., 162, *165*
Ross, S., 263, *270*
Rothweiler, M., 162, *165*
Rott, S., *289*
Rutherford, W. C., 304, *309*
Ryan, J., 123, *138*

S

Salaberry, M. R., 2, *3,* 55, 57, *62,* 275, 276,
        288
Salaberry, R., 2, *2,* 9, 19, *28,* 33, 51*n*, *62,*
        80, 81, 88, 89, *91,* 94, *96,* 171,
        181, 196, *200,* 257, *268,* 294, *308*
Sanz, C., 2, *3,* 52, *63,* 170, *181,* 198, *200,*
        208, 216, 217, *218,* 235, *239,*
        246*n*, 248, 249, *254, 255,* 264,
        265, *269, 270,* 274, 275, 276,
        285, *288, 289,* 313, 318, *322, 323*
Sato, C., 331, *335*
Sawyer, M., 90, *92*
Schachter, J., 66, *77*
Schmidt, R., 72, *77, 269*
Schmidt, R. W., 6, 7, 12, *30,* 183, *186,*
        264, *269,* 274, *288,* 302, *309*
Scott, D. R., 302, *309*
Scott, V. M., 183, 185, *186,* 197, 198, 199,
        200, 227, *239,* 274, *288*
Segalowitz, N., 72, *77*
Segui, J., 303, *308*
Shapiro, L. P., 302, *309*
Sharwood Smith, M., 7, *30,* 66, *78,* 227,
        239
Shattuck-Hufnagel, S., 302, *309*
Silva-Corvalán, C., 120, 122, *138*
Slobin, D. I., 1, *3,* 21, *31*
Smith, S., 305, *307*
Sokalski, K., 2, *2,* 33, 53, 57, *62,* 79, *91,*
        144, *165,* 171, *180,* 265, 273,
        274, 275, 276, 277, *287*
Spada, N., 67, 68, 69, 71, 72, *77, 78,* 242,
        254, 274, 275, 284, *287, 289*
Steinmetz, D., 121, *137*
Swain, M. S., 13, *31,* 37, *62,* 67, *78,* 81,
        92, 164, *166,* 243, *253,* 280, *288*
Swisher, M. V., 244, *254*

T

Terrell, T. D., 6, 27, *31,* 53, *62,* 170, *180,*
        181

Thale, D., 82, *91*
Thompson, S. A., 304, *308*
Tomasello, M., 243, *254*
Tomlin, R., 302, *309*
Trahey, M., 274, *288*
Truscott, J., 329*n*, *335*
Tuller, B., 302, *309*
Turk, A. E., 302, *309*

U

Ullman, M., 162, *165*

V

Vañó-Cerdá, A., 120, *138*
VanPatten, B., x, 1, 2, *2, 3,* 6, 9, 13, 15, 17,
        19, 22, 23, 27, *28, 30, 31,* 33, 34,
        35, 37, 38, 40, 45, 52, 54, 55, 56,
        58, *61, 62, 63,* 66, 67, 73, *78,* 79,
        83, 84, 87, 88, *92,* 93, 94, 96, *96,*
        99, 100, 101, 102, 103, 104, 111,
        113, *114,* 119, 122, 124, 127,
        135, 136, *138,* 143, 144, 146,
        149, 159, 163, 164, *165, 166,*
        170, 171, 172, 173, 174, 175,
        177, 178, 179, *181,* 183, *186,*
        187, 189, 190, 196, 197, 198,
        200, 207, 208, 210, 216, 217,
        218, 227, 228, *239,* 241, 242,
        245, 248, 249, 252, *254, 255,*
        257*n*, 258, 260, 262, 264, 265,
        269, 270, 273, 274, 275, 276,
        277, 278, 280, 281, 285, *287,*
        288, 289, 311, 313, 316, 318,
        320, *322, 323,* 329, *335*
Varela, E., 243, *253*
Villa, V., 302, *309*

W

Warden, C. A., 244, *255, 270*
Waters, G., *91*
Weyerts, H., 162, *165, 166*
White, J., 65, 68*n*, 69, 71, *77, 78,* 274, *289*
White, L., 66, 68, 69, 71, *78,* 242, *255,*
        270, 274, 275, *287, 288, 289*
Williams, J., 257, *268,* 273, *287, 289*
Wilson, A., 244, *254*
Wode, H., 66, *78,* 299, *309*
Woest, A., 162, *165*

Wolvin, A. D., 6, *31*
Wong, W., 6, 15, 23, *30,* 33, 37, 38, 45*n*,
  52, 58, *63,* 79, 88, 89, *92,* 94, *96,*
  113, *114,* 127, 136, 143, 163,
  173, 175, 190, 208, 217, 275,
  285, 314, *323*
Wong Fillmore, L., 7, *31*

X

Xiao, Y., 304, *309*

Y

Yang, J. C., 244, *255, 270*
Yano, Y., 263, *270*

Z

Zander, E., 162, *165*
Zobl, H., 66, 69, 78

Subject Index

A

Activities, 118, 167–168
Availability of resources principle, 11, 177, 296

C

Clitic, 298–299
Computer assisted language learning (CALL), 244–253
Contextual constraint principle, 17–18, 177

D

Deliberate conflict, 23–24

E

Early constraint principle, 328, 331, 333
Event probabilities principle, 17, 177
Explicit feedback, 241–253
Explicit information (EI), *see also* Structured input (SI), 35–37, 52, 183–201, 207–220, 227–239, 334
French, 187–205
Italian future tense, 207–225

F

Feedback, 71–72, 257–258, 264
CALL, 244–253

computer-delivered, 241–244
First noun principle, 15–16, 34–35, 98, 177, 187, 304–306, 328, 333
Forms, 71, 82–87, 119, 169, 241, 257, 297, 300, 313
French, 187–205
Focus on form (FoF), 170–172, 174, 176, 257–268, 298
Focus on meaning (FoM), 170–172, 174

G

Grammatical explanation, 139
Grammatical form, 9, 82, 84–87

I

Implicit feedback, 241–253
Input, 66–67, 171, 297
    comprehensibility, 66–67
    frequency, 67–68
    salience, 67, 300
Input processing, 1–3, 5–28, 33–35, 291–307, 325–332, 334
    chunking, 8
    intake, 7, 66, 297
    lexical items, 8–10
    redundancy, 88–89
    restructuring, 25–26
Input processing model, 79–91, 98, 257, 294–297, 305
Instruction
    French causative, 56, 97–116
    Spanish ser and estar, 119–141, 314

Instructional treatments, 261–262
Italian future tense, 207–225

L

L1, L2 learners, 20–24, 27, 33–35, 65, 69,
    79, 81, 89–91, 124, 144–145,
    164, 197, 198, 227, 243, 252,
    257–265, 293, 304, 306, 326,
    330, 332
L1 transfer principle, 330–333
Lexical categories, 299
Lexical preference principle, 14, 21–22,
    177, 188, 229, 331
Lexical semantics principle, 16–17, 24,
    177

M

Meaning, 84–87, 144, 169, 298
Meaning-based output instruction,
    147–165
    affective activity, 168
    referential activity, 167
Meaning-before-nonmeaning principle, 11,
    177
Meaningful output based instruction, 93
Morphology, 10, 68, 162

N

Non-semantic morphosyntactic properties,
    300
Noticing hypothesis, 302, 304

O

Output, 12–13, 26–27, 171
    activities, 167–168
Output instruction, *see* Meaning-based
    output instruction

P

Parsing, 20–21, 296, 326–327, 329–330,
    332, 333
Perception, 6
Processing Instruction (PI) research,
    73–74, 169–172, 257
    feedback, 71–72, 257–258, 264

French, 187–205
    future of, 311–322
    perceptual strategies, 313–314
    syntactic strategies, 313
Italian, 207–225
    limits, 320
Spanish, 119–141, 144–165, 227–239,
    314
    subjects, 316–318
Preference for nonredundancy principle,
    11, 177
Primacy of content words principle, 14,
    177
Primacy of meaning principle, 177, 296,
    298, 300, 301, 302
Principles, 11, 13–19, 177, 229, 295–302,
    304–306, 328–333
Processing, 6, 294, 296
Processing instruction, 1–3, 33–61, 71–75,
    93–96, 102–116, 125–141,
    143–165, 171–180, 183–186,
    208–218, 227–239, 241–253,
    257–268, 273–286, 291–307,
    332–335
    affective activity, 117, 167
    goals, 177–180
    grammatical explanation, 139
    guidelines, 75
    long-term effects, 271, 273–286
    referential activity, 117, 167
    replication studies, 52–60, 113
    short term effects, 274–275
    vs. traditional instruction, 45–52
Prosodic word, 298

R

Redundancy, 88–89
Replication studies, 52–60, 113

S

Second language acquisition (SLA), 5–6,
    11, 20, 27, 65–67, 79–80, 90–91,
    113, 119, 124, 144, 164, 170,
    176, 207, 227, 238, 242, 257,
    262–263, 271, 273, 285, 291,
    306, 326, 333, 334
    focus on form (FoF), 170–172, 174,
        176, 257–268, 298
    focus on meaning (FoM), 170–172, 174

input, 66–67, 171
  output, 12–13, 26–27, 171
Semantic-aspectual values, 119
Semantic information, 9–10
Sentence location principle, 14, 145, 177,
    229, 295
Signal registration, 302
Spanish subjunctive, 144–165, 227–239
Structured input (SI), *see also* Explicit in-
    formation (EI), 37–45, 52–61,
    69, 72, 183–200, 207–218,
    221–222, 231–239, 334
  French, 187–205
  Italian future tense, 207–225
Structured input tasks, 177–178
  surface forms, 82–84

T

Teaching
  PI guidelines, 75
Traditional instruction (TI), 45–52,
    102–116, 125–141, 143–144,
    159, 173–176, 276, 315, 334
  initial mechanical activity, 118
  meaning-based activity, 118

U

Universal grammar (UG), 8, 73